Contesting Citizenship in Latin America

Indigenous people in Latin America have mobilized in unprecedented ways. By taking to the streets, forging new agendas, and fielding political candidates, indigenous movements have come to shape national political debates about multiethnic democracies, political equality, and subnational autonomy. These are remarkable developments in a region where ethnic cleavages were once universally described as weak.

Deborah Yashar explains the contemporary and uneven emergence of Latin American indigenous movements – addressing both why indigenous identities have become politically salient in the contemporary period and why they have translated into significant political organizations in some places and not others. She argues that ethnic politics can best be explained through a comparative historical approach that analyzes three factors: changing citizenship regimes, social networks, and political associational space. Her argument provides insight into the fragility and unevenness of Latin America's third wave democracies and has broader implications for the ways in which we theorize the relationship between citizenship, states, identity, and collective action.

Deborah J. Yashar is Associate Professor of Politics and International Affairs at Princeton University and the Director of Princeton's Program in Latin American Studies. She is the author of *Demanding Democracy: Reform and Reaction in Costa Rica and Guatemala, 1870s–1950s*, as well as articles and chapters on democratization, ethnic politics, collective action, and globalization.

Cambridge Studies in Contentious Politics

Ronald Aminzade et al., *Silence and Voice in the Study of Contentious Politics*
Charles D. Brockett, *Political Movements and Violence in Central America*
Gerald Davis, Doug McAdam, W. Richard Scott, and Mayer Zald, editors, *Social Movements and Organization Theory*
Jack A. Goldstone, editor, *States, Parties, and Social Movements*
Doug McAdam, Sidney Tarrow, and Charles Tilly, *Dynamics of Contention*
Charles Tilly, *The Politics of Collective Violence*
Charles Tilly, *Contention and Democracy in Europe, 1650–2000*

Contesting Citizenship in Latin America

THE RISE OF INDIGENOUS MOVEMENTS AND THE POSTLIBERAL CHALLENGE

DEBORAH J. YASHAR

Princeton University

CAMBRIDGE
UNIVERSITY PRESS

CAMBRIDGE UNIVERSITY PRESS
Cambridge, New York, Melbourne, Madrid, Cape Town, Singapore,
São Paulo, Delhi, Dubai, Tokyo, Mexico City

Cambridge University Press
The Edinburgh Building, Cambridge CB2 8RU, UK

Published in the United States of America by Cambridge University Press, New York

www.cambridge.org
Information on this title: www.cambridge.org/9780521534802

First published 2005
Reprinted 2006 (twice), 2007

A catalogue record for this publication is available from the British Library

Library of Congress Cataloging in Publication Data

Yashar, Deborah J., 1963–
Contesting citizenship in Latin America : the rise of indigenous movements and the
postliberal challenge / Deborah J. Yashar
   p. cm.– (Cambridge studies in contentious politics)
Includes bibliographical references and index.
ISBN 0-521-82746-9 (hardback : alk. paper) – ISBN 0-521-53480-1 (pbk : alk. paper)
1. Indians of South America – Politics and government. 2. Indians of South America –
Civil Rights. 3. Indians of South America – Goverment relations. 4. Indigenous peoples–
South America – Politics and government. 5. Indigenous peoples – Civil rights – South
America. 6. Indigenous peoples – South America – Government relations. 7. Political
rights– South America. 8. Citizenship – South America. 9. South America – Politics and
government. 10. South America – Race relations. 11. South America – Social policy.
I. Title. II. Series.
F2230.1.P65Y37   2005
323.1198–dc22   2004055293

ISBN 978-0-521-82746-1 Hardback
ISBN 978-0-521-53480-2 Paperback

For My Parents,
Audrey and John Yashar

Contents

List of Tables

Acknowledgments

In the summer of 1996, I traveled to Chiapas, Mexico, to take part in a Zapatista conference entitled "The Intercontinental Conference for Humanity and Against Neoliberalism." Thousands of people from all over the world traveled to this conference, later dubbed the "Intergalactic Conference," to learn about the Zapatistas, make common cause with this movement, and strategize about a global fight for democracy and justice. The conference provided an opportunity to bear witness to extraordinary developments in Mexico. It also raised themes that resonated throughout Latin America. As I subsequently traveled to Guatemala, Ecuador, Bolivia, and Peru, I often recalled the speech read by the indigenous leader, Ana María, at the opening event. To the thousands of people who had traveled to La Realidad, Chiapas, she said:

Below in the city and the plantations, we did not exist. Our lives were worth less than the machines and the animals. We were like rocks, like plants along the road. We did not have voices. We did not have faces. We did not have names. We did not have tomorrow. We did not exist.

... Then we went to the mountains.... The mountains told us to take up arms to have a voice, it told us to cover our faces to have a visage, it told us to forget our names so that we could be named, it told us to protect our past so that we could have a tomorrow.

... Behind our black faces, behind our armed voice, behind our unnamed name, behind those of us that *you* see, behind us is *you*, behind us are the same simple and ordinary men and women that are found in all ethnic and racial groups, that paint themselves in all colors, that speak in all languages, and that live in all places.

The same forgotten men and women.
The same excluded people.

The same people who are not tolerated.
The same people who are persecuted.

We are the same as you. Behind us is you.[1]

The rights to be heard, to be seen, to be recognized, and to be respected are at the core of much indigenous organizing throughout the Americas – from Mexico, to Guatemala, to Ecuador, to Bolivia, and beyond. This book sets out to explain the unprecedented and uneven emergence of these Latin American indigenous movements. They have assumed a dominant role in social movements and have increasingly come to shape political agendas throughout the region. In the process, they have demanded a voice and a seat in places that once ignored indigenous peoples. They have struggled for equal treatment, just as they have demanded local autonomy.

I thank, first and foremost, the indigenous activists who spent so many hours talking with me about indigenous communities, movements, and politics in Ecuador, Bolivia, and Peru – the countries that form the core of this book. While those conversations took place several years ago, they are still very much alive for me. I would particularly like to acknowledge Ampam Karakras, José María Cabascango, and Leonardo Viteri, in Ecuador; Jenaro Flores, Constantino Lima, and Marcial Fabricano in Bolivia; and Bonifacio Cruz and Evaristo Nukjuag in Peru. Some among this list welcomed me into their homes; others brought me to conferences and workshops; others sat down countless times to talk with me about indigenous movements and democracy; they all opened up doors that allowed me to talk to other indigenous activists and leaders. I am indebted to them all for their insight and generosity, without which I could not have written this book.

So too, several Latin American scholar-activists helped me to navigate new and uncharted waters, helping me to decipher and to amplify the wealth of experiences, books, and ideas. In particular, I want to thank Xavier Albó, Ricardo Calla, María Eugenia Choque, Carlos Mamani, and Ramiro Molina in Bolivia and Juan Bottasso, Ampam Karakras, Diego Iturralde, Jorge León, and Galo Ramón in Ecuador. Each of these scholars helped me to better understand contemporary politics in the region and to make sense of the political similarities and differences among the countries situated in the Andean-Amazon corridor.

---

[1] This speech was reprinted in *Crónicas intergalácticas. EZLN. Primer Encuentro Intercontinental por la Humanidad y contra el Neoliberalismo*. Chiapas, Mexico. 1996, pp. 23–9.

Acknowledgments

In the United States, several people helped to lay the foundation for this project. Jorge Domínguez was the intellectual catalyst for this book. At the time, I was completing my first book on democracy and authoritarianism in Central America. Jorge asked me to write a chapter on indigenous movements and democratic governance for his co-edited volume with Abraham Lowenthal. That fateful request sparked my fascination with ethnic politics and ultimately led me to pursue the research that culminated in this book. Ted MacDonald, in turn, provided me with my first contacts in the field. I thank him immensely for introducing me to people who proved to be so consequential as I conducted the research, particularly in Ecuador and Bolivia. And to Sid Tarrow and Kay Warren, who took an early interest in this project, read my work with care, challenged me intellectually to think about the fields of social movements and anthropology, respectively, and in turn invited me to take part in seminars that proved to be enormously productive.

In the process of writing this book, I have incurred many intellectual debts to colleagues and friends who have shared their work and provided critical and insightful feedback on related articles, book chapters, and conference presentations. I thank, in particular, Jeremy Adelman, Eva Bellin, Sheri Berman, Nancy Bermeo, Alyson Brysk, Valerie Bunce, Miguel Centeno, John Coatsworth, David Collier, Christian Davenport, Jorge I. Domínguez, Kent Eaton, Susan Eckstein, Jonathan Fox, Kevin Healy, Donald Horowitz, Courtney Jung, Ira Katznelson, Arang Keshavarzian, Margaret Keck, Atul Kohli, Roberto Laserna, Abraham Lowenthal, José Antonio Lucero, Beatriz Manz, Doug McAdam, Kathleen McNamara, Tali Mendelberg Guillermo O'Donnell, Rachel Sieder, Paul Sigmund, Theda Skocpol, Lynn Stephen, Sidney Tarrow, Charles Tilly, Donna Lee Van Cott, Kay Warren, Lynn White, and Elisabeth Wood.

This book is deeply indebted to the crew of excellent researchers who helped me along the way. I want to thank those who assisted me in the gathering of materials in the United States, Ecuador, Bolivia, and Peru. Rafael de la Dehesa, Anna Dahlstein, Tyler Dickovick, Lily Jara, Esperanza Luján, Maritza Rodríguez-Seguí, Daniela Raz, Adam Webb, Jorje Valle, and Verouschka Zilveti provided assistance in scouring bibliographies, reviewing newspapers, and pulling together databases on socioeconomic indicators. Lily Jara, Verouschka Zilveti, and Maritza Rodríguez-Seguí played a particularly important role in Ecuador, Bolivia, and Peru, respectively – each of them compiling databases that were used in Part II of this book. A special thanks, moreover, to those students at Harvard and Princeton and colleagues at the Institute for Popular Democracy who took seminars with me on power and protest, social movements, and ethnic politics and citizenship. All of these seminar discussions helped to crystallize many of the ideas discussed in these pages.

This book would not have been possible without the generous support provided by the following agencies and research institutes: The United States Institute of Peace; the Joint Committee on Latin American Studies of the American Council of Learned Societies and the Social Science Research Council; the Helen Kellogg Institute for International Studies at the University of Notre Dame; the Center for International Affairs and the Milton Grant, both at Harvard University; Class of 1934 University Preceptorship in the Woodrow Wilson School at Princeton University; Princeton University's Program in Latin American Studies; Princeton's Lichtenstein Institute on Self-Determination; the Center for Advanced Study in the Behavioral Sciences summer Seminar on Contentious Politics; and the Institute for Popular Democracy in the Philippines.

Lewis Bateman is a phenomenal editor: insightful, expedient, savvy, and witty. He made it a delight to work with Cambridge University Press and found two reviewers, Charles Tilly and Elisabeth Wood, who were characteristically wise, thoughtful, and provocative. Their critiques made this a much better book than it would have been otherwise. I also want to thank Edna Lloyd who helped me format the final manuscript with great diligence, speed, and kindness; Christine Dunn for the copyediting; Becky Hornyak for the index; Prerna Singh and William T. Barndt for proofing; and Sorat Tungkasiri for sharpening the photograph pictured on the book's cover.

Finally, I turn to my family. Writing this book would not have been as fun, engaging, and thought provoking had it not been for John Gershman, my partner. John traveled with me throughout Latin America and then worked by my side in Cambridge, Massachusetts; Manila, the Philippines; South Bend, Indiana; and now Princeton, New Jersey. His unmatched intellectual curiosity, profound insight, and charming irreverence often made me look at old material in new ways; this book and my life are all the better for it. Sarah and Rebecca Yashar-Gershman, our daughters, came along relatively late in the game, both born after the research was done and at a point when I thought I needed just one more year to complete the writing. That one year turned into several more, years that have hands down been the most exciting, hilarious, warm, if exhausting years of my life.

Acknowledgments

It is to my parents, Audrey and John Yashar, that I dedicate this book. They have been an unending source of love, support, and inspiration. With their commitment to education, independence, and politics, they have always encouraged me to chart my own path and pursue big questions – even when my answers differed from their own. By their example, they have highlighted the importance of seeking that mutually beneficial, if elusive, balance between family and community, work and play. In the face of repeated uncertainty and adversity, they have embodied strength, determination, wisdom, and grace. For all this and more, I dedicate this book to them.

Deborah J. Yashar
Princeton, New Jersey
February 2004

List of Acronyms

CEB	Communidades Eclesiales de Base
COICA	Coordinadora de Organizaciones Indígenas de la Cuenca Amazónica
ILO	International Labor Organization
NAFTA	North American Free Trade Agreement
NGO	Nongovernmental Organization
UN	United Nations

Bolivia

ALAS	Asesoría Legal y de Asistencia Social
APCOB	Apoyo para el Campesino-Indígena del Oriente Boliviano
APG	Asamblea del Pueblo Guaraní
ASP	Asamblea por la Soberanía de los Pueblos
CABI	Capitanía del Alto y Bajo Izozog
CANOB	Centro Ayoreo Nativo del Oriente Boliviano
CCTK	Centro Campesino Tupak Katari
CEJIS	Centro de Estudios Jurídicos e Investigación Social
CICC	Central Indígena de Comunidades de Concepción
CICOL	Central Indígena de Comunidades Originarias de Lomerío
CIDAC	Centro de Investigación, Diseño Artesenal y Comercialización Cooperativa
CIDDEBENI	Centro de Investigación y Documentación para el Desarollo del Beni

CIDOB	Confederación Indígena del Oriente, Chaco y Amazonía de Bolivia
CIMAR	Centro de Investigación y Manejo de Recursos Naturales Renovables
CIPCA	Centro de Investigación y Promoción del Campesinado
CNRA	Consejo Nacional de Reforma Agraria
CNTCB	Confederación Nacional de Trabajadores Campesinos de Bolivia
COB	Central Obrera Boliviana
COPNAG	Central de Organizaciones de los Pueblos Nativos Guarayos
CPIB	Central de Pueblos Indígenas del Beni
CSUTCB	Confederación Sindical Unica de Trabajadores Campesinos de Bolivia
INRA	Instituto Nacional de Reforma Agraria
MAS	Movimiento al Socialismo
MBL	Movimiento Bolivia Libre
MITKA	Movimiento Indio Tupak Katari
MNR	Movimiento Nacionalista Revolucionario
MRTKL	Movimiento Revolucionario Tupak Katari de Liberación
MUJA	Movimiento Universitario Julián Apaza
NEP	New Economic Policy
SAE	Subsecretaría de Asuntos Etnicos
TAYPI	Taller de Apoyo a Ayllus y Pueblos Indígenas
TCO	Tierras Comunitarias de Origen
THOA	Taller de Historia Oral Andina

Ecuador

AIEPRA	Asociación de Indígenas Evangélicos de Pastaza
BNF	Banco Nacional de Fomento
CEDOC	Central Ecuatoriana de Organizaciones Clasistas
CEPCU	Centro de Estudios Pluriculturales
CESA	Central Ecuatoriana de Servicios Agrícolas
CONACNIE	Consejo de Coordinación de las Nacionalidades Indígenas del Ecuador

List of Acronyms

CONAIE	Confederación de Nacionalidades Indígenas del Ecuador
CONFENAIE	Confederación de Nacionalidades Indígenas de la Amazonía Ecuatoriana
CTE	Confederación de Trabajadores del Ecuador
ECUARUNARI	Ecuador Runacunapac Riccharimui (Awakening of the Ecuadorean Indian)
FEDECAP	Federación de Desarrollo Campesino de Pastaza
FEI	Federación Ecuatoriana de Indios
FEINE	Federación Ecuatoriana de Indígenas Evangélicos
FENOC	Federación Nacional de Organizaciones Campesinas
FENOC-I	Federación Nacional de Organizaciones Campesinas e Indígenas
FEPOCAN	Federación Provincial de Organizaciones Campesinas del Napo
FEPP	Fondo Ecuatoriano Populorum Progressio
FICI	Federación Indígena y Campesina de Imbabura
FOIN	Federación de Organizaciones Indígenas del Napo
FODERUMA	Fondo de Desarrollo Rural Marginal
IERAC	Instituto Ecuatoriano de Reforma Agraria y Colonización
MICH	Movimiento Indígena de Chimborazo
OPIP	Organización de Pueblos Indígenas de Pastaza

Guatemala

CERJ	Consejo de Comunidades Étnicas Runujel Junam (Council of Ethnic Communities "We Are All Equal")
COMG	Consejo de Organizaciones Mayas de Guatemala
CONIC	Coordinadora Nacional Indígena y Campesina

Mexico

CNC	Confederación Nacional Campesina
EZLN	Ejército Zapatista de Liberación Nacional
PRI	Partido Revolucionario Institucional

Peru

AIDESEP	Asociación Interétnica de Desarrollo de la Selva Peruana
CAP	Cooperativa Agraria de Producción
CNA	Confederación Nacional Agraria
CONAP	Confederación de Nacionalidades de la Amazonía Peruana
SAIS	Sociedad Agrícola de Interés Social
SINAMOS	Sistema Nacional de Apoyo a la Movilización Nacional
SNA	Sociedad Nacional Agraria
UNCA	Unión de Comunidades Aymaras

PART I

Theoretical Framing

1

Questions, Approaches, and Cases

Ethnic movements have (re)surfaced with the most recent round of democratization in Latin America, Southern Europe, Asia, and Africa. While these movements vary considerably, they have collectively challenged prevailing ideas about citizenship and the nation-state. In particular, they have questioned the idea that the nation-state, as currently conceived and constituted, serves as the legitimate basis for extending and defining democratic citizenship rights and responsibilities. Alongside an older set of demands for equal inclusion and access for all ethnic groups, we increasingly find demands for the recognition of group rights and ethnic self-determination.

The emergence of these movements in Latin America is particularly striking. While ethnic-based movements have a long history of organizing, protesting, and mobilizing in Africa, Asia, and parts of Europe, there has been no comparable pattern of ethnic-based organizing in contemporary Latin America, until recently.[1] Indigenous people in Latin America have mobilized in the past, but rarely to advance ethnic-based claims and agendas. Indeed, the cultural pluralism literature often identified Latin America

---

[1] Latin American history is dotted by famous, although scattered, rebellions, including the famous 1780s rebellion led by Tupak Amaru and Tupak Katari. As social historians continue to excavate history from dusty and faraway archives, we continue to learn of numerous localized rebellions coupled with ongoing forms of what Scott (1985) has popularized as "everyday forms of resistance." Yet, these rebellions remain the exception in Latin American history. They certainly did not emerge as national or sustained movements. And by the early twentieth century, movements rarely mobilized around indigenous-based claims. See Urioste (1992: 35) for examples of indigenous rebellions in the Bolivian Andes, C. Smith (1990) for rebellions in Guatemala, and Maybury-Lewis (1991) for a discussion of Chile, Argentina, and Brazil.

3

as the exception, the region where ethnic political debates, mobilization, and conflict did not occur.[2] It is no longer possible to sustain this position.

During the course of the last third of the twentieth century, significant and unprecedented indigenous movements emerged throughout the Americas.[3] An indigenous uprising shut down roads, occupied churches, and cut off commerce in Ecuador in June 1990 – marking the presence and strength of Ecuador's organized indigenous population and emerging indigenous agenda. An indigenous march covered 650 kilometers from the lowlands of the Bolivian Amazon to the highland capital of La Paz later that same year. Indigenous people in Chiapas confronted the Mexican state on New Year's Day 1994 and subsequently articulated a set of ethnic-based demands. Mayan Indians in Guatemala coordinated the Second Continental Meeting of Indigenous and Popular Resistance in 1991, an event that coincided with the founding of various Mayan organizations.[4] International forums celebrating indigenous resistance and culture flourished in 1992, followed by the United Nations' (UN) decision to call for an International Decade of the World's Indigenous People (1995–2004) and to finish work on the Declaration on the Rights of Indigenous People. Moreover, indigenous leaders throughout the Americas have taken a more active role in debating policy, shaping institutional design, and running for political office. In Colombia and Ecuador, for example, indigenous rights were discussed in constituent assemblies in 1990–1991 and 1997–1998, respectively. In Ecuador, Bolivia, and Guatemala, indigenous movements have fielded political candidates in local and national elections. And throughout Latin America, movements have played a key role in discussions about land reform, land use, bicultural education, and census taking, among other issues. Indeed in 1997 and 2000, indigenous movements in Ecuador were among the primary actors that took to the streets and successfully toppled two different presidents.

In short, in Latin America rural men and women are coming together as Indians in regional and national organizations and making claims denied

---

[2] See Huntington and Domínguez (1975); Young (1976); Horowitz (1985); and Gurr and Harff et al. (1993).

[3] Afrolatins have also organized throughout Latin America. For competing views on racial cleavages and their politicization, see Degler (1971); Fontaine (1985); Graham (1990); NACLA (1992); Winant (1992); Hanchard (1994); Wade (1997); Marx (1998); and Nobles (2000).

[4] The Second Continental Meeting later expanded its focus to include the resistance of Afrolatins alongside that of the region's indigenous peoples and popular sectors.

them as Indians. This is happening just as more traditional labor and peasant-based organizations have declined in organizational strength. For just as workers, women, leftists, and others have become less prone to engage in movement organizing and protest politics, we have found a burst of widespread protest among indigenous peoples in the region. It is not that Indians have not organized in the past. However, they have not organized along ethnic lines to promote an explicitly indigenous agenda. With the contemporary formation of indigenous movements in Latin America, indigenous peoples are contesting the terms of citizenship. They are demanding equal rights, but they are also demanding recognition of special rights as native peoples – with claims to land, autonomous juridical spheres, and the right to maintain ethnonational identities distinct from, but formative of, a multinational state. As such, they are opening up the debate about what citizenship entails – particularly in a multicultural context.

This book explains the uneven emergence, timing, and location of indigenous protest in contemporary Latin America: why indigenous movements have emerged now and not before; and why they have emerged in some places and not others. In the process, it speaks to several broader debates: How does state formation (un)intentionally shape political identities and the salience of ethnic cleavages? Under what circumstances can social actors mobilize around new political claims? What is the relationship between ethnicity and democracy? And how are ethnic movements trying to push new democracies in a postliberal direction?

A Meso-Level Approach: National Projects, the Reach of the State, and Unintended Consequences

To explain the timing and location of indigenous organizing in Latin America, this book begins with a simple but all-too-often overlooked observation about identity politics. Institutions matter. In particular, in the era of the nation-state, it is the state that fundamentally defines the public terms of national political identity formation, expression, and mobilization.[5] Insofar as states are the prevailing political units in our world and insofar as

---

[5] Tilly (1984) observed that social movements are fundamentally framed by their relationship to the state. He observed that the move from local fiefdoms to nation-states shifted the terrain of political action. It encouraged actors to scale up their actions from local to national levels. The point being made here parallels Tilly's key insight but focuses more specifically on the identities that are privileged rather than the scale and target of social mobilization.

they extend/restrict political citizenship and define national projects,[6] they institutionalize and privilege certain national political identities. In turn, they provide incentives for actors to publicly express some political identities over others. In this regard, states try to shape, coordinate, and channel public identities.

In analyzing identity politics, it is therefore logical to use the state as the point of departure. In particular, this book sets out to analyze how Latin American states attempted to structure society – its identities, interests, and preferences – by taking a careful look at a complex of state institutions: citizenship regimes. The latter have played a disproportionately important role both in shaping and later reflecting state-projected nationalisms. As discussed at length in Chapter 2, citizenship regimes define *who* has political membership, *which* rights they possess, and *how* interest intermediation with the state is structured. The state, in general, and citizenship regimes, in particular, play a key role in *formally* defining the intersection between national politics, political membership, and public identities. As citizenship regimes have changed over time, so too have the publicly sanctioned players, rules of the game, and likely (but not preordained) outcomes.

However, the state and citizenship regimes cannot be studied in an institutional vacuum; nor can publicly sanctioned identities, rights, and modes of interest intermediation be taken at face value. For as several key works on the state have highlighted, while we must analyze the state, we *cannot* assume that states are competent, purposive, coherent, and capable. Nor can we assume a preconstituted society that will respond predictably to institutional change.[7] To the contrary, we must analyze states and state projects in light of the *reach* of the state – understood in terms of the state's actual penetration throughout the country and its capacity to govern society. For the reach of the state can vary considerably. Not only is the state virtually absent in many areas nominally governed by it but the state's proclaimed control over governed areas is often undermined by weak and incapable institutions.

---

[6] See for example, Deutsch (1953); Weber (1976); Gellner (1983); Hobsbawm and Ranger (1983); Hobsbawm (1990); and Anderson (1991). For a review of the vast literature on nationalism, see Breuilly (1993).

[7] O'Donnell (1993); Fox (1994a and 1994b); Joseph and Nugent (1994); Migdal, Kohli, and Shue (1994); Migdal (1998 and 2001); Scott (1998); Yashar (1999); Herbst (2000); Harty (2001); and Stoner-Weiss (forthcoming) have all highlighted that states are key political institutions whose capacity and institutionalization vary among countries *and* subnationally.

Consequently, state projects do not necessarily translate into stated outcomes. With respect to national projects and political identities this means that publicly sanctioned identities do not necessarily equal private identities and preferences. People can and do have several identities and can express those identities in different forums. This is not just a pluralist or postmodern insight. It is also one that Geertz (1963) advocated in his discussion of new nation-states confronted with diverse ethnic populations. He noted that states need to encourage ethnic groups to adopt a shared civic identity before the state and to express their ethnic identities in more private forums. One does not have to agree with Geertz's policy recommendation to agree with his insight that this is possible.

Hence state projects must be assessed against the reach of the state. Where the state has unevenly penetrated society, local enclaves provide an arena for "private" identities to find public expression. We have found this dynamic with the Muslim Brotherhood throughout much of the Middle East, the Basques in northern Spain, and Catholics in Northern Ireland. We will find that indigenous peoples in Latin America also operate in this kind of context: states have privileged certain identities and interests but have been too weak to impose them. While in the Amazon, state weakness is a function of the relative absence of the state. In the Andes and rural areas in Mesoamerica, it is a function of the varied capacity of the state to penetrate into these localities and displace preexisting forms of governance. In all these areas, a certain kind of local autonomy remained – one in which ethnic identities remained salient, local authority structures evolved, and actors learned to maneuver between local ethnicities and national identities.

What can one take away from this brief discussion? For it started off by asserting the centrality of states and concluded by noting their partial and at times unintended impact.

- States privilege certain political identities – particularly through different forms of citizenship regimes. In this regard, political identities are historically contingent, institutionally bounded, and open to change.
- The reach of the state, however, shapes the degree to which states successfully impose these political identities throughout society. National projects can produce fractured responses, precisely because states confront complex societies that do not always share common experiences vis-à-vis the state. In this regard, political identities are not entirely malleable.

- Where the reach of the state is uneven, in particular, local enclaves can persist and alternative political identities and authority structures can coexist subnationally with national projects that suggest otherwise.
- By extension, where new rounds of state formation challenge (intentionally or otherwise) the autonomy of these enclaves, we should not be surprised to find resistance and, where possible, mobilization.
- In this regard, historical sequencing matters. We can assume neither that states nor societies persist independently of one another. Hence, we need to look at how states interact with society and, in turn, how society responds to and/or resists state efforts.

In short, this book argues that political identities are historically contingent, institutionally bounded, and open to change. States (and those in power) set the stage but societies do not always conform to the script. This is because even if the state can define the terms of public interaction, it cannot impose preferences or displace identities; for political identities are neither fixed nor completely malleable. Indeed, they operate differently in different arenas and at different times. The question then becomes, why do *some* identities and interests become more important at some times and not at others, in some places and not others. And when and why do those politicized identities translate into political action?

To explain changes in identity politics (in this case, the contemporary emergence of indigenous movements in Latin America), this approach leads one to hypothesize that important institutional changes might have politicized identities in new and unintended ways. This is precisely what this book finds. In the context of Latin America's indigenous movements, I argue that contemporary *changes in citizenship regimes* politicized indigenous identities precisely because they unwittingly challenged enclaves of local autonomy that had gone largely unrecognized by the state. However, I will also argue that we cannot simply infer mobilization from motives, a point drawn from scholarship on social movements and contentious politics.[8] Indeed, one must also consider two additional factors, the *political associational space* that provided the political opportunity to organize and the *transcommunity networks* that provided the capacity for diverse and often spatially distant indigenous community to scale up and confront the state. This book develops this three-pronged argument conceptually (Chapter 2), theoretically (Chapter 3), and empirically (Chapters 4–6).

---

[8] See McAdam (1982); McAdam, McCarthy, and Zald (1996); Tarrow (1998); and McAdam, Tarrow, and Tilly (2001).

Prevailing Explanations

This meso-level approach differs from the prevailing theories of identity politics. It is neither bound by local primordialism, on one end of the spectrum, nor transnational constructivism, on the other. Rather, the approach developed here consciously seeks to find a middle ground in which institutions become the historical referent for, but not the contemporary composer of, political identities. I argue that this mid-range comparative approach is more compelling, precisely because it can explain change over time and variation among cases, something that the prevailing explanations cannot (yet) do. Here I critically review five explanations that have been marshaled in recent years to explain identity politics, in general, and ethnic politics, in particular. While each approach is provocative, I find that none of them provides the adequate point of departure to explain change and variation. This is because they lack a temporal and/or spatial understanding of political identities and their relationship to the state. To these approaches I now turn.

Primordialism[9]

Primordialism is the prevailing argument most commonly voiced in policy and lay circles – although decreasingly so in academic circles where it has largely been discredited. Primordialists assume that ethnic identities are deeply rooted affective ties that shape primary loyalties and affinities. While it is not assumed that all ethnic identities lead to conflict, it is assumed that actors possess a strong sense of ethnic or racial identity that *primarily* shapes their actions and worldview. Accordingly, individuals and communities commonly advance and/or defend ethnically derived concerns – particularly when they perceive a disadvantage or long-standing abuse or ethnic slight. The emergence of indigenous organizations and protest are therefore understood as a natural expression of integral ethnic identities. Identities are fixed. They are locally rooted. They are often understood as immutable.

Primordial arguments have found their greatest renaissance among chroniclers of the former Soviet Union, former Yugoslavia, Burundi, Rwanda, and Israel/Palestine. In the first two cases, it is argued that political regimes repressed a deeply rooted sense of national identity. The subsequent breakdown of repressive political institutions enabled submerged ethno-national identities to resurface; and with that rebirth, nations have

---

[9] Geertz (1963); Isaacs (1975); van den Berghe (1981); and Stack (1986).

naturally aspired to establish their own nation-state. In the latter three cases, the ongoing conflict is analyzed as a consequence of historic antagonisms, whether within or between states. As the press would have it, there is long-standing animosity going back as long as anyone can remember that explains the ongoing and brutal conflict between primordial groups in Burundi, Rwanda, Israel/Palestine, Sri Lanka, Indonesia, and just about anywhere where ethnic conflicts appear.

Yet, primordial arguments fall short. First, they cannot be empirically sustained. Detailed case studies and comparative analyses have revealed the constructed and changing nature of ethnic identities. Identities are not fixed nor do they have natural affinities. In Latin America, for example, *Indian* is not a natural category. It is a category imposed by colonial powers; it does not recognize the diversity (and at times historical animosity) among indigenous communities. To forge an indigenous movement in the contemporary era, activists had to convince people to expand their self-identification from Quichua, or Shuar, or Totzil or something else to *Indian*. This was not a given. And in the process of organizing and protesting, those identities, interests, and preferences were open to further change. The situational and evolving terms of ethnic identities and political mobilization have been convincingly demonstrated and widely accepted by anthropologists and social historians. Consequently, one can argue that primordial *sentiments*, to use Geertz's term, are strong in some cases; but the historical explanation of that sentiment is weak.

Moreover, the primordial approach sidesteps the fundamental question of why these identities emerge as a central axis of action in some cases and not others. Ethnic/national identities and conflicts are not reclaimed everywhere, even when there are moments of political opening. Hence, even if democratization allows for the greater expression of ethnic identity, this does not mean that individuals assume that political identity. And where they do, it is not apparent that they do so for primordial reasons (as opposed to strategic ones, as discussed next). The cases of Latin America are most instructive here. Earlier rounds of democratization did not lead to the emergence of indigenous organizations or ethnic conflict – even when indigenous identities were clearly significant at the local level. Indeed, a basic claim of this book is that the politicization of ethnic cleavages is a new phenomenon in the region. Finally, even if we assume that ethnic loyalties are given, unchanging, and deeply rooted (an extremely dubious assumption to begin with), primordialist arguments provide little insight into why, when, or how these identities translate into political organizing and action in some cases and not others. For even if ethnicity is the primary identity that affects where one lives, how one votes, and where one spends money, it does not mean that individuals will join political organizations and mobilize on behalf of their ethnic group.

In short, the emergence of ethnic movements and conflicts speaks to the salience of ethnic identities; but primordial arguments fail to problematize when, why, and where identities become politically salient and the conditions under which they engender political organizations.

Instrumentalism

Instrumentalist or rational choice analyses challenge the primordial assumption that ethnic identities as such motivate collective action. Instrumentalists begin by assuming that individuals have fixed preferences, are goal oriented, act intentionally, and engage in utility-maximizing behavior.[10] These assumptions lead instrumentalists to ask a) why individuals choose to organize (along ethnic lines) and b) why they choose to act *collectively*, particularly if in the absence of doing so they can still enjoy collective benefits. This last point has been elaborated most skillfully by Mancur Olson (1965). In other words, while they question primordialism's assumptions about the naturalness of identity and the group, they share an assumption that preferences are fixed. But whereas primordialists assume that groups seek to maintain the integrity and autonomy of the group, as such, instrumentalists tend to analyze the maximization of *other* goals: generally economic resources, power, and/or security. To explain why individuals choose to act, therefore, they assess the costs and benefits alongside the positive and negative incentives. In other words, one needs to look at individual intentionality and its collective consequences.

Instrumental approaches to collective ethnic action have addressed a variety of dynamics: ethnic mobilization in Africa (Bates 1974), language choices in the post-Soviet world (Laitin 1998), ethnic conflict (Fearon and Laitin 1996; Bates, Figueiredo, and Weingast 1998), and feelings of belonging (Hardin 1995). These authors, in turn, have articulated a provocative set of arguments. Bates focuses on modernization and the ways in which it provides new opportunities for political entrepreneurs who seek to secure

---

[10] For important statements on the relationship between rational choice and ethnicity, see Rabushka and Shepsle (1972); Bates (1974); and Bates and Weingast (1995). For sympathetic but critical elaborations see Laitin (1986 and 1998); Hardin (1995); and Fearon and Laitin (2000).

11

access to scarce resources. Laitin focuses on the cascade dynamic to explain language choices in a context of relative political stability versus change. Fearon and Laitin analyze the security dilemma in light of information exchanges, signaling, and the problems poised by noise. Hardin provides a theoretical explanation of the need to belong to groups and how that can spiral into conflict. In other words, the approach has been used to explain a wide range of outcomes. In some cases political entrepreneurs play an active role. In others they do not. But in all of them, decisions are made at a microanalytic level – taking individual actors as the unit of analysis, assuming their preferences, and looking at the aggregation of individual-based decisions to explain broad macro-analytic outcomes.

But regardless of the particular argument, instrumentalist explanations of collective ethnic action share one general problem. They tend to shift the question away from why *ethnicity* (as opposed to some other identity) becomes salient to a discussion of how to maximize a particular goal (be it material gain, security, belonging, or something else). In this scenario, the politicization of ethnicity is largely instrumental to achieving other goals; the ethnic card is one tool among many. The conditions under which ethnicity becomes politicized is less relevant to these studies than modeling and predicting the utility and capacity of ethnicity for collective action.

Yet, this recrafting of the question sidesteps why ethnic loyalties become the basis for political action at one time versus another. These studies *to date* have provided little insight into how one arrives at utility functions – particularly if actors are not acting in their economic self-interest – without making post hoc arguments; why actors occasionally act in ways that appear detrimental to their material interests; and when and why ethnicity (as opposed to other categories) becomes politicized. To answer these central questions, one needs to move away from rational choice's trademark parsimony to historically grounded determinations of preferences and institutional boundaries, as found in Laitin (1998).[11] As argued in this book, indigenous movements are rational responses to changing institutional circumstances. The changing circumstances, rather than the

---

[11] Laitin (1998) persuasively discusses the broader comparative historical context that explains why individuals privilege ethnic identities in some cases and not others. Fearon and Laitin (2000) also suggest that rationalist and culturalist explanations can be bridged and can better inform one another – with rational choice, for example, underscoring the strategic calculations embedded in cultural analyses and culturalist explanations, in turn, providing a better understanding of the discourses and heuristic frames that are mobilized in situations of ethnic violence.

can't all 3 be true!

rationality, however, are the key variables to explaining why, when, and where movements emerge.[12]

Poststructuralism

Poststructural alternatives challenge the prior two approaches.[13] Despite their diversity, poststructural approaches commonly assume that identities are not given or ordered but socially constructed and evolving. Individuals do not necessarily identify with or act according to structurally defined positions, for structural conditions do not determine or define actors in any kind of uniform, unitary, or teleological fashion. Individuals are plural subjects and power is more diffuse. As subjects, they can assume a role in fashioning and reconstituting their identities (e.g., as Indians, workers, or women), although there is no agreement over the degree of choice that actors have vis-à-vis these diffused power relations.

Poststructuralism opened the door to see ethnic identities as primary and purposive without arguing that they are primordial or instrumental in nature. By challenging structural and teleological explanations, it problematized identity rather than assuming it. By refocusing on the local, analyzing discourse, and highlighting identity as a social construction, poststructural studies have heightened our sense of context, complexity, and the dynamic process by which agents (re)negotiate their identities. Indigenous identity is, from this perspective, both constituted by social conditions as well as renegotiated by individuals.

This book draws on poststructural assumptions that individuals are plural subjects with multiple configured identities; these identities are socially constructed and transmutable. But it also assumes that very real structural conditions of poverty and authoritarian rule can impede the unencumbered expression of identities and pursuit of collective action just as they can shape needs as preferences. Given the structural conditions faced by Latin America's indigenous peoples, I do not ascribe to the literary method that pushes scholarship in a discursive and relativist direction. Discursive analyses cannot speak to the comparative questions raised in this book. While

---

[12] If instrumental approaches provide an incomplete explanation of the conditions under which ethnic identity becomes politically salient for a group of people, they do provide important insight into organization building and maintenance. See Laitin (1986) and Varshney (1995). Accordingly, Cohen (1985) has distinguished between social movement theorizing that privileges strategy (discussed here) versus identity (discussed next).

[13] Foucault (1980); Laclau and Mouffe (1985); Touraine (1988); and Melucci (1989).

13

problematizing ethnicity, poststructural approaches can neither explain why it becomes assumed as a salient *political* identity *across cases* nor delineate the conditions under which people are likely or able to organize around that identity. Many poststructural theorists would argue that these questions wrongly presuppose universal explanations (where none exist). Ultimately, the poststructural distancing from generalized explanations begs the question as to why indigenous movements have emerged throughout the Americas in the past decades. In other words, it is difficult for these approaches to scale up from the individual and local to the regional and comparative.

Structural Conditions of Poverty and Inequality

A fourth approach focuses on structural or material conditions of poverty and inequality. It is a given in Latin America that indigenous populations experience ethnic discrimination, marginalization, material deprivation, and economic exploitation. "World Bank and other development agencies indicate that Indians remain the poorest and most destitute of the region's population, with the highest rate of infant mortality and childhood malnutrition and the lowest rates of literacy and schooling" (David and Partridge 1994: 38). Carlos Fuentes, speaking of the inextricable fusion of ethnic and class identities among the Mayan in Chiapas, said: "What has an extremely long lifespan is the sequence of poverty, injustice, plunder and violation in which, since the 16th century, live the Indians who are peasants and the peasants who are Indians."[14] Indeed, ethnically stratified poverty is all the more striking and onerous given that: "[e]ven before the severe adjustment of the 1980s, Latin America had the most inequitable income distribution and the highest level of poverty relative to its income of any area in the world" (Morley 1995: vi). According to Gurr (1993: 61 and 2000: ch. 4), indigenous peoples in Latin America have experienced among the highest discriminatory barriers (along economic, political, and cultural lines) in the world.

These material or structural conditions have disadvantaged indigenous communities for centuries and constitute a constant source of conflict and object of change. Resistance has assumed multiple forms from sporadic rebellions to everyday forms of resistance embedded in dances, stories, and rituals that are an integral part of indigenous communities.[15] The dance of the conquest (practiced in various indigenous communities throughout

---

[14] *New York Times* op-ed reprinted in the *Boston Globe*, January 11, 1994.
[15] For example, see Nash (1989) and Scott (1990).

Latin America), for example, has been amply studied by anthropologists who have highlighted the ways in which the dance is a vivid reminder of an ongoing process of colonization, anger against the landlord, and expression of resistance. Similarly, the Popul Vuj (the Mayan book of origin) weaves many complex tapestries of meaning, one of which is the oft-repeated phrase: "May we all rise up, may no one be left behind."

Yet, looking at structural conditions of poverty and inequality alone cannot explain the contemporary and continental-wide rise in indigenous mobilization in Latin America or elsewhere. This is because these structural conditions are constant. They coincide both with the lack of mobilization in earlier times and the rise in mobilization in the contemporary period. Moreover, differences in poverty rates do not coincide with the uneven emergence of these movements. Poverty rates, for example, are indisputably higher in the Amazon than in the Andes.[16] Yet, there is no clear correlation between poverty rates, the emergence of indigenous movements, and their strength and/or their mobilizational capacity. Relative to the Andes, Amazonian movements emerge early in Ecuador, late in Bolivia, and without rival in Peru. In other words, poverty and inequality are severe and ongoing concerns. But they are poor predictors of when, where, and why indigenous movements emerge.[17]

Globalization[18]

If the first two approaches assume actor identities, and the last one assumes structural constants, the final one does neither. Rather, this approach begins by noting that there have been changes in context, including the integration of economies, the growth of civil societies, and the development of international norms and cultures—all of which impact heavily on ethnic movements. This approach has become a growth industry for scholars and has also had an impact on studies of collective action and social movements. Increasingly, scholars have come to argue that globalization explains a new round of collective action. And in some cases, the case is made that globalization has served to heighten or advance ethnic identities (Brysk 2000).

---

[16] For Ecuador, Larrea (1996: 13) finds that poverty rates are as high as 95 percent in some Amazonian cantons.

[17] However, it must be noted that if poverty and inequality do not explain the recent rise in ethnic mobilization, one cannot begin to respond to the demands of these communities without redressing these very structural conditions.

[18] This section on globalization draws on Yashar (2002).

15

This approach has put forth several types of arguments to explain the interaction of globalization and the salience of ethnic identities. Most commonly argued is that globalization has heightened inequalities in the race to integrate markets. Economic integration, therefore, can threaten economic livelihoods, national sovereignty, and/or cultural boundaries. Protest emerges as a defensive response to integrated markets.[19] From this perspective, one would hypothesize that free markets harm indigenous ways of life and, therefore, politicize indigenous communities to take action. A second approach identifies the emergence of a transnational civil society and/or transnational advocacy networks.[20] This new transnational context provides networks, resources, information, funds, and so forth that were previously inaccessible to groups. Under these circumstances politically weak groups, including ethnic communities, have gained the opportunity and capacity to protest. They have become politically stronger with the support, information, and funding provided by various international organizations, nongovermental organizations (NGOs), funding agencies, and professional associations. A final globalization argument contends that globalization has produced new sets of norms and ideas, including human rights, and indigenous rights, and environmental rights, among others. These are increasingly instantiated in international institutions that legitimate and propagate these ideas. In turn, these ideas shape self-understandings and legitimate the demands of new social movements, including ethnic-based movements.[21]

Each of these approaches is at first blush compelling and aptly describes important movements that have gained substantial press – including the Zapatista protest against the North American Free Trade Agreement (NAFTA), indigenous protests against international oil exploration, indigenous participation in UN working groups and professional conferences, and collective efforts to pass the International Labor Organization's (ILO) Convention 169. In other words, there appears to be a descriptive fit between certain aspects of globalization and the campaigns launched by some movements.

Yet globalization approaches remain blunt instruments to address the regionwide politicization of ethnic cleavages, in general, and indigenous movements in Latin America, in particular. This is so for several reasons.

---

[19] For example, see Rodrik (1997). While Rodrik does not focus specifically on ethnic politics, his arguments about protest could logically include new ethnic movements.

[20] See Keck and Sikkink (1998) and Brysk (2000), in particular.

[21] See in particular Soysal (1994).

Conceptually, the term remains imprecise. What does it (not) cover? When did it begin? The competing and vague terms that are used do not entirely answer this question and, consequently, make it hard to ascertain if and how globalization does (not) matter. For how can one discern the causal mechanisms when the timing and sequencing of globalization are in question? Indeed, in some cases, the movements to be explained emerge prior to the onset of key moments in economic, political, and normative globalization. Secondly, even if one grants a common and bounded definition of globalization, the globalization arguments beg the question as to why globalization catalyzes collective action in some places and not others; and why ethnicity (or any political identity) becomes the primary basis for mobilization in some cases and yet not in others. When we pitch our arguments in terms of globalization, without greater attention paid to why, how, and where domestic actors can and do engage in collective action, we lose sight of the variation that exists among cases. For collective action is not universal. It remains an outcome that requires us to explain variation across and within cases. It is this very variation that we need to explain. And it this very variation that becomes a tool for discerning and substantiating arguments about when/where movements emerge and when/where they do so along ethnic lines. Radcliffe draws similar conclusions: "the transnational engagement of global organizations, states and subjects are not decided *a priori*, and leave room for agency and dynamic processes of change" (Radcliffe 2001: 20).

In light of recent research on transnational networks' influence on policy formulation, it is clear that transnationalism matters in politics and development. The mapping out of such transnational networks however relies upon a detailed *empirical* understanding of the actors involved, their means of communication and the power relationships between them (Radcliffe 2001: 27).

In short, the globalization literature thus far suffers from an ahistorical and often universalizing understanding of if, where, and how this phenomenon matters for identity politics and collective action. So too this literature suffers from the assumption, rather than demonstration, that the state is of declining relevance in contemporary politics. This book will argue the opposite. It is precisely the changing and uneven role of the state that will prove consequential to the politicization of indigenous identities in contemporary Latin America.

Seen as a whole, the ahistorical and atemporal quality of the prior approaches limits their ability to explain the *contemporary* salience of indigenous identity for political organizing in Latin America. They are too static and, as such, have a difficult time explaining change over time and variation within and among cases. Primordialists view identity as a constant and take the ethnic group as the appropriate level of analysis. They therefore negate the possibility for change over time. Instrumentalists assume given utility functions for individuals therefore placing historical context outside the model. Poststructuralists challenge historical master narratives and see identity and identity-related action as largely contingent, individuated, and nongeneralizable. Structural arguments about poverty and inequality identify long-standing conditions that cannot explain the contemporary emergence of these movements. And globalization arguments have failed to provide us with a historically and conceptually precise understanding of what globalization is, how it differs from prior periods, and why it matters in some cases but not others. In short, by assuming the appropriate level of analysis (individual, group, global) and by often assuming the ends to be achieved, these approaches find it difficult to account for how time and historical context intervene to shape and reshape identities, movements, and preferences.

As such, none of these approaches can be relied on individually to explain the politicization of and organization around indigenous identity. However, nor can they be summarily dismissed. Balancing primordialists against poststructuralists, I acknowledge the power of ethnic ties without assuming that they are primary or unchanging. Confronting instrumentalists' concern for organization building and strategy, I evaluate the conditions in which actors can and do join organizations. And in evaluating context, motives, and resources, I acknowledge the motives and opportunities identified by studies of structural conditions and globalization. To integrate a concern for identity, organizations, motive, and context, I situate these questions *historically* and *comparatively* in terms of changing *state–society relations*. Rather than presuming the identities of important actors and national context, we need to problematize both.

This book does so by advancing a comparative historical and meso-level approach that looks at changing state–society relations in twentieth-century Latin America. The rest of this book analyzes how states tried to constitute societies through citizenship regimes and how indigenous people responded in kind. I argue that citizenship regimes fundamentally *changed* in the last third of the twentieth century, with a corresponding, albeit unintentional, consequence of politicizing ethnic cleavages in the late twentieth century. Yet, if temporal changes in citizenship regimes provided the contemporary motive for indigenous organizing, they do not explain the spatial variation among and within countries in the late twentieth century. To explain why indigenous organizations emerged in some places and not others, two additional variables are introduced: *political associational space* and *transcommunity networks*. These two additional variables speak to varied opportunities and capacities that in turn help us to map out where indigenous movements were (not) able to emerge in the contemporary period. In short, while changing citizenship regimes speak to the temporal question of why indigenous movements have emerged now and not before, political associational space and societal networks speak to the spatial question of when and where they were able to do so. This argument is elaborated in Chapters 2 and 3 and substantiated in Chapters 4, 5, and 6.

The Cases and Research Design

This three-part argument is explored and evaluated against a subset of five Latin American countries that claim the largest absolute and relative indigenous populations: Bolivia, Guatemala, Peru, Ecuador, and Mexico. These countries are home to 90 percent of Latin America's estimated 35–40 million indigenous peoples and have the highest indigenous to non-indigenous ratio:[22] Bolivia (60–70 percent), Guatemala (45–60 percent),

---

[22] It is commonly stipulated that approximately 400 ethnic groups live in Latin America, composing between thirty-five to forty million people, 6 to 10 percent of the total Latin American population, and an estimated 10 percent of the world's estimated 300 or so million indigenous peoples. It should be noted that the simple question: "how many Indians are there?" leads to rather complex answers, all of which boil down to: "we do not know (and cannot know) for sure." This is because the category, indigenous or Indian, is not stable. While one can only be "Indian" if one descends from a line of indigenous peoples, not all those of indigenous descent maintain that identity. In fact, Latin American states have actively encouraged Indians to assimilate into a mestizo (mixed) culture and to adopt non-Indian practices, loyalties, and the like. To avoid discrimination and to increase chances for social mobility, many (but not all) Indians appeared to follow the state's lead. Yet some who would never claim an Indian identity in legal or mixed company do so in other spheres. Significant waves of migration, remote communities, and mistrust of researchers makes it even more difficult to gather current, reliable, and cross-national data. The lack of reliable data is a sign of the uneven incorporation of indigenous peoples into existing states and democracies. That said, the figures cited are included to give a general sense of demography. In most cases they draw on national census data that determines indigenous identity according to self-identification or primary language use. Given the incentives not to identify, these figures are probably a conservative estimate.

19

Peru (38–40 percent), Ecuador (30–38 percent), and Mexico (12–14 percent) (see Table 1.1).[23]

Moreover, these five countries claim indigenous populations of three million or more, whereas all other Latin American cases claim one million or less. Indeed, while Mexico's indigenous population (estimated at over ten million) constitutes a comparatively lower percentage of that country's total population, Mexico claims the highest percentage (around 30 percent) of Latin America's total indigenous population. Indigenous populations in the rest of the region's countries are significantly smaller – in both relative and absolute terms – constituting 10 percent or less of each country's total population (refer to Table 1.1). The five cases studied here, therefore, claim Latin America's largest indigenous populations. The majority of these communities have lived in peasantized[24] agricultural areas in Mesoamerica (which includes Mexico and Guatemala, along with the rest of Central America) and the Andes (which stretches from Venezuela to Tierra del Fuego and includes the highland parts of Ecuador, Peru, and Bolivia). A significantly smaller percentage of the indigenous population lives in the Amazon (which includes but is not limited to the lowlands parts of Ecuador, Peru, and Bolivia), where populations were historically less likely to engage in sedentary agricultural forms of livelihood. Indigenous peoples living in the Amazon, Andes, and Mesoamerica share deep poverty and structural inequality, with estimated national poverty rates for indigenous peoples ranging from 65 to 85 percent (Psacharopoulos and Patrinos 1994: 207).

---

[23] There are no agreed upon figures for indigenous peoples. The table presented here, therefore, should be read as a general indicator of differences among countries rather than a precise indication of the percentage of indigenous people living in each country. Indeed, the estimated though not terribly reliable figures in Table 1 do not reveal the ways in which indigenous communities have changed with respect to the meaning, content, scope, and form of identities, practices, or goals of indigenous peoples. Nor do these figures intend to stipulate a shared identity among indigenous peoples. Indeed, the very idea of an "indigenous people" is predicated on the arrival of "settlers" against whom indigenous peoples identify themselves and are identified. Hence there is a dual image that needs to be kept in mind. While indigenous peoples differ substantially among themselves – with respect to primary identities, practices, etc. – often leading to conflict or competition, they have often shared common opposition to those who have tried to dominate them.

[24] Indians have been and remain largely peasants. While there are important debates about how to define the peasantry (which is a changing and perhaps increasingly anachronistic category), for the purposes of this book, I highlight the general commitment to farm the land as a fundamental identity and livelihood of the peasantry. That said, it is important to note that *not* all Indians are peasants. Indigenous families have increasingly migrated to the cities and engaged in other kinds of livelihood. In some parts of the Andes, these migrant urban communities are referred to as *cholos*.

Table 1.1. *Estimates of Indigenous Peoples in Latin America, (1978–1991)*

Estimated % of Total Population	
Populations over 10%	
Bolivia	60–70
Guatemala	45–60
Peru	38–40
Ecuador	30–38
Mexico	12–14
Populations b/w 5–10%	
Belize	9
Panama	4–8
Chile	4–6
Populations under 5%	
Guyana	4
Surinam	3
Honduras	2–3
Paraguay	2
El Salvador	<2
Colombia	<2
Nicaragua	<2
Argentina	<2
Venezuela	<2
French Guyana	<2
Costa Rica	<1
Brazil	<1
Uruguay	0

Source: Mayer and Masferrer, (1979: 220–221); Stefano Varese, (1991); *Statistical Abstract of Latin America* (1993: 30, pt. I: 150); and *Statistical Abstract of Latin America* (2001: 37, Table 532: 104)

Ethnic cleavages were weak in all five cases for much of the twentieth century. This pattern abruptly changed in four of the cases by the end of the twentieth century. Indeed, significant indigenous movements emerged in Ecuador, Bolivia, Guatemala, and Mexico, but not in Peru.[25] In these first four cases, indigenous peoples mobilized beyond the local level to forge moderate to strong regional/subnational and national organizations

[25] Smith (1985); Mallon (1992); Stavenhagen (1992); Adrianzén et al. (1993); Van Cott (1994); Mayer (1996); Yashar (1998); and Brysk (2000).

21

(where strength is defined as organizational endurance, geographic scope, *and* mobilizational capacity).[26] In Peru, by contrast, mobilizing along ethnic lines has been weak and localized.[27]

To explain the politicization of ethnic cleavages therefore requires that we explain *both* why there has been change over time and variation across cases. This book is designed to answer both of these questions by using a cross between a most similar and most different systems

---

[26] Strength requires endurance, geographic scope, and mobilizational capacity. Endurance means that organizations persist over time. If organizations are ephemeral (no matter how brilliant their short shelf life) or if they "persist" but as organizational shells, I understand them to be organizationally weak. Geographically, strength means that the movement has leaders and supporters at the regional and perhaps even national level. In other words, localized movements (no matter how well orchestrated and no matter how deep their ties) are not considered strong for the purposes of this book. Finally, mobilizational capacity refers to the ability to call on supporters to demonstrate. This last indicator is the most difficult (and perhaps problematic) to measure as capacity is hard to know in advance. I have therefore used a proxy by looking at the size of past mobilizations and the perceived depth of contemporary ties to the organization. When analyzing these three dimensions of strength (endurance, geography, and mobilization), scholars and activists have generally agreed that Peru is an outlier when compared to Ecuador, Bolivia, Guatemala, and Mexico. Indigenous organizations in Peru have generally *not* emerged and when they have (and where they have "endured"), they do not have deep ties to society, are not regional and/or national organizations, and have not demonstrated mobilizational capacity. Ecuador, Bolivia, Guatemala, and Mexico, by contrast are comparatively strong on all of these dimensions. In each case, organizations have emerged with an ongoing history, with a broader geographic scope, and with the capacity to mobilize indigenous communities in the streets, highways, markets, and government buildings. In this regard, these four cases are categorically in a different situation than Peru in the contemporary period.

[27] While this book explains *domestic* mobilization by indigenous movements, it is important to note that in all of the countries discussed here, including Peru, indigenous leaders have taken a more active role in international forums to establish ties, attain funds, access information, and pressure for change at home (Brysk 2000). This international organizing has happened in and through various organizational loci, most notably the UN. In 1983 the UN, for example, created a working group on indigenous peoples that has included representation from member states and indigenous organizations to draft a declaration of indigenous rights; this working group declared 1993 the Year of Indigenous People. Indigenous peoples have formed transnational organizations such as the South American Indian Council, the International Indian Treaty Council; the Campaign for 500 Years of Indigenous, Black, and Popular Resistance; and the Amazonian Coalition (COICA). They have also gained a presence in international environmental movements, displayed with fanfare at the 1992 Earth Summit in Rio de Janeiro, Brazil. Indigenous communities have found an institutional space within transnational environmental groups that have worked in coalition around issues of equitable and sustainable development. These are striking developments and have received significant coverage. But they do not signify strength and mobilization at home, which is the focus of this book. Indeed, Keck and Sikkink (1998) and Brysk (2000) have observed that many movements turn to the international arena precisely when they are weak at home.

design. To explain change over time, this book uses a most similar systems design. Longitudinal comparisons are made within each case to explain why indigenous mobilization was weak earlier in the century but strong by the end of the century.[28] To explain variation across the cases, this book uses a cross between the most similar and most different systems designs. The cross-national comparison of Ecuador, Bolivia, Guatemala, and Mexico is a most different systems design geared toward explaining why different cases each witnessed the emergence of indigenous movements by century's end. The cross-national comparison of these four cases with Peru approximates a most similar systems design, for Peru shares certain central features with several of the cases and yet failed to witness the emergence of a significant indigenous movement by the end of the twentieth century. Peru shares with Ecuador and Bolivia basic geography, demography, and histories of populism and corporatism. Peru shared with Guatemala, a history of violent civil war. In short, the book sets out to maximize a set of comparisons to yield insight into variation over time and across cases.

The following discussion briefly introduces the cases analyzed throughout this book. While acknowledging the peculiarities of each case, the following sketch also highlights broad similarities in indigenous movement emergence in Ecuador, Bolivia, Guatemala, and Mexico, particularly when contrasted with Peru. For while differences surely exist among the first four cases, they exhibit parallel outcomes of indigenous mobilization. And while Peru certainly shares political features with each of the cases discussed here, it stands alone by not experiencing indigenous mobilization along the lines and scope found in Ecuador, Bolivia, Guatemala, and Mexico.

By the late twentieth century the Ecuadorian indigenous movement emerged as the most prominent and consequential indigenous movement in Latin America. It transformed rural organizing and shaped state policy on bicultural education, agrarian reform, and territorial autonomy.[29] With its origins in disparate organizations, the Ecuadorian movement developed two significant regional federations – ECUARUNARI (Ecuador Runacanapac Riccharimui, "awakening of the Ecuadorian Indian") of the Andes and CONFENAIE (La Confederación de Nacionalidades Indígenas de la Amazonía Ecuatoriana, The Confederation of Indigenous Nationalities

---

[28] In the case studies presented in Part II, I also highlight variation in indigenous mobilization *within* countries. Hence, I explain why indigenous mobilization is stronger in some regions of a country and not others. This draws on a most similar systems research design.

[29] Confederación de Organizaciones Indígenas del Ecuador (1989); Almeida (1992); Selverston (1994 and 2001); Trujillo (1994); and Zamoc (1994).

of the Ecuadorian Amazon) of the Amazon – that subsequently founded in the 1980s the national confederation CONAIE (Confederation de Nacionalidades Indigenas del Ecuador – the Confederation of Indigenous Nationalities of Ecuador). Among other indigenous confederations, CONAIE has become the prominent interlocutor for Ecuador's indigenous peoples, particularly following its organization of a week-long indigenous civic strike in 1990 that shut down roads, occupied churches, and cut off commerce in Ecuador. It sustained this protest capacity throughout the 1990s, contesting government policies and proposing alternatives. In 1996, following internal debates, they entered the electoral arena as part of a larger coalition and successfully fielded Andean and Amazonian legislative candidates. In 1998, they tried to shape the new Constitution. And in 1997 and 2000, they spearheaded multisector protests that toppled the government; in the 2000 protest, they were "partners" in a short-lived military-indigenous governing junta.

Bolivia's contemporary indigenous movement has also become a prominent actor in political debates. This movement has its origins in the late 1960s and early 1970s as indigenous activists began to assert autonomy within the Andean-based peasant organization and the universities.[30] These activists called themselves Kataristas to commemorate Tupak Katari, an eighteenth-century Aymara hero. By 1979, Kataristas had assumed control of the military-dominated peasant organization renaming it the Confederación Sindical Unica de Trabajadores Campesinos de Bolivia (CSUTCB); asserted greater independence from the national labor federation; and challenged the military-peasant pact. While Katarismo, as an organizational force, did not sustain political momentum or unity, it has had a lasting impact on union and electoral politics – as illustrated by the 1993 vice presidential election of Katarista Víctor Hugo Cárdenas. The Bolivian Amazon has also become an active site of indigenous organizing, marked by the 1990 march and the formation and expansion of the regional confederation, CIDOB (Confederación Indígena del Oriente Chaco y Amazonía de Bolivia – Indigenous Confederation of the East, Chaco, and Amazon). In the 1990s, these regional organizations have sustained a prominent national role – debating territorial autonomy and land reform proposals as well as proposing candidates for national and local elections. In 1990 they too marched from the lowlands of the Amazon to the highland

---

[30] Klein (1982); Cusicanqui (1984); Libermann and Godínez (1992); Mallon (1992); Albó (1994); and Ticona, Rojas, and Albó (1995).

capital (650 kilometers) to make these demands. And in the mid-1990s they also negotiated important changes in land reform policy and autonomy rights.

The Guatemalan indigenous movement has also gained recognition – although it does not rival the mobilizational strength and political impact of the Ecuadorian and Bolivian indigenous movements. The Guatemalan indigenous movement emerged with the organizing and coordination for the Second Continental Meeting of Indigenous and Popular Resistance in 1991.[31] Newly founded Mayan organizations such as Majawil Q'ij, CONIC (Coordinadora Nacional Indígena y Campesina – National Indigenous and Peasant Coordination), and COMG (Consejo de Organizaciones Mayas de Guatemala – Council of Mayan Organizations of Guatemala) proclaimed the centrality of indigenous identity for their political work. These incipient organizations challenged the predominantly class-based discourse and goals of Guatemala's popular movements and have sought to create organizations more responsive to indigenous communities and concerns. During negotiations to end Guatemala's civil war, these organizationally diverse and often competitive organizations met in ongoing national forums to participate in the peace process. These efforts culminated in the 1995 Accord on Identity and Rights of Indigenous Peoples and the 1996 Final Peace Accord. Indigenous popular organizations also formed an electoral coalition, Nukuj Ajpop, and ran a number of successful municipal and legislative candidates in the 1995 election.

Mexico's indigenous movements gained international and national attention with the Chiapas rebellion by the Ejército Zapatista de Liberación Nacional (EZLN, The Zapatista Army of National Liberation), initiated on January 1, 1994.[32] Efforts to organize and promote indigenous organizing predate the Zapatistas. Nonetheless, the historically and comparatively limited capacity of Mexico's Indian communities to constitute a significant and independent national movement led scholars to remark on the historically minor role that indigenous organizations had played in Mexico. The Zapatistas challenged this pattern. Their largely indigenous army mobilized significant support and compelled the Mexican government to engage in negotiations. The EZLN's agenda includes platforms for indigenous

---

[31] Smith (1990); Bastos and Camus (1993 and 1995); Cojti (1996); Seider (1998); Warren (1998); and Nelson (1999).

[32] Nagengast and Kearney (1990); Burbach and Rossett (1994); Collier and Lowery (1994); Fox (1994); Harvey, Navarro, and Rubin (1994); Benjamin (1996); Harvey (1996 and 1998); Stephens (1996, 1997, and 2002); Mattiace (1997); and Womack (1999).

autonomy and cultural respect alongside claims for democratization. The EZLN has engineered a political opening for Mexico's indigenous peoples by simultaneously promoting discussions between indigenous communities and negotiations with the Mexican state. In the spring of 2001, the EZLN organized a march from the remote state of Chiapas to Mexico City to speak before the Parliament and demand fulfillment of autonomy clauses in the San Andrés Accords between the EZLN and the government. In 2001, the legislature passed a very weak version of the local autonomy bill. The EZLN subsequently criticized this law for strengthening the power of local elites rather than indigenous communities.

Peru, by contrast, has not witnessed sustained national and widespread indigenous mobilization, as found in the prior four cases.[33] The low level of indigenous organizing is ironic given Víctor Raúl Haya de la Torre and José Carlos Martiátegui's early-twentieth-century arguments about Peru's indigenous core. Nonetheless, it is widely observed that "[i]n Peru, there is no Indian movement. The political proposal to organize specifically around indigenous identity is a profound failure in the country."[34] Organizing in the countryside has principally developed along different lines. On the one hand, Sendero Luminoso had until the mid to late 1990s organized quite effectively throughout much of the Peruvian countryside. Although this movement organizes indigenous peasants, it rejects demands or agendas emanating from an indigenous identity. I therefore exclude it from the universe of indigenous movements discussed in this book. On the other hand, rondas campesinas have emerged in Peru. These peasant organizations play a role in the adjudication and enforcement of justice as well as the oversight of public works. The rondas campesinas, however, have remained localized in nature and do not focus on indigenous-based concerns per se. Indeed, the emergence of Sendero Luminoso and the rondas campesinas highlight the limited role of indigenous identity as a basis for mobilization and claim making in Peru. The exceptions are more localized organizations such as the Asociación Interétnica de Desarrollo de la Selva Peruana (AIDESEP), in the Amazon, and the Unión de Comunidades Aymaras (UNCA), near the Bolivian border.

In short, while indigenous communities have mobilized and been mobilized in the past, ethnic cleavages have become significantly more

---

[33] Cotler and Portocarrero (1969); Handelman (1975); McClintock (1981 and 1989); Starn (1992 and 1999); and Seligmann (1995).
[34] Mayer (1996: 175). Translation by author.

politicized in recent years in Ecuador, Bolivia, Guatemala, and Mexico. In each of these countries, indigenous communities have organized and sustained important and consequential indigenous movements. In Ecuador these organizations have developed one national confederation that speaks on behalf of various regional federations. In Bolivia, indigenous communities have developed strong regional federations. In Guatemala, emergent and competitive national organizations have gained a voice in national forums. In Mexico, moderately strong regional organizations have emerged and have gained a significant voice in contemporary political debates. All these organizations share a commitment to organize and defend Indians as Indians – even while they have emerged with varying degrees of strength. They are fundamentally demanding both that the promise of democracy be fulfilled (to respect the individual rights of indigenous men and women) and that the state legally recognize indigenous community rights to land and local forms of governance. From this perspective, these movements have assumed an indigenous identity and focus that is not prevalent in Peru's rural organizations. Ethnic cleavages in Peru have thus far been politically overshadowed by class-based organizing and protest. Organizing has occurred within indigenous communities but is local in scope, weak in outreach, and marginalized from political debates. An explanation of the rising political salience of indigenous organizing, therefore, requires not only that we explain why it developed by the late twentieth century in Ecuador, Bolivia, Guatemala, and Mexico, but also why it remained so weak in Peru.

This book analyzes these five cases, therefore, to explain when, where, and why indigenous movements have emerged in Latin America. It does so in two ways. Part I (Chapters 1–3) refers to all five cases when conceptualizing and making the argument about when, where, and why indigenous movements have emerged in Latin America. Part II (Chapters 4–6) of the book then presents and probes three case studies in greater detail: Ecuador, Bolivia, and Peru. These three cases were chosen because they not only share the most similar historical, political, and demographic characteristics, but also because they exhibit the greatest variation in outcomes of indigenous mobilization. In other words, they most neatly fit the most similar systems research design. These chapters allow for a more in-depth analysis of variation over time, across cases, and across subnational units.

The case material throughout the book draws on various kinds of sources. First, this book makes extensive use of secondary sources on all cases. Second, I conducted research trips to all of the countries between 1995–1997.

I also drew more informally from earlier research trips to Guatemala from 1989–1990, and 1994. Fieldwork primarily included individual and collective interviews but also policy analysis and newspaper databases:

- *Elite Interviews.* I conducted over 150 interviews with indigenous leaders; peasant leaders; and ministers of agrarian reform, education, and indigenous affairs. I combined a standardized set of questions with questions written for the given interviewee. These interviews were open-ended and did not follow any particular format. When permitted, I taped interviews; this was the norm. These interviews lasted anywhere from thirty minutes to four hours; the average interview ran for sixty to ninety minutes.
- *Focus Groups.* I also conducted elective and anonymous discussion groups in Bolivia, Ecuador, and Peru. These were designed to evaluate elite observations against local experiences. As the case material in Part II will make clear, these focus groups were fascinating and fun but were ultimately methodologically problematic – given the predictable difficulty in arranging honest, open, and comparable focus groups in various rural indigenous communities with which I could only develop a short-term kind of trust. That said, these focus groups raised additional questions that I could subsequently probe in the elite interviews and elsewhere.
- *Indigenous Conferences.* I also participated in a few indigenous conferences in Mexico, Ecuador, and Bolivia. These included the five-day Intergalactic Encounter for Humanity and Against Neoliberalism, organized by the EZLN in Chiapas; a three-day conference of leaders from several Amazonian organizations and NGOs from Ecuador, Bolivia, Venezuela, and the United States that took place in Lago Agrio, Ecuador; a two-day conference of the Organización de Pueblos Indígenas de Pastaza (OPIP), that took place in the province of Puno, Ecuador; and a four-day traveling "conference" with leaders from Bolivia's CIDOB that took us to several communities in the Bolivian Amazon and Chaco. On each of these occasions, I remained a silent observer during the conferences. However, I talked extensively with the organizers of three of these trips before and after each of the meetings.
- *Policy Review.* I gathered longitudinal data on ethnicity, land distribution, access to credit, education, health, and poverty – with an eye toward discerning how indigenous social conditions and state-Indian relations have changed. In this task, I was skillfully aided by three research assistants: Maritza Rodríguez-Seguí in Peru, Lily Jara in Ecuador, and Verouchka Zilvetti in Bolivia.

- *Newspaper Studies.* I compiled a computer database of coverage of indigenous movements over the past 10 to 15 years in Bolivia and Ecuador. Given the weakness of indigenous movements in Peru, this was not relevant. Jorge Zalles and Adam Webb helped with the collection and cataloging of the data on Ecuador. Verouchka Zilvetti did the same for Bolivia.

In short, this book combines secondary sources with primary fieldwork. It therefore stands on the shoulders of others before me and was supported by those who helped me gather data in the field. By weaving these sources together, I have sought to develop a methodologically grounded, theoretically engaged, and descriptive account of the emergence of indigenous movements in Latin America.

Plan of Book

This book is divided into three parts. Part I (Chapters 1–3) lays the conceptual and analytic groundwork for this book. Chapter 2 discusses the key analytical concepts used throughout the book, namely citizenship and citizenship regimes. Chapter 3 then turns to the argument. To explain the contemporary and uneven emergence of indigenous movements in Latin America, three factors are analyzed: changing citizenship regimes, transcommunity social networks, and political associational space. While the first variable explains the contemporary motive for organizing, the latter two explain the capacity and opportunity to do so. In particular, I argue that changing citizenship regimes politicized ethnic cleavages in Latin America by challenging the local autonomy that indigenous communities had previously carved out. This challenge to local autonomy became particularly threatening to indigenous communities in the context of an incomplete (and at times contradictory) process of democratization and state reform. Indigenous movements have emerged in this mix to contest the institutional boundaries and practice of citizenship. This mobilization has proven possible, however, only where two other factors were in play: political associational space and preexisting social networks. Whereas political associational space provided the opportunity to engage in sustained legal organizing, networks provided the mechanisms, capacity, and resources for doing so.

Part II (Chapters 4–6) explores the argument developed in Part I in light of original fieldwork in three case studies: Ecuador, Bolivia, and Peru. These chapters explore how subnational variation is initially explained by variation in the three factors previously outlined: changing citizenship regimes and

29

their challenge to local autonomy, transcommunity networks, and political associational space. These chapters then explore how timing and sequence change the field of indigenous organizing for later movement organizing. In this sense, the movements cannot be analyzed independently of one another but must be analyzed against a longitudinal and national field of organizing.

The book concludes in Part III by taking up a new question: what are the political implications of Latin America's indigenous movements for the terms and practice of democracy? Chapter 7 introduces the postliberal challenge that they pose. Yet this challenge is not one that has spiraled into ethnic violence, as we have seen in other parts of Africa, Asia, and the Middle East. Rather, it is one that aims to contest and reformulate the terms of democratic and multicultural citizenship. For indeed, the postliberal challenge proposes a democratic citizenship that not only respects individual political rights but also grants collective rights to autonomy. Most indigenous movements seek to achieve these goals while respecting the sovereignty and integrity of existing democratic states. In this regard, the contemporary politicization of ethnic cleavages in Latin America has implications beyond social movements, state formation, and identity politics. For indigenous movements throughout the region have come to shape contemporary political debates about the future course and quality of democracy in Latin America.

2

Citizenship Regimes, the State, and Ethnic Cleavages

At a national scale effective citizenship is a necessary condition of democracy....
Without effective citizenship, no regime provides sufficient breadth, equality,
binding consultation, or protection of participants in public politics to qualify as
democratic (Tilly 1999: 256).

Citizenship is at the core of democracy. It is also at the core of indigenous
mobilization in Latin America and beyond. For if Indians are contesting the
terms of citizenship, they are also contesting their unequal experiences with
it. But what is citizenship? Who gets to be a citizen? And how is citizenship
experienced? These are basic questions. Yet they have been largely sidelined
in studies of third wave democracies. Indeed, democratization studies for
the most part have tended to assume that the category, boundaries, and
experiences of citizenship are given and preconstituted. While there have
been notable exceptions, most recent studies have tended to focus on the
institutions that define democracy rather than the people who take part and
the terms by which they do so.[1]

It is no longer possible to ignore citizenship (and its links to ethnicity) in democratization studies. For with the turn to competitive electoral
regimes, we have witnessed the (re)emergence of groups committed to

I want to thank my students who have taken my course, Ethnic Politics and Citizenship (1996–
2001). While they have not read this chapter, conversations in these seminars helped me flesh
out some of the ideas developed in this chapter. For parallel discussions of citizenship, see
Shafir (1998) and Wiener (1999).

[1] For important exceptions in studies of democratization, see Fox (1990 and 1994a);
O'Donnell (1993); Jelin and Hershberg (1996); Linz and Stepan (1996); and Chalmers et al.
(1997). Studies of nationalism, ethnic conflict, multiculturalism, immigration, and genocide,
by contrast, have acknowledged and explored why and how citizenship is a highly contested
good and concept.

redefining citizenship. These are not "simply" struggles to expand the suffrage to excluded groups. Rather, the new struggles have increasingly assumed an ethnonational cast and have taken two broad forms. First, in their most extreme and exclusionary form, social and political movements have formed to redefine the *boundaries* of citizenship by *restricting* membership to a given ethnonational group. Informed by nationalist ideas and international rhetoric about self-determination, groups in Eastern Europe, Africa, Asia, and the Middle East have mobilized in multiethnic polities to construct nation-states where membership is allocated along ethnonational lines. This program has often had destructive consequences as nonnationals have been excluded, often violently, from the polities that they once identified as theirs. These concerns have dominated studies of ethnic conflict (Sri Lanka, Rwanda, Ireland, Israel/Palestine) and studies of genocide (Germany, Rwanda, the former Yugoslavia). In both cases, struggles to restrict citizenship along ethnonational lines have commonly resulted in violence.

While we are perhaps most familiar with these violent conflicts, not all struggles over citizenship have resulted in violent struggles over national boundaries. A second form has occurred over the *content* rather than boundaries of citizenship in multiethnic settings. We have found that indigenous groups, in particular, have mobilized in recent years to demand a redefinition of citizenship that would maintain their rights as citizens of a polity but also accommodate their community-based demands to local autonomy. These struggles have most often been discussed in studies of multiculturalism and have tended to focus on the more established democracies, including the United States, Canada, Australia, New Zealand, and even India.[2] However, these nonviolent movements to redefine the content of citizenship are not restricted to these older democracies. Indeed, during the last part of the twentieth century, these movements also started to emerge in the new democracies of Latin America.

This book is fundamentally interested in the intersection of democracy, citizenship, and ethnic politics. But rather than focus on the most familiar cases of ethnic violence in new democracies or multiculturalism in the established democracies, it casts its gaze on the least likely region: Latin

---

[2] Multiculturalism has come to mean many things. It is used here to refer to public *policies* that recognize ethnoracial diversity and that allocate some goods/resources along those lines. It is *not* used to describe a diverse society or to refer to individuals whose parents come from different ethnoracial backgrounds.

America. Latin America has developed a reputation as an anomaly in studies of cultural pluralism, ethnic conflict, and multiculturalism. In several classic studies, it is described as the region where ethnic identities have had little political salience. Ethnic cleavages are comparatively weak; violent ethnic conflicts are rare, isolated, and small; and assimilation and miscegenation have been described as giving way to a new cosmic race, a racial democracy, or at the very least a melting pot.[3] Consequently, efforts to allocate or redefine citizenship have been understood as issues of *democratization* rather than issues of ethnic politics – whether viewed from the perspective of ethnic conflict or multiculturalism. In other words, citizenship is understood as civil and political rights – independent of any particular ethnic content or conflict. Indeed, with the transition to democracy, Latin American constitutions granted to all individuals (independent of ethnic origins) the right to participate as citizens with relatively few formal political restrictions. Compared to other regions, this equalization and universalization of citizenship is noteworthy. For whereas democratization in much of Africa, Asia, and Eastern Europe resulted in the activation and/or intensification of ethnic violence – as different ethnic groups vied for power and/or sought to carve out new nation-states – Latin America democratized with no apparent ethnic hitches – no ethnic violence; and no challenges to carve up the nation-state.[4]

---

[3] Ethnic relations in Latin America have played out historically in quite different ways from African and Asian countries. Latin American countries gained independence more than a century earlier than Africa and much of Asia. Latin American independence and national liberation movements in the nineteenth century referred to European settlers who subsequently set out to construct a nation-state coincident with the ethnicity of the conquerors. In Africa and parts of Asia, where many countries maintained colonial status through the 1950s and 1960s, independence movements developed within indigenous communities against settler populations. National liberation movements set out not only to capture state power but also to refashion a "truer" national identity. Following independence any semblance of national unity within many African countries broke down and gave way to ongoing conflict between ethnic groups, as in Nigeria, Rwanda, or Burundi. Hence, while pluriethnic states compose both Latin America and Africa, ethnic relations and conflict have played out on different terrains. In Latin America, ethnic cleavages have tended to occur between horizontal groups (white/mestizo groups that effectively occupy the state and indigenous groups that do not). In Africa, excluding important examples such as South Africa and Eritrea, ethnic cleavages since independence tend to exist between more vertically integrated groups competing, when democratic conditions prevail, to gain political power.

[4] Gurr (2000: ch. 2) highlights that whereas enthnopolitical conflict generally increased in the post–World War II period and peaked in the early to mid-1990s, Latin America followed a different path. In Latin America, there has been little ethnopolitical conflict although there was a rise in ethnic protest in the 1990s.

Most analysts, therefore, assumed that ethnicity and citizenship were nonpolitical issues in the new Latin American democracies.[5] By the end of the twentieth century, however, the entire landscape of Latin American politics shifted as indigenous movements formed to contest contemporary citizenship in one country after another. Vocal and increasingly powerful indigenous movements have emerged throughout the region. We have seen a rise in movement organizing and protest in countries as diverse as Ecuador, Mexico, Brazil, Bolivia, Guatemala, Nicaragua, and beyond. Unlike the new democracies in Africa, Asia, and Eastern Europe, these new movements did not mobilize to redefine the *boundaries* of citizenship and did not spiral into ethnic conflict (or genocide). Rather, the newly formed indigenous movements mobilized to redefine the *content* of citizenship, in ways that paralleled but cannot be reduced to the multicultural struggles found in the older democracies of North America, Australia, and New Zealand.

This book sets out to explain the politicization of ethnic cleavages in late-twentieth-century Latin America. It focuses, in particular, on explaining the emergence and proliferation of these indigenous movements in the region. I argue in this book that the erosion of prior citizenship regimes throughout Latin America unwittingly challenged local autonomy, thereby politicizing indigenous communities in new ways. The rest of this book explains these changes in citizenship regimes in light of variations in social networks and political associational space.

This chapter engages in a prior and essential task. It conceptualizes citizenship regimes (as boundaries, form, and content). In particular, it analyzes who has citizenship (the boundaries), under what terms (the forms of interest intermediation), and with what rights and practices (the content). This three-dimensional analysis of citizenship regimes not only makes clear why one cannot reduce citizenship to democratization but also why one should not analyze it absent a concern for social cleavages and state capacity, more broadly. This discussion thus provides the conceptual framework for the analytical concerns of the rest of this book: namely why and how indigenous movements are contesting the contemporary terms of citizenship in Latin America.

---

[5] See Linz and Stepan (1996) for an example of scholars who see ethnonational issues at play in all democratizing regions save Latin America.

Conceptualizing Citizenship: The Who, How, and What

Who Can Be a Citizen? Drawing Boundaries

Who is in and who is out? – these are the first questions that any political community must answer about itself (Walzer 1993: 55).

We live in a world of bounded and exclusive citizenries. Every modern state identifies a particular set of persons as its citizens and defines all others as noncitizens, as aliens.... In global perspective, citizenship is a powerful instrument of social closure.... Every state claims to be the state of, and for, a particular, bounded citizenry, usually conceived as a nation (Brubaker 1992: ix–x).

So who is and should be a citizen? Who is included and what is the legitimating mechanism for doing so? Should boundaries be tied to the state system and, if so, should citizenship be restricted to certain categories of people? As discussed next, the question of who is eligible to be a part of a political community is fundamentally tied to the boundaries that are drawn – both vis-à-vis the resident population (a question of restrictiveness) and vis-à-vis those who reside beyond those state borders (a question of the primacy of state borders). For boundaries are drawn both within states as well as between them. These boundaries are drawn to define and uphold the relevant political community and have implications for the public (generally national) identity.

Four principles (the Aristotelian ideal, *jus sanguinis*, *jus soli*, and universality) have been used to define the relevant political community. Viewed together, these four principles provide a framework for thinking about how different states allocate citizenship. While each principle privileges a different template for determining the political community for citizenship, they each have implications for national perceptions of public identities and ethnonational relations in multiethnic states, including those in Latin America. As with all frameworks, however, these four principles serve more as heuristic markers rather than absolute descriptions of the principles used by all cases. Some cases fall neatly into one category. Others bridge categories. I elaborate on these four ways of allocating citizenship, in order of increasing inclusiveness (see Table 2.1).

The Aristotelian Ideal The first principle used to define who can be a citizen builds on normative beliefs about who is capable or fit. Drawing on political theorists such as Aristotle and J. S. Mill, this approach evaluates

Table 2.1. *Principles for Allocating Citizenship*[a]

		Restrictive Identities	
		Yes	No
	Yes	*Jus Sanguinis* National descent National sovereignty	*Jus Soli* Territorial and civic community State sovereignty
Primacy of State Borders	Not Necessarily	*Aristotelian Ideal*[b] Those who are fit/capable	*Universal Citizenship* Open borders

[a] While scholars of immigration have tended to focus on the columns in Table 1, theorists of citizenship have tended to focus on the rows. See Rubio-Marín (2000) and Honig (2001) for efforts to bridge these divides. Honig (2001) analyzes how categories of foreignness have defined and valued what it is to be a citizen.
[b] This category can theoretically apply either to open or closed borders. In practice, however, it has been defined by states.

who is capable of reason and who is able to calculate the general will of the community as a whole. While this principle can theoretically be used to include all human beings, it has historically been used to restrict citizenship *within* existing states to white, property-owning males. Those who "fit" this Aristotelian ideal were granted full citizenship rights. Those who did not were relegated to either secondary or tertiary status; they were subjects rather than citizens. This principle was obviously not confined to Athenian times. It has been widely applied in the twentieth century to exclude groups deemed unfit to assume the rights and responsibilities of citizenship. Women, Indians, blacks, slaves, and Jews, among others, have commonly been denied the full status of citizenship. These groups were commonly described by political elites as lacking reason, as tied to particular interests, and/or as lesser beings; they were consequently excluded from full citizenship rights. Indeed, Shklar (1991) reminds us, in her powerful discussion of citizenship in the United States, that citizenship has historically been defined and valued precisely in terms of those who were excluded. It was democratic for the few; it was undemocratic for the many.

In Latin America, this principle has been used at different times to deny citizenship to women, Indians, and Blacks. As revisionist historians of the past couple of decades have so clearly illustrated, the arrival of Columbus and the ensuing conquest by Spanish and Portuguese settlers occurred at the expense of many indigenous communities that were subsequently subordinated to the political authority of newly created Latin American states and the spiritual authority of the Catholic Church.[6] Military expeditions against the indigenous population were particularly brutal in Uruguay, Argentina, and Chile and, to a lesser degree, in Brazil.[7] These same countries, similar to many others in Latin America, enacted legislation to attract European immigration, arguing that this would improve the racial composition and, therefore, the economic and political prospects of the new states. Latin American nation-states treated indigenous peoples as heathens, a threat to security, an impediment to economic development, and a source of cheap, if not free, labor. The various states enacted corresponding, if at times internally contradictory, policies to address these fears, perceptions, and goals. They killed those perceived as a threat to an emerging nation-state, isolated and/or denied the existence of those in remote areas, coerced populations for their labor, and/or promoted a policy of assimilation. Where and when it became difficult to repress or formally exclude these social groups, literacy requirements were used effectively to exclude the majority of these same groups. Literacy requirements were in place until 1945 in Guatemala, 1970 in Chile, 1979 in Ecuador, 1980 in Peru, and 1985 in Brazil and effectively excluded many indigenous men and most indigenous women from taking part in elections and exercising their political voice (Lapp 1994: 3). Remarkably, no sustained or widespread organization or mobilization occurred in Latin America to extend citizenship to *Indians*, until recently.

Democratization scholars who focus on the extension of the suffrage are generally looking at those cases where the Aristotelian principle of fitness has been used historically to exclude certain categories of people. And indeed, with the third wave of democratization in Latin America, states have rescinded restrictive literacy clauses (where they still existed) and have consequentially extended formal citizenship to indigenous peoples. In other regions, as well, we find the declining legitimacy of Aristotelian evaluations

[6] See Maybury-Lewis (1991) and Mallon (1992) for a discussion of the varied ways in which nineteenth-century states set out to control indigenous communities through violence, isolation, and assimilation. See Stern (1992) for a sobering discussion of the need to adopt a more nuanced understanding of the colonization of the Americas and the multiple roles and actions of the colonizers and indigenous peoples in this process. See Yrigoyen (2000) for a discussion of the trajectory of different legal systems in Latin America.

[7] See Stavenhagen (1988: 29) and Maybury-Lewis (1991).

of who is and can be a citizen. Most dramatically, we have seen in South Africa the dismantling of apartheid and the extension of citizenship rights to all South Africans, regardless of race and ethnicity. Ironically, it is in this period of *more* democratic access to citizenship that indigenous mobilization in Latin America has grown in strength and power. We return to this point in Chapter 3.

Jus Sanguinis[8]   While it is no longer acceptable to exclude people according to the Aristotelian principle of fitness, we commonly accept the rights of states to extend and restrict citizenship according to the principle of national descent or kinship. Indeed, the prevailing type of citizenship operates according to the principle of *jus sanguinis*. Rooted in nineteenth- and twentieth-century ideas about the nation-state, this ideal type is predicated on the idea that the fundamental political community is based on descent or ethnonational origins. Citizenship, therefore, should be restricted to the ethnonational community. Each nation should have a state, each national should be a citizen of his/her nation-state, and each nation-state should allocate citizenship rights along national lines. In short, states and citizenship are and should be the political manifestation of ethnonational identity.

Germany is the prototypical model of *jus sanguinis*; but this principle applies to a broader range of cases. In countries that apply this model, those presumed to share a common lineage are automatically extended citizenship rights (even if they are born and live abroad). Those who are presumed to herald from other national backgrounds, are commonly denied these rights in their new home countries. Consequently, those countries with multiethnic populations that use this principle of determining citizenship face a serious challenge. Guest workers who have resided in Germany for generations, for example, have demanded the right to become citizens – a status that is highly restricted.[9]

Moreover, in much of Africa and Asia, this principle has given way and informed the ethnic conflicts that have emerged – leading some ethnic groups to mobilize to demand either inclusion (where it is denied), to create their own polity (so that nation and state coincide), or to fight to gain control of the state that now excludes or marginalizes them. In many cases, they appeal to international norms about self-determination. It is striking that citizenship in cases of *jus sanguinis* assumes a primordial community that can

---

[8] The discussion of *jus sanguinis* and *jus soli* draws extensively on Brubaker (1992).
[9] Brubaker (1992); Soysal (1994); and Rubio-Marín (2000).

and should govern itself. As such, those sharing ascriptive characteristics are in; those who do not are out.

This principle is foreign to Latin America. As a region populated largely by immigrants, it is hard to sustain the principle of *jus sanguinis*. And in a region where ethnic identities are understood to be malleable, it is hard to maintain a rigid and legal analysis of identity and citizenship. Indeed, Latin American states have promoted policies that encourage indigenous people to shed their "Indian ways" and to assimilate into a mestizo (or mixed) culture. In doing so, they gain the possibility of becoming full citizens – although for most indigenous people, citizenship has proven elusive in practice.

Jus soli   *Jus soli* provides an alternative way of allocating (and restricting) citizenship in this age of sovereign states. The principle of *jus soli* grants citizenship along territorial lines. *Jus soli* begins with the assumption that a community is primarily defined by geography and civic ties. States therefore generally extend citizenship to those who are born in a given territory. They naturalize those migrants who meet a set of conditions, including knowledge of and commitment to the principles of a given state. Citizenship is self-consciously tied to ideas of civic inclusion, equality, freedom, and fraternity. In other words, there is no claim that the political community is one of blood, kinship, and descent. Rather *jus soli* sanctifies the individual and her *political* allegiances and civic ties to a given state. Today this form of citizenship is common in the Americas – but can also be found to one degree or another in Britain and France.[10]

Given this territorial and liberal/civic understanding of citizenship, it is perhaps no surprise that many of these states have come to include ethnically diverse populations. And in the ex-colonial countries, these immigrant populations have come to reside on lands that were once populated and governed by indigenous peoples. It is in these states that the multicultural debates have found greatest resonance – with Indians often demanding a certain degree of autonomy and immigrants and former slaves demanding greater inclusion. The Latin American cases discussed in this

---

[10] *Jus soli* is not an absolute and, therefore, varies according to national norms. Whereas some countries automatically grant citizenship to those born in a given territory (e.g., United States, Britain), others grant citizenship to children of immigrants only when they turn eighteen and only if they are still residents of the country (France). See Brubaker (1992) for a discussion of the exceptions and details in the British case (81 fn. 14) and France (ch. 4).

book fall squarely into this camp. Indigenous people in Latin America have questioned the degree to which this liberal, civic, and territorial basis of citizenship is in fact inclusionary. Or, more precisely, they have challenged the consequences of this form of inclusion – for cultural identities, local autonomy, and land ownership. Ironically, *land*, which indigenous peoples claim as *theirs*, has become the contemporary territorial basis for determining access to citizenship in the *national* polity.

Universal Citizenship/Open Borders The fourth principle for allocating citizenship builds on the idea that the fundamental political community is humanity writ large – independent of fitness, national identities, or territorial boundaries. Citizenship should be a universal good – with no political restrictions. Universal access and open borders should define a world system. This principle remains an unrealized project that could take various forms – including the existence of states that agree to open up borders and access to citizenship; or the creation of a world government to which all would belong. In this model, passports would become obsolete, or at the very least their role would change. While this fourth approach to citizenship remains (at present) no more than an ideal, some of its ideas are approximated at a global level in UN ideals of *human* rights (Soysal 1994) and at a regional level within the European Union (EU) (Weiner 1999). In its purest form, this ideal type is based on universalism – no individual is excluded (regardless of race, ethnicity, ideology, or capacity); everyone is a citizen. This last type of citizenship is a political project rather than a political reality – as it is implemented nowhere. As such, it is not discussed at length here. But when juxtaposed against the prior three models, it helps to highlight where citizenship inheres, how restrictive it is, and the central role of the *state* in this process.

Prevailing Citizenships, Prevailing States *Jus sanguinis* and *jus soli* are the prevailing forms of allocating citizenship today. Juxtaposing them against the fourth principle of universal citizenship/open borders places in sharp relief the fact that these prevailing modes of allocating citizenship are predicated on and reinforce the state system. Both presume that the state is the natural and preferred basis for determining the political community. In this regard, citizenship becomes a way of defining who is "in" and who is "out." It is a form of "social closure," as noted by Brubaker (1992: ch. 1). And it is the state that is understood as the final arbiter in determining and allocating these rights (see Table 2.1).

Jus soli and *jus sanguinis* are therefore not just about extending citizenship as a form of inclusion but also about delimiting membership in the state system. Some people have citizenship in a given state; others do not – a *political* decision that has more often than not had an *ethnic* bias. *Jus sanguinis* makes this explicit by stating its ethnocentric bias. For this practice of allocating and determining citizenship according to national membership remains exclusionary precisely because we do not live in a tightly contained world where nations and states coincide in a neat way.[11] There are many more self-proclaimed nations than states. Self-proclaimed nation-states often have, in fact, multinational populations. Colonialism, war, refugee flows, and migration patterns (both forced and voluntary) have further complicated the fit between nations and states. Indeed, in the postcolonial world, one could say that there is a poor fit between states and nations and between country residence and national membership. Consequently, the construction of nation-state boundaries and citizenship provides a way of excluding not only those beyond national borders but also those nonnationals residing within them. Otherwise stated, *jus sanguinis* provides the logic for treating nonnational residents as second-class citizens (even when they have lived in these countries for several generations). These problems are not restricted to authoritarian times but are prevalent in many contemporary democratic regimes that extend citizenship according to this principle. The question of *who* can be a citizen is an ethnic question – pure and simple. And often the ethnic movements and conflicts that emerge in these cases are about who can become a citizen and how that happens.

Jus soli, by contrast, claims to be ethnoblind, when it comes to the allocation or extension of citizenship. And comparatively speaking, access to citizenship is more open and accessible to those *residing in* a given state territory. However, this should not blind us to the fact that *jus soli* begs the question of who can legally emigrate to that country.[12] And of particular importance for this book, it presents other kinds of challenges for ethnic

---

[11] For a similar point with respect to dual citizenship, see Carens (2000: 162–6).

[12] *Jus soli* is *not* a policy of open borders. Indeed, these countries often have rather restrictive laws for immigration, residence, travel, and visas – even while they have comparatively liberal citizenship laws. The story of Jews who were trying to escape the Holocaust but were turned away from many Allied states that operated on the principle of *jus soli* is a horrifying example of how strictly these same states protect their borders. Similarly, political and economic refugees from Mexico, Central America, and the Caribbean have more often than not been turned away from the United States – one of the prototypical cases of *jus soli*.

groups residing in their borders. These challenges have less to do with access to formal citizenship (which is theoretically granted to those born in a given country) and more to do with how citizenship is experienced once it is granted.[13]

In other words, while discussions of *who* can be a citizen might lead one to conclude that *jus sanguinis* and the Aristotelian principle are ethnocentric and *jus soli* is ethnoblind, discussions of *how* citizenship is experienced lead one to question this simple dichotomy. Indeed, if one is to make sense of ethnic mobilization in *jus soli* states (i.e., those in the Americas), then one must consider other aspects of citizenship (form and content) and compare them against the experiences of its citizenry.

How Do Citizens Relate to States? Different Forms of Interest Intermediation

There are competing principles, therefore, for determining membership in any given polity. But what form does the relationship take between citizens and the state?[14] What are the terms of *interest intermediation*? Who is the subject of citizenship? And who is the object of state norms, rules, and regulations? It is now commonplace among scholars of democratization to assume the primacy and relevance of the individual. Yet as comparativists once highlighted, and as political theorists continue to do so, interest intermediation can privilege the collectivity just as it can privilege the individual.[15]

---

[13] See Yrigoyen (2000: 206–8) for a discussion of the Latin American legal tradition that presumed correspondence between one nation, one state, and one law – thereby negating the juridical existence of Indians.

[14] For the rest of the chapter, I assume that states are sovereign entities vested with the power to decide who can be a citizen.

[15] Comparativists once tackled these questions with an eye toward analyzing competing *institutional* arrangements of interest intermediation. They analyzed pluralist modes of interest intermediation (that privileged the individual) against corporatist and consociational forms of doing so (that privileged the group). This fascination stemmed from a profound realization that countries in Europe, Latin America, and the Middle East often institutionalized state–society relations in radically distinct ways from the classic liberal democracies in Great Britain, the United States, and both of their former colonies. With the recent round of democratization, comparativists have regrettably lost interest in these questions as liberal ideas gain ascendancy. For an exception in comparative politics, see Janoski (1998). For particularly important normative debates in political theory on the topic of individual and group rights, see the edited volumes by Kymlicka (1995) and Shapiro and Kymlicka (1997).

Political theorists and philosophers, unsurprisingly, have pursued these questions with the greatest vigor. Debates about liberalism and communitarianism, in particular, speak to this question – albeit from a largely normative rather than empirical perspective. Liberals privilege the individual as the primary unit or subject of political life. The individual possesses certain rights and responsibilities and, in large part, acts to maximize *personal autonomy*, interests, and capacities. She is free to do so provided that she does not harm others. While individuals rely on the state to maintain law and order and to establish relations with other states, individuals seek to keep the state to a minimum. It is this freedom to actualize individual liberties free from state intervention that is the hallmark of contemporary democratic citizenship, according to prevailing liberal political norms.

The individual, in either the utilitarian or the contractual liberal view, is the sovereign author of her life who pursues her private rational advantage or conception of the good. The role of politics in this approach remains negative: only to aid and protect individuals from interference by governments in exercising the rights they inalienably possess and in return for which they have to undertake certain minimal political duties (pay taxes, vote periodically, obey the law, serve in the military). Consequently, citizenship, in the liberal view, is an accessory, not a value in itself (Shafir 1998: 10).

Liberalism therefore is an individual affair. Rights and responsibilities inhere in the individual. And it is the individual who relates to and is regulated by the state. Ethnicity and multiculturalism are irrelevant to a discussion of citizenship and the formal mechanisms of interest intermediation. While any individual has the right to participate in ethnic (or any other) associations, ethnic groups should not be privileged in designing the institutions of interest intermediation. This school of thought has become hegemonic in political theory, comparative politics (including American politics), and policy circles.

But citizenship has obviously not been confined theoretically or empirically to a set of individual rights and responsibilities. Groups have also assumed a formal political role in defining some state–society relations. Theoretically speaking, communitarians question the assumption that we can analyze individuals outside of the social context. Indeed, communitarians argue that identities, interests, preferences, meanings, and capacities are socially constructed and are rooted in communities. Interest intermediation and political mobilization cannot be understood, therefore, independently of the community, for individuals do not operate independently and autonomously from their community context. From this starting point, communitarians argue that we need to privilege the community as the basis for understanding political subjects and their relationship to the state.

The communitarian philosophy has an empirical correlate in countries that have institutionalized corporatism, consociationalism, and/or legal pluralism. Each of these forms of interest intermediation and representation privileges the group as the primary political actors. Hence we find that corporatist systems privilege labor and business in their negotiations with the state. The underlying idea is that these groups should have a monopoly of representation for their sector and should have collective representation in shaping economic policy. Consociational systems set out to institutionalize interest intermediation and representation in societies deeply divided by social cleavages such as ethnicity, race, religion, and/or political ideology; in these cases, states do not allow the accumulation of individual decisions to decide who their executive and legislators will be but allocate these offices depending on group identities, quotas, alternation in power, veto rules, among other things. Finally, multiethnic countries with legal pluralism institutionalize systems where different groups maintain jurisdiction over their own communities – according to different and at times contrary legal precepts. What all of these cases share is that groups rather than individuals are the political subjects who have the right and responsibility to take political action. Under these circumstances, the state obviously must play an active role to determine which groups are privileged (and which ones are not), what the rules are, and how national politics is regulated. At base, states actively intervene to create more equal outcomes among groups rather than focusing exclusively on providing equal opportunities for individuals. It is the state-sanctioned group, therefore, that maximizes *autonomy* rather than the individual.

These two classical frameworks, therefore, have quite different ways of looking at state–society relations, with very distinct ways of thinking about the role that ethnicity plays in defining citizenship – with communitarians seeing it as primary and liberals seeing it as secondary.[16]

---

[16] That said, a new generation of liberals has tried to evaluate how states can accommodate a group-based understanding of ethnicity and ethnic rights within the liberal tradition. See for example, Guttman (1994); Taylor (1994); Kymlicka (1995); Williams (1998); and Carens (2000). Kymlicka (1995) notes in his edited volume, for example, that it is not that culture does not matter for liberals; but the idea is that in liberal democracies, national cultures should be able to "accommodate" and "incorporate" other ethnic groups through a process of assimilation. This, at least, is the self-understanding in countries such as France (Brubaker 1992), the United States (Kymlicka 1995: 23–4), Australia (Chesterman and Galligan 1997),

These debates are rooted in Western thought and context. They are not restricted, however, to the West. These foundational questions are relevant to the new democracies in Latin America, Africa, Asia, the Middle East, and Eastern Europe – even if comparative scholars of these regions have more often than not ignored the liberal-communitarian debate that speaks to the philosophical foundations of ethnic diversity and democratic representation. But the questions that these theories raise cannot be ignored. What is the central unit of political life? To what extent should these institutions be informed by liberal or group principles? Should communities be granted special (i.e., different) rights by virtue of being a community? What are the appropriate institutions to mediate between citizens and states? And does the state have the capacity to enforce one type of citizenship or the other? These questions and answers are at the heart of democratic institution building and social policy. In the process of addressing these issues, regime-founding actors have made decisions about the appropriate form of citizenship and the corresponding relationship between society and state. In general, the liberal/pluralist version has been ascendant in the advanced industrial and developing world. This is increasingly so with the third wave of democracy, but was not historically the case.

What Does Citizenship Entail? Content and Marshall's Trilogy of Rights

The third component of citizenship speaks to content. What does citizenship entail? While it is common to note that citizenship entails rights and responsibilities between citizenry and state, the actual content of that relationship has varied over time. Most studies of democratization have failed to take these changes into account. As they discuss democratization in the third wave, they have tended to equate citizenship with the extension of the suffrage and civil rights. However, as T. H. Marshall (1963) made

and Latin America (Wade 1997). As noted in the following section, Kymlicka argues that in addition to the protection of civil and political rights for different individuals, liberal democracies still need to incorporate some group-differentiated rights – provided that they do not grant these groups the right to engage in internally restrictive practices. He observes that the countries classically identified as liberal democracies (United States, Canada, etc.) have done precisely that by granting some combination of self-government rights, polyethnic rights, and special representation rights (see Kymlicka 1995: chs. 2–3). As Yashar (1999) and Carens (2000: 2) note, however, these theoretical discussions within liberalism, while fascinating, have been distinctly divorced from empirical context – making it unclear how relevant they are to actual political debates and how one would in fact implement a multicultural and group-based version of liberalism.

clear in his masterful study (if idealized picture) of Great Britain, the twentieth century has witnessed the standardization of three different kinds of rights: civil, political, and social.

- Civil rights refer to "the rights necessary for individual freedom" and have come to include, among other things, freedom of association, expression, faith, and religion as well as freedom to own property, engage in contracts, and seek justice; these rights are backed up by the courts (71).
- Political rights refer to the right to take part in government – whether by participating in a legislature or local government or by exercising the right to suffrage (72).
- Social rights refer to "the whole range from the right to a modicum of economic welfare and security to the right to share to the full in the social heritage and to live the life of a civilized being according to the standards prevailing in the society. The institutions most closely connected with it are the educational system and the social services" (72). By assuring a certain standard of living (through welfare programs in housing, education, and health), social rights helped to raise up the impoverished and provide them with the opportunity and the resources to act equally as citizens in the political realm. It is not that all people should live as equals, but that all should live above a certain line. In this regard, Marshall acknowledged and accepted that citizenship provides the architecture for legitimating social inequality (70, 106).

Marshall derived these rights from the British experience but projected that they would be extended (in this order) in other cases as well.[17] The scope, sequencing, and depth of citizenship in other cases, however, have not occurred in the sequential and nonconflictual ways outlined by Marshall. For if in Europe citizenship rights were extended sequentially and relatively slowly, in the developing world, they have generally been granted sparingly, simultaneously, in a different sequence, and/or intermittently.[18] In other words, there is no simple and universal logic to the content of citizenship in the twentieth century. By the end of the twentieth century, the idea of social *rights* was everywhere challenged by conservative politicians and neoliberal

---

[17] Marshall assumed that citizenship coincided with and bolstered the idea of a common civilization. In this regard, his argument assumed that citizenship is a trilogy of rights restricted to a given ethnonational community that shared a given "civilization." This point is made in passing in several points in this classic text but is not a point on which he elaborated.

[18] Also see O'Donnell (2001).

economists who successfully reframed it as an expensive and unsustainable entitlement rather than a fundamental right of the citizenry. By the end of the twentieth century, the social rights that Marshall outlined as a sign of humanity's progress were dismissed as a dispensable luxury. To further complicate the picture, several advanced industrial countries have extended political, civil, and even some social rights to noncitizens residing in their country. In other words, the content of citizenship has been subject to enormous variation across time and across region.

Given this variation, any discussion of citizenship must account for the content of citizenship and the rights that are upheld in any given state. Marshall's categories of three rights provides an extremely useful framework for doing so. For the trilogy of citizenship rights makes abundantly clear that we cannot reduce citizenship to suffrage, as many democratization studies have presumed, but must identify rather than assume its content.

Citizenship Regimes

Who has access to citizenship? What rights does citizenship entail? What are the appropriate institutions to mediate between citizens and states? To what extent should these institutions be informed by liberal or group principles? These questions and answers are the stuff of democratic institution building and social policy. Each of the third wave democracies has had to make decisions about these issues. In the process of doing so, they have defined the boundaries, form, and terms of citizenship. In doing so, they have put in place patterned combinations that I refer to here as "citizenship regimes." To recap, a citizenship regime refers to the patterned combination of choices about the three fundamental questions posed in this chapter:[19]

- Who has access to citizenship? Is this based on the principle of "fitness," *jus sangunis, jus soli*, and/or open borders?
- What is the form of citizenship? In particular, what are the primary modes of interest intermediation? Are they based on liberal/pluralist

[19] I borrow the phrase "citizenship regime" from Jenson and Phillip (1996). They use the term to refer to the varying bundles of rights and responsibilities that citizenship can confer. I use the term in a more expansive sense. In Yashar (1999), I used the term to refer not only to the content of citizenship but also to its accompanying modes of interest intermediation. Upon reflection, I have decided to expand the scope of the term further to also refer to *who* has access to citizenship.

Table 2.2. *Citizenship Regimes in Latin America*

	Corporatist	Neoliberal
Primary Characteristics		
Civil Rights	Yes (w/ constraints)	Yes
Political Rights	Varies	Yes
Social Rights	Yes	Limited
Interest Intermediation	Corporatist	Pluralist
Privileged Unit	Class	Individual
Context and Cases		
Regime	Democratic or Authoritarian	Democratic or Authoritarian
Time Period	Mid-20th century	1980s on
Cases	All – to varying degrees	All

principles that privilege the individual or corporatist/consociational/ communitarian principles that privilege the group.

- What is the content of citizenship rights? Drawing on T. H. Marshall, content refers to the civil, political, and social rights extended to the citizenry.

There are various combinations that could take place and that have in fact done so. In the twentieth century, corporatism and neoliberal citizenship regimes have been the most significant (see Table 2.2). These two citizenship regimes are neither equal to nor derivative of political regime type (democracy and authoritarianism).

Corporatist citizenship regimes were constructed by Latin American states in the mid-twentieth century.[20] Latin American countries started to extend social rights (including labor rights, pensions, subsidies, credit, health care, education, and the like) and institutionalized corporatist modes of interest intermediation for workers and peasants in particular. As such, states privileged collective units and offered corresponding social programs to address collective concerns. Importantly, corporatist citizenship regimes did not necessarily extend political rights alongside these social ones given that they were constructed by both democratic and authoritarian regimes. Military regimes in fact had a rather ambiguous relationship to

---

[20] I use the terms *corporate* and *corporatist* to refer to state-designated forms of political representation and mediation between the state and societal groups. I do not use the term to suggest the presumed closed nature of indigenous communities, as discussed in Wolfe's classic (1957) article.

corporatism. The military in Peru and Ecuador actually initiated these corporatist projects, although the same could not be said for the militaries in the Southern Cone and Central America.

In the third wave democracies, states have tended to promote neoliberal citizenship regimes.[21] The expansion of political and civil rights has tended to coincide with the decline in social rights and the promotion of liberal or pluralist modes of interest intermediation. Organized social sectors (such as workers and peasants) have lost their state assurance of a basic standard of living and similarly have lost their main institutional means of accessing and occasionally influencing the state. Seen as a whole, neoliberal citizenship regimes in the third wave of democracy, and particularly in Latin America, have celebrated the individual as the political subject of citizenship. This book analyzes why and how this development sharpened the very ethnic cleavages that liberalism should theoretically have accommodated.

While citizenship regimes have such distinct consequences for state–society relations, they share one important feature. They both assume the irrelevance of ethnicity and the prevalence and salience of some other kind of identity. As argued in the following chapters, this assumption was misplaced. For while all Latin American states tried to remake Indians into other identities (peasants, nationals, individuals), these were only partially successful endeavors. Indeed, by the end of the twentieth century, ethnic cleavages were repoliticized and indigenous identities became politically salient. To understand these developments, we must look at citizenship regimes in light of existing social cleavages and the reach of the state.

Concluding with Social Cleavages and the State

This chapter has argued that the boundaries, form, and content of citizenship regimes matter. They provide the formal institutional context within

---

[21] I use the term *neoliberal* to define this citizenship regime for three reasons. First, I want to distinguish it from T. H. Marshall's description of earlier British liberal citizenship regimes where civil and political rights were extended first, but social rights were not yet on the political agenda. The sequencing of citizenship rights that Marshall identified, while perhaps applicable to the late-nineteenth-century liberal periods in Latin America, does not apply to the contemporary Latin American context, where social rights were dismantled and civil and political rights extended. Second, I want to distinguish it from the liberal periods that marked the second half of nineteenth-century Latin American politics. Finally, I want to link the contemporary neoliberal citizenship regimes to the contemporary neoliberal reforms that have redefined Latin America's political economies and dismantled many of the social programs that were once tied to social rights.

which societal actors operate. In this regard, they fundamentally define formal aspects of state–society relations. But should one generalize from the institutions of different citizenship regimes to the experiences within them? For if most democratization scholars and contemporary political regimes have privileged a liberal understanding of citizenship, they have also assumed that the *experience* of citizenship at any given point in time is, for analytical purposes, more or less constant among citizens of a given state.[22] At any one point in time, citizens are assumed to have equal rights and responsibilities. But the formalism associated with this approach, which assumes that each citizen gains certain rights, independent of a set of social cleavages and conflicts, falls prey to the very shortcomings once noted by Schattsneider (1975) in his criticism of legal formalism. They mistake institutions for practice and formalism for experience. Indeed, studies of democracy have done precisely this by taking citizenship as a given institution that is extended and experienced equally by all individuals. Schattsneider noted: "The flaw in the pluralist heaven is that the heavenly chorus sings with a strong upper-class accent."[23] In other words, liberalism (or pluralism, according to Schattsneider) assumes an equality that belies differential opportunities and experiences. As Foweraker and Landman (1997: 13) have also noted: "citizens may enjoy equality before the law, but the law 'is silent on their ability to use it' (Bendix 1964)." For these reasons, it would be shortsighted to elevate citizenship regimes to a new kind of formalism.[24]

To tackle how citizenship regimes matter, therefore, we must situate them in the context of the societal cleavages, inequalities, and tensions that exist in society. Societal cleavages and inequalities can compromise, hinder, and at times undermine the political equality promised by citizenship. Different social groups do not necessarily identify with the national political community, gain equal representation or voice in the prevailing forms of interest intermediation, and/or encounter equal access to the rights acknowledged by a given citizenship regime. These points are eloquently and convincingly made by a diverse set of scholars, whose work has greatly influenced the kinds of arguments made in this book. This list includes, but is not

---

[22] Important exceptions include O'Donnell (1993); Fox (1994a and 1994b); Foweraker and Landman (1997); and Yashar (1999).

[23] Schattsneider (1975: 34–5); cited in Williams (1998: 76).

[24] Also see Wiener (1999: 199).

limited to, Marx,[25] T. H. Marshall,[26] Walzer (1983 and 1993),[27] and Young (1995).[28] One does not have to agree with their distinct (and different) policy recommendations to appreciate the eloquence, power, and implications of their arguments about citizenship and inequality. Despite fundamental differences in ideological orientations, all of these scholars note that while citizenship legally grants equal rights, in practice these rights can be and have been minimized and blocked for significant parts of the citizenry. This tension can result from the inequalities posed by capitalism (Marx and Marshall) and/or the persistence of social exclusions (Walzer and Young). In short, citizenship regimes can grant formal equal rights for an officially defined political community, but they cannot do away with unequal experiences – vis-à-vis citizenship regimes, other citizens, and the state. For given

[25] Marx argued that citizenship was epiphenomenal. It did not and could not extend equal political rights insofar as it was *derivative* of material conditions that were at their core unequal. So long as capitalism prevailed, material conditions would generate inequality among classes. So long as material inequality persisted, political equality of individuals would remain ideational rather than actual.

[26] T. H. Marshall observed that there is an inherent and deep tension between capitalism and democratic citizenship. The former creates economic inequality while the latter creates political equality. He argued that these two systems would always be in tension with one another. While a supporter of both, he argued that extreme economic inequalities undermined the capacity of the impoverished to act as political equals. In particular, extreme economic inequalities made it difficult for individuals to take part in a "civilized" life – which he saw as the *sine qua non* of citizenship. Marshall therefore saw the need to tame and counteract the extreme inequalities that capitalism could and had created.

[27] Walzer argued in his classic 1983 book, *Spheres of Justice*, that the extension of formal citizenship holds great promise but does not result in equality. He wrote that it would result in a world where no particular group would dominate in all spheres; some groups would prevail in some spheres; other groups would prevail in other spheres. He called this social equilibrium "complex equality." "No one would rule or be ruled all the time and everywhere. No one would be radically excluded." In 1993, Walzer observed that this ideal form of complex equality had not occurred. The inclusive democracies of the late twentieth century had reproduced inequalities that existed previously in all spheres of society, by systematically disadvantaging certain groups through stereotyping, discrimination, and disregard.

[28] Young (1995) argues that despite citizenship's formal equality, historically marginalized and excluded groups do not operate on a level playing field in public debates. Citizenship grants these groups the right to vote and to organize, but it does not actually grant an equal *voice*. This is not least because the public sphere is not a neutral-free zone. Powerful groups have defined the rules and called them neutral. However, the rules and associated norms in fact reflect, if not favor, the practices, discourses and interests of some groups over others. As such, historically marginalized groups come to the public sphere with distinct disadvantages – finding it difficult to speak out and to be heard.

different social backgrounds and social contexts, experiences are uneven, social marginalization can persist, and other kinds of exclusions and in-equalities can result – particularly for subordinated or marginalized ethnic groups.

If I draw explicitly on these authors for their insight into the tension between citizenship and social inequality, the same cannot be said for their assumptions about state capacity. Marshall, Walzer, and Young have all ar-gued that the state has intervened or should do so to address the tension be-tween citizenship's political equality and societal inequalities: be it through social rights (Marshall); neocorporatist forms of representation (Young); or greater education and civic life (Walzer). At base, all of these scholars trust that the state has the capacity to play this corrective role. Given their focus on the advanced industrial democracies, this political analysis and policy recommendation perhaps are compelling.

They are right to highlight the potentially corrective role of the state. And they are right to pinpoint that state intervention can perhaps allevi-ate the tension between citizenship and social inequality. However, they are wrong to assume that state capacity exists. State capacity cannot be assumed but has to be empirically substantiated. This is true for all cases, but par-ticularly for the new democracies, where one does not always find a fully functioning and capable state. In this context, it is not only that other social cleavages and practices can seriously compromise the ideals of liberal citi-zenship (a point forcefully made by Marshall, Walzer, and Young). It is also, fundamentally, that states cannot always deliver on the political promise to correct this situation.

Most political constitutions of Latin America have guaranteed the basic bundle of citizenship rights since Independence, but there exists "an appreciable gap between protection on paper and environment in practice" (Panizza 1993: 209).

The failure of the rule of law leaves a yawning gap between the formal legal structure and the real reach of the law, between rights-in-principle and rights-in-practice, and this gap ... is of fundamental importance to the relationship between citizenship rights and social movements (Foweraker and Landman 1997: 20–1).

Indeed, as we will see in the cases of Latin America, the incomplete and uneven reach of the state has compromised indigenous peoples' access to and experiences with different types of citizenship regimes. In the ab-sence of a state that can actually govern across a territory – what Michael Mann (1986: 59) refers to as infrastructural power – citizenship regimes are compromised, at best, and sacrificed at worst. Under these circumstances, it is not only that citizenship regimes might fail to deliver on the promise of unified political communities, equal political rights, and standardized forms of interest intermediation, but they might also mask the local autonomies and deep social inequalities that already exist.

3

The Argument

INDIGENOUS MOBILIZATION IN
LATIN AMERICA

The Latin American anomaly has yet to be explained. Why were ethnic
cleavages weak in Latin America? Why did they reverse course at century's
end, as indigenous mobilization proliferated throughout the region? And
why have significant regional and national movements emerged in all cases
except Peru? This chapter addresses the contemporary and yet uneven
emergence of indigenous movements in Latin America by analyzing the
five cases outlined in Chapter 1: Ecuador, Bolivia, Guatemala, Mexico, and
Peru. I compare these cases cross-temporally and cross-nationally.

This chapter highlights the role of citizenship regimes vis-à-vis existing
social cleavages and uneven state penetration – as conceptualized and discussed in Chapter 2. I argue here that different types of citizenship regimes
first diffused and then activated ethnic cleavages. Earlier citizenship regimes
unintentionally enabled indigenous communities to carve out spaces of local autonomy, with limited interference from the state in matters of local
governance. Subsequent citizenship regimes, however, threatened the autonomy that had been secured and, consequently, politicized ethnic cleavages. Hence we must trace the comparative historical arc of citizenship
regimes and the associated patterns of state formation to understand the
politicization of these ethnic cleavages and the *motive* for organizing. Where
autonomy was possible, ethnic cleavages were weak. Where autonomy was
subsequently challenged, ethnic cleavages became more salient.

This comparative historical discussion of citizenship regimes explains
why ethnic cleavages have become more politicized in the contemporary
period but were comparatively weak in earlier periods. But this variable
alone does not explain when and where those cleavages translated into

This chapter is a revised and expanded version of Yashar (1998 and 1999).

indigenous organizations. For as theories of social movement and collective action have made clear, alongside motives one must also consider the *capacity* and *opportunity* for organizing.[1] One must therefore ask not only why indigenous people would want to organize along indigenous lines, but also when they confronted the opportunity to do so, and where they had the capacity to mobilize accordingly. In Latin America, the preexistence of transcommunity networks provided the capacity to organize while political associational space (freedom of association and expression) essentially provided the political opportunity to do so.

This chapter makes the case that only where these three factors (changing citizenship regimes that challenged local autonomy, transcommunity networks, and political associational space) came together did indigenous movements emerge. As Tables 3.1 and 3.2 lay out, these three factors concatenated in Ecuador, Bolivia, Guatemala, and Mexico by the end of the twentieth century and gave rise to significant indigenous movements in each country. These three factors did *not* appear together in Peru, where political associational spaces were elusive and community networks were weak – thereby working against indigenous organizing beyond the local level. This chapter develops this three-pronged comparative historical argument against the five most densely populated indigenous countries in Latin America.

The Motive: Changing Citizenship Regimes, States, and Autonomy

The politicization of ethnic cleavages and the motive for organizing resulted from the shift in citizenship regimes and the challenge to local autonomy that ensued. Latin America essentially experienced an arc of citizenship regimes that moved from corporatist citizenship regimes toward neoliberal ones, as noted in Chapter 2 (and summarized in Table 2.2). While corporatist citizenship regimes advanced civil and social rights (and at times political rights) alongside class-based forms of interest intermediation, neoliberal citizenship regimes advanced civil and political rights alongside pluralist forms of interest intermediation.

Both corporatist and neoliberal citizenship regimes profoundly and intentionally reshaped state institutions and resources, as well as the terms of public access to them. Because of the uneven reach of the state, however, they had unintended consequences. Thus, in attempting to restructure

---

[1] See McAdam, McCarthy, and Zald (1996); Tarrow (1998); and Gurr (2000: ch. 3).

Table 3.1. *Emergence of Indigenous Movements in Latin America: Scoring of Variables and Cases*[a]

	Motive/Incentive Changing Citizenship Regimes that Challenge Local Autonomy		Capacity Transcommunity Networks	Opportunity Political Associational Space[b]	Outcome Indigenous Movements
	For Highland Peasants	For Lowlands/ Amazon			
Ecuador	+	+	+	+	Strong National Confederation
Bolivia	+	+	+	+	Strong Regional Confederations
Mexico	+	N/A	+	+	Significant Regional Movements
Guatemala	+	N/A	+	+	Significant National Movements
Peru	+	+	–	–	Weak/Rare Local Movements

[a] Changing citizenship regimes explain the contemporary politicization of indigenous identities. This variable is therefore key to explaining variation over time: namely, why indigenous movements emerge in the contemporary period but not earlier. Networks and political associational space are used to explain variation in capacity and opportunity, respectively, within the contemporary context of politicized indigenous identities. These two variables are therefore used to explain variation among the cases: namely why indigenous identities emerge in all cases but Peru. They are also used to explain subnational variation within the five cases.

[b] This column focuses on the changing political associational space in the more state-penetrated highland regions of the Andes and Mesoamerica. This is because in the Amazon, low state penetration for most of the century meant that there has been a relatively constant opportunity for political organizing.

society into class-based federations with social rights, corporatist citizenship regimes unwittingly provided autonomous spaces that could shelter rural indigenous communities from state control. And for their part, neoliberal citizenship regimes, setting out to shatter corporatism's class-based model and social rights and replace them with a more atomized or individuated set of state–society relations, in fact challenged the indigenous local autonomy that corporatism had unintentionally sheltered. As such, corporatist and neoliberal citizenship regimes had foundational projects for state and society that were consequential but unevenly institutionalized. From the top looking down, these projects restructured society in radical ways. From the bottom looking up, however, these new projects of state formation and interest intermediation have been contested at many steps along the way. This section juxtaposes the formal goals and the unintended consequences of these two citizenship regimes as a way to explain both why ethnic cleavages were once weak and why they subsequently became politicized.

Corporatist Citizenship Regimes and Local Autonomy

It is commonly acknowledged that Latin American politicians, in both democratic and authoritarian regimes, set out to address the social question in the mid-twentieth century with corporatism. As the working class and peasantry started to mobilize for resources, inclusion, and justice, political parties and the state sought to capture political support and to control the masses with the creation of new modes of interest intermediation and social rights. Corporatism did not necessarily grant free and universal suffrage. But it did create and/or promote labor and peasant associations that 1) structured, and often monopolized, official representation, 2) received state subsidies, and 3) were controlled by the state. A new type of state–society relations, therefore, was adopted that a) institutionalized a new mode of class-based interest intermediation and that b) extended social rights through the extension of social policies designed to provide a modicum of social welfare (including education, health, credit, subsidies, and the like).[2] In other words, at mid-century, Latin American countries started to institutionalize corporatist citizenship regimes.

---

[2] For classic perspectives on Latin American corporatism, see Malloy (1977). For a seminal comparative analysis of Latin American corporatism, see Collier and Collier (1991). Also see Collier (1995).

Table 3.2. *Emergence of Indigenous Movements in Latin America: Description of Variables and Cases*

	Motive/Incentive Changing Citizenship Regimes that Challenge Local Autonomy		*Capacity* Transcommunity Networks	*Opportunity* Political Associational Space	*Outcome* Indigenous Movements
	For Highland Peasants	*For Lowlands/ Amazon*			
Ecuador	Eroding corporatist citizenship regime in mid-1970s culminates in 1980s with neoliberal citizenship regime in 1980s and 1990s	State development programs, beginning in 1960s but particularly in 1990s	Peasant unions and church networks	Political opening from 1978 on	*Strong National Confederation* CONAIE (founded in 1985) composed of the highland organization ECUARUNARI (founded in 1972)[a] and the lowland organization CONFENAIE (founded in 1980)
Bolivia	Military-Peasant Pact (1960s) and Banzer dictatorship (1970s) erode corporatist citizenship regime; culminates in neoliberal citizenship regime in 1980s–1990s	State development programs, beginning in 1960s but particularly in 1990s	Peasant unions, church networks, and NGOs	Brief political opening 1970–1971; political opening from 1978/1982 on	*Strong Regional Confederations* Kataristas in the highland organization CSUTCB (emerged in 1970s); and the lowland organization CIDOB (first founded in 1982)[b]

Mexico	Erosion of corporatist citizenship regime beginning in 1940s culminates in neoliberal citizenship regime in 1980s and 1990s	N/A	Peasant unions and church networks	Partial political opening from 1988 on	*Significant Regional Movements* particularly EZLN (emerged in 1994)
Guatemala	Dismantling of corporatist citizenship regime after 1954 coup	N/A	Peasant union is repressed after 1954; churches create new networks 1960s–1980s	Uneven political opening from 1985/1992 on	*Significant National Movements* including Majawil Q'ij, CONIC, and COMG (founded in 1990s)
Peru	Overthrow of Velasco regime in 1975 coup; reverses much of corporatist citizenship regime and culminates in neoliberal citizenship in 1980s and 1990s	State development programs, beginning in 1960s but particularly in 1990s	Fragmented peasant unions; fragmented church networks	Growing restrictions, 1980–1992; 1992 autogolpe; end of civil war in 1990s provided greater associational space	*Weak Regional Movements* AIDESEP (founded in 1980) and UNCA (founded in 1983)

---

[a] ECUARUNARI was founded in 1972, although it subsequently wavered between a class-based and ethnic-based agenda. While it adopted an ethnic agenda initially, it pursued a class-based agenda from 1977–1985, after which it adopted an explicit identification with and primary concern for an "ethnic" agenda.

[b] The founding dates for these two regional organizations is somewhat arbitrary. The Kataristas first started to emerge in the early 1970s but their organizing efforts were cut short by the Banzer dictatorship; they assumed a public face and gained public notoriety in 1979. CIDOB was founded in 1982 as a subregional organization but expanded in the 1980s to encompass all of the Bolivian lowlands.

Less commonly explored, or even questioned, are the ways in which indigenous peoples were affected by the corporatist project. I argue in this book that corporatist citizenship regimes unwittingly institutionalized autonomous spaces for indigenous peoples.[3] Relatively unmonitored local spaces were created where indigenous people could sustain their local indigenous identities and forms of governance. So too they gained institutional mechanisms to access the state and its resources. As such, many indigenous communities survived and grew beyond the de facto reach of the state.

The new modes of interest intermediation and the new social programs fostered this autonomy in the following ways. Labor laws freed Indians from slave labor, debt peonage, and other forms of repressive labor control. Accordingly, these laws provided Indians with a degree of freedom previously denied them. The laws recognized indigenous peoples as candidates for citizenship rather than objects of local control. Land reforms alongside other social programs granted indigenous communities land titles and social services and, in the process, provided them both with a basis for securing a basic standard of living (i.e., social rights) and with the geographic space to secure cultural practices and political autonomy. Moreover, peasant federations, as the primary mode of interest intermediation, provided Indians with institutional avenues for accessing and interacting with the state.

Land reforms in Mexico (1934), Bolivia (1953), Guatemala (the short-lived reform of 1952), Ecuador (1964 and 1973), and Peru (1968), for example, weakened landed elites' control of the countryside, redistributed significant tracts of land, and provided incentives for Indians to register as peasant communities.[4] This registration reorganized the countryside along

---

[3] Some scholars working on social movements and oppositional consciousness have underscored the importance of "free spaces" (see, in particular, Evans and Boyte [1986]). A more recent round of scholarship has emphasized, in particular, that physical segregation and the capacity to talk in unmonitored spaces can ironically provide the free spaces for oppositional consciousness and mobilization (see Groch 2001 and Morris and Braine 2001: 30–1). This general idea maps onto the argument developed in this book. Indigenous people were removed from the centers of power but were also alienated from it. As such, they had the spaces to maintain and develop ideational and political autonomy. While this argument broadly parallels the ideas about "free spaces," I have chosen not to use this term, which was developed for the United States and presumes a commitment to democracy (which I did not find) rather than autonomy (which better describes the de facto practices found in many indigenous communities).

[4] See McClintock (1981: 61) and Eckstein (1983) for comparative land reform data.

state-regulated corporatist lines, with many peasant communities joining peasant federations in hopes of gaining access to land and the state. These corporatist reforms brought with them the creation and expansion of social services in the areas of agricultural support, infrastructure, education, and health. Access to land and these services were often gained through corporatist associations.

In other words, the corporatist citizenship regime recognized Indians' freedom from elite control, recatalogued Indians as peasants, and as such, granted them rights and access previously denied them. The state and union organizations imposed a peasant identity on Indians as the ticket for political incorporation and access to resources. With the distribution of land, extension of agricultural credits, and provision of agricultural subsidies, peasants developed a new relationship with the state, one that subordinated them into official channels in exchange for clientelistic rewards. While the actual implementation of these reforms was quite uneven within and across countries, they generated political ties with those rural sectors that had gained (or hoped to gain) access to land and the state.

The registration of peasant communities and the growth of peasant federations, in particular, fostered the fiction that the state had turned Indians into peasants and stripped indigenous ethnicity of its salience. Official political discourse promoted assimilation into mestizo culture and extended resources to rural citizens insofar as they identified and organized as peasants. Until recently, studies of corporatism highlighted the strong reach of these corporatist institutions and their capacity to control and remake these social sectors. Latin American corporatist states presumably centralized state–society relations.

Yet this enterprise was compromised by the absence of a rationalized bureaucracy, the failure to establish authority, and a lack of monopoly of the legitimate use of force. For in contrast to Weber's classic definition of the state, many of Latin America's central political institutions remain weak, commitment to those institutions remains questionable, and the territorial scope of those institutions remains ambiguous.[5] This is nowhere more apparent than from the vantage of the countryside. From that perspective, it is difficult to argue that there is a single human community (as opposed to

---

[5] Weber (1946: 78) argued in his classic definition of the state: "The state is a human community that (successfully) claims the monopoly of the legitimate use of physical force within a given territory." In Latin America, however, as in most of Africa, Asia, and the Middle East, this standard is still largely unmet.

many), that the state claims a monopoly of the legitimate use of force, or that the territory is clearly defined. National identities, borders, and legitimacy are all in question and often in flux.[6] Indeed, Latin America remains very much in the throes of state formation, where the identities, borders, and legitimacy of the state are highly politicized and contested processes, particularly in the countryside. Even in Guatemala, where the military state of the 1970s and 1980s was presumed omnipotent and omnipresent, the state was unevenly institutionalized, thereby leaving spaces for autonomous action.[7]

Hence, despite official statements and institutions of corporatist control, large areas of the country operated beyond the reach of the state. Authoritarian enclaves were dominated by patronage and clientelist networks. Caudillos and landlords at times deployed their own paramilitary forces, created their own political rules, displayed greater allegiance to subnational politics than to national politics, and/or deployed state institutions for their benefit.[8]

The weak reach of the state had implications for both those areas that were targeted by corporatist citizenship regimes (the Andean and Mesoamerican highlands) and those that were not (the Amazon). Studies of the Amazon have long noted the failure of states to govern the Amazon – leaving large swaths of territory and significant numbers of Indians beyond the political and military control of the state. States did not actively seek to harness the Amazon region until the latter part of the twentieth century. Prior to that they had mapped out boundaries that de facto included Indians as members, though not necessarily citizens, of the given state.[9] With this de facto policy of disregard, Indians did not gain access to state resources but they did maintain substantial, if not complete, political autonomy from the state – leaving indigenous authorities and practices to govern social, political, economic, and cultural relations therein. And while colonization schemes beginning in the 1960s (which in some places coincided with land reforms) did pose a threat in some places, these schemes did not initially change the circumstances for most indigenous communities in the

---

[6] State formation is a process of political mapping. As Scott (1998) has argued, it requires a situation of mutual intelligibility. The state must be able to read, identify, and defend the territory it governs. Those governed should be able to identify (with) and depend on the state for basic functions.

[7] Yashar (1997b).

[8] Fox (1994a and 1994b); Joseph and Nugent (1994); Nickson (1995); and Hagopian (1996).

[9] See Ruiz (1993); Santos-Granero (1996); and Smith (1996).

Amazon, which remained beyond the reach of the colonists or who reset-
tled in areas not yet claimed by them. In short, while corporatist citizenship
regimes granted access to the state and social rights, the uneven reach of the
state de facto undermined the centralizing program and allowed for local
authorities – indigenous and otherwise – to act with relative autonomy in the
Amazon.

The uneven reach of the state also had an impact on the capacity of Latin
American countries to incorporate those areas most affected by the corporatist citizenship regimes. In the agricultural highlands of Bolivia, Peru, and
Ecuador as well as the rural areas in Mexico and Guatemala, the state could
not assert the pervasive control that the overwhelming majority of studies
of corporatism have tended to assume.[10] To the contrary, indigenous communities managed to carve out a degree of local autonomy that remained
beyond the reach of corporatist institutions. Indeed, due to labor laws,
land reform, and credit programs (fundamental components of the corporatist citizenship regimes in the countryside) Indians secured the spaces in
which they could institutionalize indigenous community practices at the local level.[11] In more ways than one, the distribution of inviolable communal
lands to registered peasant communities provided Indians with the physical
space not only for farming but also for securing governance by traditional
indigenous authorities and the public expression of cultural ties. In this way
the legal registration of communities and granting of community-based
property created a legally defined, state-sanctioned, geographic area that
allowed for the growth and/or maintenance of politically autonomous local
enclaves, indigenous culture, and political practices. Otherwise stated, land
reforms (which extended social rights in the countryside) masked the maintenance of indigenous autonomy and in some cases even engendered the
(re)emergence of indigenous leaders, the (re)constitution of communities,
and the expression of (evolving) indigenous identities at the community
level.

In Mexico, for example, the land reform accompanied the creation
of a national peasant federation, the Confederación Nacional Campesina

---

[10] Rubin (1997), for example, highlights how corporatism in Mexico is much more porous
than commonly portrayed and that alternative spaces for organizing were therefore present
for social movement formation and political contestation.

[11] In Eugen Weber's classic (1976) study of nation building, he illuminates how the French
state turned peasants into Frenchman. I suggest here that Latin American efforts to turn
Indians into peasants in fact created the space in which they could defend and develop a
local indigenous identity.

(CNC), and distributed property in many forms. Of these, the distribution of *ejidos* (communally owned land) unwittingly provided the greatest latitude for local indigenous autonomy – they were community based, inalienable, and, while regulated, often beyond state control.[12] In Bolivia the National Revolutionary governments of the 1950s and the subsequent military governments between 1964 and 1974 also incorporated Indians into the state as peasants. As in Mexico, they depended on alliances and pacts with peasant federations, which were expected both to deliver votes to the government and to control the local communities. Contrary to the hopes of politicians and military officers, Bolivia witnessed the maintenance of *ayllus* (kinship groups governed by a set of local-level indigenous authorities) in several regions in the Andean countryside.[13] In Ecuador the 1937 community law and later the 1964 and 1973 land reforms defined indigenous men and women as peasants and gave them access to the state insofar as they represented themselves as peasant communities and/or unions. Greater state penetration, land reforms, and freedom of movement often increased indigenous peasant independence from local landlords and, moreover, enabled indigenous communities to strengthen and (re)construct local public spaces for community authority structures and customary law.[14] Indeed, the number of registered peasant communities skyrocketed in the 1960s and 1970s.[15] However, at the local level, many indigenous communities continued to maintain some form of indigenous practices and institutions. These clientelist and corporatist arrangements were most advanced in Mexico and Bolivia, followed by Ecuador; the broad outlines of these arrangements endured in these three countries until the 1980s. Short-lived state efforts to incorporate the peasantry and pass land reform programs also occurred in Guatemala (1944–1954) and Peru (1968–1975).

Corporatist citizenship regimes, therefore, created a dynamic dualism, with identities shifting according to the locale. Before the state, Indians assumed identities as peasants – thereby gaining access to the social services and goods (in other words, *social rights*). Within the community, peasants assumed their identities as Indians – thereby securing local cultural

---

[12] Fox (1994a); Mattiace (1997); Rubin (1997); Harvey (1998); and Napolitano and Leyva Solano (1998).

[13] Rivera Cusicanqui y Equipo THOAS (1992); Ticona, Rojas, and Albó (1995); and Ströbele-Gregor (1996).

[14] Guerrero (1993).

[15] Zamosc (1995).

enclaves.[16] Location mattered for the expression of identity. Where the state incompletely penetrated local communities (nowhere more evident than in the Amazon), Indians sustained and asserted varying degrees of political autonomy by retaining authority systems and customs.[17] For even if states did not respect indigenous jurisdiction in these communities, indigenous communities often did.

Shifting Citizenship Regimes and Challenging Local Autonomy

This particular balance in state–society relations, however, would not survive the century. Military and economic elites did not necessarily accept the rising power of class (including peasant) federations, and economic constraints made it difficult for states to sustain social programs that had extended the host of social programs associated with the corporatist citizenship regimes. Moreover, states increasingly responded to economic pressures to open up markets that had protected or ignored indigenous lands. As elites started to *erode* corporatist citizenship regimes and to try to gain command of national territories, they politicized ethnic cleavages by challenging the two types of autonomy that had developed 1) among the peasantized and corporatirized areas of the Andes and Mesoamerica and 2) within the Amazon.

The erosion of corporatist citizenship regimes began as early as 1954 in Guatemala and culminated throughout the region with the replacement of corporatist citizenship regimes with neoliberal citizenship regimes in the 1980s and 1990s. Indeed, by the end of the twentieth century, citizenship regimes had changed radically as neoliberal ideas came to define the rights of citizens and the predominant mode of interest intermediation. With the third wave of democracy and the economic crises of the 1980s and 1990s, in particular, politicians throughout the region started to advocate individual autonomy and responsibility, a program based on granting individual political and civil rights (but not necessarily social rights), the emasculation

[16] This duality is captured by disciplinary differences in the social sciences. Political scientists working on this period have highlighted the centrality of class, the peasantry, and corporatist organizations, as if they displaced community autonomy and ethnic identities. Anthropologists have historically focused on the local level and, in turn, have highlighted community autonomy and ethnicity, often at the expense of broader patterns of state–society relations.

[17] Corporatist citizenship regimes barely penetrated the Amazon. Amazonian Indians rarely formed part of peasant federations, and states did not have the resources to control them. Consequently, Amazonian Indians had even more autonomy than Andean and Mesoamerican Indians.

of corporatist organizations, and the promotion of free markets in land and labor. The last of these amplified the challenge to local autonomy that had begun in earlier periods and provided the language that movements would use to challenge neoliberalism and to articulate a postliberal challenge. The rest of this section lays out how changing citizenship regimes politicized ethnic cleavages and provided the motive for organizing in two regions differentially affected by the state.

Eroding Corporatist Citizenship Regimes and Politicizing Ethnic Cleavages in the Andes and Mesomerica   One wave of ethnic politicization occurred in the very areas that had been explicitly targeted by the corporatist citizenship regimes: the Andes and Mesomerica. In these areas – which had been formally granted labor freedoms, social rights in the form of land and social services, and peasant-based representation – Indians eventually confronted the erosion of corporatist citizenship regimes and a corresponding challenge to local autonomy. In some cases this was a slow process (as in Ecuador, Bolivia, and Mexico); in others it was a sudden reversal (as in Guatemala and Peru). But in all cases, it eventually resulted in the political project and economic "imperative" associated with the neoliberal citizenship regimes of the 1980s and 1990s.

In Ecuador, Bolivia, and Mexico the weakening of rural peasant programs was a slow and steady process. The military government in Ecuador initially extended these corporatist rights but subsequently backpedaled on their promises. In Mexico, it was a slow process that occurred over decades as the state decreased its commitment to the land reform program initially passed in the 1930s. In Bolivia, the military governments of the 1960s sought to reassert control over the peasantry in the "Military-Peasant Pact," which essentially imposed leaders on peasant federations and imposed stabilization packages during the 1970s.

In each of these cases, there was a steady erosion of corporatist citizenship regimes – which resulted in the steady weakening of state-sanctioned peasant federations, the slowing down of land reform commitments, and increasing efforts by the state to control local politics. In each case, Indians started to organize along ethnic-based lines – with particularly important organizing efforts in each case in the 1970s.[18]

---

[18] Indigenous movements did not emerge immediately following the motive provided by the changing citizenship regimes. As argued here, two other variables (networks and political associational space) were also necessary as they provided *capacity* and *opportunity*, respectively.

Neoliberal citizenship regimes were implemented in Ecuador, Bolivia, and Mexico in the 1980s and 1990s and delivered the final coup de grace against corporatist citizenship regimes, in general, and local autonomy, in particular. While neoliberal citizenship regimes did not cause indigenous mobilization in the first place, they did subsequently catalyze *additional* mobilization (and shaped the political agendas that emerged). Neoliberal citizenship regimes resulted in reduced ministerial budgets for ministries of agriculture; social services; and economic programs, including protection of peasant lands, access to credit, and agricultural subsidies. Real wages in the agricultural sector steadily declined from the 1980s and by 1992 had declined by 30 percent in Latin America as a whole.[19] By the mid-1990s, land reforms had been proposed to privatize land markets in Mexico (1991 – with the decision to dismantle the constitutional protection of communal held lands, ejidos), Ecuador (1994 – with the land reform proposal), and Bolivia (1996 – with the land reform proposal). All of these were designed to make previously inalienable lands open for sale. In short, indigenous communities definitively lost their interlocutors with the state, land security, and social resources. Under these circumstances the ability to maintain local autonomy and secure a stable relationship with the state seemed increasingly remote.

In Guatemala and Peru (in contrast to Ecuador, Bolivia, and Mexico), the overthrow of corporatist citizenship regimes did not occur slowly but took place suddenly in counterreform coups in 1954 and 1975, respectively. In post-1954 Guatemala and post-1975 Peru, militaries repressed peasant unions, weakened and even reversed land reform distribution, and weakened social programs that had granted social rights to this sector. In other words, they reversed the corporatist citizenship regimes that had incorporated Indians into the polity and promised to support indigenous communities as economically viable entities. With the turn to civilian rule (an uneven and torturous process in both cases), states neither recognized social rights from earlier periods nor supported the formation of corporatist peasant federations. To the contrary, they enacted reforms that further cut state-run social programs – except for targeted safety net programs – and delimited the spaces for class-based organizing. Neoliberal reforms, in particular in Peru, further inserted instability into the countryside as poverty and inequality rates soared in the 1980s and 1990s. In Guatemala and Peru, local

---

[19] Urioste (1992); Conaghan and Malloy (1994); de Janvry et al. (1994); Lustig (1995); Morley (1995); and Wilkie, Contreras, and Komisaruk (1995: Table 3107, 990).

autonomy was challenged not only by the reversal of state reforms in the 1950s and 1970s, respectively, but also by subsequent civil wars that ravaged the countryside in both countries through the 1980s and part of the 1990s.

Both the slow (Ecuador, Bolivia, and Mexico) and sudden (Peru and Guatemala) reversal of corporatist citizenship regimes have had significant consequences – not least for indigenous peoples. In sum, class-based federations have lost political and social leverage throughout the region, and consequently Indians have lost their formal ties and access to the state. Most dramatically for Indians, states have slowed down (in some cases reversed) land reforms, privatized land markets, liberalized agricultural prices, eliminated agricultural subsidies, and diminished credit programs.[20] The reforms threaten a communal land base that the state had once made inviolable.[21] In other words, they have threatened the social rights that had been extended with the earlier corporatist citizenship regimes.

In all five cases, the weakening of corporatist modes of interest intermediation and the dismantling of rural programs (including land reforms, credit programs, and the like) have further increased uncertainty about property regimes among peasants in Mesoamerica and the Andes. Liberalizing states have made it clear that they will not maintain (in Mexico, Ecuador, and Bolivia) or reestablish (in Guatemala and Peru) special forms of property rights, credit, and subsidies for peasants. Consequently, the contemporary period challenges the poor's access to the state and its resources. In all five countries, one's status as a peasant now provides limited political purchase – as peasant programs are dismantled and peasant organizations weakened. Rural organizing and protest respond to this material uncertainty, as peasants fear indebtedness, declining incomes, and the loss of land. The *indigenous* character of the contemporary movements, however, extends beyond material concerns for land as a productive resource. The potential loss of land also affects the *viability* and *autonomy* of local indigenous political institutions that had operated in, and assumed, a relatively well-defined and stable geographic space.

In this context of reduced spaces for local autonomy and access to the state, ethnic cleavages have been politicized. Indigenous movements – particularly those that mobilize in the countryside – have protested the state

---

[20] Conaghan and Malloy (1994); de Janvry et al. (1994); Morley (1995); and Urioste Fernández de Córdova (1995).

[21] These reforms (particularly efforts to privatize land markets and to privilege the individual over the corporate unit) echo late-nineteenth-century Liberal reforms that were incontrovertibly detrimental to indigenous peoples.

reforms that have placed restrictions on the inalienable *community rights* and de facto *local autonomy* that they had secured earlier with corporatist citizenship regimes. Indigenous movements, in short, have come to demand that the state officially recognize indigenous communities. In Mexico as well as Guatemala, we find separate efforts to negotiate autonomy for the Mayan populations residing on either side of the border.[22] In Bolivia, indigenous activists have worked to recognize, reconstitute, and/or register the ayllus (communal organizations) that have dotted the Andean countryside;[23] through the *Ley Inra*, this became legally possible.[24] In Ecuador, indigenous movements and NGOs have started to dialogue and initiate projects to strengthen and/or reconstitute systems of elders that have receded in importance over the years.[25]

Promoting Development and Politicizing Ethnic Cleavages in the Amazon
A second type of indigenous movement occurred in areas that had fallen beyond the scope of corporatist citizenship regimes. In the Amazon, as noted previously, the state has historically been weak – with limited impact on policy, social services, infrastructure, government access, or institution building. Corporatist citizenship regimes did not find significant institutional expression in the Amazon. While the state expanded in the three decades after World War II in the Andes, the Amazon remained relatively marginalized from contemporary politics, the market, and the state's role in each. Colonization programs did develop, starting in the 1960s, but they affected pockets of the Amazon, not the region as a whole. As such, incidents of colonization were interpreted as isolated events, rather than collective slights.

[22] For discussions of autonomy debates in Mexico, see Ojarasca (1995); Díaz-Polanco (1997); Mattiace (1997); and Stephen (1997).

[23] Ayllus often claim sovereignty over discontinuous land bases. This geographical spread poses a challenge to Western ideas of state formation, which generally assume that continuous areas coincide with a single political administration.

[24] Several interviews with each of the following people between May–August 1997: Constantino Lima, Aymaran nationalist activist since the 1970s; Carlos Mamani, María Eugenia Choque Quispe, and Ramón Conde, researcher-activists at *Taller de Historia Oral Andina* (THOA); and Ricardo Calla, former-director of *Taller de Apoyo a Ayllus y Pueblos Indígenas* (TAYPI). Also see Molina and Arias (1996), Albó and Ayllu Sartañani (n.d.).

[25] Based on several interviews with José María Cabascango of ECUARUNARI, several interviews with Luis Maldonado of *Centro de Estudios Pluriculturales* (CEPCU), three interviews with Fernando Rosero, Director of the United Nations Volunteers (March 11, 1997, March 18, 1997, and May 7, 1997), and one interview with Congressman Luis Macas (May 6, 1997). All interviews conducted between February 1997 and May 1997.

These colonization programs and the expansion into the Amazon, how-ever, have become increasingly consequential. Development programs have encouraged colonization by Andean peasants (indigenous and nonindigenous) and the expansion of cattle ranching, logging operations, and oil exploration. In many cases, foreign companies took advantage of these development schemes alongside domestic migrants and domestic companies. Whether international or national in origin, these developments have challenged indigenous communities in the Amazon that had remained relatively independent from the state and had sustained political and economic control over vast land areas. Indigenous movements have emerged to oppose these developments and, in the process, have demanded that the state recognize indigenous territories. In Ecuador, for example, the first indigenous organization formed in the 1960s among the Shuar in order to protect their lands against colonization plans. This pattern was replicated throughout the Ecuadorian and Bolivian Amazon as colonizers, oil companies, cattle grazers, and loggers started to penetrate the region. These Amazonian movements assumed particular visibility in the 1980s and 1990s when states accelerated programs to promote more open land markets in the Amazon – culminating in significant marches in Ecuador (1992) and Bolivia (1990).

Throughout Latin America (including Peru), therefore, the contemporary period has challenged the space for indigenous local autonomy that was secured during the prior corporatist citizenship regimes and its associated developmentalist state. In Mesoamerica and the Andes, the state has supported the dismantling of corporatist forms of representation, agricultural subsidies, and protection of communally and individually held lands. In the Amazon, the state has increased its presence and promoted colonization by Andean nationals and foreign companies. In both cases, the state's challenge to land tenure and use has threatened material livelihoods and indigenous forms of autonomous local governance – both of which had depended on more stable property relations. In this context, indigenous movements are asserting the right to new administrative spheres with a certain degree of political autonomy at the local level. This is not just a call for more land, although that is certainly a core component of the demands. It is also a demand that the state recognize and respect autonomous indigenous political jurisdiction and authority over the communities that inhabit that geographic space.

These movements gained momentum in the context of neoliberal citizenship regimes. They were not caused by them but they were spurred on by them. For as Richard Chase Smith wrote, in the years prior to neoliberal hegemony:

> The issues of land and ethnic identity coalesced the ethnic federations. In each case, a particular group felt its collective land base and identity threatened by both state policies of colonization and integration and by the expanding capitalist market economy. Virtually every ethnic federation began as a meeting of headmen or representatives of different settlements of a particular ethnic group who were looking for common strategies to defend the land and their nationality (Smith 1985: 17).

Smith was insightful and prescient. While he was talking about the Amazon in 1985, his observations resonate throughout Latin America as a whole.

The Capacity: Transcommunity Networks

Movements, however, do not emerge mechanically as new needs and motives present themselves. They must build (upon) organizational capacity to initiate and sustain a movement. Organizational capacity must be demonstrated (rather than assumed), particularly for indigenous communities, which are often separated by great distances, and for indigenous identities, which have historically been more clearly defined by and embedded in *local* communities. In the absence of ties between and among communities, it is extremely difficult to scale up demands, to organize, and to launch protests.

Networks provide this organizational capacity.[26] They fostered the communication and cooperation that was essential for transcending geographic dispersion, language barriers, and cultural unfamiliarity (and in some cases hostility). In doing so, networks provided the forum for future indigenous leaders to meet, share common experiences, develop a common language, identify common problems, and articulate common goals. In turn, indigenous men developed ethnic identities that referred not only to their local Indian communities but also to a transcommunity indigenous identification. This "indigenous" identity was a product more than a cause of the first generation networks that were in place. It did not necessarily include a close national identification with all indigenous communities. Indeed, as elaborated in Part II, Andean and Amazonian indigenous movements in Ecuador and Bolivia (and even Peru) formed separately and did not

---

[26] I thank Arang Keshavarzian for his insight into networks and suggestions for improving my argument, not all of which I have been able to incorporate.

necessarily or easily translate those regional ties into national ones. Indeed, different historical experiences had resulted in very different cultural norms, understandings of autonomy and land, and styles of negotiation. Without networks, it was impossible to bridge these divides.

Networks, therefore, constitute a second part of the explanation about indigenous movement formation in Latin America insofar as they provided the organizational capacity necessary to build indigenous movements. I take networks to refer to the repeated exchanges and resulting relationships that are constructed among individuals or social units by formal and informal institutions. Networks can take many forms. The one distinguishing feature that proved essential for indigenous movement formation was geography. Only where *trans*community networks were in place could and did indigenous communities possess the organizational capacity to forge broad indigenous movements. The existence of these networks more than their organizational features (vertical or horizontal; coercive or cooperative; social, political, economic, cultural, and/or religious; etc.), proved key to explaining *where* indigenous leaders possessed the organizational capacity to build indigenous movements.[27]

This argument builds on the vast literature on networks (and its kindred literature on social capital and civil society). Granovetter (1995) argued that the capacity to secure jobs is best explained by personal contacts and networks, rather than by education, training, or skill. Social movements theorists have also made similar arguments about movement building (McAdam, McCarthy, and Zald 1996; Tarrow 1998). McAdam, for example, found that churches played this role in the development of the civil rights movement in the United States and that personal contacts played this role in explaining who joined Freedom Summer (McAdam 1982 and 1988). Putnam (1993) has looked at the civic networks that have engendered more effective governance. And Varshney (2002) analyzes how networks of civic engagement shape trajectories of ethnic violence. In general, networks enable people (or communities) to interact, to exchange information, to build social capital, and to mobilize for change. They help to overcome distances that otherwise might appear insurmountable. And in so doing, they provide the basis for building movements. In Ecuador,

---

[27] These other organizational features of networks do not explain movement emergence, although they probably do provide insight into the *types* of movements that did emerge. Further work is needed to explain why some networks lead to unified movements in a given area and why others lead to competitive ones. In this regard, the discussion of networks still requires further analysis, as also noted by Podolny and Page (1998: 73).

Bolivia, Mexico, and Guatemala, networks provided the spaces within which indigenous leaders built ties, developed trust, gained leadership skills, and forged new ideas. These networks allowed for "brokerage," which McAdam, Tarrow, and Tilly (2001) discuss as a relational mechanism that connects sites, creates new collective actors, and/or speaks on their behalf. The very social interaction that occurs through and by brokers can create autonomous spheres in which actors can identify their shared circumstances, scale up their reference group to transcend local geography, and recast identities (e.g., assuming an identity as *Indians* rather than solely as distinct indigenous communities).

Networks and movements, therefore, are analytically and temporally distinct. They cannot be reduced to one another. Indigenous activists drew on *existing* networks to build *new* movements. These movements, in turn, had very different organizational identities and goals than the networks on which they built. Indeed, indigenous movements often severed ties to the prior networks and, in some cases, critiqued these networks for subordinating indigenous peoples. Consequently, the existence of prior networks does not equal the formation of new ones; rather, older networks provided the basis for generating new ones.

The state, unions, churches, and NGOs have played a crucial role in this regard.[28] While pursuing their respective missions, these institutions (unwittingly) provided links that have become a basis for forging translocal (and subsequently transnational) indigenous identities and movements. The state, for example, attempted to mobilize support and control rebellions within peasant communities, as part of the corporatist and populist developmental policies previously discussed. With the passage of land reforms, states attempted to construct a loyal national peasantry, to weaken more localized ethnic identities, and to forge a nation-state. In Mexico and Bolivia, where these processes were most advanced, peasant unions were linked to corporatist state-parties that promised access to land, economic support, and social services. In Ecuador, the state agrarian reform program promoted rural organizing, resulting in a significant increase in the registering of rural *comunas*, cooperatives, and associations. This state-sanctioned rural organizing in Mexico, Bolivia, and Ecuador engendered cross-community networks that were later used in these countries to organize indigenous movements – in some places tied to and in some places autonomous from the peasant unions.

---

[28] See Brysk (2000) for a discussion of the transnational dimensions of these networks.

Guatemala's democratic regime (1944–1954) and Peru's military reform government (1968–1975) also passed land reforms and encouraged peasant organizing, but subsequent counterreform governments in Guatemala (1954) and in Peru (1975) undermined this process. As a consequence, the Guatemalan and Peruvian peasantry of the 1980s and 1990s has not sustained transcommunity peasant networks as a result of patron-client ties with the state, as in Mexico, Bolivia, and Ecuador. The Guatemalan and Peruvian states have been hostile to peasant demands and have attempted to localize, disarticulate, and repress rural organizing efforts. Consequently, Peru has never really achieved and sustained a national peasant network – except briefly (if then) during the Velasco government (1968–1975).[29] In the absence of sustained political liberalization and a more sustained developmentalist state in the Peruvian countryside, it has been difficult to construct a national peasant movement. And in the absence of these kinds of networks, it has been difficult to construct an indigenous identity and organization that transcends its more localized referent. Guatemala, unlike Peru, did subsequently organize an opposition peasant movement on the basis of networks constructed by the Catholic Church.[30] In Guatemala, many post–Vatican II clerics and lay persons organized Christian Base Communities (CEBs) in the countryside. Many CEB members subsequently forged a new peasant movement and used the base communities to reconstruct intercommunity networks that had been repressed by the military.

In Latin America, more broadly, churches have helped to construct and strengthen rural networks between communities not only in Guatemala but also in Mexico, Bolivia, and Ecuador.[31] Churches often provided the means of communication, the locus of interaction, and literacy skills that linked one community to another. So too, church leaders inspired by liberation theology created CEBs that encouraged activism and created lay leaders that could travel between communities to address local and national problems. Catholic and Protestant churches played a crucial role in constructing networks in Chiapas, Mexico. Bishop Samuel Ruiz, for example, organized indigenous fora, brought resources to indigenous communities, and encouraged more active forms of localized organizing. In Bolivia and Ecuador, a more heterogenous church presence – Salesians, Franciscans, Protestants,

---

[29] Cotler and Portocarrero (1969); Handelman (1975); McClintock (1981); and Seligmann (1995).

[30] Little has been written on the impact of liberation theology and theologians on the Peruvian countryside. See Peña (1995).

[31] See Brown (1993); Chojnacki (1995); Floyd (1995); and Santana (1995: chs. 6–7).

Summer Institute for Linguistics (SIL), etc.[32] – also played a particularly important role in the Amazon in bridging significant differences between communities, addressing literacy, providing radio services, and organizing against land invasions.[33] Again, while churches were active in Peru, they never managed to sustain *trans*community ties – in large part, as we shall see, because of the repression that ensued in the countryside.

In short, states, unions, churches, and, more recently, NGOs (particularly in Bolivia) have provided networks that enabled indigenous communities to transcend localized identities and to identify commonly trusted leaders. In some cases these networks were internationally inspired and supported (Brysk 2000); in many they were not. In all cases, however, these networks built literacy skills and cross-community social capital that enabled indigenous leaders to move between communities, build support, and develop frames that resonated within and across communities. In turn, indigenous leaders gained access to information and resources that enabled them to communicate with the state. When confronted with changing rural–state relations that threatened property relations and local autonomy, these networks provided the organizational bases for coordinating significant indigenous mobilizing from the 1970s on.

The Political Opportunity:[34] Political Associational Space

If state reforms politicized indigenous identity and networks provided the organizational capacity, indigenous movement organizing would still

---

[32] See Castro Mantilla (1996: 20) for a chart on the SIL in Latin America – including where it began working, contracts, and ministries.

[33] In Bolivia, church influence largely occurred centuries earlier through missions that created nuclear settlements; these settlements became the centers of indigenous organizing in the 1970s and 1980s. In Ecuador and Peru, church influence occurred much more clearly through boarding schools, where future indigenous leaders met one another and acquired leadership and communication skills that were later used to organize regional indigenous organizations in the Amazon. In both cases, churches along with NGOs provided the networks, resources, and skills for indigenous organizing in the region. I thank Diego Iturralde and Sergio Delgado for first bringing these patterns to my attention in an interview held in La Paz, Bolivia on October 20, 1995.

[34] See McAdam (1996: 27). McAdam lays out four dimensions that constitute political opportunity structures: the degree of political opening; elite alignments; presence of elite allies; and the state's capacity and propensity to use repression. In the case of Latin America's indigenous movements, elite alignments and access to elite allies do not uniformly play a role in movement *formation* – even if they do affect *policy success*. Consequently, I rely more on McAdam's first and fourth dimensions to analyze movement emergence.

only emerge in the presence of one more variable: political associational space. The need for associational space is painfully obvious (particularly for scholars of social movements) but often overlooked in discussions of ethnic politics, as it is all too common to assume that ethnic cleavages naturally translate into political organizations and protest. Political associational space (in conjunction with changing citizenship regimes and transcommunity networks), however, proved crucial to the emergence and growth of indigenous movements.[35]

So what is political associational space? Political associational space refers to the de facto existence of freedom of association and expression. It is not reducible to regime type; it is not equal to democracy.[36] To the contrary, political associational space can exist (to varying degrees) in different political contexts, including the following: where states are virtually or largely absent (as in the Amazon); in democratic regimes where states protect civil rights *in practice*; and in transitional regimes where authorities initiate a process of political liberalization that includes a decline in repression and a corresponding increase in respect for civil rights. The common denominator in these three contexts is that the state does not trample on the capacity to associate and to speak out.

---

[35] One might point out that where political associational spaces have been closed off, innovative activists have been known to create them (see, e.g., Keck and Sikkink 1998; Navarro 1998; Tarrow 1998; and Tilly 2002). They have used "nonpolitical" fora to engage in political activities; and/or they have built alliances with domestic elites and/or international activists to overcome political obstacles. This exceptional heroism on the part of some activists is incontrovertible. However, the examples are noteworthy precisely because they have been the exception. In general, closed political associational spaces have worked against movement building – particularly in indigenous rural areas where activists could not organize, speak out, and mobilize without incurring repression against them and their communities.

[36] As commonly noted, political liberalization is not synonymous with democratization. Democratization can coincide with political crackdowns – as in Peru and Guatemala in the 1980s. Moreover, political liberalization can occur independently of democracy – as in Brazil during the *distensão* period and Mexico in the 1990s. Empirically speaking, while political liberalization has provided the political opportunity for movement organizing in the Andes and Mesoamerica, the same cannot necessarily be said of electoral or formal democracy, per se. See Eisinger (1973) for a discussion of the curvilinear relationship between democracy and protest. Eisinger noted that protest is *least* likely where democracy is both foreclosed and fully achieved. It is in the spaces in between, where democracy fulfills only part of its promises, that social groups are most likely to protest. See Davenport and Armstrong (2002) for a statistical analysis of the relationship between democracy and repression.

It is also important to make clear that associational space is *not* the same as networks. The former refers to the political opportunity to organize while the latter refers to the existing capacity to do so. These two variables can affect one another but do not necessarily covary. During times of political closure networks can persist (as with military-dominated corporatist associations and churches). Moreover, associational space does not necessarily translate into the existence or growth of social networks.

Empirically speaking we can see how political associational space has mattered in both its de facto and de jure forms. In the Amazon, where the state has historically been weak (in many places relatively absent), a generalized associational space existed independent of changes in the national political regimes. Even when national governments deployed repression in other areas, this violence rarely affected the Amazon in a direct way. In this regard, associational space existed de facto and was relatively constant in the Amazonian regions.[37] Amazonian indigenous communities had the opportunity to organize transcommunity movements absent state regulation, control, and repression (although they often confronted local forms of oppression from landlords and churches).

In the Andean and Mesoamerican regions, where the state had incorporated and penetrated the highlands to a greater degree than that found in the lowland areas of the Amazon, political associational space has been more variable. It fluctuated in tandem with periods of national political closure and political liberalization. During periods of political closure and militarization, states restricted freedom of association in these regions and, therefore, closed off opportunities for legal organizing among communities. This type of closure occurred in Bolivia in the 1970s; Guatemala from 1954 through the mid-1980s and sporadically again in the 1990s; Peru from the mid-1970s through much of the 1990s (with a brief opening at the end of the 1970s and early 1980s). During these periods of political closure, indigenous organizing did not emerge or simply dissipated. Indeed, Jenaro Flores of Bolivia and Demetrio Cojti of Guatemala, both prominent indigenous leaders who helped to cofound indigenous movements in their respective countries, commented on separate occasions that political closure preempted incipient efforts to organize indigenous movements and weakened those that had started organizing during earlier and more open

---

[37] Again, Peru is a partial exception in this regard and is discussed at greater length in Part III.

times.[38] Where, however, political liberalization legally and practically resulted in the freedom to organize, there was greater opportunity to mobilize along indigenous lines.

In the Andean and Mesoamerican regions, a strong correlation exists between indigenous organizing and the extension of political associational space. National political associational space was extended the furthest in Bolivia (late 1970s and early 1980s) and Ecuador (late 1970s); and it is in these two countries that we find the first two and strongest movements in the region. National political associational space was extended the least in Peru (with an ongoing and violent civil war for much of the 1980s and 1990s) and it is here that indigenous movement organizing was largely foreclosed. Guatemala and Mexico pose intermediate cases of indigenous movement organizing, with indigenous movements emerging in a context of rather uneven processes of political liberalization and political associational space. In Guatemala, a staggering history of repression in the 1970s and early 1980s gave way to the extension of some political associational space in the mid-1980s and mid-1990s. Indigenous movements emerged in these periods of relative political opening, although their growth and strength was hampered by a rise in political violence in the late 1980s and again the late 1990s. Mexico also extended political associational space in the 1990s, although it did so against a less repressive background than in Guatemala. During 1995, 1996, and 1997 research trips, indigenous leaders generally stated that political liberalization had created a more propitious environment for organizing. And indeed, the establishment and growth of indigenous movements largely coincides with or follows the increased respect for civil liberties.

Only where associational space was in evidence did national indigenous movements emerge, including CONAIE in Ecuador, CSUTCB and CIDOB in Bolivia, COMG in Guatemala, and the EZLN in Mexico. Each of these movements built on preexisting dense social networks that allowed for both the construction of *transcommunity* ties and the creation of *panethnic* movements (as illustrated by quadrants II and IV in Table 3.3). Where these networks did not exist, it was close to impossible to organize beyond the local community level – particularly when combined with nonexistent or limited associational space. Where, however, widespread repression

---

[38] Several interviews in 1995 and 1997 with Jenaro Flores in La Paz, Bolivia and one interview in February 1996 with Demetrio Cojti in Guatemala City, Guatemala.

Table 3.3. *Latin American Indigenous Movements in the Context of Contemporary Challenges to Local Autonomy*

Political Associational Space	Preexisting Networks	
	Low	High
No: Closure/Militarization	No indigenous mobilization, as in Peruvian Andes	Panethnic movements but politically constrained in Bolivia 1970s (Andes); Ecuador 1970s (Andes); Guatemala 1970s–1980s; and Mexico 1970s–1980s
Yes: Amazon: Relatively Constant Andes: Political Liberalization	Localized and mono-ethnic mobilization occurs in isolated cases everywhere, including the Peruvian Amazon	Panethnic regional and/or national mobilization in Bolivia and Ecuador (Andes and Amazon); Guatemala 1990s; and Mexico 1990s[a]

[a] Mexico has experienced national political liberalization, as noted in the text. However, political associational space remains uneven – with increased (although fluctuating) political associational space at the national (and international level) and increased and ongoing political closure at some local levels.

continued and freedom of association was foreclosed, political closure pre-empted indigenous movement formation.

Peru falls into this latter category. Several anonymous 1997 interviews in Peru also commented on the insurmountable obstacles that authoritarian rule and civil war, in particular, posed for indigenous and peasant organizing. The violent civil war closed off avenues for freedom of organization and expression. Moreover, it destroyed existing organizations and obstructed the formation of trans-community networks that have proved so important elsewhere. In this context, sustained regional and national indigenous organizing has proved elusive in all but some isolated locations in the Peruvian Amazon, as discussed in Chapter 6.

In short, shifting citizenship regimes challenged local autonomy and politicized ethnic cleavages. Social networks provided the capacity to organize beyond local communities and to scale up efforts into regional and national indigenous organizations. And political associational space provided the necessary political opportunity for doing so. For these reasons, the existence and interplay among these three causal factors best explain the contemporary and uneven emergence of Latin America's indigenous movements.

Concluding with Second-Generation Movements: Learning, Modularity, and Strategy

One could end the story here. Challenges to local autonomy politicized ethnic cleavages. Movements emerged where activists could draw on existing resources in a context of political spaces for association. This outline explains the first wave of organizing that occurred in Ecuador, Bolivia, Mexico, and Guatemala. Were these conditions to extend to Peru, then we would forecast that significant indigenous organizing would occur there as well. The findings in this book lead to these conclusions. But it is important to note that the emergence of these movements (and the political successes that they subsequently have had) have also shifted the circumstances within which other social movements operate and the shape of the movements themselves.

For the first generation of indigenous movements gained a degree of success that no one predicted. They have at times successfully pressured states to engage in policy discussions about democratic representation, land reforms, territorial autonomy, constitutional reforms, peace accords, bicultural education, and international loans, among others. In several of these cases, these discussions have translated into legislation and, in a smaller subset, into the implementation phase. In other words, these movements have become new interlocutors with the state, have gained national and international notoriety, and have delivered goods to their community.

These successes have not gone unnoticed. Indeed, the successes of these early movements have actually contributed to the growth of a second generation of indigenous movements that have *followed, learned from,* and *replicated* the language adopted by the first round. This second generation has not necessarily mobilized to defend local autonomy, as in the first-generation cases. Rather they have observed the successes of indigenous movements before them, and the failures of many other types of movements, and strategically decided to use ethnic identities as the marker for mobilization. In other words, indigenous movements that were once *new* have become a prototype for *modularity* and a *duplication* of sorts. These second-generation movements have started to label their movements as ethnic or indigenous – to gain a toehold into national and international debates.

These second-generation movements do not necessarily have common goals. They include coca growers who initially lost their jobs in the national mines and have turned to coca production for their livelihood; youth who want to increase their professional opportunities and help their community; and scholars who have traveled to international conferences and gained increased knowledge, contacts, and resources, etc. All of these movements mobilize Indians. Most mobilize for noteworthy causes. But the rationale for mobilizing as Indians appears to be tied to the knowledge gained by learning what others have done and how they have succeeded. It is strategic behavior not because it is inauthentic but because the activists could have chosen to do otherwise. Their choice to mobilize along *ethnic* lines is a consequence of the successes of those that have preceded them.

Hence timing and sequence matter. The first generation of movements set the stage for the second. And the second generation of movements has in turn emerged according to a different logic and with a different set of demands. In other words, they are modular, in the sense highlighted by Tarrow (1998) and borrowed from Anderson (1991). Their identity is no less authentic. But the process of politicization and the adoption of that identity are different – in many ways because these movements could have mobilized along different lines. For many of these activists, their ties to the *community* are less clear; their migratory context appears more prevalent; and their discourse more calculated and strategic.

So too, once indigenous movements became prevalent, international funding agencies, NGOs, and the like developed important programs that aided existing movements where they existed, and occasionally catalyzed movements where they did not. Movements borrowed strategies from one another and examined comparative successes/failures. Brysk (2000) highlights the various linkages that exist between indigenous movements and transnational forces and the ways in which these ties have increased the chances of success in one campaign after another. She also highlights (2000: 21) how indigenous movements across borders have mimicked successful protests. Apparently, Ecuadorian activists examined videos of the 1990 Bolivian indigenous march before launching a protest later that same year. The first generation of indigenous organizing was therefore consequential for those movements that followed – opening the door for more cross-movement and cross-border interaction. In short, we cannot look at indigenous movements in Latin America outside of a comparative historical context. Historical changes in state–society relations politicized ethnic cleavages. And the emergence of these movements in turn has become a reference for new rounds of movement formation and agenda setting.

Viewed together these first- and second-generation indigenous movements pose fundamental challenges that Latin America's democracies are beginning (or will need) to tackle. They are forcing Latin America's new regimes to confront the limited reach of prior rounds of state formation, to address the indeterminacy of the current round of democratic institution building, and to consider how new democracies might reform states more effectively to accommodate plural identities, political units, and administrative heterogeneity. Part II elaborates on why and how these movements have emerged. Part III elaborates on the implications of these movements for democracy and the postliberal challenge.

The Cases

4

Ecuador

LATIN AMERICA'S STRONGEST
INDIGENOUS MOVEMENT

Ecuador claims Latin America's strongest, oldest, and most consequential indigenous movement, CONAIE. CONAIE first gained national and international notoriety in 1990 with a protest that shut down commerce for a week and forced the government to negotiate with them on several issues. By the end of the twentieth century, it had sustained this power of mobilization and parlayed it into a national force to be reckoned with when debating development policy, bicultural education, and institutional design. Moreover, several of its regional and national leaders have been elected to the national legislature and appointed to national office. Indeed, they took part in drafting the country's new Constitution in 1997–1998. Dramatically, CONAIE also helped to topple two national governments (Presidents Bucaram in 1997 and Mahuad in 2000). In a country where civil society is notoriously weak (Pachano 1996), the strength of Ecuador's indigenous movement is all the more striking.

This chapter explains the emergence of Ecuador's indigenous movements. It seeks to strike a balance between delineating the common origins of these movements and presenting the organizational stories that make these movements so unique in Ecuadorian history. Drawing on the framework outlined in Chapter 3, this chapter illustrates how the Ecuadorian state unintentionally granted pockets of local autonomy to indigenous people, only later to challenge that very autonomy through changing citizenship regimes. This change in citizenship regimes catalyzed indigenous communities to mobilize, beginning in the 1960s on through the present day. However, only where existing transcommunity networks and political associational space were *also* present were indigenous communities able to organize in defense of their autonomy (at first) and on behalf of their democratic rights (somewhat later).

Table 4.1. *Indigenous Peoples in Ecuador*

Region	Ethnicity[a]	Language
Amazon	Shuar-Achuar	Shuar-Chicham
	Secoya	Paicoca
	Siona	Paicoca
	Huao (Huaroni)	Huao Tiriro
	A'I (Cofán)	A'Ingae
	Quichua	Quichua Shimi
Andes/Sierra	Quichua	Quichua Shimi
Coast	Awa	Awapit
	Chachi	Cha'Palaachi
	Tsachila	Tsafiqui

[a] The original table uses the term *nationality* for this column. Given that I restrict the term *nationality* to those people looking to form their own *state*, I have changed this column's heading to *ethnicity*, so that concepts are used consistently throughout the book.

Source: Information taken from CONAIE (1989: 283).

Ecuador's *national* indigenous movement did not emerge fully formed, however. Indeed, it was the culmination and merging of two distinct regional indigenous associations in the Andes and Amazon – reflecting the weight of ethnically diverse and distinct geopolitical zones (see Table 4.1).[1]

While both of the regional associations can and will be explained by the concatenation of changing citizenship regimes, networks, and political associational space, it is also important to recognize the regionally specific institutional dynamics in which these variables played out. State–Indian relations in the two regions were markedly distinct. The Ecuadorian state

---

[1] Ecuador is a small country estimated at about 13 million people. But it is far from homogeneous. The country is divided into three geo-ecological zones: the Amazon (lowlands), the Andes (the Sierra or highlands), and the Coast. These three geographic areas have different types of economies, political dynamics, and relations to the central state. While the capital (Quito) is based in the highlands, it has experienced significant political competition from the coast (in particular, the city of Guayaquil). Hence, the Andes and the Coast have dominated national politics. The Amazon has remained, until recently, a distant zone – in terms of state formation, political incorporation, and governance. The emergence of Ecuador's national indigenous movement would shift that dynamic. While indigenous movements have emerged in all three zones, the most significant are based in the Amazon and the Andes. While indigenous peoples constitute less than 1 percent of the coastal population, they constitute about 38 percent of the Amazonian population and an estimated 10–40 percent of the Andean population (depending on one's definition and methodology). See Pallares (1997: 113–18) and Andolina (1999: 8) for a discussion of the figures.

has actively sought to incorporate and control indigenous communities in the Andes since colonial times. Yet, it largely neglected the Amazon and its indigenous population until the second half of the twentieth century. Consequently, the carving out and defense of local autonomies in both the Andes and Amazon in the late twentieth century would assume different forms and meanings. While Andean indigenous communities sought to defend the private and communal landholdings acquired through corporatist policies, Amazonian indigenous communities sought to maintain their de facto control over vast territories that the state had initially ignored and subsequently granted (through corporatist and then neoliberal policies) to new colonizers and developers. In short, indigenous movements emerged in both the Andes and the Amazon to defend local autonomy but the precise ways in which that process unfolded differed.

This chapter therefore presents three analytic narratives. Parts I and II analyze the formation of the two regional indigenous organizations in the Andes (ECUARUNARI) and the Amazon (CONFENAIE).[2] Part III turns to the subsequent formation of CONAIE, Ecuador's national, and Latin America's strongest, indigenous confederation.

Part I: The Ecuadorian Andes and ECUARUNARI [3]

Ecuador's political history is geographically circumscribed. State formation, the organization of the economy, and the capacity to govern vary by region. These processes were the most advanced in the Andean highlands, with corresponding consequences for the majority of the country's indigenous people who live in this region. Beginning with the colonial period, indigenous people were declared subjects of the state, property of landlords, and members of churches that displaced them from their lands, limited their freedom of movement and cultural expression, and curtailed their autonomy. While independence nominally offered the opportunity to institutionalize juridical equality, indigenous people remained second-class

---

[2] Ecuador has also developed a coastal indigenous federation that forms part of CONAIE. The coastal organizations, however, are not discussed in this chapter. They appear to have been largely organized by the national federation rather than the reverse. As such, they are not discussed at any length here because their narrative is derivative rather than constitutive of the founding of CONAIE. For one of the few discussions of these coastal organizations, see CONAIE (1989: 235–57).

[3] Also see Pallares's (1997) wonderful dissertation on the politicization of indigenous identities and their translation into indigenous organizations in the Ecuadorian highland.

citizens throughout the nineteenth and much of the twentieth century. The creation of corporatist citizenship regimes at mid-twentieth century occurred against this backdrop as a means to standardize state–society relations and incorporate citizens into a national, political, economic, and social project. Corporatism would prove to be highly consequential for indigenous people and for the movements that eventually emerged at century's end.

Corporatist Citizenship Regimes and Carving out Local Autonomy

Ecuador's corporatist citizenship regime was forged by three foundational laws that spanned four decades and several administrations. These laws included the 1937 *Ley de Organización y Régimen de las Comunas* (*Ley de Comunas*), the 1964 land reform, and the 1973 land reform.[4] These reforms were designed, among other things, to standardize local organization and, in the process, to make Indians into Ecuadorian peasants. These institutional changes were consequential – remapping the countryside and providing new institutional access to the state. This section argues, however, that they did not entirely remake local identities, affinities, and practices. Despite state efforts to subordinate Indians to a national project, indigenous communities often survived. They responded to state initiatives but with priorities that were distinct from those laid out by state officials. State efforts to incorporate them into the state were often turned into local initiatives to carve out or legalize local autonomy. Indeed, while the 1937 law initially had a limited impact, it would subsequently become an important means for indigenous communities to secure autonomy from local elites (landlords, churches, and local officials) and from the state. In this regard, laws designed to incorporate Indians into a corporatist form of citizenship also provided the tools for securing enclaves of cultural, political, and material autonomy. This local identification and initiative was largely ignored by the state but would prove fundamental to the indigenous movements that emerged in the Andes in the 1970s and 1980s.

---

[4] The discussion of these three laws draws largely from Barsky (1984: 31); Wray (1993: 12); Santana (1995: 24–31); Zamosc (1995); and Torres Galarza (1995: 48–9). I thank Galó Ramón (April 28, 1997) and Cecilia Viteri (February 27, 1997) for discussing the concept and practice of contemporary comunas.

1937 Ley de Organización y Régimen de las Comunas The Ley de Comunas and the corresponding *Estatuto Jurídico de las Comunidades Campesinas*
provided the juridical basis for subsequent institutional efforts to build a
corporatist citizenship regime. The 1937 law sought to stamp the countryside with a set of standardized political institutions and governance structures. It nominally homogenized rural communities (that might have had
different labels) by juridically acknowledging and labeling them as comunas, the smallest political-administrative unit in Ecuador. Comunas were
peculiar to peasant communities and distinct from municipalities.[5] The comuna refers to a local *peasant* community that has fifty or more permanent
residents and is governed by the *cabildo* (a five-person rotating executive
council or governance structure).[6] As such, the law incorporated indigenous people along class-based lines. However, that incorporation did not
grant equal political status or access to the state, for literacy restrictions effectively kept many, if not most, indigenous people from voting in national
elections.

The 1937 law encompassed many goals, including a political project to
supplant traditional indigenous communities with more "modern" forms of
governance (Wray 1993: 12–15). While the law did not specifically target
indigenous communities per se (Barsky 1984: 31), its efforts to institutionalize state control over the countryside (with its large indigenous population)
were evident. The Ministry of Social Welfare and later the Ministry of Agriculture (MAG) thus assumed responsibility for registering and regulating
these communities. And while the comuna had the right to directly elect
local community leaders, MAG gained the right to veto those decisions.
The law, therefore, granted an alternative form of community organizing,
authority, and electoral process but maintained the state's right to regulate
community choices.

In this context, the state attempted to lure local communities to register as comunas in exchange for access to state institutions and resources.

---

[5] Cecilia Viteri highlighted this particular point. She noted that the existence of municipalities
and comunas institutionalized a dual mode of state–local relations. This institutional context
reinforced the political marginalization of indigenous people who were not only incorporated through different political institutions than other Ecuadorian citizens but who also
remained barred from voting due to literacy requirements. Interview on February 27, 1997,
Quito, Ecuador.

[6] While the cabildo is ideally responsible for day-to-day decisions, a community-wide assembly is responsible for making broader community-wide decisions.

The request for land titles, public schools, and state-financed credit, for example, required that the community have juridical personality. Status as a comuna provided one way for communities to make these legal requests. Some communities did file for this status after the law was first passed. However, the law was only partially accessed and institutionalized in the countryside, a situation that did not change dramatically until decades later.

Indeed in the years immediately following its legislation, the 1937 law did not have a uniform or pervasive impact on indigenous communities and/or the new comunas. The state's weak control over the countryside meant that comunas retained a certain degree of autonomy to decide local affairs. In some cases, this decision-making authority was within the confines of the law. In others, it reflected the weak oversight of the state. In the matter of indigenous customary law, for example, the state retained an effectively ambiguous position.[7] While the state appointed *tenientes políticos*, or political officers, who were legally responsible for adjudicating conflicts in the community and serving the interests of the national state, these tenientes políticos did not always follow the letter of the law (Wray 1993: 33–5, 44–5). Nor did they always determine legal matters within the community. In this context, many indigenous communities de facto followed their own political traditions within their communities, where possible. Accordingly, the law institutionalized territorial integrity and created the possibility of political jurisdiction thereof.[8]

The *Ley de comunas*, in effect, makes the communal *Cabildo* the defender and the guarantor of the integrity of territory pertaining to the community and it enables the *Cabildo* to conduct all operations designed to augment communal property or to review and make decisions regarding the division of communal property (Santana 1995: 119).

---

[7] Rodrigo de la Cruz (1993: 75) and Wray (1993: 18–19).

[8] To say that indigenous communities exercised an important degree of local autonomy does not mean, however, that decisions over authority were uniform or uncontested. Historically, community elders assumed positions of leadership in the community. However, with the Ley de Comunas and the official recognition of the cabildo system, older leaders confronted increasing competition from younger and often more educated leaders who could more effectively mediate with outsiders – particularly the state. This gave way to different outcomes: in some cases it led to ongoing communal conflict over authority. In others, communities divided roles with elders governing internal community affairs and the elected younger members serving as interlocutors vis-à-vis the state and outsiders. In others, a new generation of rotating and elected leaders displaced the leaders altogether. See Wray (1993: 31) and Stavenhagen and Iturralde (1990).

The new comunas, however, did not have total autonomy, even where the national state was weak. In Ecuador, three powerful local forces – the landed elite, the Catholic Church, and the just-mentioned tenientes políticos – were commonly referred to as the holy trinity, and often dominated the countryside.[9] With the end of the *tributo de indios* in 1857, these local power holders were able to penetrate and control indigenous communities while the latter had little recourse to the state to defend any issues that might arise. The landed elite subsequently bound indigenous peasants to systems of *concertaje, huasipungo,* and *yanapa* – whereby indigenous peasants agreed to work for the landlord in exchange for land use; advance wages, grains or animals; and the right to water, wood, and straw as available in the rivers, woods, and fields, respectively.[10] Like elsewhere in Latin America, this system led to abuse and often resulted in lifetime indebtedness to the landowner (Hurtado 1980: 48; Carrasco 1994: 483). Through the mid-twentieth century, therefore, this holy trinity, circumscribed the power of the national state *and* the autonomy of indigenous communities, a situation that did not fundamentally change with the 1937 Ley de Comunas (Lucero 2003: 26).

The Ley de Comunas therefore guaranteed *legal* possibilities for local autonomy. The radical possibilities offered by this law, however, were not realized until the 1964 and 1973 land reforms, which fundamentally weakened the power of local elites and provided greater incentives (access to land and services) for indigenous communities to register with the state.

Populist Militaries and Corporatist Land Reforms If the 1937 Ley de Comunas provided the juridical basis for creating corporatist rural communities, the 1964 and 1973 land reforms provided the material basis for consolidating a corporatist citizenship regime. Populist military governments (1963–1966 and 1972–1979) oversaw this corporatist project, drawing on the developmental recommendations from the UN's Economic Commission on Latin America and the U.S. Agency for International Development – both of which called for a transformation of the oligarchic system of landholding and rural labor markets (Conaghan

---

[9] Carrasco (1994: 483) and Guerrero (1995).

[10] *Huasipungueros* worked on the haciendas in exchange for the use of hacienda land. *Yanaperos* worked on haciendas in exchange for the use of water and pastureland. See Hurtado (1980: 49) and Barsky (1984: 151–2).

91

and Malloy 1994: 39; Pachano 1996: 41). The military advanced land reforms that set out to promote development, increase social support, and ward off radical agendas. In the process, they institutionalized a corporatist citizenship regime that incorporated Indians as peasants – extending greater civil and economic rights, although not political ones. In fact, applications to register as comunas rose significantly following the land reforms, as communities appealed for land and resources (Barsky 1984; Zamosc 1995).

The 1964 land reform primarily promised civil rights by attempting to reorganize material and political power relations in the countryside. The military regime concluded that economic development required replacing the *hacienda* system with more productive farms and less exploitative labor relations. Accordingly, the land reform eliminated the huasipungo and yanapa – systems that had effectively tied indigenous families to the hacienda. While the 1954 census suggested that only 7 percent of Andean rural families were *huasipungueros*, the abolition of this system was an important precedent (Barsky 1984: 44, 151–2).[11] It freed indigenous people from semifeudal working conditions – thereby granting them civil rights previously denied them – and it outlined certain mechanisms for gaining access to land.[12]

Social programs in education, health, social security, and infrastructure also accompanied the land reform. Together they represented the military regime's efforts to build ties with the peasantry and to solidify their basis of political support. Moreover, the military promoted organizing within the rural communities (Barsky 1984: 205). The military regime, therefore, created an economic and social opening for communities previously dominated by landlords and excluded from social programs. Yet the first land reform had a less significant impact on land distribution – with the greatest growth in medium-size landholdings of 20–99 hectares – than its successor (see Table 4.2).

If the first land reform was noteworthy for granting civil rights, the second land reform provided a noteworthy advance in social rights for the peasantry. General Guillermo Rodríguez Lara's government (1972–1976)

---

[11] With the elimination of the huasipungo system also came the elimination of the right to access the landlords' lands, water, and other natural resources (Bebbington et al. 1992: 119; Korovokin 1997: 25; and Pallares 1997: 139–40).

[12] If huasipungueros had worked for more than ten years, then they were to gain title to that land. If they worked less than ten years, the huasipungo could pay off the difference to gain title (Barsky 1984: 151–2).

Table 4.2. *Distribution of Agricultural Lands, Ecuador (1954 and 1974 Censuses)*

Size of Landholding in Hectares	1954 Census				1974 Census			
	# of Cases	% of Cases	Land Mass	% of Total Land Mass	# of Cases	% of Cases	Land Mass	% of Total Land Mass
<5	251,696	73.26	432,100	7.23	344,931	66.82	538,286	6.64
5–19.9	57,650	16.78	566,800	9.48	95,878	18.57	926,815	11.44
20–99	27,702	8.06	1,138,700	19.05	64,505	12.50	2,661,148	32.85
100–499.9	5,087	1.48	1,156,300	19.35	9,478	1.84	1,675,132	20.68
>500	1,427	0.42	2,683,163	44.89	1,422	0.28	2,300,103	28.39
TOTAL	343,562	100.00	5,977,063	100.00	516,214	100.00	8,101,484	100.00

Source: Ecuador: Instituto Nacional de Estadística y Censos (INEC); Censos agropecuarios de 1954 and 1974.
Elaboration: Lily Jara, 1997.

decided to promote a more serious land redistribution[13] and rural development plan that included rural schools, health, irrigation, electrification, potable water, infrastructure, and other social programs (Guerrero 1995: 61). With rising oil export revenues, the state suddenly had the cash to expand these services to the rural poor.[14] These social programs, particularly the land distribution, signaled the state's commitment to a minimum standard of living for rural citizens – a basic indicator of the extension of social rights. In these ways, the state increased its presence in the local communities and inscribed a more corporatist and centralized form of interest intermediation.

While data is scarce and inconsistent, it is undisputed that the land reforms overwhelmingly targeted the Andes.[15] By one account, the Andes claimed an estimated 75.3 percent of the beneficiaries who received 69.4 percent of the land adjudicated by the agrarian reform (Barsky 1984: 314).[16] Officially, the state redistributed an estimated one-quarter of the total area of haciendas larger than 100 hectares between 1954 and 1982. Moreover, landowners began to sell off their lands for fear of expropriation. "In 1954, large haciendas [larger than 100 hectares] monopolized more than three-quarters of the total area, but by the mid-1980s, agricultural land was distributed in similar proportions among large, medium, and small farms" (Zamosc 1994: 43). Chimborazo, the Ecuadorian province with the largest Quichua-speaking population, evidenced significant changes in land tenure patterns following the 1973 land reform.[17] In short, it is open to debate as

---

[13] Various studies of Chimborazo, for example, have noted that no substantial changes occurred following the 1964 land reform. See Silva (1986); Bebbington et al. (1992: 114, 118); and Korovkin (1997).

[14] Ibarra (1992: 175–6) and Guerrero (1995: 61).

[15] There are no official, published, and (dis)aggregated land reform records for the period following the land reform. Ecuador has had three *censos agropecuarios* (1954, 1974, and 2002). These censuses, however, do not provide the data to analyze adequately the impact of the 1973 land reform. Nonetheless, there is scattered information (published and unpublished) in various state ministries and agencies. These were analyzed in the database on land distribution that was compiled for this project by Lily Jara (1997).

[16] By 1974 the land reform had targeted 1) the provinces of Chimborazo and Bolívar (which claimed among the most outdated and unproductive haciendas; 2) the cantons of Cayambe and Pedro-Moncayo (where state-owned public lands had been transferred but not yet legalized); and 3) the rice zones on the Coast (where much of the land transfer had already happened but required other kinds of support) (Barsky 1984: 238; Bebbington et al. 1992: 121; and Zamosc 1994: 42–3).

[17] Guamote, for example, had the highest cantonal levels of land concentration in the country. By 1979, the land reform had transformed Guamote into a campesino economy (Bebbington et al. 1992: 123). While Guamote experienced perhaps the most dramatic cantonal changes,

to why Rodríguez Lara introduced these reforms, but it is clear that he enacted a reform that opened up new material opportunities for indigenous rural communities.

The significance of land distribution was multifold. It provided some indigenous communities with secure land titles. It increased access to resources from the state. And it marked the end of the holy trinity that governed the countryside. These were significant changes that granted indigenous peoples and communities a degree of autonomy, opportunity, and participation that had not existed previously. For despite the fact that these reforms were implemented by a military regime, they increased local resources and local power. Indeed, alongside the land reforms, the state also increased social spending. Numbers for primary schools, primary school attendance, mortality rates, infectious diseases, access to clinics, and health figures improved during these years (Jara 1997).[18] This rise in social expenditure was facilitated by the banana and then oil booms, which simultaneously generated increased employment and increased demand for agricultural goods (Zamosc 1994: 44).

These corporatist measures were not undertaken to address "indigenous issues." To the contrary, Rodríguez is quoted as having said: "[In Ecuador] there is no more Indian problem. We all become white men when we accept the goals of the national culture."[19] It is not surprising therefore that the land reform (particularly the second one) had unintended consequences for indigenous peoples. For the land reform did more than construct corporatist ties with the countryside. It also created a space in which indigenous communities could secure more local autonomy to sustain and strengthen local practices and authority systems. In this context, appeals for community legal

the land reform also had a serious impact on the north and central parts of Chimborazo (Bebbington et al. 1992: 121); interviews with Diego Iturralde, October 20, 1995 and August 13, 1997; Tixan focus group and anonymous person working at a development NGO on March 14, 1997; and Fernando Rosero, March 20, 1997 and April 28, 1997.

[18] Larrea (1992); Younger et al. (1997); and data compiled by Lily Jara (1997), who analyzed education and health data from the Ecuadorian Ministry of Education and Culture (1965–1995); the Ministry of Finance and Public Credit (1966–1990); the Central Bank of Ecuador (1948–1983); and several state agencies that procure and provide health services. Improvements, however, were not absolute. Younger et al. (1997) have documented the wide discrepancies that exist between urban and rural areas. And even where schools and clinics are present, these institutions often lack books, supplies, and personnel. Moreover, Larrea (1992: 248) observes that in the 1970s, while the ratio of inhabitants per physician decreased from 2,909 in 1970 to 1,188 in 1982, the ratio of hospital beds per thousand inhabitants also declined from 2.6 in 1970 to 1.8 in 1981.

[19] Cited by Chad Black (1998: 7) from article published in *Christian Science Monitor*.

recognition increased significantly following the land reform.[20] In point of fact, the land reform and related programs encouraged the formation of comunas, associations, and cooperatives, for only an organized community with legal recognition could successfully appeal for land and/or credit.[21] Consequently, throughout this period, the number of rural comunas, associations, and cooperatives increased accordingly and developed a certain degree of autonomy from the holy trinity that had regulated rural politics.[22] Zamosc (1995) notes that predominantly indigenous cantons demonstrated through 1985 a preference to register as comunas. This form of organizing is the most administratively onerous, with the most responsibilities but also the most autonomy to govern. Simultaneously, the Ecuadorian Institute for Agrarian Reform and Colonization (IERAC) was promoting communal land titling, which enabled newly recognized comunas to regulate and govern communal lands.[23] But Pallares (1997) observes that in the context of state efforts to remake the countryside in its image, indigenous communities asserted an important degree of local control. Her observations are apt.

Once the traditional hacienda was dissolved, indigenous peasants sidestepped the government's encouragement of state-planned cooperatives, and drew upon a 1937 law which established the legal and political legitimacy of Indian communities and protected their right to land. Communities proliferated for obvious reasons. To qualify legally as a community, community dwellers had to assign some land to communal use. In turn they would be protected by the law as legal communities, and would have a much better standing in cases of disputes with individual landowners and possible land expropriation. Another reason behind the growth of communities was the dissolution of traditional local power relations after the demise of the hacienda. After the land was reappropriated in the 1963 reforms, community structures helped to reorganize power locally, replacing the vacuum left by the hacienda. Elected councils pursued social integration and some degree of political

---

[20] Ramón (1994: 179); Zamosc (1995); Pallares (1997: 143–5); and Natalia Wray, interview, November 23, 1995, Quito.

[21] Gonzalo Ortiz Crespo, interview, March 11, 1997, Quito and Benjamín Tovar, former Director Nacional de Desarrollo Campesino, MAG, interview, December 1, 1995, Quito.

[22] See Carrasco (1994: 485); Guerrero (1995: 56–7, 60–3); and Zamosc (1995). See Zamosc (1995: 45–6) for a concise discussion of the difference between comunas, cooperatives, and associations. As noted, comunas were first legalized in 1937 with the Ley de Comunas. Cooperatives have their roots in the 1930s but gained steam with the 1966 Law of Cooperatives that accompanied the land reform. Associations are the newest and least onerous kind of organization regulated by a 1978 Accord.

[23] Korovkin (1993: 12) reminds us that even where land was communally titled, it tended to be farmed on a family (and not a communal) basis. Nonetheless, it is the comuna (not the state or the market) that assumed responsibility for allocating the lands to families.

autonomy, utilizing both consent and coercion to achieve community goals (Pallares 1997: 143–4).

But indigenous communities also served a larger purpose. The idea of community, its survival and reproduction, lent a tangible meaning to indigenous peasants' struggles, enabling the framing of what mestizo bureaucrats perceived as merely material demands into cultural claims. The joint pursuit of land for the community provided a common history and identity; its final acquisition signified both the end of the struggle, abuse, repression and death, and the beginning of a shared, uninhabited space for cultural reproduction (Pallares 1997: 144–5).

If we take Chimborazo province (1927–1991) as an example, 62.3 percent of all comunas recognized since 1937 were recognized between 1965–1991. Moreover, some 72.5 percent of existing cooperatives were recognized between 1965 and 1974 and 94.3 percent of associations were recognized between 1975 and 1991 (Bebbington et al. 1992: 135). Viewed historically and collectively, these were significant advances for indigenous communities (increased access to lands and state resources, declining control of hacendados, and greater legal spaces for local autonomy). In other words, the corporatist citizenship regime (based on the 1937 Ley de Comunas and the 1964 and 1973 land reforms) granted a form of social and civil rights that had not existed previously.

The Erosion of Corporatist Citizenship Regimes: Between Promise and Practice

The corporatist citizenship regime therefore was meant to incorporate and control but unintentionally also granted the space for physical, material, social, and cultural autonomy – particularly with the recognition of comunas and the distribution of the land on which these communities were located. In this regard, the corporatist citizenship regime unwittingly institutionalized indigenous communities just as the state was seeking to privilege peasant and national identities. As discussed next, the state soon backed away from the social rights provision that was first promised with these reforms. This state retreat threatened the local autonomy that had recently been promised and that was fundamental to the survival of these communities. In terms of land reform distribution, indigenous communities increased access to lands, but often acquired lands of questionable quality and insufficient size (Korovkin 1997b: 36–8). Moreover, the land reform did not solve the problem of *minifundismo* (micro plots of land). Minifundismo remains significantly higher in cantons with majority indigenous populations than in others (Zamosc 1995: 31–42). By 1984, the land reforms had distributed only 32.6 percent of the 2,510,000 hectares originally targeted (Barsky 1984: 317). Indeed, by the end of military rule, the land reform was stymied. It was modified in 1974 and in 1979 to respond to landlord demands (Barsky 1984: 239).[24] Before handing power over to the newly elected civilians, the military finally buckled under pressure from the Chamber of Agriculture, and the government foreclosed options for accessing land through land reform (Barsky 1984: 246).

If land was unevenly distributed, so too was credit unevenly disbursed. In these years, credit was granted but not in the numbers or direction that was needed. In the late 1970s the military government announced El Fondo de Desarrollo Rural Marginal (FODERUMA), which was to channel agricultural credit, infrastructure, and services to the poorest people and to collaborate with community organizations when doing this work (Korovkin 1993: 25). Grindle (1986: 58), citing a 1979 World Bank study, notes that the percentage of public agricultural credit accessed by low-income producers increased in the 1970s. That said, credit still favored largeholders and the funds for smallholders were never adequate. Consequently, the program was criticized heavily by the peasant and indigenous organizations that emerged.[25]

The land reform therefore raised expectations that were unevenly met. It promised more social rights (land, credit, and education) than were ever actually delivered. In the end, the military retreated from the very citizenship regime that it had institutionalized. By the end of the 1970s and certainly throughout the 1980s, social resources became scarce commodities that were accessed unevenly by different ethnic groups. By the end of the 1970s, it was clear that indigenous people were formally equal members of society but were effectively denied equal experiences – limited access to the state (through literacy requirements), resources, land, and dignity. Indeed, Pallares (1997: ch. 3, esp. 180–1) recounts that with the "freedoms" associated with the land reforms came the emergence of new forms of racism and discrimination – excluding from, segregrating within, or discriminating against Indians in public spaces, including schools, hospitals, workplaces, markets, and state offices. According to Pallares (1997: ch. 3, esp. 130–2), land reforms replaced one form of racial subordination with

---

[24] In 1979, for example, the military government passed the *Ley de Fomento y Desarrollo Agropecuario*.

[25] See CONAIE (1989: 125–234, passim) and Chiodi et al. (1990: vol I, 354).

another. It weakened some identities but imposed others. It promised equality but delivered inequality. And in the mix, Indians remained subjects of discrimination and racism.

In this context, indigenous communities started to demand respect, inclusion, and autonomy. They started to organize for equal treatment in state offices, schools, courts, buses, public areas, and the like. In these new circumstances it was not the landlord that was held responsible for the harsh times. It was the state that had promised a form of incorporation and security and then stepped away from the plate. In this process, local indigenous communities started to target the national state (rather than local authorities in the holy trinity) and in so doing scaled up their own identities. They were no longer community X fighting against landlord Y but they were Indians making demands on the state to maintain their lands (and therefore their material and political autonomy), their access to resources (and therefore their rights as equal citizens), and their dignity (and therefore their identity as Indians). Pallares (1997: 180–94) finds that these sorts of demands first increased following the land reforms that abolished the huasipungo system and granted formal civil and economic equality (although suffrage was not extended until much later).

In short, the military's corporatist citizenship regime oversaw a form of rural incorporation that was a marked but uneven change. The land reforms and accompanying programs recognized Indians as citizens – granting them more material and political autonomy than before. However, as ethnic "subordinates" they were granted unequal access to social programs and the state; so too they had unequal experiences under the subsequent democracy. With the explicit challenge to local autonomy that ensued, local indigenous communities were politicized to organize in defense of their homes and their land. Local and regional efforts at indigenous organizing, however, occurred only in the presence of transcommunity networks and political associational space.

Transcommunity Networks and Political Associational Space

Indigenous peoples started to mobilize for change – a greater form of political inclusion, greater access to social resources, and greater local autonomy. These demands initially emerged as isolated grievances by comunas that had registered as local communities but had been denied equal access. They eventually scaled up into provincial, regional, and later national organizations. This process of scaling up, however, was not given, particularly because indigenous peoples did not necessarily assume common identities or automatically command the means to communicate with one another.[26] Indeed, the process of scaling up required the preexistence or formation of social networks among the comunas.[27] Churches and unions, in particular, provided this social infrastructure. While these organizations sought to harness indigenous communities for their own ends, each in turn provided the networks subsequently used by indigenous organizers to forge an Andean indigenous movement. Without exception, each Andean indigenous leader interviewed for this project began his or her account of the movement by referring to some combination of union organizing in the 1940s–1970s, and church activism in the 1960s and 1970s. This section therefore outlines the ways in which unions and churches served to create the mobilizational networks among previously dispersed communities.

Rural unions in Ecuador emerged as important pressure groups for the land reforms that were passed in 1964 and 1973. The *Federación Ecuatoriana de Indios* (FEI – the Ecuadorian Federation of Indians), founded in the mid-1940s, was arguably the first significant organization in the country-side.[28] There are indications that FEI did initiate projects that reflected ethnic-based concerns. Dolores Cacuango, for example, worked with FEI in the mid-1940s to establish a number of schools in Cayambe where indigenous teachers would teach in Quichua (Chiodi et al. 1990: vol. I, 339). Yet, despite FEI's namesake and Cacuango's noteworthy efforts, FEI was essentially a Marxist-inspired organization tied to the Communist Party. It initially brought together two different tendencies – one privileging class struggle, the other promoting indigenous identities and concerns.[29] In the initial years, the materialist approach came to dominate the organization. Ultimately, FEI did very little to promote an indigenous identity, to discuss

---

[26] While all highland Indians speak Quichua, they in fact come from quite distinct ethnic groups that do not necessarily identify with one another. The common identification as Indians, therefore, is a reflection of historic and contemporary state policies as well as mestizo practices that identify and treat all Indians from the highlands as one. See Pallares (1997) for an extremely thoughtful discussion of how ethnicity, race, and the highlands intersect in Ecuador.

[27] In Chimborazo, Bebbington et al. (1992: 157) have demonstrated the predominance of comunas as the basis of subsequent regional organizing.

[28] This discussion of FEI is based on CONAIE (1989: 31–3); Guerrero (1993); Korovkin (1993); Pallares (1997); Black (1998); José María Cabascango, interview, November 27, 1995; and Natalia Wray, interview, November 23, 1995.

[29] Natalia Wray, interview, November 23, 1995, Quito.

indigenous rights, and to modify the terms of citizenship for Indians. To the contrary, it primarily sought to mobilize Indians as semiproletarianized rural workers, to awaken a class consciousness, and to create an ally of the Ecuadorian working class (with the *Confederación de Trabajadores del Ecuador*, CTE, in particular). With a primary concern for class exploitation and land tenure issues, FEI worked largely with rural workers tied to the huasipungo system.[30] FEI was committed to abolishing the huasipungo system and sought to create a salaried rural proletariat that would subsequently form part of a broader class-based front. Unsurprisingly, the leadership of this organization was largely nonindigenous – although there were local indigenous leaders within FEI (Black 1998: 14).

FEI was among the first to call for land reform. Following the land reform, they encouraged indigenous communities to register as cooperatives.[31] FEI therefore provided a partial organizational infrastructure for subsequent indigenous organizing. Insofar as it pressured for land reform, it helped to create "free" economic agents who could demand political inclusion and economic equality. Insofar as it helped to create links among communities, it initiated a dialogue across communities. For even if the national leaders understood these struggles as issues of class, local indigenous people often interpreted them in ways that *also* incorporated an ethnic understanding of local issues (CONAIE 1989: 276).

It is necessary to reiterate the fact that although the struggle and demands of the *campesino* unions were dominated by the viewpoint of the mediators, who undertook a new form of organization similar to that of unions and turned to union demonstrations such as strikes, the indigenous mobilizations did not lose an ethnic character. In this way, the community provided the foundation for unionism and the existing unity and solidarity was reinforced by kinship networks (*redes de parentesco*) and loyalties that conformed to our process of historical-cultural development. Furthermore, for us, the indigenous, the claims to land were of double significance, we used them as the basis for our subsistence, but also as *Pacha Mama* (Mother Earth), the source of our culture (CONAIE 1989: 276).

But insofar as it sought to impose a class-based identity without incorporating local indigenous concerns and forms of governance, it proved to be

---

[30] FEI was strong in Cayambe and Cotopaxi but less so in Chimborazo; it was weak or nonexistent in Imbabura, Tungurahu, and Loja (Pallares 1997: 198).

[31] According to Natalia Wray the formation of cooperatives (rather than comunas) created friction between FEI and some indigenous communities over who was a member, what their responsibilities were, and how to make decisions (Natalia Wray, interview, November 23, 1995, Quito).

shortsighted. Following the first land reform, FEI therefore declined in importance; for the huasipungos with whom they had worked were now "free agents." Consequently, FEI did not develop into a significant national organization – even less so following the 1964 land reform (CONAIE 1989: 33, 276).

If FEI diminished in importance in the 1960s, the Federación Nacional de Organizaciones Campesinas (FENOC) emerged as a more important rural federation in the same years and worked primarily in the Andes and the Coast.[32] With its institutional roots in the *Confederación Ecuatoriana de Obreros Católicos*, CEDOC (the Ecuadorian Confederation of Catholic Workers – founded in 1938) they also began organizing rural workers in rural unions.[33] The Catholic Church promoted FENOC as an alternative to class-based organization by the left (Black 1998: 14). FENOC remained tied to CEDOC, later renamed the *Central Ecuatoriana de Organizaciones Clasistas* (De la Cruz 1993 and Pallares 1997: 218). FENOC, unsurprisingly, was internally divided by the Christian Democrats and Socialists. While the Christian Democrats dominated in the first years, the Socialist wing eventually came to dominate the federation by the mid-1970s.[34] With this move to the left and a more explicit class-based agenda, FENOC changed strategies. It moved from a more moderate approach (of organizing committees and negotiations for land reform) to a more aggressive approach (of organizing land seizures to pressure for these changes). With the implementation (1973) and then paralysis (1979) of the land reform, and the subsequent crisis of socialism (end of 1980s), FENOC initially lost much of the scattered organizational strength that it had established in the countryside.

The Vatican II Catholic Church also played a significant role in creating networks among indigenous communities. The progressive wing of the church (distinct from the more conservative wing that had earlier formed part of the holy trinity) played this key role in the countryside by shifting the unit of organizing from the worker or cooperative to the community (in contrast to FEI and FENOC, which had tried to organize rural workers into unions and cooperatives as the basic unit of organizing) (Korovkin 1993: 14).

---

[32] This discussion of FENOC draws on de la Cruz (1993); Zamosc (1994); Santana (1995); Pallares (1997: 218); Black (1998); and Pedro de la Cruz, FENOC's president, interview, December 8, 1995.

[33] De la Cruz (1993); Santana (1995: 126–7); and Black (1998).

[34] Zamosc (1994: 46); Pedro de la Cruz, interview, December 8, 1995, Quito; and Black (1998: 20).

The land reforms, in many ways, facilitated this work. They did so by weakening local landlords and promoting community-based organizations. In this context, the progressive church found a legal, national, and more democratic local space in which to work. This is a position that the church was well positioned to fill, particularly as rural unions such as FEI began to lose political momentum in the countryside.

The traditional mediators' loss of influence, especially due to their lack of sensitivity to the globality of indigenous aspirations, left an opening so that we could see that we had to be the ones to directly struggle for the solutions to our own problems. In this manner, the Church (influenced by the Second Vatican) came to convert itself during the 60s into a mediator, replacing the work that leftist parties had been carrying out through FEI. Likewise, other institutions related to the Church, like CEDOC and its affiliated subsidiary FENOC, held this role within a union framework (CONAIE 1989: 278).

Various denominations therefore began to organize the countryside and take up social issues. Following the legislation of the two land reforms, and informed by Vatican II, the Catholic Church began to engage in "social action" in rural communities. The *Fondo Ecuatoriano Populorum Progressio* (FEPP) worked with marginalized rural communities (not individuals). Founded in 1970 by Monseñor Cándido Rada, FEPP sought to provide credit, technical assistance, training, legal services, and community building. The credit program was seen as an essential way to help campesinos with land purchases and agricultural production – particularly important with the opportunities that were presented between 1973–1979 with the second land reform. FEPP also placed a great emphasis on community training. By 1981 FEPP supported 230 projects and by 1985 it was working with about 330 groups in fifteen provinces (Gavilanes 1995: 28, 30–2, 65, 67, 68, 86, 141).

The *Misión Andina* also had an important impact on local communities and the ties among them. The Misión Andina (which started off as a UN program and was eventually nationalized in 1965) worked primarily in isolated and impoverished indigenous communities and by 1969 had worked in one way or another with about 6 percent of the rural population in the Andes. Apart from providing tools for better production and training for new professions, the Misión also directed a leadership training program. This work helped to bridge the isolation that existed between indigenous communities, to promote organizing, and to train leaders who would play a key role following the two land reform laws (Barsky 1984: 32–40).

Through the *Central Ecuatoriana de Servicios Agrícolas* (CESA) the church also supported the local organizing process and provided technical support related to the land reform.[35] CESA was founded in 1967 and was financed by el Fondo Populorum Progressio with support from the Ecuadorian government. CESA advanced the idea of land reform by distributing some of the church lands.[36] Their work also supported FENOC's organizing process in the countryside (Santana 1995).

It is in this context that Catholic churches influenced by Vatican II began to work closely with indigenous rural communities and to promote their more active participation in running local affairs. In most interviews with indigenous leaders, the church was described as a kind of catalyst for them – either because a progressive priest encouraged them and supported them in educational pursuits; or because churches organized schools where they developed skills and contacts. Moreover, the churches often actively began to promote local and provincial organizations: "The church's objective was to prepare rural indigenous catechists and rural organizers (*animadores*) and in doing this Catholics organized courses, seminars, meetings, etc" (Santana 1995: 181).

Monseñor Proaño of Riobamba, in particular, was the most well-known Catholic priest to work among the indigenous.[37] Influenced by liberation theology and concerned about class-based inequalities, Proaño promoted and supported indigenous organizing within and between communities in the province of Chimborazo.[38] He created research-action centers that provided ethical support to Indians, and CEBs, among other things. Miguel Lluco recalls that Proaño and his pastoral team played an important role in the formation of the *Movimiento Indígena del Chimborazo* (MICH) an indigenous federation in Chimborazo, and ECUARUNARI, the Andean indigenous organization.[39] Lluco later

---

[35] This discussion of CESA draws on Santana (1995: 178–80) and Gonzalo Ortiz Crespo, interview, March 11, 1997, Quito.

[36] Gonzalo Ortiz Crespo, interview, March 11, 1997.

[37] Father Juan Bottasso, interview, November 17, 1995; José María Cabascango, interview, March 19, 1997 and March 26, 1997; and Miguel Lluco, interview, April 30, 1997, Quito.

[38] See Bebbington et al. 1992: 152–7. Santana (1995: ch. 6) and Father Juan Bottasso (Interview, November 22, 1995) observe that Proaño was known for his work with indigenous people but that he primarily promoted a class-based line. Only in 1986 did Proaño begin to speak about the "indianization" of the church (171).

[39] Miguel Lluco, interview, March 26, 1997, Quito. Carmen Yamberla, president of FICI, the provincial indigenous organization of Imbabura, also recalls the advisory role that Proaño played in her own community interview on March 12, 1997 in Otavalo, Ecuador.

became president of ECUARUNARI and a national deputy in the Ecuadorian Congress.

Proaño also assumed an important role with the popular radio programs. He founded the Escuelas Radiofónicas in 1960 (Espinoso 1992: 186; Korovkin 1997b: 30; Black 1998: 25–6). Daily programs were aired in Spanish and Quichua to teach basic literacy, math, agricultural techniques, hygiene, and health. Facilitators in each community would instruct the communities nightly. The programs were aired in thirteen provinces but, apparently, had the greatest impact in Chimborazo – greatly increasing literacy and social networks (Chiodi et al. 1990: vol. 1, 357; Bebbington et al. 1992: 182–4; Korovkin 1993: 14 and 1997b: 29–30).

The programs promoted not only literacy but also increased consciousness about shared conditions, according to Father Juan Bottasso.[40] Alongside these programs, indigenous communities started to discuss the importance of land reform and indigenous organizing. "It provided them with legal advice in their struggles against hacienda owners and helped them to achieve official recognition of their communities" (Korovkin 1997: 30).

In turn, the Catholic Church helped organize indigenous organizations, such as ECUARUNARI and its member organizations.[41] Whereas FEI had played an organizing role at the local level, the church took local organizing and diversity even more seriously and integrated indigenous, religious, and material interests. In this regard, it played a crucial role in providing the networks for indigenous organizing beyond the community level (Korovkin 1997b: 30).

In short, the 1960s and 1970s were a time of active organizing in the countryside. Rural unions and church-affiliated organizations started to mobilize in the countryside. While these organizations intended to mobilize for their own ends (class or ecclesiastical), they had the unintended effect of also providing the networks for indigenous communities to mobilize against the very state that had promised to incorporate them but then failed to do so.

The ability to mobilize these preexisting networks depended on *political associational space*. The populist military regime of Rodríguez Lara (1972–1976) first created this political opportunity. Even though he denied the existence of an indigenous problem, his policies and rhetoric (at least during the initial years of his regime) created an auspicious and

---

[40] Father Juan Bottasso, interview, November 22, 1995, Quito.
[41] See CONAIE (1989: passim) and Korovkin (1997b: 30).

feasible environment to organize along ethnic lines. He deployed a populist rhetoric that seemed favorable to civic organizing. He even went so far as to fund the first organizing meetings that resulted in the foundation of ECUARUNARI, the first Andean-wide indigenous organization (Pallares 1997: 154, fn. 37). Hence, while militaries in the Southern Cone were repressing civil societies and closing off avenues for organizing, the Ecuadorian military (along with its Peruvian counterpart) were encouraging corporatist kinds of organizations. With the 1973 land reform, the political opportunity to organize increased even further, insofar as the regime appeared supportive of the peasantry and its claims. Ultimately, a deeper political associational space did not emerge until the 1980s; however, it clearly had its origins in this period of populist military rule – with corresponding consequences for forging what would become Ecuador's regional indigenous movement.

Forming the Regional Andean Federation

ECUARUNARI emerged in 1972, drawing on preexisting networks and taking advantage of the political associational space provided by Rodríguez Lara. It aspired to become the first large federation of indigenous people in the Andes. In fact its mobilizational capacity and indigenous claim making would place it center stage by the 1980s. However, its successes on both fronts were not preordained in the early 1970s. For it emerged early relative to the challenges to indigenous local autonomy that developed great force in the 1980s and early relative to a deeper and more sustained political associational space that emerged with democratization in the 1980s. As a result, ECUARUNARI became caught up in the 1970s in the land reform struggles and class-based organizational debates in popular circles. In this regard it was initially not so dissimilar from other peasant unions that were working to organize around the land reforms. This class-based focus occurred even while locally it started to work with and respond to indigenous communities who were now the victims of discrimination, racism, and marginalization. ECUARUNARI's public and national commitment to *indigenous* affairs, however, did emerge, consolidate, and stabilize almost a decade later as challenges to indigenous local autonomy became more apparent and as negotiations with its Amazonian counterpart took off. This section briefly highlights ECUARUNARI's origins and circuitous path as it wavered between and reshuffled its commitment to class- and ethnic-based agendas.

ECUARUNARI was founded during an auspicious political moment. As noted, the military government of Rodríguez Lara gave funding to ECUARUNARI for its first Congress (Pallares 1997: 154, 268). Shortly thereafter Rodríguez Lara passed the 1973 land reform. In other words, the military allowed and even supported the formation of ECUARUNARI – although it is far from certain that they realized the direction that ECUARUARI would take and the impact that it would have.

The *ability* to organize within and among distinct communities, however, was a product of the networks (particularly parish organizing) left in the countryside, a point noted in most interviews on the subject. Indeed, parishes with progressive priests formed the first communities that organized and joined ECUARUNARI. According to ECUARUNARI documents, the church did so to wrest control from FEI, and its ties to the Communist Party (CONAIE 1989: 214). According to José María Cabascango (a leader in ECUARUNARI and CONAIE) ECUARUNARI was first founded in Chimborazo, Cañar, Azuay, and Pichincha, all places where Monseñor Proaño and the progressive church were organizing.[42] Wray observes that ECUARUNARI forged nuclei of *"catequistas de base"* that promoted a new reading of the bible. Although ECUARUNARI was never an ecclesiastic organization, Cabascango notes that the progressive church and progressive catechists played a hand in promoting provincial-level organizations in the countryside.[43] Hence, on the basis of their ties and contacts, it was possible to form the regional organization, ECUARUNARI. A similar dynamic played out within the local chapters that formed part of ECUARUNARI. In Pichincha, for example,

The juncture that opened within the progressive sectors of the Catholic Church and within private institutions provided us with access to physical spaces in which we held meetings, capacity-building courses, etc. In sum, it enabled us to create a dynamic process and to consolidate certain actions of the Organization (CONAIE 1989: 149).

ECUARUNARI had its organizational roots in the Catholic Church. However, over time, indigenous leaders began to assert the need for more autonomy from the church. Alongside this push for organizational independence, ECUARUNARI's leaders began to discuss what it meant to be

---

[42] CONAIE (1989: 163) and José María Cabascango, interviews, March 19, 1997 and March 26, 1997, Quito.

[43] Jose María Cabascango, interview, November 27, 1995, Quito.

indigenous (CONAIE 1989: 280, 314). But the ethnic line did not immediately win out.

Indeed, ECUARUNARI's goals and political identity were projects in
formation. From the start, ECUARUNARI had a directorate headed by indigenous men. It mobilized largely indigenous peasants with a focus on land
reform and redistribution. Nonetheless, the organization wavered between
an emphasis on ethnic- versus class-based demands. Both were relevant.
The balance between them, however, shifted over time. While an ethnic-
emphasis dominated in the first few years (around 1972–1977), it shifted
to a more explicit class-based agenda at its fourth congress (1977–1985),
which included alliances with other popular/class-based organizations.[44]
Indeed, Cabascango recalls that in the early 1980s, the organization focused on *campesinos* and class struggle. Many referred to class struggles in
Central America, particularly Nicaragua, for their inspiration. And Black
(1998: 19) notes that there was little programmatic difference in these years
between ECUARUNARI and FENOC. Yet, this class emphasis did not go
unchallenged. While the explicit *national agenda* was a "class"-based one,
this did not necessarily reflect the *multiple actions* taken at the national level
and the primary political agendas at the *local level* (Pallares 1997). Indeed,
at the national level, ECUARUNARI was advocating a class-based agenda
but was also reaching out to forge alliances with the lowland Indian organizations (first the Shuar and then CONFENAIE) – a point that is picked
up in the next two sections. Moreover, at the local level, activists were often
prioritizing antiracist work and the search for local autonomy by appointing
or electing indigenous tenientes políticos – both of which can be seen as
more explicitly ethnic-based demands (Pallares 1997: 220–43, 252–8, 292,
302). In other words it was pursuing a dual strategy.

Despite its almost exclusively campesinista rhetoric, after 1977 ECUARUNARI was
actually conducting a dual strategy: to the left and popular sectors, the organization
was the voice of the highland peasant, whereas with lowland organizations and state
actors, organization activists were negotiating positions as Indians (Pallares 1997:
252–3).

Zamosc (1994: 48) similarly observes that "[a]t the grass roots, the key
element was revitalizing the traditional organizational framework – the local
communities and the cabildos, which began to coalesce into *federaciones de
comunidades* and *uniones de cabildos* in parishes and *cantones*."

---

[44] CONAIE (1989: 218–30); Pallares (1997: 209–15); and Andolina (1999: 68).

This dual strategy (of working with class-based organizations while also encouraging the growth of indigenous ones) eventually gave way to a nationally explicit *ethnic agenda* once again in 1985. As elaborated in Part III of this chapter, this organizational convergence around an indigenous agenda coincided with and was strengthened by three factors. First, the explicit move away from a corporatist citizenship regime and toward a neoliberal citizenship regime in the 1980s was interpreted by indigenous leaders as a fundamental and state-initiated challenge to indigenous community survival. As such it spurred indigenous communities to mobilize in order to defend their land base, access to resources, and corporatist-based ties to state institutions. In this context, ECUARUNARI was forced to consider indigenous issues as not just local grievances but issues of national import – one that required a national response directed at the national state. Second, during these years, ECUARUNARI had strengthened networks and initiated dialogues with its Amazonian counterpart, CONFENAIE, and was influenced by the latter's agenda – not just for land but territory; not just for equality but also autonomy. Finally, the 1980s marked an overall deepening of political associational space – which granted greater opportunities for sustained and explicit organizing around issues that had been understood politically as private (rather than public) affairs. Together, these three factors provided the motive, capacity, and opportunity for ECUARUNARI to adopt a more explicit ethnic agenda in the 1980s.[45]

Before discussing these transregional interactions with CONFENAIE and their culmination in the national confederation, CONAIE, it is essential to discuss the organizational developments in the Amazon. This chapter turns now to that task.

Part II: The Ecuadorian Amazon and CONFENAIE

A second pattern of indigenous organizing developed in the Ecuadorian Amazon. This pattern diverged from its Andean counterpart because of a radically different history of state–Indian relations. For if the Ecuadorian state actively sought to incorporate and control Andean Indians, beginning with the colonial period, it made no parallel and sustained effort in

---

[45] Pallares (1997: 210–14) and Andolina (1999: 69) suggest that ECUARUNARI's ultimate shift toward an explicit indigenous agenda resulted from the negotiations with the lowland Indians, pressure from local activists, and the political opening that recognized Indians as cultural actors (granting a political "wedge" to protest) but denied them other more material-based rights.

the Amazon until the 1960s. Hence, whereas Andean Indians carved out local autonomy despite state efforts to the contrary, Amazonian Indians largely maintained this autonomy given the uneven and weak penetration of the state. Therefore, to highlight and explain why changing citizenship regimes (and the associated challenges to local autonomy), political associational space, and networks were causally consequential in the Amazon, it is necessary to chart out the different ways in which these factors combined against this different history of state–Indian relations.

At a Distance: Relative Autonomy

Indeed, the Ecuadorian state has never successfully incorporated the territory and peoples that comprise the Amazon – although it has always had greater presence in the north than the south (CONAIE 1989: 41).[46] Lured by vast and rich resources, the colonial state did initially attempt to settle the area and bring it under the control of the colonial government. Successive uprisings by Amazonian Indians, however, effectively quashed these efforts and prevented the state from establishing political control over this economically attractive area (Hurtado 1980: 32). Hence, the Ecuadorian state has largely neglected the Amazon since the colonial period. While included on official maps of the area, there has been little evidence until recently of state political commitment to, and control of, the area. Indeed, state projects to promote agriculture, build infrastructure, develop schools and clinics, register citizens, build armies, and so forth, have rarely targeted the Amazon. Similarly, political parties and elites have overwhelmingly ignored this region. Even official census material has, until recently, chosen to neglect this area. Unsurprisingly, then, political ideologies, political parties, political patrons, and state officials were weak currents in the Amazon. In other words, the state was attempting to build a sense of national identity in the highlands and the coast, but there was no parallel effort to do the same in the Amazon. Consequently, the state, as an institutional and political presence, was virtually absent in the Amazon.

---

[46] While claiming nearly half (45.8–46.2 percent) of the country's total landmass, the Amazon claims extremely low population density (Corkhill and Cubitt 1988: v and CONAIE 1989: 37). Approximately 2.5–4 percent of the national population resides in the Amazon, one-third of whom are indigenous. CONAIE (1989: 35) estimated that there are 285,000 people living in the Amazon, of which just over 100,000 are indigenous. Most indigenous people in the Amazon are Shuar or Quichua.

In this context, many indigenous communities in the Amazon were relatively removed from the citizenship regimes and state-building processes attempted in the rest of the country in the nineteenth and first half of the twentieth century,[47] although they did not necessarily escape from the predatory presence of haciendas.[48] With little effort to delimit territories, to establish citizens, or to set up a governmental apparatus, the Amazonian indigenous peoples remained beyond the reach and control of the Ecuadorian state. Largely isolated and dispersed communities were constituted by extended families that developed and sustained their own political systems. As such, indigenous peoples throughout much of the Amazon shared relative political autonomy from the state to run their affairs in the way decided by each community.

Without competition or threat from the Ecuadorian state, indigenous peoples maintained relatively unchallenged control over the space in which they lived. Distinguished by language, dress, customs, and political systems, among other things, different indigenous peoples have lived in geographically distinct areas – although there has clearly been migration and interaction among communities. Loose boundaries exist among these various peoples – although the significance and consciousness of these boundaries has depended on the proximity to and competition from other peoples. When indigenous peoples remained relatively isolated from one another, there was less need or reason to delimit territorial boundaries. When indigenous peoples resided in relative proximity, there was greater need/desire to define boundaries between peoples. As Barth (1969) indicated in his classic essay, boundaries are never fixed and immutable. In the Ecuadorian Amazon, peoples surely passed over and between boundaries – at times as part of normal business, at times leading to conflict. The very importance of territorial boundaries however remained essential to defining differences between peoples and the practices lived therein.

---

[47] The state did initiate a few projects. Ruiz (1992) notes that the state supported oil exploration in the 1920s, and following the 1940s war with Peru the state militarized parts of the Amazon (Ruiz 1992: 456–60).

[48] From the end of the nineteenth century to the 1920s, the Amazon became a global reserve for caucho. Little information exists on the impact of the caucheros on the indigenous peoples of the Amazon (Ruiz 1992: 454–6). In some areas, they coerced indigenous people to work for them, as in Napo, where Indians were forcefully incorporated into the hacienda system (CONAIE 1989: 39–42, 45). And in some cases indigenous peoples were lured by high wages to work for oil companies (until 1949 when Shell left) (Ruiz 1992).

If space was bounded between peoples, it was much more fluid and less proprietary within indigenous communities. To varying degrees, the territory was a space to reside, fish, and hunt. Communities were essentially defined by extended families or a group of extended families. They were largely dispersed, autonomous, and itinerant (Ruiz 1992: 452) – moving not infrequently to take advantage of different ecological niches and needs. Hence, while a family did not have title or exact boundaries to delimit what was theirs, patterns of use defined the right to reside there – even if only temporarily. In many cases, the most immediate loyalty and community ties were defined by the extended family. Political decisions were therefore decentralized and political power was multicephalous. In short, communities were relatively autonomous within a bounded territory and largely autonomous from the state. As discussed in the following text, prior to the 1960s, this left the field open for random colonizers to try to exploit the natural resources and for churches to try to proselytize within the scattered indigenous communities.

Political Associational Space: A Relative Constant in the Amazon

Given the state's weak presence in the Amazon, swings between military and democratic governments had little political impact/relevance for those residing in the region. In this regard, political associational space was relatively constant in the Amazon. As one indigenous teacher said: "We almost don't take notice of what is happening with the government of the mestizos."[49] Changes in regime and levels of repression have had faint echo in this region. In this regard, the political associational space or opportunity to organize was analytically present – insofar as the state put up relatively few obstacles to collective action. For this reason, the causal story outlined next focuses on the state reforms that challenge local autonomy (thereby politicizing indigenous communities) and the networks that were in place (thereby making organizing a feasible response).

The Motive: Challenging Local Autonomy

In the second half of the twentieth century, the state's relationship to the Amazon and the indigenous peoples there changed with the implementation and then erosion of the corporatist citizenship regime (culminating in

---

[49] Stated during an anonymous group interview in Pastaza on May 3, 1997.

the implementation of a neoliberal citizenship regime in the 1980s). The state actively began to encourage colonization in order to relieve pressures for land reform within the highlands. The state passed several laws to oversee the migration of highland peasants to the Amazon (including the 1964 Law of Agrarian Reform and Colonization; the 1973 New Agrarian Reform Law; the 1977 Law of Colonization of the Amazon Region; and the 1981 Law of Forestry and Natural Areas and Wildlife Conservation [Luque 1998: 6]).

Colonization was an ongoing process but accelerated noticeably with the 1964 land reform – particularly because Amazonian indigenous peoples did not hold title to lands used. The state "opened up" the Amazon to rapid colonization by those willing to clear, farm, and graze the otherwise pristine jungles. Agriculturalists first lay claim to land. Small farmers and rural workers from the Andes moved to the Amazon, often moving together to settle and develop lands in new agricultural centers. Large landowners, particularly cattle ranchers, also lay claim to vast expanses of land and cleared the forest to create grazing pastures. In both cases, the colonizers claimed untitled lands, cleared the jungle, and engaged in farming and cattle grazing. In both cases, indigenous peoples that had lived on and off these lands (but did not have legal title to them) were displaced.

Colonization was extensive. By one account over 2,500,000 hectares were distributed to over 55,000 families between 1964–1985 (see Table 4.3).[50] Given that the 1989 population in the Ecuadorian Amazon was estimated at 285,000 people, it is evident that colonization generated a significant influx into the region. By 1984, the colonization program had distributed 22 percent more land than targeted, although to 24.5 percent fewer families than targeted (Barsky 1984: 317). As such, colonization tended to favor larger landholders (i.e., African Palm plantations and cattle grazing).

These waves of colonization politicized indigenous communities that were displaced or affected by them. Indeed, the first round of indigenous organizing among the Shuar in Morona Santiago in 1964 and the Quichua in Napo in 1968, for example, was a reaction to this first round of colonization, as discussed in the following text. The new colonizers, settlements, and predatory use of the Amazon challenged and affected the space and ways in which indigenous communities did and could live (Bebbington et al. 1992: 65).

---

[50] By a different account, IERAC, adjudicated 1,012,546 hectares of land and distributed it to 29,048 families between 1964 and 1979 (Barksy 1984: 317).

Table 4.3. *Ecuador: Number of Families/Beneficiaries and Hectares of Land Distributed through Colonization and Land Reform (1964–1985)*

Year	Colonization		Land Reform	
	Families	Hectares	Families	Hectares
1964 (Sept.–Dec.)	728	17,614	831	2,194
1965	2,686	97,821	12,617	56,614
1966	2,708	92,123	4,712	26,795
1967	1,567	58,416	4,452	25,154
1968	1,408	43,043	1,884	20,983
1969	1,535	59,623	3,463	20,736
1970	2,295	92,629	1,110	6,903
1971	1,505	56,732	2,391	19,520
1972	1,920	69,939	1,838	17,401
1973	2,783	121,049	1,932	23,805
1974	2,778	138,214	2,930	24,453
1975	2,417	93,324	3,413	39,784
1976	3,397	159,158	5,430	62,333
1977	2,798	135,699	4,621	73,911
1978	2,463	143,759	5,857	47,037
1979	2,876	151,736	9,048	87,681
1980	2,190	125,097	1,799	65,135
1981	2,533	83,000	4,979	39,575
1982	2,124	104,294	2,939	25,846
1983	4,097	328,472	6,705	32,337
1984	6,250	245,628	2,332	35,324
1985 (first semester)	2,418	85,302	1,272	13,160
TOTAL	55,476	2,502,672	86,555	766,681

Source: Elaborated by Lily Jara drawing on Almeida (1988: 33, Table 2).

State-supported oil exploration also sparked a significant challenge to indigenous communities and catalyzed the second round of indigenous organizing. With the 1967 discovery of large oil reserves in the Amazon and the 1982 changes to the hydrocarbon law, foreign oil companies started to return to the Amazon (Kimmerling 1993: 13, 19, 21). Indeed, with membership in OPEC from 1973–1992, the military made exploration and defense of these areas an issue of national security (Sawyer 1996: 27).

As part of this security measure, the military began building state agencies and sending state officers – that is, appointed political officers (tenientes políticos), police, military, and judges. Yet the increased presence of "law and security" did not translate into greater democratization, equality before the law, and protection in these areas. To the contrary, interviewees always highlighted the ill treatment and discrimination that they suffered at the hands of military officers and the courts. Cases brought before the political officer or the judge were generally dismissed or unfairly processed. Moreover, the presence of these new forces directly challenged the autonomy of local indigenous authorities to determine the course of local affairs. In short, the state's presence in the Amazon did not translate into either a capable or democratic state.[51]

Unlike the earlier round of colonization, oil exploration did not require title to vast tracts of land, per se. Oil companies had a primary interest in subsoil rights and infrastructure (roads, pipelines, etc.), consequently their claims were apparently more targeted and less intrusive than the vast agricultural colonization efforts that had occurred previously. "According to Ecuadorian law, all petroleum reserves are state property, regardless of who owns topsoil rights" (Kimmerling 1996: 35 – my translation). The state, however, rarely regulated the oil companies to assure that they lived up to environmental and civil code regulations (Kimmerling 1996: 13–143).

Ecuadorian law is replete with rights and obligations that, in theory, protect the lands and peoples in the Amazon from environmentally destructive petroleum development. In practice, however, the law does not play an effective role in protecting the human rights and the environment in the petroleum camps. . . . The result has been a broad non-fulfillment of the environmental and human rights laws pertaining to those that live there (Kimmerling 1996: 79).

As would become apparent, the oil companies actions would also have a detrimental environmental impact on the surrounding forests, rivers, lands and, therefore, people.[52] Kimmerling (1993) reports on the serious environmental consequences of unregulated oil exploration – not only occupying indigenous lands but also scaring off forest animals and polluting the rivers. In other words, they were destroying livelihood for indigenous communities. *The New York Times* provides a chilling account of the hazardous practices and deleterious environmental consequences associated with prior rounds of oil exploration in the Amazon. This resulted in a 1993 class action suit levied in the United States against Texaco for harm done in Shushufindi, one area in the Ecuadorian Amazon. The suit sought "compensation and restoration of their contaminated lands and waters" (Lu 1998: 1). While a U.S. judge dismissed the case in 2001, and while the terms of the case

[51] See Kimmerling (1996: 13–143) for a discussion of Ecuadorian laws and their lack of application, misapplication, or discriminatory application.
[52] See *Diario Hoy*, December 15, 1993, 8A.

are complicated (given prior agreements with the Ecuadorian state, abiding by past environmental standards that were clearly inadequate, signing a relatively minimal cleanup agreement with the state in 1995, charges of scapegoating, etc.), the associated environmental impact has been indisputably harmful, as reported quite vividly in a disturbing *New York Times* article on Texaco and Shushufindi.

The center estimated that 30 billion gallons of toxic waste were dumped into the environment. It said that while 1.4 billion barrels of crude were extracted, 17 million barrels had been spilled during Texaco's tenure here – 1.5 times the amount spilled by the Exxon Valdez disaster. The plaintiffs say that the damage was never remedied.

In the oil-drilling region, open flames roar out of pipes jutting over murky pools, burning off gas to separate water from the crude oil. The soil is covered with a salty crust and is green and yellow in places. Its surface crumbles when poked with a stick, releasing the heavy odor of petroleum. Clouds of steam rise in this hellish, strangely lunar slice of the Amazon. The trees near the pools are leafless, their branches brittle.[53]

As the environmental consequences became apparent, indigenous communities were increasingly politicized – seeking to defend their communities and to secure better relationships with the state. Organizations emerged among the Cofán and Siona-Secoya in Napo and among the Quichua, Achuar, and Shiwiar in Pastaza.

State-sanctioned development plans therefore sparked significant waves of agricultural colonization and oil exploration, both of which resulted in nonindigenous claims to lands that had previously been used by indigenous communities. These developments posed a clear threat to indigenous material and political autonomy and survival. Indigenous organizations emerged to combat what was seen as predatory and environmentally destructive land grabbing. To do so, they used legal measures affiliated with the land reform and other state statutes to form rural organizations and to gain legal title to the land. To gain access to the state, voice collective demands, and gain collective access, the state required that territorially bounded groups register as associations, comunas, cooperatives, or centers. There was no legal status that allowed a collectivity to gain recognition and rights as a group of indigenous peoples.[54] Hence the indigenous organizations that emerged used these state-defined groups to define their

---

[53] Diane Jean Schemo, "Ecuadoreans Want Texaco to Clear Toxic Residue," *The New York Times*, February 1, 1998, A12.
[54] Natalia Wray, interview, November 23, 1995, Quito.

legal collective identity and to initiate legal proceedings to title the lands on which they had lived and off of which they had been pushed. They used the land reform and *Ley de Tierras Baldías* to form groups and demand the recognition of communal lands.[55] In these ways, indigenous people in the Amazon started to organize to defend their land and their collective autonomy.

Mobilizing Networks

The emergence of these organizations, however, was not an automatic response to these changing conditions. Indeed, the capacity to organize required the existence or construction of networks between communities. These networks were strongest where the churches had tried to proselytize.[56]

Prior to the 1960s, the state effectively yielded the Amazon to the churches. They left it to the churches to tame those that were considered "savages" and "beasts." While the churches also confronted resistance from indigenous communities, they were more perseverant than the state. Jesuit, Salesian, Franciscan, and other missionaries independently penetrated the Amazonian jungles in search of indigenous communities that they could convert to Christianity and bring into the fold. Diaries and testimonials indicate that the missionaries tended to view the Indians as "savages" and in the beginning took it upon themselves to "christianize" and "civilize" them. The Ecuadorian state sanctioned this mission by signing a bilateral agreement in 1888 with the Holy See to divide the Amazon into four vicariates granted to the Jesuits, Salesians, Dominicans, and Franciscans (CONAIE 1989: 28).

While Catholic orders largely dominated this effort in the nineteenth century, they were increasingly joined in the twentieth century by Protestant (evangelical) orders (Stoll 1990 and Brown 1993). The SIL became the cause célèbre. The SIL signed a *convenio de cooperación* with President Galo Plaza in 1952, arrived in 1953, and made rapid strides into the jungle. With an interest in bringing the bible to indigenous people, they translated

---

[55] Natalia Wray, interview, November 23, 1995, Quito.

[56] The presence and role of the church in the Amazon is discussed in Stoll (1990); Bebbington et al. (1992); Bottasso (1993); and Brown (1993). Information was also gathered in interviews with Father Juan Bottasso, November 17, 1995 and November 22, 1995; Valerio Grefa, November 29, 1995 and March 18, 1997; and FOIN group discussion, December 6, 1999.

the bible into various indigenous languages.[57] In the 1950s, they began working with five indigenous groups in the Amazon region: the Quichua, Shuar, Huaorani, Siona-Secoya, and the Cofán. They began working with the Quichua of the Andes in the early 1970s (Chiodi et al. 1990: vol. I, 343–51).

Assuming many of the responsibilities and rights associated with the modern state, the Catholic and Protestant missions tried to create nucleated and settled communities out of itinerant and fragmented indigenous communities or families. By building churches, schools, and health facilities, the churches attempted to lure indigenous families to settle in these church-designated centers. Once families and communities settled in these areas, they developed an increasingly dependent relationship on these missions for resources and norms. Hence, if indigenous peoples in the Amazon were relatively autonomous from the state, they were not necessarily autonomous from the churches. In the 1960s and 1970s, however, a few indigenous communities converted these very tools of control into organizational resources used against the colonizers.

The churches provided the indigenous movement's future leaders the space to build social capital among them, the Spanish language skills to communicate across communities and with the state, and the resources to start to do so. In short, it provided them with the networks to organize. In countless interviews, leaders noted that the churches remained ambivalent toward and suspicious of the indigenous organizations that they (intentionally and unintentionally) helped to found. They tried to maintain control and in some cases they directly attempted to undermine these emerging organizations. But even in these cases, the contacts and skills that were supposed to acculturate and christianize Indians were often used subsequently to organize Indians, to demand local autonomy, and later to voice demands for territory.

Forming Local Federations

Several local federations emerged. I introduce the first and most important among them: *Federación de Centros Shuar*; *Federación de Organizaciones Indígenas del Napo*; and *Organización de Pueblos Indígenas de Pastaza*.

---

[57] SIL was expelled in 1981 following protest by indigenous communities and rumors that SIL was affiliated with the CIA (CONAIE 1989: 39).

Federación de Centros Shuar   The Shuar were the first to organize along indigenous lines – both in the Amazon and in Latin America as a whole.[58] Located in the southern Amazonian province, Santiago Morona, they were almost entirely independent of the Ecuadorian state. In 1894, however, Salesian missionaries, moved into the area and established missions and schools (CONAIE 1989: 41).

Colonization was initially sporadic but increased noticeably in the second half of the 1950s, 1960s, and 1970s with state-organized colonization projects. In the 1960s colonos and cattle grazers encroached on the spaces in which the Shuar had lived. Father Shutka (who arrived in Ecuador in 1960) worked with the Shuar to find a way to defend themselves against colonizers. Rather than negotiating a contract with the government on behalf of the Shuar, a meeting was called in September 1961 with delegates from each of the Shuar sectors. These delegates were young Shuar men who had studied in the Salesian boarding school, spoke Spanish, and had a basic understanding of the law, according to Bottasso. The meeting ended with the decision to form nine "centers," and to appoint authorities from the strongest families in each sector – a task that Shutka apparently assumed. Indeed, the Federation's own narrative acknowledged that Shutka was responsible for coming up with the idea to form centers to facilitate the communal work that was needed (CONAIE 1989: 91). Shutka described the monthly meetings that occurred between 1961 and 1962 in which there were leadership and training courses. After the centers had agreed on their statutes, the people elected their own leaders, according to Shutka. Five of the centers experimented with cattle grazing (Bebbington et al. 1992: 78).

With the foundation of the centers, small schools and clinics were set up in each locale. To maintain contact among the various centers, the mission organized literacy and religious programs on the radio.[59] In discussing this period, Shutka proudly noted that the missionary visits to different sectors, the radio programs, the schools, and the formation of centers helped to found communities and to establish interaction among them – helping to

---

[58] The narrative about the Shuar foundation is largely based on two interviews with Father Juan Bottasso, November 17 and November 22, 1995, and one interview each with Father Shutka, November 24, 1995 and Ampam Karakras, November 26, 1995. Also see Bottasso (1993); Santana (1995: ch. 3); and Hendricks (1996).

[59] CONAIE (1989: 92) and Hendricks (1996: 136). According to Shutka (Interview, November 24, 1995), the radio was left by the wife of a departing U.S. ambassador and radio programs were later supported by the Ecuadorian Ministry of Education. Eventually thirty-one communities had radios and seventy-five centers had radio schools.

overcome isolation, fragmentation, and animosity. Reflecting on this pe-riod, Father Juan Bottasso said, "Father Shutka was very paternalistic. At that point, we all were."[60]

In 1964, the Shuar founded *The Federación de Centros Shuar* (the Shuar Federation, or Federation of Shuar Centers). With advice from Shutka, the federation decided to use the colonization laws to secure land titles. They bought cattle (with funds raised from abroad) and grazed the land to prevent outsiders from encroaching any further. While the Shuar ini-tially tried to legalize individual titles, they eventually decided that it would be best to secure collective titles to land – in order to make it more diffi-cult for individuals to sell their lands to outsiders and more likely that the Shuar could maintain communal integrity.[61] They secured collective titles and promoted cattle grazing. By the mid-1970s the Shuar Federation was describing its mission as follows:

It has two fundamental goals: the recognition of the Shuar culture as a system constitutive of Ecuadorian society, that is "the self determination of the Shuar group as part of a new concept of the Pluralist Ecuadorian State"; and the achievement of economic self-sufficiency, as the foundation for a development free of external pressures and influences...(CONAIE 1989: 90–1).

The Salesians, therefore, played a central role in the founding of the Shuar Federation. Their schools trained a generation of Shuar leaders who spoke the same language, came to know each other, gained access to ideas and resources, and witnessed the ways in which the church had formed its own centers throughout the region. Hendricks (1996: 150) notes that to date, all Federation presidents have been teachers trained in the mission schools. In short, the missions created a network among Shuar families that had lived more isolated from one another. The Shuar Federation, however, ultimately cut off its ties with the church and eventually adopted an anticlerical stance. It came to organize not only those influenced by Catholicism but also those influenced by Protestantism.

The titling of land, creation of Shuar Centers, and cattle grazing pro-vided the Shuar with the resources to defend their lands and to garner re-sources for their communities. The act of defending, however, transformed the political, social, and economic organization of the Shuar. The titling of

---

[60] Juan Bottasso, interview, November 17, 1995, Quito.

[61] CONAIE (1989: 91). Bottasso claimed that the idea to title lands collectively came from the missionaries rather than the Shuar because the Shuar had been more accustomed to working in family units.

land and formation of centers presumed a more settled and nucleated social life. Cattle grazing changed the economy from one that had primarily focused on horticulture and fishing. And, the Shuar became increasingly dependent on the organization to provide social, economic, and political services (Hendricks 1996: 135–6).

The Shuar became a referent for subsequent indigenous organizing in the Amazon. In particular, their organized response to outside colonization, their decision to defend their lands by turning to cattle grazing and legalizing their title to them, and their use of the radio to communicate between isolated communities, were strategic and tactical tools that were employed by subsequent movements.[62] Moreover, Shuar leaders were to assume national prominence in subsequent efforts to build regional and national indigenous offices. The first president of the Shuar Federation, Miguel Tankamash, also became the first president of the Amazonian regional federation, CONFENAIE, and later was president of Ecuador's national indigenous federation, CONAIE.

Federación de Organizaciones Indígenas del Napo The second significant indigenous organization emerged in Napo with the founding of the Federación de Organizaciones Indígenas del Napo (FOIN).[63] According to a FOIN document, the indigenous peoples of Napo were displaced and exploited throughout the 1900s. Indians first retreated further into the jungle with the arrival of whites who sought to use Indian labor to search for gold or produce caucho or coffee. Indians retreated further with the 1922 arrival of the Josephine mission that began to lay claim to land (FOIN n.d.: 1–2).

In 1959, the state built a road between Puerto Napo and Puyo, which facilitated the arrival of colonos. Indeed, between 1962–1982, the population of NAPO is said to have quadrupled from 25,582 to 115,118 inhabitants (CONAIE 1989: 40). With the building of the road, "The life of our peoples changed a lot from that point on" (FOIN n.d.: 3). The wave of colonization and the corresponding commercialization of land presented Indians with two choices: they could either leave their lands to the colonos, who were purchasing them; or they could legalize their own title to land, purchasing

---

[62] Bebbington et al. (1992: 78) and Taylor (1996: 223, 228–9, 248).
[63] This discussion about FOIN draws primarily from interviews with FOIN leaders (past and then present) – Cristóbal Tapuy, Ignacio Grefa, Blas Chimbo Chong, and Víctor Coyafeo – on December 6, 1995.

the land from IERAC (the Ecuadorian Institute of Agrarian Reform and Colonization) (FOIN n.d.: 3).

The Napo Indians launched various efforts to contain and end abuses by the colonos and the authorities. They turned to the churches for support. The Josephine mission first assumed this role. The Josephine missionaries supported the organization of an agricultural workers union (between 1958–1960) to legalize landholdings (CONAIE 1989: 47). These initial efforts failed when the organizers suspected the mission's ulterior motives (i.e., to christianize the Indians and to create settled centers) (FOIN n.d.: 3–4). The churches, however, continued in Napo and engaged in leadership training (between 1966 and 1968) (FOIN n.d.: 5). Many of those who later became indigenous leaders were trained in Josephine and evangelical missions. According to ex-FOIN president, Ignacio Grefa, a group of teachers, many of whom had been educated in the missions, were largely responsible for the organizing and in June 1969 they founded the *Federación Provincial de Organizaciones Campesinas del Napo* (FEPOCAN – The Provincial Federation of Peasant Organizations of Napo).[64]

The relationship with the mission remained rocky, however. On the one hand, the new indigenous leaders were beneficiaries of the missionaries' education and training. Cristóbal Tapuy, for example, was trained in the Josephine mission and later became president of FOIN; the regional organization, CONFENAIE; and the national organization, CONAIE. He noted that the mission provided a good education. It taught him Spanish and how to talk to the authorities and provided him with the tools to identify and solve problems. In short, the mission schools provided him and others with invaluable skills.[65] Those same leaders, on the other hand, also criticized the mission's effort to control them and keep them subordinated. Tapuy, Ignacio Grefa, Blas Chimbo Chong, and Víctor Coyafeo all acknowledged the role of the missions in training future leaders but also noted that the church had no intention of "raising their consciousness" and encouraging independent thought and action. There was no figure similar to Shutka who came to encourage indigenous organizations in their drive to organize along ethnic lines for local autonomy. Indeed, these leaders criticized the mission for having deceived the communities – amassing large tracts of land, creating dependence on the mission, and encouraging passivity and

[64] Ignacio Grefa, ex-president of FOIN, December 6, 1995, Tena, Napo, Ecuador. Also see CONAIE (1989: 47) and (FOIN n.d.: 5).
[65] Cristóbal Tapuy, ex-president of FOIN, interview, November 24, 1995, Quito.

submission. "FOIN emerged with the superficial help of the Josephines. They wanted to keep us in a subordinated position."[66] The missions, in turn, responded that the leaders were communists.[67]

The first objective of the organization was to defend the land and to fight against abuse by the authorities.[68] Faced with colonization, they promoted the titling of their lands. However, they rejected individual titles, fearing that this would provide further channels for outsiders to seduce individuals into selling their lands. Instead, they pushed for collective titling in order to make sales more difficult. They argued that each community (which if it did not exist would need to be formed) would include its members (*socios*) and then decide the allocation of lands – that is, which lands would be worked communally and which lands would be worked by an individual family. But whether worked communally or individually, the land belonged to the community and, as such, could not be sold without communal consent.[69] Members also argued that they should assume responsibility for resolving disputes within the community – in order to avoid the perennial abuse and fines that state authorities tended to levy – and in speaking before the authorities on behalf of the community when there were disputes with colonos (FOIN n.d.: 6).

As the original name, FEPOCAN, suggests, organizers first modeled their response on peasant organizations in the Andes. FEPOCAN initially attempted to build unions to defend their right to the land. Cristóbal Tapuy notes that this effort failed. It was difficult to impose entirely new organizations on old ones. And as the left was relatively weak in the Amazon, it was relatively uncomplicated to shift away from this union focus and to highlight the role of ethnicity as the central organizing theme.

If the organization originally adopted union structures, it had already developed a character quite distinct from the traditional peasant organizations. By demanding collective lands and by building an organization that sought to adjudicate disputes within and between communities, they had highlighted their differences as "Indians." Beginning in 1973, leaders began to refer to the organization as the Federación de Organizaciones Indígenas

---

[66] Cristóbal Tapuy, ex-president of FOIN, interview, November 24, 1995, Quito.
[67] Ignacio Grefa, Blas Chimbo Chong, and Víctor Coyafeo, group interview with FOIN members, December 6, 1995, Tena, Napo, Ecuador.
[68] Ignacio Grefa, interview, December 6, 1995, Tena, Napo, Ecuador and FOIN (n.d.: 5–6).
[69] Ignacio Grefa, Blas Chimbo Chong, and Víctor Coyafeo, group interview with FOIN members, December 6, 1995, Tena, Napo, Ecuador and FOIN (n.d.: 5–6). Cristóbal Tapuy made similar points in conversations held in December 1995, Tena, Napo, Ecuador.

del Napo (FOIN – the Federation of Indigenous Organizations of Napo), a name that was approved in their 1978 congress, and legally recognized in 1984 (FOIN n.d.: 6). FOIN's principal demands have been the following:

For us it is clear, that our people and culture cannot be maintained without a physical space that allows us to reproduce ourselves biologically and socially and therefore the principal work of the Federation from its beginning has been the defense of our territories. It has attempted to provide solutions to numerous land conflicts, whether they be with *colonos* or companies, especially companies working in African palm, logging, etc. In the last few years problems of this nature have been aggravated, since it is no longer just *colonos* and companies that seek to take over our territory, the State with an incongruous policy of environmental protection, the Law of Forest Patrimony and through the creation of ecological reserves is limiting our physical space (CONAIE 1989: 48).

Organización de Pueblos Indígenas de Pastaza The third significant Amazonian indigenous organization formed almost ten years later in Pastaza.[70] Geographically sandwiched between Morona Santiago (where the Shuar Federation is based) and Napo (where FOIN is based), the Organización de Pueblos Indígenas de Pastaza (OPIP) emerged in the late 1970s largely in response to the expansion of oil company activities.[71] These oil companies and colonization patterns threatened their lands, lifestyles, and environment, and challenged local political autonomy.[72]

The Ecuadorian government granted oil exploration and drilling rights to AngloSaxon Petroleum, a subsidiary of Royal Dutch Shell at the end of the 1930s (Muratorio 1996: 373). However, full-scale and long-term oil exploration did not occur until decades later. Oil companies began lobbying for state-granted rights to drill and market oil. The state saw oil exports as a means to generate economic growth and welcomed oil exploration. Indeed, it did so with a minimum of regulation. In this context, oil companies often tended to displace indigenous communities and to pollute their rivers.

---

[70] This discussion of OPIP draws on interviews in 1997 with leaders, Leonardo Viteri, César Cerda, Antonio Vargas, and Tito Manuel Merino Gayes. Insight also comes from participation in the March 6, 1997 OPIP assembly, and several group discussions on May 2, 1997 and May 3, 1997 in a community outside of Puyo, Pastaza.

[71] Penetration in this area began with the Dominicans in 1877. The construction of a road in the 1930s benefited the Royal Shell Oil Company and encouraged waves of colonization. An OPIP narrative notes, however, that the most significant colonization occurred after the 1964 land reform (CONAIE 1989: 79).

[72] Cesar Cerda, president of OPIP, interview, May 6, 1997, Quito, and group discussions, May 2, 1997 and May 3, 1997, outside of Puyo, Pastaza.

Consequently, they posed a concrete and formidable threat to indigenous community survival – formidable because they had state backing, funds, and were left unregulated. So too the roads that were built were seen as a mixed and dangerous blessing. They made it easier to travel but also made it easier for others to come. In one anonymous 1997 group interview in a community outside of Puyo, Pastaza, the male community members discussed how roads were dangerous: they brought illnesses, noise, alcohol, easy exit for children and therefore a declining respect for elders, easier migration to the city and with that an increasing embarassment about being "Indian," an increasing dependence on others, and increasing interest in foreign fashion and trends, among other things. The community then started to discuss the various ways in which roads served to undermine indigenous cultures, increase dependence and fascination with foreign cultures, and increase state control of the communities (through educational and health programs that denigrate indigenous cultures). One person summarized the group sentiment: "In this sense, the road has killed us. It has brought us no benefits. It has killed our culture." Another person said a few moments later, "It is for these reasons that we do not want the oil companies."[73]

Recalling the first OPIP congress and the motives for attending, Tito Manuel Merino Gayes recounted that with the arrival of the oil companies, there was increased public discrimination, a development that denied Indians from Pastaza their citizenship rights and their corresponding capacity to defend their land. Discrimination had always been a problem. With the arrival of the colonos and their grab for land, however, discrimination became more pervasive. Merino recalled, for example, that colonos began to purchase cattle as a means to secure land previously used by Indians – as the law indicated, those who worked the land for five years could claim it. The cattle however, predictably began to disturb indigenous-held lands. When indigenous people went to the courts to denounce destruction of property, they were generally derided. Their cases were lost, often before they had even been filed. With the arrival of Shell, their access to land was further challenged as the oil company, in the presence of the military, missionaries, and businessmen, claimed the land as if it were theirs.[74]

---

[73] Group interview, May 2, 1997, outside of Puyo, Pastaza.

[74] Tito Manuel Merino Gayes, interview, April 3, 1997, Alishungu, Pastaza. Merino was the General Coordinator of the OPIP 1992 march from Puyo to Pastaza and a leader of *Promoción y Organización de OPIP* between 1990–1993.

Quichua organizers in Pastaza founded OPIP to defend their lands (CONAIE 1989: 87–88). But the Pastaza leaders did not overwhelmingly build on church networks, as with the earlier round of indigenous organizing. As a second-generation movement, they drew on the experience, skills, and networks of their movement predecessors – the Shuar Federation and FOIN. FOIN, in particular, would help to provide those networks.[75]

If OPIP has drawn on prior organizational strategies, their political strategy for gaining legal recognition of lands has been different. The Shuar Federation and FOIN used the agrarian reform and colonization laws to gain legal title for collective lands (at the level of the center) and therefore had to demonstrate that they were *working* the land. This required them to settle in nucleated communities and either to engage in agricultural production and/or cattle grazing. OPIP took a different course. They proclaimed that independent of the agrarian reform and colonization laws and independent of "working" the land, the indigenous communities had a right to their *territory*. This right derived from historical use rather than contemporary legal acts and applied to indigenous peoples who had lived in and off the land. "With or without title, we are the legitimate owners of the indigenous territories of Pastaza," stated Cesar Cerda, President of OPIP.[76]

OPIP placed "territorial" demands on the political map with the thirteen-day march from Puyo to Quito in 1992.[77] The 2,000-person march, which followed various unsuccessful attempts to gain state recognition, demanded the state's legal recognition of their territorial rights – conceived as one territory that would be administered by OPIP.[78] The decision to organize this physically demanding march highlighted the underlying

---

[75] CONAIE (1989: 79); Juan Bottasso, interview, November 22, 1995; and Antonio Vargas, interview, March 4, 1997.

[76] Cesar Cerda, president of OPIP, interview, May 6, 1997, Quito.

[77] *Diario Hoy*, August 24, 1990: A3. These demands for territory predated the 1992 March. OPIP submitted a proposal to President Rodrigo Borja in 1990 for indigenous territorial rights and self-government.

[78] *Diario Hoy* (May 3, 1992) reported that prior to the March, the indigenous organizations and the government had reached loggerheads over how to define and apportion lands. A key sticking point had been that the government wanted to apportion land to communities based on population, while OPIP wanted land distributed to particular nationalities (Quichua, Shiwiar, and Achuar) according to ancestral claims to the land. Another point of conflict emerged over subsoil rights with the government declaring that these are state rights and the indigenous groups demanding direct control over them. Finally, while the government sought to talk about land as an agricultural property, OPIP sought to define these lands as territories with a historic claim to a particular space.

belief that Ecuador's democratic institutions were not including or respecting indigenous people.

The members at a 1997 OPIP assembly repeated similar refrains. They
noted discrimination, poor application of the laws, lack of information, and
the military's presence in their communities.[79]

Remarkably, President Rodrigo Borja formally transferred land titles in
Pastaza to Shiwiar, Quichua, Achuar, and Záparo communities under the
aegis of OPIP, AIEPRA (*Asociación de Indígenas Evangélicos de Pastaza*), and
FEDECAP (*Federación de Desarrollo Campesino de Pastaza*). The land grants
totaled 1,115,475 hectares.[80] The grant is restricted to surface rights for
cultivation only and is inalienable; both the existing claims of settlers and
the government's subsoil rights remain intact.[81] The government, however, did not grant the territory as a single unit; nor did it recognize OPIP
as the organization responsible for all of the territory.[82] The state recognized nineteen different blocs and gave lands to state-recognized comunas (defined by the 1937 law of communities). While Ortiz Crespo, then
Secretary of the President and chief negotiator with the OPIP delega-
tion, highlighted the delivery of lands to communities, Merino and Vargas
of OPIP highlighted the recognition of nineteen blocs that do *not* coincide geospatially with the areas covered by OPIP's twelve member
associations.[83]

This decision was monumental but highlighted the tension between
1) state efforts to regulate, standardize, and govern these areas in Pastaza;
2) OPIP's effort to assert its power as interlocutor before the state and
representative governing body in Pastaza; 3) local communities that have
now gained certain legal rights independent of OPIP; 4) the twelve associations that compose OPIP; and 5) the presence of oil companies that still
want to gain subsoil rights to the lands whose topsoil has been granted to
Indians. In this context, OPIP has assumed the role as interlocutor for the
communities vis-à-vis the state, oil companies, and outside bodies. It has
coordinated the planning and management of natural resources – through
training workshops and research in each of the twelve associations that form

---

[79] OPIP assembly, April 3, 1997, Alishungu, Pastaza.
[80] Selverston (1994: 146 and 2001: 45).
[81] As reported in *Diario Hoy*, May 15, 1992: A1.
[82] Tito Manuel Merino Gayes, interview, April 3, 1997 and Gonzalo Ortiz Crespo, interview, March 11, 1997.
[83] Antonio Vargas, interview, March 4, 1997; Gonzalo Ortiz Crespo, interview, March 11, 1997; and Tito Manuel Merino Gayes, interview, April 3, 1997.

OPIP. Moreover, it has played an advisory role – even to those few communities in the territory that are not part of OPIP. But OPIP does not have legal authority to govern the communities.[84] While the state does not necessarily sanction the communities' and OPIP's governing role, OPIP has laid out the agenda to do this work.[85] The point, according to Merino, is that the state should fulfill its legal rights and role vis-à-vis the community *and* should recognize and respect indigenous customs within the territory.

With OPIP's increased stature within Pastaza, it assumed a role in negotiating with the state and the oil companies. The nineteen territorial blocs recognized by Borjas do not correspond to existing indigenous communities or associations but do correspond to subsoil blocs being conceded to oil companies. This situation created the chance for oil companies to negotiate directly with communities rather than OPIP. The subsoil concessions created internal conflict within many indigenous communities about what is in their collective interest and how best to interact with the oil companies.[86] In this context, OPIP has tried to scale up negotiations – that is, to speak on behalf of its twelve member associations, which have adopted conflicting positions.

Even with these conflicts over strategy, OPIP has come to play a key role in the region. Indigenous communities in Pastaza look to OPIP to negotiate with the state and to play a proactive role in developing and sustaining indigenous communities. As such, OPIP has developed projects to promote ethnic identity, education, and sustainable and alternative development strategies.

Forming the Regional Federation

The three local organizations mentioned have been the most prominent within Ecuador (although outside of Ecuador, the Huaorani case has become particularly well known). Yet, a number of other organizations

---

[84] In the community discussion held outside of Puyo, Pastaza on May 2, 1997, one person explained that the community determines affairs within the community; OPIP or one of its twelve member organizations regulates affairs among indigenous communities in Pastaza; and the state addresses other types of issues.

[85] Cēsar Cerda, president of OPIP, interview, May 6, 1997, Quito.

[86] *El Comercio* (December 15, 1993: 10A) reports accusations by OPIP leaders that ARCO attempted to buy off and sign separate agreements with certain weakly organized indigenous communities, with the goal of dividing the opposition. Also see *Diario Hoy* (December 20, 1993), which indicates that OPIP accused ARCO of starting and lavishly funding a new organization called DICIP to divide the indigenous population.

also emerged in the Amazon to address the same basic issues of political autonomy, cultural survival, and land defense, including other organizations among Quichua, Siona and Secoya, and Huaorani communities in Napo and Sucumbíos, in particular (Burke 1997: 13).

The 1960s through the 1980s, therefore, were a time of organization building. By 1984, lands had been adjudicated for several communities – including the Siona-Secoyas, Cofanes, Huaoranis, Achuar and Shuars, and Alamas – totaling approximately 760,000 hectares and affecting almost 6,900 families (Barsky 1984: 299). As this organizing spread throughout the Amazon, prominent indigenous leaders started to discuss the possibility of forging a regional federation to represent all indigenous peoples in the Amazon. They had the motive (challenge to local autonomy), the networks (preexisting organizations), and the opportunity (not only was the Amazon relatively free of state repression but also by the late 1970s it was apparent that political associational space was opening in Ecuador). Indeed, democratization began in 1979 and the new civilian administrations voiced a more open cultural policy toward Indians (a point that is discussed further in the last section of this chapter). Under these circumstances, the moment seemed auspicious for forming a regional body. This was not inevitable but it was certainly possible.

CONFENAIE was formed in 1980 by OPIP, FOIN, Asociación Independiente del Pueblo Shuar (AIPSE), and Jatun Comuna Aguarico (JCA), following several years of discussion. The goal was to coordinate among organizations, to defend cultures, and to defend land, which was seen as the foundation of everything else.

All of these objectives were asserted insofar as a people without culture cannot exist, a people without territory cannot live, a people without a language that is part of the culture, would not be a people. For that reason it has been stated concretely that one of the primary objectives is to defend the culture and the land, create consciousness of the unity of all of the indigenous of the Amazon, and to also promote coordination with other organizations in the sierra [Andes] in order to come to form an organization that brings together all of the indigenous of Ecuador (CONAIE 1989: 100).

CONFENAIE sought to defend land and indigenous cultures (CONAIE 1989: 99–101; Kimmerling 1993: 13). With this as a goal, CONFENAIE called not just for the end of colonization, the expulsion of African palm companies, and social programs (education, health, infrastructure, etc.), but they also demanded a percentage of the proceeds from oil and mining companies (CONAIE 1989: 103–4).

129

Discussions and decisions taken at its Sixth Congress illustrate the types of demands articulated by this organization. Valerio Grefa, the president at the time, called to establish self-government, to fight for land rights, and to occupy historically relevant social spaces. The Congress in turn called for an indigenous Amazonian parliament. The Congress also critiqued what they saw as the handover of 90 percent of the Amazon to transnational companies that in turn exploited resources and harmed the environment.[87]

CONFENAIE therefore brought together indigenous people from throughout the Amazon – overcoming seemingly insurmountable problems of language, infrastructure, and the like – in order to mobilize for greater political autonomy and the defense of their lands. While CONFENAIE has experienced its own internal battles (and in fact has often been surpassed by its constitutive organizations, such as OPIP), it came to play a key role in forging Ecuador's most prominent national indigenous federation, CONAIE. This is the focus of the final part of this chapter.

Part III: Forming the National Confederation, CONAIE

CONFENAIE and ECUARUNARI emerged as *the* regional indigenous organizations in the Amazon and Andes respectively. Each emerged to defend local autonomy and demand equal rights of inclusion. In the late 1970s and early 1980s, indigenous activists from ECUARUNARI and CONFENAIE started meeting to discuss the formation of a national federation.[88]

---

[87] See *Diario Hoy* (February 8, 1991: 7A). Also see *Diario Hoy* (October 28, 1991) where CONFENAIE president, Valerio Grefa, criticized IERAC's continued opening of the Amazon to outside settlement, and demanded the return of such ecologically sensitive lands to their indigenous inhabitants. Also see *Diario Hoy* (November 25, 1993) for the discussion of a subsequent CONFENAIE convention in Pastaza. There the organization also called for the establishment of an indigenous parliament with 100 elected leaders and three-year terms. Among the goals declared were the development of the juridical idea of territories; the defense of territorial rights; and the promotion of sound environmental management. CONFENAIE tried to make clear that they were *not* calling for the establishment of a parallel state.

[88] The exact date of those first meetings between CONFENAIE and ECUARUNARI seems open for discussion. According to Pallares (1997: 241) ECUARUNARI first met with the Shuar in the 1970s to learn from them. She then notes that the first effort to coordinate discussions among highland and lowland Indians took place in 1977 at the First Conference of Indigenous Peoples in Sucúa (Lowlands). Macas marks the first discussions in 1979 (interview, May 6, 1997). CONAIE (1989: 261) and Andolina (1999: 72–3) date this first meeting in 1980. And José Maria Cabascango (interview, November 27, 1995) states that discussions between the Andean and Amazonian organizations began about 1981 – to discuss their joint political project.

These conversations culminated with the founding of the *Consejo de Coordinación de las Nacionalidades Indígenas* (CONACNIE – The Coordinating Council of Indigenous Nationalities)[89] in 1980 and subsequently the Confederación de Nacionalidades Indígenas del Ecuador (CONAIE) in 1986. CONAIE has no real counterpart in other Latin American cases. Insofar as it claims representation of all Indians in the country, it has gained a dominant position in negotiations with the state, and it has developed national powers of mobilization.[90]

Between 1980 and 1986, CONACNIE discussed and debated several issues, including the identity, goals, and strategies that would define the national indigenous movement. One of the issues dealt with having to represent distinct identities of indigenous peoples from the Amazon and the Andes – not to mention the differences among the communities in each region. To forge a national indigenous organization required the adoption of a shared identity that did not naturally exist. Indigenous leaders needed to find a common denominator that would encompass the otherwise distinct and diverse cultural, historical, and social traditions between the regions. Some Andeans felt little affinity with Amazonian Indians (who had been portrayed as "savages" in national Ecuadorian imagery) and therefore wanted ECUARUNARI to emerge as the national federation (rather than forge a new national organization). Some Amazonians felt that their Andean counterparts had lost much of their indigenous heritage and cultural identification. In other words, not all communities naturally wanted to take part in a national indigenous federation. In this context, the role of networks and shared leadership proved essential in creating the ties among communities, scaling up identities, and creating a baseline of trust (or at least familiarity) within a broader movement.[91]

The ability to arrive at a shared understanding rested on the existence of networks left in place by unions, churches, and NGOs, as discussed in Parts I and II of this chapter. These organizations had provided the framework for forging a transcommunity identity, leaders that would

---

[89] CONAIE (1989) and Pallares (1997: 287 ff., 347–58, ch. 5).

[90] See Lucero (2002) for a discussion of other national indigenous organizations in Ecuador and the issues related to national unity and representation.

[91] In the end, the regional organizations agreed to refer to themselves as "indigenous nationalities" to highlight their common historical ties to the land and yet their diverse cultures. See Lucero (2003) for a discussion of how the adoption of the word nationalities played a role in helping to forge CONAIE as a *national* confederation, despite significant regional differences.

be respected between communities, as well as providing the resources to mobilize. With the formation of CONAIE, the national organization publicly and actively recognized this diversity. In this spirit, CONAIE proposed in 1988 a Preliminary Draft of the Law of Indigenous Nationalities of Ecuador, which called for a plurinational state (Black 1998: 22).[92] CONAIE has worked to promote this unity, although differences remain.[93]

A second related issue had to do with the articulation and understanding of land as the central demand shared by both regional organizations.[94] As discussed previously, the 1970s witnessed a parallel threat to local autonomy (as the state failed to follow through on land promises in the Andes and as development projects initiated incursions into Amazonian indigenous lands). Yet at the end of that decade, the two regional organizations maintained distinct conceptions of the land on which they lived and worked. From the start, CONFENAIE understood land primarily in terms of ethnic survival and integrity – it was not only livelihood but also the very basis for ethnic identity, governance, and the future. CONFENAIE therefore called for territory in order to encompass their material-political-cultural demand. As noted in Part I, ECUARUNARI's leadership came into these discussions still heavily (although not exclusively) influenced by a class-based analysis of land as a productive resource to be secured. As discussed in the following text, however, state-initiated reforms (from a corporatist to a neoliberal citizenship regime) in the 1980s brought the Andean conception closer to that of their Amazonian counterparts as

---

[92] The draft law proposed the following. While CONAIE would play a role in national dialogue, the unit of mobilization would still remain the community. Cabildos and community assemblies would remain the local site where indigenous families would gather to discuss, interpret, frame, and decide their participation (if, when, how) in the regional and national movements. The power of local leadership, therefore, would be respected. The regional and national movements would serve to scale up concerns without, ideally, erasing local autonomy – although in practice it seems that the regional federations declined in importance in the wake of CONAIE's founding.

[93] The tensions between the Amazon and the Andes have remained despite the existence and power of the national federation and national claim making. This has been evidenced by several events including debates over future presidents of CONAIE (with loyalties tied to regional affiliations). Moreover, some argue that CONAIE's position as the national confederation has come at the expense of the regional federations that compose it.

[94] Natalia Wray, interview, November 23, 1995, Quito; José María Cabascango, interview, November 27, 1995; and Luis Macas, interview, May 6, 1997, Quito.

reforms *directly challenged the land base on which indigenous communities had survived.*

No one can escape it. If there is a land conflict, this is a community problem. The central issue, therefore, is how to *recover the lands* and strengthen the *comunas* so that power is returned to the communities. . . . It is important, therefore, to maintain the concept of the territoriality of the community (Luis Macas, interview on May 6, 1997).

In the context of these 1980s reforms, CONFENAIE's vision of land began to resonate more with ECUARUNARI, which began to move away from its more class-based focus and toward a more explicitly ethnic-based position. In other words, CONAIE not only responded to a set of local and regional demands to defend local autonomy but also changed the field of political organizing within its constitutive regional organizations. By the mid-to-late 1980s, both CONFENAIE and ECUARUNARI were arguing that the loss of land was tantamount to the loss of culture and indigenous identity.

Hence, the bridges that were built between lowland and highland Indianistas and highland campesinistas during the 1980s were possible due to a common agreement, by the late 1980s, that there was no strict dichotomy between material and cultural demands. This premise became the starting point for a new common language in which the concepts of nationalism, plurinationalism, and self-determination would take on importance, while existent constructions of nation and democracy would be challenged. In this new perspective, there was a cultural dimension to all material needs and demands, and cultural issues/policy could not be kept separately from the material needs of the population (Pallares 1997: 349).

In this regard, there was a fusion of material and cultural demands – with the former understood as the lifeline for the latter. This final part of the Ecuadorian case study explains how CONAIE emerged in a context of changing citizenship regimes and political associational space.[95]

[95] CONAIE's (1989: 277–9) account of its own emergence largely corroborates the tripartite comparative argument developed in this book. While they obviously do not use the same analytical frame, their origins story does highlight 1) that the struggle for land and to defend local autonomy provided the motive; 2) that church and union networks provided the capacity; and 3) that political associational space in the 1980s provided the opportunity. A summary of their official story goes as follows. They argue that with the land reform, the left lost its organizing mandate in the countryside, which had been to demand the redistribution of land and to serve as an interlocutor between rural communities who needed land and the state that had the power to grant these titles. Once land was distributed (as far as it went), the left became less relevant (which I would add resulted from the erosion of the corporatist citizenship regime) and the comunas became the main interlocutor with the state. Out of this experience and the struggle for land, indigenous communities had gained

Neoliberal Citizenship Regimes: Extending Political Rights,
Retracting Social Ones

Ecuador's national indigenous movement, CONACNIE and then CO-
NAIE, was forged in the 1980s as Ecuador's new civilian administration
revamped the country's citizenship regime – away from corporatism and
toward neoliberalism. The new civilian administrations extended political
rights and oversaw socioeconomic reforms that fundamentally replaced redistributive policies and corporatist institutions with neoliberal ones. Most
dramatically for the country's indigenous communities, basic policies and
programs that had secured community access to land (and provided supporting social services) were reduced, at best, and cut, at worst. As such, the
prospects for indigenous community autonomy and integrity were placed
at risk.

By example, President Jaime Roldós, the first president to assume office following the populist military period of the 1970s, implemented the
agrarian development promotion law.[96] The law not only slowed down the
agrarian reform but also punished land invaders by disqualifying them from
subsequent adjudication of lands. The law also legitimated the public use of
force against land invasions, which resulted in an increase in violence against
indigenous protestors (Korovkin 1997b: 37; Pallares 1997: 171–5). This
reform therefore cut short corporatist policies that promised indigenous
communities the land on which they had lived and worked. Redistribution
was largely confined to the least productive land. Indigenous communities
thus confronted unpromising futures: with little prospect for securing title
to productive land and uncertain prospects for securing unproductive land.

increased organizational capacity and a clear awareness that they needed legal titles for
land to defend their local autonomy. In this context, the Catholic Church moved in and
started to organize along lines inspired by Vatican II. They started to organize indigenous
peoples to create their own organizations and to speak out. Young indigenous men and
women with greater educational experience emerged as leaders. Education provided them
with tools for organizing; it also highlighted that Indians could acquire educational degrees but would not be equal members of Ecuadorian society. These leaders returned to
their communities and started to work with them to defend land rights, to demand local
autonomy, and to demand equal rights as equal citizens. While the land reforms and organizing by unions and churches occurred during the military period, the *discussions* to form
a national *indigenous* federation occurred during the period of political liberalization that
coincided with the administrations of Roldós and Hurtado – even though it was founded
during the comparatively more conservative/repressive civilian administration of Febres
Cordero.

[96] The military regime actually passed the agrarian development promotion law in 1979 but
left implementation for the new civilian administrations.

In either case, the land reform was no longer a venue for securing a space within which communities could sustain ongoing material and political autonomy. In short, the end of the land reform increased the uncertainty and instability of land tenure and holdings. As such, indigenous communities confronted a question not only of how to survive economically but also how to maintain the lands on which the communities maintained their political, cultural, and social practices.

The subsequent economic crisis that hit the Latin American region as a whole further jeopardized the integrity of these communities. Democratically elected presidents reversed many redistributive policies associated with the prior corporatist period. As is well documented for Latin America, the 1980s and 1990s witnessed a decline in state services as countries attempted to put their financial house in order following decades of high but unsustainable growth. In Ecuador, the discovery and export of oil fueled an unsustainable and shortsighted development policy. With an increase in state revenues in the 1970s, the state had gained an increased capacity to invest in social programs, including land reform, rural credit, education, and health. And even during the first civilian administration, Roldós announced a National Program for Rural Development, as part of his National Development Plan, which partially targeted the rural poor (Barsky 1984: 277). With the 1980s economic crisis, however, the state lost its revenue base. Accordingly, it sharply curtailed expenses for social programs. By doing so, it essentially minimized the social rights extended during the earlier corporatist citizenship regimes and reduced the support services for rural poor (i.e., indigenous) communities.

Presidents Jaime Roldós (1979–1981) and then Osvaldo Hurtado (1981–1984) implemented stabilization measures as part of a move toward fiscal constraint and austerity (Conaghan and Malloy 1994: 110–14).[97] Reflecting on this situation, Hurtado observed that "1982–1983 was a very difficult winter that had a destructive impact that was generalizable for agriculture; campesinos were also very affected. And after 1984, public spending also contracted, all of which must have affected the rural sector. As a result of the economic crisis, there was decreased spending for the rural sector."[98] Ortiz (1992: 122–3) also observes that the crisis after 1982 most severely

---

[97] Osvaldo Hurtado was Roldós's vice president but assumed office following Roldós's death in a plane crash.

[98] Osvaldo Hurtado, vice president and then president of Ecuador. Currently president of CORDES. Interview, December 1, 1995, Quito.

hit Andean campesinos who had been producing agricultural goods for the domestic market. Indeed, the decline in agricultural prices hit the peasant sector hard. The average price of onion, corn, wheat, and potato, for example, declined an estimated 66.8 percent between 1975 and 1986 leading to a significant decline in market earnings for indigenous peasants of the highlands and the terms of trade (Ramón 1990; also see Ortiz 1992: 123).

These initial changes were but a prelude to the significant and draconian economic reforms undertaken by the second civilian administration of President León Febres Cordero (1984–1988).

The adjustment policies begun in 1982 under the Christian Democratic government of Osvaldo Hurtado became draconian during the Conservative administration of León Febres Cordero and were largely maintained by Social Democratic President Rodrigo Borja. Government measures sought to eliminate stimulus programs, abolish protection and subsidies, reduce price controls, promote exports, open up the economy to the international market, reduce public spending, devalue the currency, and foster increases in interest rates. . . . In the 1980s, the annual growth of the agricultural GNP averaged 4.9 percent, indicating that in aggregate terms the agricultural sector did better than the rest of the economy . . . however, . . . the success story belonged to the agricultural exporters and the agro-industrial producers of the Costa and the northern Sierra. . . . The crisis of the 1980s in the countryside hit the peasant economy, and most brutally in the poorest areas of the highlands. Caught in the crunch of inflationary increases in the price of all basic necessities, reduced opportunity for obtaining credit, exorbitant interest rates, and contraction of state supports and services, the market-oriented peasants found their situation worsening as the real prices paid for their products deteriorated and the cost of the mostly imported agricultural inputs was driven up by the devaluations (Zamosc 1994: 51–2).

Febres Cordero reversed statist reforms and employed repression to temper resistance. During his first year, he engaged in a process of deregulation that included lifting price controls on a range of agricultural commodities including fertilizers and other agricultural inputs.[99] While Febres Cordero could not sustain his basic economic policy, the deregulation on price controls for agriculture continued through the next administration of Borjas, which was considered more progressive.[100] In this context, basic agricultural inputs skyrocketed between 1980–1988 (almost eightfold for seed, twelvefold for fertilizer, and almost ninefold for machinery and equipment) (Racines 1993: 111) while prices for agricultural products such as corn

[99] Whitaker and Green (1990: 30–1) and Conaghan and Malloy (1994: 142–3).
[100] Thoumi and Grindle (1992: 73) and Conaghan and Malloy (1994).

136

remained relatively stable, not including 1984–1985, with an increase of 60 percent. This led to a decrease in purchasing power for indigenous communities (Rosero 1991: ch. 5).

If the civilian governments cut back on subsidies and agricultural inputs, they also cut back significantly on total public expenditures (current outlays and investments) for agriculture (Colyer 1990: 281). This was evident in figures for credit as well as social service outlays. In the areas of credit, for example, Korovkin (1993: 25 and 1997) notes that by the early 1980s, FODERUMA's budget constituted 0.1 percent of national credit provided by the national bank, el Banco Central, of which it was a part. Laying insult to injury, FODERUMA spent less than half of its designated funds between 1978 and 1985 (Korovkin 1993: 26). Younger et al. (n.d., esp. table 37) also found that access to credit was extremely tight and overwhelmingly benefited large landholders. On the basis of 1994 and 1995 surveys and data from the Banco Nacional de Fomento (BNF, the National Development Bank), they found that very few landholders (3 percent or less of all agricultural homes) gained access to credit extended by BNF.[101] Because the coast claims the overwhelming majority (75–86 percent) of annual agricultural credits and because the overwhelming majority of Indians live in the Andes, it is reasonable to conclude that the percentage of credit allocated to Indians declined for these same years.

A similar decline occurred in the areas of social sector spending – as evidenced by outlays for education.[102] A state-sponsored poverty study reveals that between 1982 and 1994, educational expenses as a percentage of

---

[101] The BNF, the state bank that was to have provided credit to small producers, does not disaggregate its data. Hence, one does not know if/when credit is allocated to individuals or groups (i.e., comunas), if/when credit targets small farmers versus large farmers, and whether creditors are indigenous or not. That said, the percentage of credit allocated to agriculture experienced a secular decline from 1968 to 1994 (Jara 1997, who analyzed data from the BNF, Boletines Estadísticas, 1966–1975, 1970–1989, and 1984–1994).

[102] The decline in education expenses is apparent but difficult to document precisely – in part because there are multiple figures for education expenses: those initially allocated and those subsequently readjusted and authorized following expenses – and because the numbers provided by the Ministry of Education and Culture and the Ministry of Finance and Public Credit do not coincide exactly. Yet, regardless of which figures one looks at, there is a secular decline in the percentage of the budget allocated for expenses from 1980 (with a high of 33.02 percent) to 1996 (with a low of 14.25 percent). As for actual amounts expended, figures are available beginning in 1987; there is a significant decline from 1989 to 1995 and a significant rise reported in 1996. Finally, the percentage of the GNP reported in Jara (1997: Table E.11) also indicates a decline from a high of 4.6 percent in 1981 to a low of 2.7 percent in 1996.

Table 4.4. *Ecuador: Central Government Social Sector Expenditures (1980–1993)*

Year	1980	1985	1988	1990	1993
Budget Shares (% of total expenditures)					
Social Sectors	41.0	32.7	34.4	28.6	27.5
Education	33.1	24.5	23.6	18.5	19.9
Health/Community Development	6.9	7.3	9.7	8.2	5.4
Other [a]	7.4	1.7	2.2	5.9	15.4
Total Expenditures/GDP	14.2	15.1	13.8	14.7	14.0
Social Sectors/GDP	5.8	4.9	4.8	4.2	3.9
Real Spending Per Capita (1985 constant thousand sucres)					
Social Sectors	7.2	5.8	5.5	4.8	4.4
Education	5.8	4.4	3.8	3.1	3.2
Health/Community Development	1.2	1.3	1.6	1.4	0.9
Other	1.2	0.4	0.4	0.9	3.1

[a] The World Bank (1995b: 190) notes that the rise in "other" includes social spending programs that target the poor, such as the social investment program, FISE. FISE was created in 1993 and finances "small-scale social investments aimed at poverty alleviation based on an institutional design similar to social funds operating in other LAX countries" (World Bank 1995a: 1).

Source: World Bank (1995b).

the GDP fell from 5.1 percent to 2.9 percent. Similarly, health figures for the same dates fell from 1.8 percent to 0.9 percent (Larrea et al. 1996: 12). A World Bank study (1995b: 190) paints a parallel picture with social sector spending (determined as real spending per capita) declining from 7.2 percent in 1980 to 4.4 percent in 1993 (see Table 4.4). The decline in education expenses, moreover, coincided with an increase in enrollment for primary, secondary, and higher education. "The result was a severe deterioration in the quality of education . . ." (World Bank 1995b: 191). In assessing basic services by ethnic composition of a given canton in 1990, the study found:

The strongly indigenous Cantons [where more than 50 percent of residents speak indigenous languages] are worse off with respect to any of the recorded social and service variables, both when compared to other Cantons in the rural and those in the urban areas (World Bank 1995: 29).

In its current form the poor in Ecuador benefit little from the social security system because the poor's coverage is low and benefits reaching them are minimal (World Bank 1995b: 17).

It is not just that the indigenous poor suffered a decline in access to state resources, but they are indisputably the worst off on any economic score of poverty. While poverty reports differ based on the instrument used to measure poverty, they have all concluded that poverty rates are higher in rural areas and disproportionately higher for indigenous peoples.

In short, given eroding corporatist institutions and policies, indigenous communities were increasingly vulnerable: they were fast losing access to state resources and were encountering greater and more devastating poverty. *Land security* was at risk and with it an entire way of life. With the implementation of a neoliberal citizenship regime, in particular, the land that had been secured through the Ley de Comunas and land reforms was in jeopardy. The Ley de Comunas had provided indigenous communities with the legal mechanism to define a territorial space in which local leaders could govern and serve as interlocutors vis-à-vis the state. The land reform provided some available lands to establish more of these comunas and to sustain them with the rise in supporting social policies (such as credit, price controls, and subsidies). In the 1980s, the decline in these services coupled with the challenge to the comunas was an attack on the last space in which indigenous communities had created autonomy. In the late 1970s through mid-1980s, therefore, the recently founded regional indigenous confederations, CONFENAIE and ECUARUNARI, converged around a set of concerns for land and territory.

Land became and remains one of the central demands of CONFENAIE and ECUARUNARI. Yet the fight for land referred to two distinct understandings of the land. For the Amazonian Indians who had maintained a significant degree of political, economic, and social autonomy from the state, the demand for land meant the fight to delimit territorial spaces in which Amazonian Indians could live according to their own practices. In this sense, the demand included land as a productive resource and as political-social space in which practices could be defended. For the Andean Indians, the demand for land initially drew on the demands voiced by campesino organizations – the demand for a plot of land to farm. During the 1980s, the struggle for land expanded to include the protection of local spaces of autonomy – focusing on the right of the comuna to govern itself.[103] With the neoliberal reforms of the 1980s, the need to defend and

---

[103] FICI (1994: 3–4); José María Cabascango, interviews, March 26, 1997 and April 23, 1997; and CONAIE (n.d.).

legalize access to lands became all the more compelling. And those Andean leaders in ECUARUNARI who had initially seen land as a largely productive material resource were convinced by their peers in ECUARUNARI, CONFENAIE, and CONAIE that land was also a cultural and political basis for indigenous survival. As the 1980s progressed, the *ethnic* agenda within ECUARUNARI therefore became dominant, and land and local autonomy became a common demand.

Land demands have come to represent, therefore, a defense of the very space in which indigenous people define and govern themselves. This expanded understanding of land "is the fundamental base for the physical and cultural survival of our peoples" (FICI 1994). Similarly, Luis Macas, former president of CONAIE, states that,

We reaffirm that the land is the indispensable condition for life, for the existence of the people, and for its development; without this basic element it is impossible to have the conditions to educate a child, to have health and to reproduce our culture (Macas 1992: 24).

The points that we have demanded . . . are precisely the right to the land, to the soil. For us, land is the indispensable condition needed to develop ourselves, for being able to reproduce ourselves socially, economically, and politically. We repeatedly state that without land, without this material base upon which to establish ourselves, the indigenous *pueblos* cannot speak of education, nor of culture, nor of any other element (Macas 1994: 175).

The land demand has come to include the respect for individual and collective rights. Individual rights refer to the right to own land, the right to equal rights, the right to equal services. Collective rights include the right for indigenous peoples to gain legal recognition, to end discrimination, to claim collective lands or territories, and to achieve respect for their authorities and legal traditions. ". . . as individuals and as pueblos that have the same rights and the same obligations as any other Ecuadorians. For this reason . . . we have demanded the recognition of local authorities in certain provinces" (Macas 1994: 177).

Political Associational Space through Political Liberalization

As these new civilian administrations were cutting back social rights, effectively challenging the local autonomy of indigenous communities, they also extended the political opportunity for organizing. Constitutionally speaking, the transition from authoritarian rule coincided with a marked expansion of the suffrage. The democratic transition in 1979 granted suffrage rights to Ecuador's indigenous men and women of legal age, constituting the first time in the country's history that literacy requirements had not been used to exclude them. No longer would indigenous peoples necessarily be sidelined from elections or dependent on corporatist institutions to have a voice. As such, the new democratic period constitutionally granted indigenous people unprecedented avenues for electoral participation.

Alongside this expansion of the suffrage, the new civilian administrations, particularly the first two, were supportive of a more multicultural policy toward indigenous peoples. Roldós and Hurtado initiated what Pallares (1997) refers to as neo-indigenismo – a policy designed by nonindigenous officials to incorporate Indians into the state without necessarily promoting earlier forms of assimilation. Roldós and Hurtado did so through discrete symbolic and cultural acts. Both Roldós and Hurtado, for example, incorporated indigenous references into their inaugurations. Roldós spoke Quichua for a few minutes and called for a multicultural nation; Hurtado wore a presidential sash with writing in Shuar (Pallares 1997: 326–7). Moreover, both promoted a diverse cultural policy with funding for various cultural events and the promotion of a National Literacy Program (Pallares 1997: 309–10, 327).[104]

This cultural policy and, in particular, the literacy programs created a new political opportunity for organizing (and in some cases provided the social capital and skills for a new generation of leaders).[105] In an interview

---

[104] During the Roldós/Hurtado administration, the state intiated a rural literacy program. In 1982 Hurtado made bilingual education official in indigenous communities and created the Department of Rural Education (DER). In 1985, he also created the Project for Bilingual Education. While León Febres Cordero froze most pro-indigenous policies during his administration (1984–1988), Borja's administration (1988–1992) reinitiated a more open stance, as witnessed by the founding of the National Directorate of Indigenous Bilingual Intercultural Education (DINEIB) (Pallares 1997: 309–10). Borja turned over the directorship of this program to the national indigenous movement, CONAIE, in 1988. Thereafter CONAIE submitted a national plan for indigenous education (that emphasized bilingual education and called for CONAIE's participation and administration of funds at the local level). In 1988, in an agreement with the Ministry of Cultural Education, CONAIE was responsible for coordinating the National Literacy Campaign in those communities in which they worked. See Selverston (1997) and Black (1998: 26).

[105] Interviews with Rosero (March 18, 1997) and Macas (May 6, 1997) all emphasized the role of education. Also see Selverston (1997) and Pallares (1997: 241–2) for a discussion of the important role of indigenous intellectuals who had access to education and resources. Pallares (1997: 242) notes, in particular, the importance of an indigenous intelligentsia from

with Hurtado, he highlighted how this literacy program supported both indigenous communities and the growth of the indigenous movement. Indeed, he noted that a number of important indigenous leaders had worked in the literacy programs, including Luis Macas, who later became president of CONAIE and a representative in Ecuador's national legislature. Hurtado commented further: "the literacy program was a mobilizing structure where leaders got to know each other, and to work with and create experimental elements."[106] It is important to note, and perhaps ironic, that this literacy program coincided with an overall decline in education expenditures, as noted previously. Luis Macas concurred with Hurtado's suggestion. In thinking about the emergence of these movements and in thinking about their role and endurance in the 1980s, Macas concludes that,

The democratization process definitively had an impact on the organizing process. . . . The bilingual education programs, while initiated during the military period, flourished during the democratic period. . . . And the recognition of territories in Pastaza during the Borja administration would never have happened had it not been a democratic government. We have gained this space under democracy. It is not that the government gave us this space, in fact it has often tried to close those spaces. . . . But I think that if there had not been a democratic system, this process definitely would have brought the advances of the indigenous movement to a standstill (Luis Macas, interview, May 6, 1997).

Yet if political associational space increased during the 1980s as a whole, indigenous activists remained suspicious of the democracies that had been founded. Indeed, not all activists saw the new democratic regime as unambiguously positive. Given that prior democratic regimes had succumbed to *caudillismo* and corruption while the preceding military regimes had advanced land reforms and social programs, it was not immediately apparent to indigenous leaders what electoral politics and civilian rule would offer.

By the mid-1980s, Ecuador's indigenous movements remained critical and disdainful of democratization. Not only had the new democracies implemented disadvantageous socioeconomic reforms that challenged local autonomy, but they also failed to institutionalize channels for participating in national politics – which in turn made indigenous people turn even more forcefully to local indigenous communities and authority structures.

Otavalo and Saraguro. While they did not necessarily travel throughout the countryside, they played a key role in founding the national organizations and in developing a presence at the international level.
[106] Hurtado, interview, December 1, 1995, Quito.

The main and ill-trusted avenue for national participation occurred through political parties. However, there were no historical or contemporary reasons to trust political parties.[107] Political parties had never represented indigenous peoples. They did not fight for the land reforms in the 1960s and 1970s, and they played no part in the push for democratization. Indeed, many indigenous communities had had a more direct access (through corporatist channels) to the state during the prior populist military regime. With the new rounds of democratization, political parties offered but a passing interest in indigenous communities – coming to their communities during campaign time; ignoring these communities once in office. As such, they appeared as catchall parties for political elites interested in capturing national power and coffers. Political parties were viewed neither as reliable nor trustworthy interlocutors.

Consequently, a disdain for democratic elections and political parties deepened as indigenous leaders and communities observed political parties seek their votes without offering voice. Indigenous leaders tried to run for office but were shut out by political parties and granted limited resources to do anything if elected.[108] By the mid-1980s, indigenous organizations called for an abstention from the 1986 elections.

Hence, the 1980s offered a time of political opening and disappointment. In interviews in 1995 and 1997, some argued that democratic and authoritarian periods differed little – because the military still enters their communities when there are mobilizations; the government still cheats; and they are still marginalized. Others argued that it was fundamentally different as it offered the chance to vote, organize, push for bicultural education, and act as citizens. The point to emphasize here is that the civilian administrations provided political opportunities for civic organizing – even if the democracies that they governed were viewed as shallow.

It is in this contradictory mix between new citizenship regimes (which were narrowing social rights and extending political suffrage) and political liberalization (which was granting greater political associational space to organize, albeit in the context of a shallow democracy), that *indigenous struggles for local autonomy and national representation* increased in *political* importance. It became important to defend the land base to maintain the integrity and

---

[107] See Pachano (1996: 153–69) for a discussion of the regime transition, political parties, and changes in citizenship rules. Also see Hurtado (1980: 128) who notes that political parties have historically been quite weak in Ecuador – ceding ground or failing to gain ground when confronted with (military) caudillos.

[108] Cabascango, interview, March 26, 1997; see Pallares (1997: 351–5).

cultural survival of indigenous communities. And as it became apparent that national political channels were effectively foreclosed, indigenous leaders at all levels (local, regional, and national) became increasingly important. Indigenous activists increasingly worked to bolster local indigenous governance structures[109] and to empower the national confederation, CONAIE. While CONAIE initially brought together two regional federations with quite distinct understandings of local autonomy, it would come to represent these diverse organizations in dramatic and unprecedented ways. The neoliberal reforms, indeed, catalyzed CONAIE to mobilize national protests to defend the country's diverse kinds of local autonomy.

Taking Center Stage

The year 1990 marked the public christening of the movement.[110] In May of that year, CONAIE orchestrated a ten-day mobilization that blocked roads, cut off commercial transport, and occupied churches. Cotopaxi, Chimborazo, Tungurahua, and Bolívar were among the most active.[111] The protest was labeled the *Levantamiento Nacional Indígena*, the National Indigenous Uprising, and included not only those associated with CONAIE but also members from *Federación Nacional de Organizaciones Campesinas e*

[109] The importance of strengthening local indigenous governance structures was repeated in interviews with Fernando Rosero, March 11, 1997 and March 18, 1997; Roberto Conejo, March 12, 1997; Luis Maldonado, March 12, 1997; Galo Ramón, March 20, 1997; and José María Cabascango, March 26, 1997 and April 23, 1997. Also see Maldonado (1996: 6–8). For example, discussions at CEPCU, a local indigenous NGO in Otavalo, raised this issue around the Laguna de San Pablo and highlighted the desire to find ways in which the cabildo could function effectively within and outside of the community. FICI, the regional indigenous organization from Imbabura, also stated the need to defend and foster local communal government and political autonomy, as outlined in their 1994 Ley Orgánica: "The first objective should be to obtain and strengthen local powers with concrete proposals from the population that guarantee a real participation of the people in local decisions" (FICI 1994: 3). Finally, Cabascango (November 27, 1995) speaking about ECUARUNARI as a whole, stated that the leadership was trying to find ways to strengthen local autonomy and practices. As interviewees noted, this process is complicated by the fact that the indigenous families are increasingly moving or migrating to urban areas, thereby changing the centrality and proximity of community leaders, structures, and customs.

[110] See *El Comercio* – May 29, 1990: B4, May 30, 1990: A1, June 4, 1990: B6, June 5, 1990: B4, June 12, 1990: A1, August 27, 1990: A5; *Diario Hoy* – June 15, 1990: 1A, June 22, 1990: 1A, June 23, 1990: 5A, June 28, 1990: 1A, June 29, 1990: 1A, July 2, 1990: 4A, August 9, 1990: 4A; *El Universo* – August 27, 1990: 1S12; Rosero (1991); Almeida et al. (1992); León (1994); and Zamosc (1994).

[111] Ortiz (1992: 101); León (1994: 51); and Zamosc (1994: 37–8).

Indígenas (FENOC-I), *Federación Ecuatoriana de Indígenas Evangélicos* (FEINE), and independent communities.[112]

The defense/reacquisition of land, inflation (and its impact on prices and agricultural inputs), the high cost of living, and government indifference precipitated the mobilization (Rosero 1991; León 1994: 71, 82; Zamosc 1994: 50). However, the protest became a forum for CONAIE to articulate its agenda in a national setting. It did so by espousing "16 points" (León 1994: 18–19, 62).[113] León (1994: 61) notes that the national demands fell into the following categories: 1) ethnicity – the right to be recognized as a multiethnic population with equal rights (i.e., no ethnic discrimination); 2) citizenship – equal rights to services; and 3) class – rights as peasants to land, fair prices, and so forth.

CONAIE's Sixteen Points

1. A public declaration that Ecuador is a plurinational country (to be ratified by the constitution).
2. The government must grant lands and titles to lands to the nationalities.
3. Solutions to water and irrigation needs.
4. Absolution of indigenous debts to FODERUMA and the National Development Bank.
5. Freezing of consumer prices.
6. Conclusion of priority projects in Indian communities.
7. Nonpayment of rural land taxes.

---

[112] With the formation of CONAIE and its increasing ability to shape political discourse, other campesino organizations reconsidered their objectives and methods of organizing. Pedro de la Cruz recalls some of the changes that occurred within FENOC. In 1989, FENOC split in two, apparently over whether they should explicitly include "ethnic" issues as part of their agenda. One of the organizations amended its name to FENOC-I; the "I" announced the incorporation of *lo indígena* (the indigenous) in their work. In a 1995 congress, Pedro de la Cruz, a Quichua Indian from Cotacachi, Imbabura, was elected president of the organization (Pedro de la Cruz, interview, December 8, 1995). He observed that they were still affiliated with the labor organization CEDOC but were working to establish greater autonomy. Their traditional land demands remain. But they have incorporated a cultural element that recognizes the pluri-ethnic composition of Ecuadorian society and, accordingly, the different meaning that land has for different peoples. FENOC-I subsequently incorporated the demands of the small Afro-Ecuadorian population and changed its name to FENOC-IN (where N stands for black or *negro* in spanish).

[113] Local communities articulated their own agendas, as well. They complained about and identified solutions for inflation, land conflicts, and agricultural production; infrastructure; the right to direct control over certain public entities; and antidiscrimination; among other demands (León 1994: 19, 63–8 and Pallares 1997: 363).

8. Expulsion of the Summer Institute of Linguistics.
9. Free commercial and handicraft activity.
10. CONAIE protection of archaeological sites.
11. Officialization of Indian medicine.
12. Cancellation of government decree that created parallel land-reform granting bodies.
13. The government should immediately grant funds to the nationalities.
14. The government should grant funds for bilingual education.
15. Respect for the rights of the child.
16. The fixing of fair prices for products.

Source: English Translation in Pallares (1997: 363); Spanish Version in León (1994:19)

The 1990 levantamiento was more than the "typical" peasant mobilization demanding land and credit. It was and came to represent the first national mobilization of "Indians." It had a significant impact on the national imaginary even though negotiations with the state stalled.[114] In countless interviews, participants, supporters, and antagonists pinpointed the ways in which the mobilization changed the presentation of self and the interpretation of ethnic relations. Cabascango observed,

The 1990 uprising catalyzed a process of consciousness raising. Before 1990, civil society almost did not recognize that there were Indians. There was racism and segregation and society did not pay attention to that which was indigenous. Even with our own communities, some people did not want to be Indians and they began to lose touch with their community. The 1990 uprising, however, increased our sensitivity to these issues. It affected governing circles and civil society (José María Cabascango, interview, November 27, 1995).

The protest and demands highlighted the centrality of indigeneity and land in ways that had not been seriously considered by national politicians and the nonindigenous citizenry. The protest forced a respatialization of politics, home, and community, according to León (1994: 54–5). Indigenous participants occupied spaces that were not "theirs" and by example redefined their right as citizens to be there.

---

[114] In the course of negotiations, OPIP started to articulate a more "radical" position – calling for the recognition of territories, political autonomy, and the right to participate in discussions about oil exploration in indigenous areas. See Ortiz (1992); Ruiz (1992); and Pallares (1997: 372–3). Ortiz argues that OPIP's position paralyzed the negotiations and ultimately weakened the movement. OPIP's subsequent demands raised fears of separatist intentions and challenges to national sovereignty. OPIP denied that this was the case.

The uprising was not confined to communities affiliated with CONAIE. Indeed, the uprising catalyzed other indigenous communities to join the protest and to voice their demands vis-à-vis the state.[115] Their participation revealed the widespread demands for inclusion, access, and autonomy. Moreover, it revealed the importance of local-level decision making, for the decision to participate was taken precisely at the local level.[116] And it assumed a more generalized nature. It did not only focus on land. It did not only mobilize those in CONAIE but also served as the spark for other organizations to mobilize and to make demands of the national government (León 1994: ch. 3, 86). In the process, CONAIE emerged as a central political player that year.

If 1990 demonstrated CONAIE's power of mobilization, 1994 demonstrated its power of negotiation as it debated, protested, and then renegotiated a law on agrarian reform.[117] The Ecuadorian legislature tried to privatize property relations with the 1994 Agrarian Development Law. CONAIE had opposed this law during prior consultations but their concerns were initially disregarded.[118] The law undermined the *intent* of earlier land reforms. It effectively stopped land redistribution, targeted

---

[115] One such example is the *Unión de Organizaciones Populares "Inca Atahualpa"* located in Alausí, Chimborazo. Inca Atahualpa was established in 1988 in circumstances quite distinct from those described in the text. Through the early 1980s they remained subordinate to haciendas and the tenientes políticos (as the land reforms distributed few if any lands in this area). The organization, therefore, did not emerge to defend autonomy (which it did not have) but to achieve community status, to impose order, to create governing mechanisms in a region characterized by rising conflict and crime, and to gain access to state resources. It did not identify primarily as an ethnic organization, even if it incorporated ethnic concerns into its work. As Francisco Buñay, then president, said: "We are a peasant organization and not necessarily an indigenous one. But yes, we incorporate identity and culture into our work with peasants." That said, the organization did support CONAIE's 1990 mobilization. And one of its leaders, Anselmo Lluilema, even videotaped the march for the organization. This discussion draws on a joint interview with four of the Unión's elected leaders on March 17, 1997; two different group discussions with community leaders who are members of the Unión on April 21, 1997 and April 22, 1997; and individual interviews with Carlos Díaz, March 31, 1997, Anselmo Lluilema, March 31, 1997, and Francisco Buñay, April 22, 1997. All interviews took place in Tixán.

[116] Carrasco (1993: 30); León (1994: ch. 5). Also based on focus group discussions in Tixán.

[117] For coverage of the debate over the *Ley de Ordenamiento Agrario and the Desarrollo Agrario* bill, see *Diario Hoy* – May 6, 1994: 6A; May 10, 1994: 5A; May 12, 1994: 5A; May 13, 1994: 2A, 4A, 6A; May 14, 1994: 5A; May 15, 1994: 4A; May 16, 1994: 1A; May 17, 1994: 5A; May 18, 1994: 5A, 8A; May 18, 1994: 2A; May 19, 1994: 7A; May 23, 1994: 4A; May 30, 1994: 7A; June 2, 1994: 6A; June 4, 1994: 5A; June 10, 1994: 2A; and June 14, 1994: 1A, 3A.

[118] See *Diario Hoy*, September 20, 1993: 5A.

large export-oriented farms for credit, privatized water rights, and created the mechanisms (majority vote) for selling previously inalienable indigenous lands (Andolina 1999: 212), all of which was seen as an affront to social equity and a challenge to the integrity of indigenous communities. In response, CONAIE called a 1994 protest, *Movilización por la Vida* (Mobilization for Life). CONAIE demanded 1) the withdrawal of the agrarian reform bill in favor of an alternative bill; 2) sufficient funding to resolve land disputes; 3) channeling of 1 percent of oil revenues through CONAIE for indigenous development along with the revocation of still unused oil concessions in indigenous territory, as determined by a joint commission of the government, CONAIE, and ecological and human rights groups; 4) appointment of a national director of bilingual education proposed by indigenous organizations, and sufficient resources for such programs; 5) respect for human rights, including the prohibition of private security forces in the countryside; 6) funds to reconstruct several villages damaged by natural disasters; and 7) recognition of CONAIE as the representative of indigenous and peasant interests.[119] Luis Macas, then president of CONAIE, explained the decision to protest:

> ... the CONAIE Extraordinary Assembly, which took place on June 7th and 8th in Riobamba, decided to organize the days of struggle, entitled MOBILIZATION for LIFE, as a means of rejecting the Agrarian Law that was approved by the Congress and the President, considering that it was an unconstitutional, antisocial, racist law. ... It eliminated the definition of the social function of the land and water at the same time that it *opened doors for the disappearance of communal lands, the base and sustenance necessary for the survival of indigenous peoples.* Definitively, it was an instrument in favor of the landlords and worsened inequality, violence, and injustice in the countryside (Macas 1995: 31, emphasis added).

The nationwide protests forced the government to retrace its steps. In response, the government formed a commission with 50 percent participation by indigenous leaders to reform the Agrarian Development Law. CONAIE negotiated "credit for small farmers who produce for the local market, state control of water resources, continuation of land redistribution, development of indigenous agricultural knowledge, and a *two-thirds majority vote required for indigenous communities to sell their community land*" (Andolina 1999: 213, emphasis added). In other words, they defended access to basic resources (credit, water, and land) and put in place strict measures for selling what had previous been inalienable community lands – all

---

[119] As reported in *Diario Hoy*, May 26, 1993 and Pacari (1996).

of which were designed to support the reproduction and integrity of indigenous communities. CONAIE's success in negotiating with the state reflected and consolidated its role as a widely acknowledged political actor.

CONAIE decided to enter electoral politics in 1996. This decision reversed strategy and approach because the organization had expressed a general disdain for the electoral process in Ecuador. It had protested the 1990 elections and had encouraged people to cast a null vote in 1992 (Andolina 1999: 210). CONAIE had also declared that they would not field candidates. The decision was contested and reflected a complicated set of internal negotiations.[120] In 1996, CONAIE chose to form part of a national coalition called, *Movimiento de Unidad Plurinacional Pachakutik Nuevo País* (MUPP-NP) (also called the *Movimiento Nuevo País-Pachakutik*). The coalition comprised CONAIE, the *Coordinadora de Movimientos Sociales*, and the *Movimiento de Ciudadanía por un Nuevo País*.[121] The coalition won eight seats – including provincial and national deputies (Mijeski and Beck 1998: 4). Among those elected to congress were Luis Macas, former president of CONAIE, and Miguel Lluco, former President of ECUARUNARI. The electoral success was striking as MUPP-NP elected over seventy candidates at the local and national level and won seven of every ten races it entered.[122] Former-CONAIE leaders were also discussed and chosen for national-level political appointments during both the short-lived Abdala Bucarám administration (1996–1997, 6 months) and the Fabian Alarcón administration (1997–1998, interim president). While the entry into formal politics was not free of conflicts, it was a noteworthy achievement.[123] CONAIE

---

[120] The decision to take part in the elections was an apparent response to a (renegade or uncoordinated) decision from the Amazon. At CONAIE's 1993 congress, the confederation chose to participate only in local and provincial elections. However, independent of (or contrary to) this decision, several Amazonian leaders chose to participate in national elections through the newly formed *Movimiento Pachakutik*. The Pachakutik Movement gained support in the Amazon and essentially forced CONAIE to reconsider its political strategy (Mijeski and Beck 1998: 3 and Andolina 1999: 219–21). A compromise was reached and CONAIE eventually ran an electoral campaign with the *Movimiento de Unidad Plurinacional Pachakutik* and *Nuevo País*.

[121] *Diario Hoy*, August 24, 1996.

[122] Pallares (1997: 544) and Mijeski and Beck (1998: 4) – both cite the *Washington Post*, July 23, 1996.

[123] With the entry into formal politics, several conflicts emerged over political alliances, appointments to ministries, charges of corruption and opportunism – particularly leveled against Amazonian leaders, and tensions between Pachakutik, CONAIE, and Nuevo País. For a discussion of some of these conflicts, see *Diario Hoy* (June 13, 1996: 3A); Mijeski and Beck (1998: 5); and Andolina (1999: 225–32).

has emerged, therefore, as a significant political actor. It is Latin America's most powerful indigenous social movement. It has also achieved an unprecedented voice in national political debates – although its success in this realm is far from assured given uneven electoral results since 1996 (Mijeski and Beck 1998).

Conclusion

Ecuador's indigenous movement emerged to contest the ways in which state reforms challenged local autonomy in the 1960s and 1970s. On the basis of regional networks and in the context of political associational space, indigenous activists in the Andes and Amazon organized regional indigenous associations and, ultimately, forged CONAIE, a national confederation that has gained national and international recognition. As the Ecuadorian state moved definitively from a corporatist to a neoliberal citizenship regime in the 1980s and 1990s, CONAIE decided to move beyond the defense of local autonomy and toward a redefinition of democratic citizenship. CONAIE participated actively in the Constituent Assembly, which was held from December 1997 to May 1998. They won 10 percent of the seats and were the third largest political force in the assembly (Andolina 1999: 231, 313). While they were not entirely successful in the 1998 Constituent Assembly, their partial successes were striking. The resulting Constitution did include a chapter on collective rights for indigenous people. However, the document did not outline guarantees for these rights nor did it recognize the country as a plurinational state (Andolina 1998 and 1999; Mijeski and Beck 1998). So too, the role of its former leaders in the national legislature has been noteworthy. Miguel Lluco, for example, oversaw the signing of ILO Convention 169, which advocates many of the indigenous collective demands proposed but not passed in the Constituent Assembly. Former CONAIE leader, Nina Pacari, became a vice president in the national legislature.

It is all the more ironic, then, that CONAIE would begin the second millenium with the least democratic of acts. Opposed to the conservative economic policies of then-president Jamil Mahuad, they formed an alliance with the military and helped to overthrow the government in 2000. CONAIE did not mobilize as an indigenous movement alone. Indeed, it acted on behalf of a broad set of popular demands that opposed neoliberal fiscal policy. In the immediate aftermath of the coup, a Junta composed of CONAIE, the military, and a former Supreme Court judge governed the country. Shortly thereafter, however, the military outmaneuvered CONAIE and turned the executive mantle over to then vice president, Gustavo Noboa. True to his word, Noboa continued with the very policies that had led CONAIE to protest in the first place.[124] And CONAIE's image as a defender of democracy and Indian rights was placed under greater scrutiny.

CONAIE's actions in 2000 also highlighted the growing pains of a social movement organization that had entered but not necessarily made peace with electoral politics. For when CONAIE mobilized against Mahuad, they also mobilized against the Congress, where several Pachakutik (and former CONAIE) leaders were serving as elected officials. At the time of this writing, the same tensions exist as CONAIE moved from supporting to protesting the Lucio Gutiérrez administration, a government that had appointed former CONAIE leaders Luis Macas and Nina Pacari as Ministers of Agriculture and Foreign Relations, respectively. As such, CONAIE has given birth to Ecuador's most noteworthy indigenous politicians but does not necessarily support the multiple political currents that have emerged in the process.

In the grand scheme of things, CONAIE must be credited for promoting a more democratic, inclusive, and pluri-ethnic politics. Against all odds, it mobilized indigenous people and gave them a political voice. As the region's most powerful indigenous movement, it forced Ecuadorian politicians to take note of indigenous people and to grant them the hearing that they had been denied. It placed discussions of culture, autonomy, land, territory, and education on the national political agenda – forging new debates about citizenship. Having done so, it opened the door for a new generation of national indigenous leaders to pursue these issues in the formal electoral arena. In the process, indigenous people have become powerful political actors with many voices, not just one.

---

[124] CONAIE protested the economic policies pursued by President Mahuad – particularly the dollarization of the economy. Noboa continued with the dollarization of the economy leading many to question what had changed, if anything.

5

![decorative bar]

Bolivia

STRONG REGIONAL MOVEMENTS

Indigenous people constitute the majority in Bolivia. They have been treated, however, as a minority in the contemporary period. Politicians have sought to use them as pawns in a political process that has essentially granted them a subordinate position. The Bolivian National Revolution of 1952 sought to do precisely that – to incorporate peasants while denying them their indigenous identity. Contrary to elite mestizo expectations, however, indigenous peoples did not entirely assimilate into a dominant culture nor did they accept the late-twentieth-century policies that increasingly threatened their survival.

Significant regional indigenous movements emerged in the Andes and the Amazon initially to defend their local autonomy and, ultimately, to demand an equal position in the democracy that was forged in the 1980s and 1990s. These movements gained national recognition with their mobilizations as well as their initiative in policy debates. Indeed, by the end of the twentieth century, indigenous movements had organized communities throughout the country and had fundamentally changed the terms of political discourse. They had taken part in reform discussions for land reform, territorial autonomy, municipalization, educational reform, and census taking, among other issues.

This chapter explains the emergence of Bolivia's two regional indigenous movements by analyzing changes in citizenship regimes, political associational space, and organizational networks. As in Ecuador, these three variables explain the motive, opportunity, and capacity, respectively, of Bolivia's first indigenous movements. By tracing these three variables across time and subnational regions, this chapter makes four claims – the first two of which parallel those made in the discussion of Ecuador. First and most importantly, this chapter provides further evidence for this book's main argument that indigenous movements initially emerged to defend local autonomy from state policies associated with changing citizenship regimes. Indigenous activists were able to organize, however, only where they could capitalize on political associational space and transcommunity networks. Second, this chapter also argues that subnational variations emerged between the Bolivian Andes and Amazon precisely because the organization and therefore defense of autonomy occurred against distinct regional patterns of state formation (as also occurred in Ecuador). While the *retreat of the state in* the countryside reversed corporatist state policies that had previously and unintentionally protected local community autonomy in the Andes; the penetration of the state into the Amazon challenged indigenous territorial autonomy that had previously survived in the absence of a historically viable state. In both the Andes and the Amazon, indigenous mobilization ensued therefore to defend, and extend, these distinct forms of local autonomy. These two broad comparative claims parallel those made in the Ecuadorian chapter.

Third, the Bolivian case study provides *additional* leverage to analyze how variations in the degree of local autonomy from the state also had distinct *geographic* and *temporal* patterns even *within the Andes*, where two rounds of indigenous organizing occurred in two distinct Andean departments with varying degrees of local autonomy. As this book's main argument suggests, Andean indigenous organizing first occurred precisely in those Andean regions (La Paz, in particular) that had sustained significant local autonomy from the state (and haciendas) and subsequently were most immediately threatened by changing citizenship regimes and corresponding state policies. In this regard, this chapter reinforces claims made in Chapters 1 and 3 about the uneven reach of the state, the unwitting emergence of local enclaves of political autonomy, and the corresponding mobilization of local movements to defend that autonomy. However, this chapter in turn highlights that geography is not destiny and that time and sequence can shift strategic calculations for indigenous communities in less autonomous regions. Indeed, with the emergence and initial success of the first-generation of indigenous movements, other self-identified indigenous movements followed in the less autonomous regions. This later generation of indigenous organizing appeared to be more strategic in their indigenous discourse – more aware of how an indigenous discourse proved to be a more useful way to secure material and political ends than had other forms of class-based organizing. These movements were still responding to the impact of changing citizenship regimes, political associational spaces extended by democratization, and existing networks. But their incentive was not necessarily to defend indigenous communities, as with the first round, but in most cases to create a new economic safety net for those disenfranchised by privatization schemes.

Finally, the conclusion discusses how the vagaries of Bolivian democracy and electoral politics have at times weakened the organizational momentum and policy achievements of Bolivia's indigenous movements. The regional organizations that emerged in the Andes and the Amazon ultimately were divided by partisan competition, made clear once the organizations entered and faltered in the electoral arena. As such, the organizations lost some of their cache and organizational base – first in the Andes in the mid-1980s and later in the Amazon in the 1990s.

Given the regional and temporal variation in the Bolivian case, the chapter is divided as follows. Part I explains the emergence of Bolivia's Andean indigenous organizations – recounting both the macrohistorical developments and the microregional variations that have taken place. Part II explains the emergence of Bolivia's Amazonian indigenous organization, its successes in the mid-1990s, and the obstacles it faced at decade's end. The conclusion ends with a discussion of the ambiguous relationship between democratic politics and social movements. While democracy extended greater political associational space, it also provided the context in which partisan competition and the lure of political office divided some movements that had previously maintained a more united front.

Part I: The Bolivian Andes: The Kataristas and Their Legacy[1]

In the 1970s and early 1980s, the Katarista movement gained prominence in Bolivia. A young group of Aymara men started to proclaim the importance of their indigenous culture, identity, and cosmology. They asserted the importance of reclaiming their dignity, their past, and their future. With grand words and deeds, they captured the imagination of many Aymara men and women. In the university, communities, political elections, and union politics, they began to announce the importance of being Aymara. Through language, symbols, and political competition, they sought to force Bolivia not only to reflect on its decision to reject its Indian past but also

---

[1] I use the word *legacy* to refer both to the legacy on which the Kataristas drew and the legacy that they bestowed.

to embrace that Indian past as part of a contemporary and forward-looking politics. While some Kataristas focused on urban politicking, others focused on capturing the peasant movement. The latter would prove the most successful, experiencing a meteoric rise in mobilizational, organizational, and leadership capacities by the end of the 1970s.[2]

Why and how do we explain the emergence (and later decline) of this movement, one that would fundamentally redefine organizational politics, discourse, and policy in Bolivia; one that would reject a class identity and proclaim the centrality of their previously maligned indigenous identity? Part I adopts a comparative historical frame that focuses on changing citizenship regimes. In particular, it explains how the erosion of corporatist citizenship regimes that were created in the aftermath of the 1952 Revolution challenged local autonomy and motivated indigenous communities to mobilize.[3] However, only where indigenous activists could capitalize on both preexisting networks and political associational space did indigenous movements emerge.

The Corporatist Citizenship Regime: National Federations, Local Autonomy

The 1952 Revolution represented a critical juncture in Bolivia.[4] As in Mexico, the revolution occurred on the heels of popular mobilization in the city and countryside and marked the formal demise of an old elite and the rise of a new class tied to the political party, the *Movimiento Nacionalista Revolucionario* (MNR). The MNR came to power and did so, in no small measure, on the shoulders of a radically mobilized peasantry. Following the revolution, rural mobilization escalated, particularly in La Paz, Oruro, and Cochabamba but also in the north of Potosí and Chuquisaca,

---

[2] Rivera (1987: 37) notes that there were was an indigenous movement that emerged between 1910–1930 and primarily fought to regain access to communal lands, gain recognition of indigenous authorities, gain access to social services, secure representation in the legislature, and abolish obligatory military service and tribute. While perhaps a precursor to the late-twentieth-century indigenous movements, this earlier movement did not acquire the national stature of the movements discussed in this chapter.

[3] For histories of earlier state efforts to control and/or abolish indigenous communities, see Pearce (1984: 313–16); Rivera (1987: 18–19); and Antezana Salvatierra (1992: 73–176). However, despite these efforts, local forms of authority persisted (Weeks 1947: 6 and Rivera 1987: 26–7). For accounts of historic distinctions between the highlands and the valleys of Cochabamba, see Platt (1982); Godoy (1990); Klein (1992); and Larson (1998, particularly ch. 9).

[4] See Malloy (1970); Dunkerley (1984); and Klein (1992).

as peasants began refusing to work for landlords, occupying lands, and demanding expropriation (Dunkerley 1984: 66–7). In this context, the MNR implemented a series of populist measures that included the attempt to organize society into class-based groups, the growth of social services, land reforms, and various efforts to become a one-party regime (again, like Mexico). Political science texts have tended to focus on the nationalization of the tin mines (the country's primary export earner) and the consolidation of a significant labor movement. And indeed, this was the primary focus of much of the MNR project – or at least the left wing of this conglomeration of forces. However, there is a *rural* side to this revolution, and its resulting corporatist citizenship regime, that is more consequential for explaining the indigenous movements that subsequently emerged in the 1970s.

The MNR fundamentally attempted to incorporate the countryside into the political system. It did so by extending citizenship rights; in particular, universal suffrage was passed, without restrictions. Moreover, the MNR started to allocate political positions to peasants, at various levels of government – including the legislature and executive. Rural education was also expanded – according to official figures, leading to an increase in the rural student body by 564 percent between 1952–1974 (Albó 1983: 6). Party and state officials attempted to coax the image of a national polity and downplay any reference to Bolivia's multiethnic indigenous population, which was an overwhelming majority of the population. Accordingly, they referred to Indians as "peasants." Indeed from the 1952 revolution on, most official documents, union documents, and public discourse highlighted the class identity of Indian peasants as the primary and perhaps sole public identity – with the assumption that indigenous identity would subside. This class-based transformative project was publicly institutionalized in two ways: land reform measures and corporatist peasant unions.

With the 1953 land reform, the new politicians tackled an extremely high concentration of landholdings (see Table 5.1).[5] The World Bank reported, according to Eckstein (1983: 108), that Bolivia had the highest Gini Index for land concentration in Latin America: "Four percent of the landowners held 82 percent of the land." Rivera (1987: 64–7) also reports that prior to the land reform some 8 percent of landholders held 95 percent of the country's cultivable land; of that, only 0.8 percent had been cultivated. While

---

[5] Eckstein (1983: 108); Dunkerley (1984: 19); and Rivera (1987: 64).

Table 5.1. Distribution of Agricultural Property in Bolivia before Land Reform

Size of Farms in Hectares	Farms		Total Area of Farms		Total Cultivated Area		Ratio Cultivated Area/Total Farm Area
	No.	%	Ha.	%	Ha.	%	
Less than 10	59,988	(69.4)	132,964	(0.41)	65,981	(10.2)	49.6
From 10 to 500	19,437	(22.5)	1,467,488	(4.48)	344,385	(52.6)	23.5
More than 500	6,952	(8.1)	31,149,398	(95.11)	243,892	(37.2)	0.8
TOTAL	86,377	(100.0)	32,749,850	(100.0)	654,258	(100.0)	2.0

Source: Rivera (1987: 67). Based on data from the Department of Planning and Coordination of the Republic of Bolivia, 1970: 410.

70 percent of landholders held less than .5 percent of the cultivable land.[6] Land reform was a means, therefore, to challenge the oligarchy and its control of the countryside.

The land reform had several goals but was primarily designed to reallocate land ownership.[7] The reform distributed land in three ways: 1) those who could demonstrate land use/occupation prior to 1953 on lands that had no outstanding claims to ownership, gained the legal right to that land; 2) *latifundios* that claimed ownership of large tracts of land but did not work that land directly, had those lands expropriated and, in turn, distributed to their tenant farmers; and 3) colonization was promoted in the outer-areas of the Andes and Amazon to encourage migration away from more densely populated Andean regions (World Bank 1996b, vol. 2: 161–2).[8] Jorge Múñoz, a scholar of land reform processes in Bolivia, concluded that the program was largely successful, distributing approximately one-third of the country to poor campesinos.[9] In a World Bank report that Múñoz helped to draft, it was reported that "[b]etween 1955 and 1993, CNRA [Consejo Nacional de Reforma Agraria] affected 20,547,000 hectares and benefited some 548,776 families in the six Andean departments of the country (see appendix 5-2, table 5-7)" (World Bank 1996b, vol. 2: 163–4).[10] Perhaps more significant than land distribution was freeing up the rural labor force, according to Albó. It is estimated that over 70 percent of the economically active population worked in agriculture with over 80 percent of the total population living in two departments, La Paz and Oruro (Dunkerley 1984: 18, 20). Whereas workers sometimes were compelled to work some three to five days out of the week for a landlord, the land reform gave them the resources to work for themselves (Albó 1983: 34). Hence the land reform and freeing of the labor force created a new kind of autonomy in the countryside – greater formal freedom from landlords, greater access to lands, and the

---

[6] Dunkerley (1984: 19) also highlights severe inequalities in land distribution but presents different figures, based on the 1950 *Censo Nacional Agropecuario*. According to his data, over 60 percent of properties were landholdings under five hectares and totaled just over .06 percent of all lands cultivated. By contrast, just over .06 percent of properties were farms of over 1,000 hectares but they claimed over 47 percent of all cultivated lands.

[7] See Heath (1955: 3) and Dunkerley (1984: 72–3).

[8] The last of these will be discussed in the section on the Amazon.

[9] Jorge Múñoz interview, May 31, 1997. Twenty-five years after the reforms, the Ministry of Peasant and Agropecuarian Affairs indicated that 569,913 titles had been distributed to some 404,976 beneficiaries (Albó 1983: 27–34).

[10] Urioste and Baldomar (1998: 152) cite different figures. They claim that between 1953 and 1996, the CNRA granted forty-three million hectares to 618,000 beneficiaries.

greater corresponding space to negotiate daily life according to individual and community norms.

The land reform policy coincided with an effort to create corporatist modes of interest intermediation – part of which included the institutionalization of peasant unions that were formed in decades prior to the MNR governments. The revolutionary government followed the example of the Mexican revolution and attempted to build strong peasant unions that institutionalized support for the party, created mechanisms for the state to try to control peasants, and identified the union as the main interlocutor between peasants and the state: "It soon became apparent that the *sindicato* [union] would replace the hacienda as the central mechanism of social control and become the principal interface between government and the rural masses" (Dunkerley 1984: 74). As part of this effort, the MNR immediately created a Ministry of Indian and Peasant Affairs, which was subsequently renamed the Ministry of Peasant Affairs – an indication of the MNR's commitment to turn Indians into peasants.[11]

The creation of corporatist modes of interest intermediation entailed more than the construction of state institutions. It also entailed the effort to homogenize local community institutions into national peasant union structures. In this vein, the MNR attempted to transform all indigenous communities into "agrarian unions" and create a federated structure (Albó 1994: 57).[12] It sought to create a union for each province, a federation for each department (state), and a confederation for the entire country. To some degree or another this did occur. Certainly, we find that the MNR was able to create the federations and confederations. But the more interesting question is how effective they were in creating local level unions that tied local communities to the union (and by extension to the MNR and the state).

To "turn" the indigenous communities into agrarian unions, the MNR provided concrete incentives. As in Ecuador, only those rural inhabitants

---

[11] Prior to the revolution, the Bolivian state had formed an *Instituto Indigenista Boliviano* in 1941, but it did not adopt an autonomous political role in the country, according to Castro Mantilla (1996: 25).

[12] While the MNR was creating a federated union structure and seeking to incorporate indigenous communities into it, maintained that it was promoting indigenous authorities and communities as part of the land reform effort. The reform stated a commitment: "to restore to the indigenous communes the lands which were usurped from them, and to cooperate in the modernization of their agriculture, respecting and making use of their collectivist traditions insofar as possible" (Heath 1955: 10, quoting from the preamble to the agrarian reform). Heath observed, however, that few indigenous groups knew of this commitment in the reform.

who were organized into unions had the chance of gaining access to land and other resources. While this favoritism was not legal, state bodies did little to correct or punish the MNR for disproportionately benefiting union members (Heath 1955: 8). Incentives included "1500 percent discounts on certain price-supported goods, and which were given, together with arms and ammunition, to win allegiance to the Party. The opportunity to buy sugar at 50 bolivianos a pound when it was selling everywhere at 800, lured many men to sign their names" (Heath 1955: 8).

Efforts to create a widespread federated union movement were only partially successful, however, and varied by region (between the valleys of Cochabamba, the highlands, and the north of Potosí), according to Rivera (1987: 101–2). These regions varied with respect to the degree of hacienda presence and the inverse strength of indigenous communities. Where haciendas were most prevalent (i.e, in the valleys of Cochabamba), the haciendas had historically succeeded in subordinating indigenous communities to the patrón, and in displacing indigenous structures and authorities; in turn these communities were the ones most likely to become integrated into union structures. The reasons for this seem apparent; the state provided concrete gains for doing so, including the distribution of the expropriated hacienda lands on which they worked. Moreover, these communities possessed fewer organizational resources to combat union efforts to control them. Hence, union organizations were particularly vital and became even more so in the valleys of Cochabamba (a development that predated but was significantly advanced by the MNR revolution) (Ticona, Rojas, Albó 1995: 55). In short, in these regions, the creation of union networks essentially displaced the patrón as the mediator with the state and inserted union structures to perform this mediating role as interlocutor between community and the state. Simultaneously, the severance of patrón control provided local-level communities with a greater degree of local autonomy than previously.

While clearly not the intention of MNR organizers, these agrarian unions in Cochabamba became powerful in their own right – demanding land, governing at the local levels, affirming the peasants' place in the Bolivian nation, and demanding the peasant's right to citizenship. They became self-governing institutions at the local level – both within ex-haciendas and in campesino communities (Calderón and Dandler 1984: 45). Hence, while the MNR-based unions used a class-based rhetoric, they functioned in practice as a modernized version of a traditional communal organization (Albó 2002: 75).

In the highlands where haciendas had been considerably weaker, union penetration did advance but with less success than in Cochabamba. Union structures often displaced indigenous authorities as intermediaries between local indigenous communities and the state. Yet the reach of the state was less extensive. While the state did manage to establish control over Provincial Federations and Centrales (influencing leadership and direction), it was not able to control local communities (at the communal and subcentral levels), which often maintained significant autonomy from the state-sponsored corporatist peasant federation. Even though the names of community organizations changed to accommodate the union nomenclature, the roles that these unions played often varied little from the role that indigenous communities had played at the local level. In this region, hence, there was a form of syncretism – an accommodation of union nomenclature and a displacement of "indigenous leaders as interlocutors" but a basic maintenance of indigenous customs and practices at the local level. Accordingly, apparent accommodation in fact left indigenous authorities with significant control over this process. In many cases, they simply inserted union structures into preexisting indigenous community authority systems (or ayllus – kinship groups governed by a set of local-level indigenous authorities).[13] Indeed, in many communities, preexisting indigenous authority systems simply took on the names established by union organizations (Albó 1984b: 408 and 1997: 6; Hurtado 1986: 30, 58). As Albó states, and as I loosely translate: "Internally, traditional organizations continued to function; externally, however, they were known as union organizations."[14]

A third pattern emerged in the north of Potosí, where the two authority structures (union and ayllus) remained in conflict. In contrast to the two prior Andean regions, where union structures made significant although different inroads into these communities, in the north of Potosí, preexisting indigenous authority structures often fought off the penetration of union organizations into their communities, even while union organizations

---

[13] There is no predefined set of contours that define and regulate a community. The Bolivian landscape highlights how varied these communities have been, particularly in terms of size and geographic scope. For example, some are quite small, referring to one unit; in these cases, union structures coincided with the scope of ayllus. However, in other cases, ayllus were quite large and encompassed several communities – often geographically discontiguous ones. In some of these cases, the adoption of union nomenclature and organizations to mediate with the state did, over time, diminish the jurisdiction of these larger ayllus and increase the jurisdiction of their constitutive communities (cf Albó 1997: 6).

[14] "De cara adentro, seguirá siendo la organización tradicional; de cara afuera, se llamará central sindical" (Albó 1984: 417).

often did assume the mediating role between communities and the state.[15] Indeed, Albó (1997: 6) observes that even where there was a change in nomenclature to accommodate the MNR imperative of union organizing, indigenous communities at the local level often remained the predominant and central mode of governance. This is not to say that indigenous community structures did not change in this region, as of course they did. Rather, it is to say that they were less willing to succumb to the MNR's and later the military's imperative to incorporate the communities into a union structure. Ayllus in this region consolidated their hold over physical spaces through the land reform law, which distributed land to them with *títulos proindiviso* (Rivera et al. 1990: 20 and 1992: 62).[16]

In short, the MNR sought to transform the countryside but could not do so by fiat. Indigenous authority structures persisted to varying degrees behind the institutional shell of the peasant union federation. As such, indigenous authorities often maintained and promoted *local* forms of self-government (Urioste 1989: 242; Healy 1996; Ströbele-Gregor 1996; Albó 1997). Indeed, community leaders governed transactions over property disputes and transactions – much more so than state officials and institutions (World Bank 1996a: vol. I, 34).

The territorial jurisdiction of these communities was also not recognized . . . but in reality this [territorial jurisdiction] was maintained through traditional authorities, frequently coupled with a new style of organization, called a "campesino-union" [but very different from the classical worker unions] (Albó 1997: 22).

Forty years of sindicatos have failed, however, to eliminate traditional indigenous organizations such as the ayllu from the institutional landscape of Bolivia. Pockets of traditional leadership and organizational forms persisted in regions such as Oruro, Potosí, Chiquisaca, Beni, and Santa Cruz, despite the pervasive political, social, and economic pressure to weaken and marginalize them. In some areas, they have continued side by side with the sindicatos in a pragmatic modus vivendi. *The sindicatos had served outward relations and representation while the ayllu handled the "internal" matters of indigenous and community affairs* (Healy 1996: 256, emphasis added).

---

[15] See Rivera (1990 and 1992) and Ticona, Rojas, and Albó (1995).

[16] In a 1990s study of the ayllus and their relationship with the state, anthropologists found a) that ayllus were progressively stronger the further south one traveled from the south of Oruro to the north of Potosí. Moreover, they found that ayllus tended to exist and understand themselves as a separate political unit, independent of the state. Indeed, many members of ayllus in the region were ill-informed about the role and responsibilities of the state and were dissatisfied with the low levels of state support in the areas of education, health, and development (Molina and Portugal 1995). Also see Ayllu Sartañi (1995).

This corporatist form of citizenship regime persisted for several decades. Its urban and rural institutional components became the backbone of MNR rule, incorporation, and efforts at control.[17] Insofar as the corporatist citizenship regime granted local community autonomy, mobilization around ethnic cleavages was limited.

Within the peasantry this homogenizing and "civilizing" approach was at first accepted and internalized enthusiastically as the path of liberation. Thankful to the MNR for its agrarian reform, for massification of the Spanish-speaking culture through the rural schools, and for having made suffrage universal, these peasants kept the MNR in power at the polls and helped to put down subversive efforts. However, they maintained their difference (Albó 1994: 58).

Yet the corporatist citizenship regime was eventually challenged in the 1960s and 1970s through the creation of the Military-Peasant Pact – a pact that not only challenged the role of the MNR as mediator between community and state, but which also limited the autonomy of indigenous communities as well as the resources promised by the MNR. This erosion of the corporatist bargain ultimately challenged local indigenous autonomy and catalyzed a new generation of indigenous leaders to demand their rights as Indians, as Indian communities, and as Indian citizens. To explain why, when, and where these movements occurred, we must look at the interaction of three factors: when and where the erosion of the corporatist citizenship regime challenged local autonomy and provided the motive for organizing; when political associational space provided the opportunity to organize against these reforms; and where transcommunity ties provided networks for building regional and national organizations.

Erosion of the Corporatist Citizenship Regime: Take I

In 1964, the military government of General Rene Barrientos displaced the MNR from rule and sought to rupture the corporatist bargain. In particular, Barrientos attempted to rupture ties between the MNR and the peasant movement in order to link the peasant movement more clearly to the military government. The new military government institutionalized what is commonly referred to as the Military-Peasant Pact. The military sought to impose union leaders on communities and stifle community autonomy and activity. According to Jenaro Flores, who became the leader of the Andean indigenous movement, the military named peasant leaders who provided

---

[17] Rivera (1987: 105–6) and Albó (1994).

their support in response to payments and threats (i.e., that they would take away their land and/or that they would be labeled as communists).[18]

The Military-Peasant Pact futher eroded the legitimacy of the unions as an organic link or interlocutor between the state and local indigenous communities.[19] Moreover, the pact increasingly came to represent a union structure that maintained ties to the military but that was divorced from the communities that it claimed to represent.[20]

The military governments claimed a peasant base, articulated a discourse of strong peasant support, and deployed significant patronage to create and sustain ties with the peasantry, or at the very least with the peasant leaders who served as interlocutors between state and community.[21]

Nonetheless, by the mid-1960s the military was reallocating budgets and resources away from peasant interests and toward agro-business (Eckstein 1983: 115–16).[22] Over time, the actual impact of the land reform came into question. Not only did the land reform not provide the technical support once promised (Albó 1983: 7), but over time it actually benefited fewer people (i.e., those in agro-business) who received larger tracts of land.[23] Credit policy also favored the larger landholders (Albó 1983: 63 and Eckstein 1983). Moreover, the institutional mechanisms for overseeing the land reform, particularly the titling of lands, was inefficient, with competing levels of government responsible for different stages of the process and with sufficient ambiguity about who had jurisdiction at various stages to lead to incomplete, unsynthesized, and often conflicting land-titling records.[24]

The state's declining commitment to the peasantry was also evidenced by several political decisions. For example, the state merged the Ministry

---

[18] Jenaro Flores, interview, October 24, 1995.

[19] Jenaro Flores, interviews, October 30, 1995 and May 26, 1997 and Víctor Hugo Cárdenas, interview, June 19, 1997.

[20] Dunkerley (1984: 132–3); Rivera (1987: 112–13); Jenaro Flores, interviews, October 30, 1995 and May 26, 1997; and Víctor Hugo Cárdenas, interview, June 19, 1997.

[21] Dandler (1984: 39–40); Dunkerley (1984: 132–3); Gamarra and Malloy (1988: 20); and Jenaro Flores, interviews, October 30, 1995 and May 26, 1997; and Víctor Hugo Cárdenas, interview, June 19, 1997.

[22] Eckstein (1983: 125–9) highlights the ways in which foreign creditors – foreign capital, the United States Inter-American Agricultural Service, and the IMF influenced and/or oversaw this shift away from peasant-oriented policies and toward large farmers.

[23] See Albó (1983: 42); Eckstein (1983); and Dandler (1984: 35).

[24] World Bank (1996; vol. 2, 163); Múñoz and Lavadenz (1997); Urioste and Baldomar (1998: 152); Isabel Lavadenz, interview, August 5, 1997; and Jorge Múñoz, interview, May 31, 1997. This has been particularly a problem in Santa Cruz, Chapare, and northern La Paz (World Bank 1996; vol. 2, 163).

of Peasant Affairs with the Ministry of Agriculture. By 1969 the Ministry of Agriculture received a declining percentage of the national budget: "Between 1967 and 1973, the portion of state agricultural resources allotted to the Ministry of Agriculture (and in the relevant years, to the Ministry of Peasant Affairs as well) dropped from 24 to 4 percent (USAID 1974: 189)....Thus, post-1964 governments have restricted the activities of a ministry which, in conjunction with the revolution, was established to address peasant interests" (Eckstein 1983: 115–16). Moreover, the government announced stabilization measures and tax proposals, including the 1968 tax on the agrarian sector, that were disadvantageous for indigenous peasants (Gamarra and Malloy 1988: 30 and Albó 1991: 311).[25]

The effort to convert the 1952 MNR pact with the peasantry into the Military-Peasant Pact was most successful in those rural areas where the state had already been most successful in incorporating the peasantry and where patron–client ties had been most clearly established – namely, Cochabamba. Here, state-controlled unions had most successfully penetrated local communities and displaced already weakened indigenous authority structures. Hence, while Cochabamba was historically the site of the most active peasant organizing, it was also the site of the most consistent support for the regime.[26]

The limits of that support, however, were demonstrated by the military regimes' ongoing chipping away at the corporatist citizenship regime in the countryside. In 1974 the military government enacted a monetary devaluation on the order of 666 percent. The government also announced an economic package that resulted in a 100 percent increase in prices for manufactured staples such as sugar, rice, noodles, flour, and oil. This was coupled with frozen prices for agricultural goods. Parallel to this, the military government tried to impose peasant leaders at the VII departmental congress of peasants (Dunkerley 1984: 209–10 and Hurtado 1986: 63–4).

These measures were followed by urban protests, demonstrations, and strikes. Within days of announcing the economic package, some 20,000 peasants initiated protests that blocked off several key highways (Hurtado 1986: 64–5). Rivera (1987: 120) reports that they were protesting the fact that the government was reneging on the corporatist agreements first

---

[25] Various independent left peasant organizations emerged in this context, including the Independent Peasant Block (Albó 1991: 311 and Ticona 1996: 10).

[26] It is also often claimed that because Barrientos originated from Cochabamba and was able to speak to the people in Quechua, that he created strong ties there (Malloy and Gamarra 1988: 18).

institutionalized with the 1952 revolution; the price rise affected precisely those crops that had been rationed by the 1952 revolution. Moreover, they protested their declining influence, which contrasted with their capacity in the 1950s to influence some key government decisions. After negotiations short-circuited, the government responded by massacring those who had blocked the highways (Dunkerley 1984: 212–13; Hurtado 1986: 65; Rivera 1987: 122).

The military government acted to defuse tensions and incorporate the peasantry back into the state-dominated peasant union prevalent in the countryside. Combining repression with clientelist gifts, the government weakened opposition in Cochabamba. Through the 1970s, an active form of peasant organizing occurred in Cochabamba, largely through the state-dominated peasant federation.

The state's actions did not have the same impact in other Andean regions, however. In La Paz, peasants had already started to voice resentment of the Peasant-Military Pact for imposing new institutions and leaders and for reneging on the promises made with the 1952 MNR revolution. They interpreted the repression in Cochabamba as further evidence of the need to mobilize autonomously. Indigenous peasants in La Paz, therefore, started to mobilize along ethnic lines to demand the right to local autonomy and to an autonomous organization.

The question remains: Why would these two regions, Cochabamba and La Paz, have such distinct reactions to the erosion of the corporatist citizenship regime? Autonomous indigenous organizing emerged *first* in La Paz, precisely because La Paz had historically maintained a greater degree of autonomy from the state and, therefore, had maintained more autonomous political and cultural identities (Hurtado 1986: 228). This was particularly so among the Aymara in Aroma, La Paz (as well as parts of Oruro). Indigenous communities had maintained indigenous authority systems to a degree not found in Cochabamba.

The Aymaras have relatively greater autonomy vis-à-vis the State, which could control unions at the central and subcentral level, in addition to the departmental and national level, but failed to perforate the community's union which, although isolated in its localism, maintained itself as even more impermeable to the influence of the State in comparison to the unions in the valleys. *So when the scheme imposed by the MNR and the military pact deteriorated and started to crack, it became much easier for the Aymaras to move to the offensive. As Albó notes, the Aymara communities had greater organizational reserves with which to reemerge* (Hurtado 1986: 229, emphasis added).

This regional difference maps onto the subregional historical variations mentioned previously. While indigenous community structures in La Paz maintained a significant amount of their community integrity under the weight of government-imposed union structures and relatively weaker market penetration, indigenous communities in Cochabamba were often displaced by union structures and market forces that had more successfully subordinated and/or displaced indigenous community institutions in prior periods. In this context, the region of La Paz was structurally more predisposed to organize around "Indian" demands – particularly once military reforms threatened to undermine the levels of local autonomy secured with the corporatist citizenship regime.[27]

In short, the impulse to organize along indigenous lines came from the erosion of citizenship regimes and the challenges that it posed to local autonomy. Yet the impulse or motive to organize did not translate everywhere into indigenous movements. Only where political associational space also combined with the capacity to activate and build on preexisting indigenous community networks did indigenous movements emerge. Where these factors (challenges to local autonomy resulting from the erosion of corporatist citizenship regimes; political associational space; and networks) combined in areas of strong local indigenous authority structures, indigenous movements emerged – as in La Paz.[28] Here, a new generation of indigenous leaders mobilized around and for indigenous identities.

Building the Katarista Networks in the City: Schools and Unions[29]

The move to organize publicly around an indigenous identity first emerged in discussions among several Aymara youth from the provinces of La Paz,

[27] The highlands (where La Paz is located) depended more than other regions on subsistence farming. The highlands remained the site of poor land–producer ratios and limited resources. Moreover, they lacked technical and economic assistance, education, health services, among a long list of other state-promised services that remained nothing more and nothing less than promises (Hurtado 1986: 238). La Paz's resource-poor environment meant that any changes in resource allocation or land defense directly affected the lifeline (not just the livelihood) of these Andean peasants.

[28] Where these factors combined with weaker local indigenous authority structures – as in Cochabamba – indigenous movements did not take off until *much* later – a point to which I return later in the text. In these cases, a second generation of indigenous movements emerged.

[29] This section draws on Hurtado (1986); Rivera (1987); Cárdenas (1989); Albó (1991); and Mornissen (1995). It also draws on several 1995 and 1997 interviews with Jenaro Flores, Víctor Hugo Cárdenas, and Constantino Lima, who were key actors in the indigenous movements that emerged.

who had migrated from the rural areas to the capital to pursue secondary and university degrees. These young activists drew on and built the first network. Youth came into contact with one another, gained a common political language that enabled them to communicate among themselves and to their communities. Inspired by the writings of Fausto Reinaga, they began to discuss the ways in which they had been discriminated against as Indians and the rights that they should have as Indians. They came to see their plight as the result of racial discrimination, exploitation, and segregation. By organizing movements and political parties, they sought to rectify this situation. These incipient discussions became known in the secondary schools as the *Movimiento 15 de Noviembre* (November 15th Movement) and in the university as *Movimiento Universitario Julián Apaza* (MUJA, the University Movement, Julián Apaza).[30] Yet, these movements actually cloaked two very different approaches to indigenous organizing and indigenous rights.

One approach advocated the development of an Indian movement that solely organized, represented, and advocated Indian rights. This group largely came from Pacajes, La Paz and became known as the *Indianistas* (Hurtado 1986: 262). They identified the source of their subordination in racism. Their strategy for change was to create greater Indian representation in and influence over the state. Constantino Lima recalls that this movement was quite vocal in denouncing racism and in demanding their rights as Indians. Most Indianistas were young, recently urbanized Indians who started organizing in urban barrios to gain support for the party (and later parties) that they formed.[31] They chose to organize through political parties – first in 1960 as the *Partido Acción Nacional* which, after various divisions, relabelings, and reorganizing, was renamed the *Movimiento Nacional Tupak Katari* in 1968 and finally the *Movimiento Indio Tupak Katari*

---

[30] Ramón Conde Mamani, interview, June 25, 1997 – student leader of MUJA. Conde notes that MUJA was founded in 1971 but claims that MUJA was most prominent during the period 1978–1985 (a period of political opening). At its height, it had about forty members, of whom twenty were very active. MUJA largely engaged in urban-based work at the university. They sought to increase awareness and pride of indigenous identity and to distinguish between a criolla/mestiza national identity and Indian national identity. They also engaged in university politics to shape the terms of fellowships and matriculation. MUJA did engage in some rural-based work. They attended peasant congresses and tried to inject an ethnic discourse and set of demands into an otherwise more class-based agenda. According to Conde, the majority of its members migrated from and maintained ties with rural communities.

[31] Constantino Lima, interviews, June 16, 1997 and July 15, 1997.

(MITKA) in 1978. Constantino Lima explains that this renaming reflected two important debates. First, they chose to see themselves as a movement and not as a party. The latter suggested that they were only a "part" while they wanted to project the image that they were the "whole" and in motion. Second, they chose after much debate to insert the word *Indian* into the name of their organization as a way to project the centrality and importance of their subjugation as Indians and their need to struggle against this racism.[32] "As Indians they subjugated us, as Indians we will liberate ourselves."[33] Most organizing occurred in the city. While Lima denies any great distinction between military and civilian leaders (noting that they have all tried to subjugate Indians), it is striking that organizing efforts by Indianistas were most clearly successful during periods of political opening.

Yet even during times of political opening, the *Indianistas* did not gain widespread support. Clearly their urban focus delimited the potential scope of their partisan outreach given the then relatively low (although increasing) numbers of urbanized Aymaras; but this observation begs the question as to why they did not cultivate a sustained and strong following among this group. From a comparative perspective, it appears that the most telling explanation is rooted in the weakness of transcommunity *networks*. The Indianistas failed to draw upon and or build networks that would enable them to build a movement, to scale up their indigenous identity, and to sustain their support.

The second and more influential approach (and counterpart to the Indianistas) was adopted by the *Kataristas*, who more successfully drew on transcommunity networks. Their leaders also emerged in the context of discussions and organizing at the secondary and later university circles of Aymaras who had come to the capital to conduct their studies. But the Kataristas subsequently built on and captured the union networks of the countryside. These indigenous activists (who largely came from Aroma, La Paz) saw their struggle in different ideological and strategic terms (Hurtado 1986: 262). Ideologically, they agreed that colonialism had oppressed them for centuries. While the colonial period ended in 1825, a new period of internal colonialism ensued that continued to oppress and exclude Indians, even with the MNR revolution (Cárdenas 1989: 386). But they refused to reduce their struggle to either a racial issue or a class issue. Rather, the Kataristas, and Víctor Hugo Cárdenas (who three decades later served

---

[32] Constantino Lima, interviews, June 16, 1997 and July 15, 1997.
[33] Constantino Lima, interview, July 15, 1997.

as Bolivia's vice president, 1993–1997), in particular, sought to highlight the more complex reality of ethnic and class exclusion; Indians, by virtue of being Indians, were discriminated against just as Indians who were peasants confronted additional and equally central forms of exploitation (Cárdenas 1989: 383, 387–8, 399).

In this context, Kataristas began to organize along the intersection of ethnic and class lines. They rejected both the class-based line of *criollo* Marxists and the Indianista line (who were seen as racists looking more toward the past than toward the future).[34] Instead, they returned to their communities of origin, began to organize at the local level, and worked to gain positions of leadership in their local union organizations. The idea was to gain control of the military-controlled peasant union, and to grant their communities both greater autonomy from the state and access to the latter's resources. In the process, they did not simply seek to gain control of preexisting organizations (ones that often merged with the traditional indigenous institutions, as mentioned previously), but also to create spaces to express and legitimate their indigenous practices and customs. Accordingly, young activists proposed inside *and* outside their communities the importance of using the *wiphala*, the multicolor flag; of playing indigenous musical instruments at events; and of commemorating indigenous martyrs.[35] Hurtado (1986: 230) notes that the Kataristas often found communities that knew little of or were little inspired by the history or symbolism of Tupak Katari. Nonetheless, they taught this history to link the contemporary challenge up to historical patterns of resistance. Jenaro Flores stated that in 1969, he and three other men (Adolfo Salazar, Antonio Quispe, and Tomás Santos) decided to commemorate indigenous martyrs and decided to erect a monument of Tupak Katari in the main plaza of Ayo-Ayo (in the Province of Aroma, La Paz);[36] they did so during President Torres's military government, which was considered democratic and tied to the people, according to Flores. These acts represented the symbolic shattering of the MNR's projection of a Bolivian (and hence homogeneous) "peasantry" and the assertion of the centrality of "indian-ness."[37] In this context, Kataristas announced: "Ya no somos los

---

[34] Víctor Hugo Cárdenas, interview, June 19, 1997.
[35] Jenaro Flores, interview, October 30, 1995 and Albó 1991: 312.
[36] Jenaro Flores was born in Sica Sica in the Province of La Paz, the same region as Tupak Katari (Albó 1984: 53).
[37] Víctor Hugo Cárdenas, interview, June 19, 1997 and Jenaro Flores, interview, October 30, 1995 and May 26, 1997.

campesinos de 1952" (We are no longer the peasants of 1952) (Albó 1991: 312).

The Aymara who formed the nucleus of these movements shared several characteristics. They had come to the city to gain an education and while there had not only gained increased exposure to racism but also to new ideas that advocated pride in being Indian. In the university, these new leaders also developed networks that would later be mobilized for indigenous organizing. They came from communities in La Paz that were the least well integrated into the market and union structures and, as such, saw the Military-Peasant Pact as an imposition from above that sat uncomfortably on top of indigenous authority structures, which not only survived but resented efforts to control and co-opt them (cf. Hurtado 1986: 32–4; Rivera 1987: 115). By 1968 they started to make some advances in securing local elected positions in the unions and to challenge, from below, the Military-Peasant Pact. In this endeavor, Jenaro Flores emerged as the leader.

La Paz, therefore, would follow a different trajectory than Cochabamba. In La Paz, the indigenous leaders that started to mobilize for change would come from communities that had sustained their indigenous authority structures and felt subordinated and manipulated by the Military-Peasant Pact. The virtues of the pact seemed distant to these communities, which saw it as an imposition. In this context, they would fight to gain greater local autonomy from it by trying to capture positions within the state-dominated peasant federation. In Cochabamba, by contrast, indigenous community institutions had been seriously weakened by market penetration and union organizing and there was a weaker impetus to defend community autonomy, which had shallower historical roots there. The Cochabamba communities would organize along indigenous lines only after the La Paz communities had done so with some success.

Degrees of Political Associational Space and Movement Emergence

While the commitment to organize an indigenous movement, to retake control of their communities and, eventually, to regain control of the national peasant movement was apparent by the late 1960s, its execution was stymied by two factors: opportunity and capacity. The opportunity was directly tied to the process of political opening and closure that the country experienced – with particularly acute and repressive closures during the military governments of Hugo Banzer Suarez (1971–1978) and Luis García Meza (1980–1981). Through their repressive practices they

171

Table 5.2. *Collective Protests in Bolivia (1970–2002)*

Government	Dates	# of Events	Months in Office	Monthly Average
Ovando-Tórres	1/1/70–8/20/71	734	19.6	37.45
Banzer[a]	8/21/71–7/21/78	952	83.1	11.46
Pereda-Padilla	7/22/78–8/6/79	269	12.5	21.52
Guevara-Gueiler	8/7/79–7/17/80	357	11.3	31.59
García Meza	7/18/80–10/10/82	481	26.8	17.95
Siles (UDP)	10/11/82–8/4/85	1,825	33.8	53.99
Víctor Paz (MNR)	8/5/85–8/6/89	1,180	48	24.58
Jaime Paz (MIR)	8/7/89–8/6/93	968	48	20.17
Sánchez de Lozada (MNR)	8/7/93–8/6/97	631	48	13.15
Banzer (ADN)	8/7/97–8/6/01	1,364	48	28.42
Quiroga (ADN)	8/7/01–2/28/02	185	6.8	27.21
TOTAL		8,946	385.9	23.18

[a] The Banzer government divides into two periods. A civil-military government from August 1971 to November 1974 was followed by a purely military government from November 1974 to July 1978. Protests per month were relatively similar across the two periods – 12.40 and 10.63, respectively.

Source: Laserna Roberto and Miguel Villarroel, eds. *Bolivia: 32 años de conflicto social*. Cochabamba: Ceres. 2004: Table 23. Printed with permission from authors.

severely constrained political associational space and delegitimated the official unions – consequently providing a reason to join the opposition. As Table 5.2 demonstrates, the average number of monthly protests dropped accordingly. Conversely, during the military and civilian governments of Alfredo Ovando Candia/Juan Jose Torres G. (1969–1971), Walter Guevara Arce (1979), Lidia Gueiler Tejada (1979–1980), and Hernán Siles Zuazo (1982–1985), there was greater political associational space and a corresponding rise in the average number of monthly protests.

The Kataristas found their first great opportunity to organize with the death of Barrientos and the political opening associated with the military governments of Ovando and later of Torres (1969–1971). Ovando oversaw various national-populist measures. He derogated the 1965 Law of State Security and extended basic civil rights, including the rights associated with union organizing. These expanded civil and union rights did not travel easily, however, to the countryside, where the military government maintained the basic structure of the Military-Peasant Pact (Hurtado 1986: 42). With the military government of Torres that followed shortly thereafter, there was a bit more opening to the countryside, as Torres tried to gain peasant support. In this regard, he effectively extended political associational space, albeit during military rule.

It is precisely during this period that the Kataristas started to organize energetically to form peasant organizations that were autonomous from the Military-Peasant Pact. They started to organize publicly – proudly using a discourse and wielding flags that announced the centrality of their indigenous identity. They also started to reorganize the national peasant confederation, the Confederación Nacional de Trabajadores Campesinos de Bolivia (CNTCB) (Rivera 1987: 112).

A new generation of leaders started to displace those leaders who had previously supported Barrientos – first in the provincial unions of La Paz and later in more senior positions in several departments. Jenaro Flores, was elected Secretary General of his community (Antipampa Collana in Aroma Province) in 1969 and shortly thereafter was elected to the same position at the subcentral level. By 1970, these new leaders had assumed some key positions throughout the Department of La Paz, namely in Aroma, Pacajes, Carñavi, and elsewere. But they also displaced Military-Peasant Pact leaders at the departmental levels in La Paz, Oruro, and Potosí (Hurtado 1986: 36). "Jenaro Flores Santos and Macabeo Chila were appointed to senior executive posts in the departmental federations of La Paz and Oruro, respectively. Roughly the same thing was happening in other departments and, at the Sixth National Congress of the CNTCB held in Potosí on 2 August 1971 (a few days before the fall of Torres), Jenaro Flores was selected Executive Secretary of the most important peasant federation in Bolivia" (Rivera 1987: 112).

To draw the youth into community and union affairs, Flores advocated the creation and extension of soccer leagues. Soccer leagues helped to build and extend networks to a sector, the indigenous youth, who would not naturally have become involved in the new wave of organizing without some other incentive (Hurtado 1986: 37).

To create an autonomous space from the state, the Kataristas also founded the *Centro Campesino Tupak Katari* in 1971, which was designed as a civic and sociocultural center. At base, they hoped to create links between urban and rural Aymara, to maintain cultural ties, and to create and sustain a support base for the Kataristas within the CNTCB. They did so through the radio, which was the most effective means of reaching out to a dispersed set of communities (Hurtado 1986: 52–4). Parallel radio efforts were initiated by other independent development agencies and church-affiliated research-advocacy groups, including the *Centro de Investigación y Promoción del Campesinado* (CIPCA), which broadcast history courses through the Radio San Gabriel radionovelas about events and personages such as Julián Apaza, union organizing, and other allegories.[38] CIPCA conducted research and promoted development among the Aymara. As part of the participatory and grassroots efforts, they also wrote radionovelas that presented Aymara history in Aymara. Xavier Albó, who was one of the three cofounders of CIPCA, emphasized the importance of these radio programs. They helped to highlight that problems confronting communities were not only local issues but also national in scope.[39] Similarly, they put out popular education pamphlets (Hurtado 1986: 256–9; Healy 1996: 261).

CIPCA, in fact, created a hospitable working environment for many who became and/or worked with the Kataristas. Víctor Hugo Cárdenas, first worked at CIPCA and emerged in the 1970s as an important spokesperson for the Kataristas. An educator, he spoke with great fluency and authority. In one of his several radio interviews, he explained that Indians have been subjugated continuously since colonial times. Rejecting official national history, he observed that with independence from Spain, Bolivia entered a period of neocolonialism that has continued to this day – despite the land reform and literacy laws. He observed, however, that one cannot reduce the exploitation to either an ethnic or class one, that they form part of a more complex and interrelated context in which Aymaras find themselves dominated as Indians and as peasants. In other words, he cautioned that one cannot reduce ethnicity to class or vice versa (Cárdenas 1989).

This period of political opening was short-lived and so too was the initial period of public indigenous organizing. Following Torres's overthrow by Banzer in 1971, the new military government antagonized the Kataristas and thwarted indigenous organizing (Albó 1983: 75 and 1991: 300; Mayorga 1988: 23–4). In this way, Banzer closed political associational space. At

---

[38] CIPCA was founded in 1971 by three Jesuits committed to working with the peasantry – although it soon became a research/advocacy center dominated by non-Jesuits. CIPCA first started working in the department of La Paz but in the second half of the 1970s also started to work in Cochabamba, Charagua (amongst the Guaraní), and Santa Cruz. Xavier Albó, interview, August 2, 1997.

[39] Xavier Albó, interview, August 2, 1997.

the worst moments of repression during the Banzer government, several Kataristas went into exile, their public political meetings were suspended, and union organizations that had gained a modicum of autonomy during the Torres government were harnessed by the military state. As later stated in the 1983 CSUTCB manifesto: "the coup which installed Banzer in power once more halted the independent development of the rural union movement and our organizations were left without leaders."[40] Yet, while political efforts to regain control of the regional and national peasant unions were stymied, efforts at the local level were sustained – in part because local union positions were often simply indigenous organizations with new labels, in part because the state's regional and national organizations rarely penetrated the local levels effectively (and therefore political associational space was curtailed but not destroyed at the local level), and in part because some of the Kataristas managed to sneak back into the country to continue organizing (Hurtado 1986: 58). Flores noted that it was difficult to work in the communities during this period. Hence they worked through the local indigenous authorities and/or the local union organizations.[41]

While peasant organizing per se was foreclosed, cultural and intellectual urban activities coming out of the university continued. Those in exile were able to use radio programs and cloaked language to get their message across to Aymaras in the highlands and to avoid government censure (Rivera 1987: 116–17). The *Centro Campesino Tupak Katari* (CCTK), for example, continued, until 1975 when it was closed, with its Aymara radio programs – presenting Kataristas themes through a discussion of Aymara history of struggles, demands, and memories (Hurtado 1986: 54). Moreover, churches and NGOs involved in rural development, including Oxfam, England and USA, NOVIB, and Bread for the World, provided networks through which the Kataristas mobilized communities and sustained their contact with them (Hurtado 1986: 58).

In this period of political closure, the Kataristas issued their first public document, the *Manifiesto de Tiwanaku*, in 1973, signed by the CCTK, the MINK'A Center, the National Association of Peasant Teachers, the Association of Peasant Students of Bolivia, and the PUMA Cultural Center. Tiwanaku is a sacred site in Aymara history and was chosen self-consciously

---

[40] CSUTCB's 1983 Political Manifesto, published in Rivera (1987: 197).
[41] Jenaro Flores, interview, June 10, 1997.

to symbolize the historic ties to indigenous culture, history, religion, and politics (Hurtado 1986: 58).

The manifesto is a complex document. As many actors and analysts of this period stress, the document highlights the intersection of indigenous and class struggle – drawing on and refining the ideas promoted by the indigenous/peasant wing of the Katarista movement. It celebrates an indigenous past and criticizes colonialism for dividing indigenous communities, assimilating them into a presumed mestizo culture, and imposing an uneven and inappropriate form of development. But the criticism is not just historical in focus. It also criticizes the 1952 MNR Revolution, including the land reform, universal suffrage, and educational policy, for having promoted individualism, power mongering, and co-optation.[42] So too it criticizes the national parties who claim to speak on behalf of the peasantry for using the peasantry as an electoral resource to be mobilized and manipulated without more sustained or fundamental participation. In turn, the peasant unions are portrayed as locally representative of the communities but nationally co-opted:

Although peasant unions at grass roots levels and in many of their regional organizations authentically represent the peasants, peasant unionization at [the] departmental and national level has often been used to further interests which are entirely foreign to our class. All the defects of urban party politics have been introduced into the rural areas through pseudo-leaders who have self-appointed themselves as peasant representatives. These leaders have corrupted and continue to corrupt our Aymara and Qhechwa people while the government looks on in a benevolent and indifferent manner. They are the people who have introduced sectarianism, political intrigue, nepotism, economic and moral corruption, personal ambition, hatred between brothers, false leadership and the lack of representativity into the countryside. But nothing has done as much harm as paternalism – the naïve expectation that solutions come from outside, from above. It is we the peasants ourselves who must develop the country and particularly the rural areas. Politically they have tried to treat us like children and both governments and bad leaders have always tried to offer us as "gifts" or "charity" what in reality should be given us out of justice.

It is a blot on our unblemished Inca history that our alienated peasant leaders should have proclaimed all recent Presidents of our country to be "Peasant Leaders." It would be best for us peasants if governments and political parties were to leave us

---

[42] This claim was repeated again in the CSUTCB's 1983 Manifesto, published in Rivera (1987: 196).

176

to elect our own leaders freely and democratically so that we could formulate our own socioeconomic policy inspired by our own cultural roots.[43]

Kataristas organizing clandestinely at the local levels used the Manifesto to inspire, train, and form cadre. This was often done under the auspices of the CCTK (Hurtado 1986: 60). The idea was to forge an autonomous peasant organization with a strong basis in indigenous culture to effect these changes. As stated in the documents: "There has been no revolution in the countryside; it has yet to be achieved. But there must be a revolution, one which holds up once again the banners and ideals of Tupak Katari, Bartolina Sisa. . . . The starting point of the revolution should be our people."[44]

With the 1974 massacre in Cochabamba (discussed previously), many of the Katarista organizations had to go underground and rural organizing became all the more difficult. While radio programs continued in Aymara, such as those broadcast by CIPCA (Rivera 1987: 126), and some Kataristas continued to operate within the government-controlled unions, the Kataristas' ascent was stymied by the closure of political associational space.

With the political liberalization that began in 1977, however, the Kataristas (who were both actors in pushing the political liberalization and beneficiaries of it) started to regain their public strength and, indeed, to recapture the national political positions that they had gained just before the crackdown. This is not to say that the political liberalization was clearly demarcated. Indeed, the period retrospectively described as the period of political transition (1978–1982), was one of great flux, with seven military governments and two civilian governments (Gamarra 1995: 15). Yet despite this instability, there was an opening of political associational space – particularly when compared to the Banzer military government (1971–1978).

Accordingly, there was the classic resurgence of civil society in 1977. One finds massive mobilizations against the regime, with the Kataristas taking an active role in the protests. In August 1977, the Kataristas issued the second Manifiesto de Tiwanaku. That same year, Flores and other Kataristas also started to reappear in public and reclaimed their positions in the CNTCB, based on the 1971 Potosí conference, which the military

---

[43] Manifiesto de Tiwanaku (1973), published in Rivera (1987: 174–5).
[44] Manifiesto de Tiwanaku (1973), published in Rivera (1987: 176).

government had overturned. The Kataristas also renamed the peasant federation, the CNTCB-Tupak Katari, highlighting the importance of Katarista currents. Before the fall of the Banzer government, they started to recapture union positions and, with the fall of the regime, gained complete control. By 1978, the Kataristas were poised to reemerge and gain control of the peasant movement. In March 1978, Flores was reelected Executive Secretary of the National Congress of the National Confederation of Peasant Workers of Bolivia – Tupak Katari.

Flores succeeded in gaining control of the main peasant federation; in overseeing the initial unification of various peasant federations and renaming the unified peasant confederation as the Confederación Sindical Única de Trabajadores Campesinos de Bolivia (CSUTCB);[45] and in initiating a more equal relationship with the dominant labor movement, the *Central Obrera Boliviana* (COB). According to Flores, the new peasant federation differed sharply from the old peasant federation, with communities actually electing their representatives (rather than accepting leaders imposed from outside).[46]

This was the beginning of the short-lived glory days for the Kataristas. While the CSUTCB could not be equated with a "Katarista Federation," in its initial years Kataristas dominated the important executive positions in the confederation. Flores, for example, was elected as Secretary General of the CSUTCB, a post that he held until 1987. Hurtado (1986: 142) observes that the CSUTCB's official history, the one that was propagated, was coterminous with the Katarista version of peasant indigenous struggle and ascent.

In 1979, the CSUTCB demonstrated its independence from the government. With the announcement of an International Monetary Fund (IMF)–recommended economic package simultaneously to freeze prices for agricultural goods and increase prices for fuel, transport, and basic consumer goods, the CSUTCB organized a national road blockade with local peasant unions blocking off thirty roads in every department in the country. The blockade paralyzed the country for over a week and was reported to be the largest peasant mobilization since the 1952 Revolution. Indeed, it was reported that the leaders could not always control mass-based mobilizations, which often preceded and accelerated at a faster pace than what was being

---

[45] The CSUTCB included the *Confederación Tupak Katari*, the *Confederación Independiente, Sector Huaynapaco*, and *the Federación Julián Apaza* (Hurtado 1986: 139).
[46] Jenaro Flores, interview, October 24, 1995.

advocated (at least publicly) by its national leaders (Dunkerley 1984: 273–4; Hurtado 1986: 160–85; Healy 1989: 3). The demands were not particularly ethnic in origin. They were clearly tied to material demands to regain access to resources that were being denied them. But it would be incorrect, therefore, to dismiss the movement as nothing more than an ethnically cloaked class movement.

Indeed, the Katarista leadership in the CSUTCB spearheaded several initiatives that politicized and publicized ethnic identities in unprecedented policy debates. In 1979, the CSUTCB began calling for a plurinational state (Albó 1991: 316). At the *Primer Congreso Político Indio*, held in November 1982, the leaders denounced discrimination against indigenous people.[47]

In their 1983 Political Manifesto, they also denounced efforts to reduce them to either a peasant or an Indian movement:

We, the current leaders, refuse to accept and will never accept class reductionist ideas which transform us to the status of mere "peasants." Nor do we accept ethnic reductionism which transforms our struggle into a confrontation between "Indians" and "whites." We are the heirs of great civilizations. We are also heirs to a permanent struggle against all forms of exploitation and pressure. We want to be free in a society where exploitation and organized oppression do not exist, in a state which, recognizing all national groups, develops our different cultures and authentic forms of self government.[48]

... [O]ur oppressors have attempted systematically to strip us of our historical identity by a variety of methods. They tried to make us forget our true origins and reduce us to mere peasants with no personality, history or identity. However, our entire history has demonstrated that we know how to resist such attempts. In this struggle for liberation we have held on to our character as Aymara, Qhechwa, Camba, Chapaco, Tupiwarani, etc. and we have learned that we can achieve liberation without losing our cultural and national identity, without being ashamed of what we are; we will recover our lost dignity.[49]

Indeed, for these reasons, they denounced the 1953 Land Reform once again not only for promoting individualism but also for fragmenting their community-based organizations.[50] The same manifesto declares that the rural unions that emerged in the wake of the land reforms were borrowed

---

[47] *Presencia*, November 24, 1982.
[48] 1983 Political Manifesto of the CSUTCB, published in Rivera (1987: 191).
[49] 1983 Political Manifesto of the CSUTCB, published in Rivera (1987: 200).
[50] 1983 Political Manifesto of the CSUTCB, published in Rivera (1987: 191).

and misplaced forms of organizing – imposed on top of and/or alongside traditional indigenous organizations.

Moreover, the CSUTCB proposed an Agrarian Reform Proposal in 1983–1984 that introduced ethnic demands into policy debates. Víctor Hugo Cárdenas is reputed to have drafted the proposal, in consultation with Xavier Albó and Silvia Rivera. However, it has also been stated that the proposal was drafted with significant consultation with and participation by indigenous communities – turning to communities for their input and feedback (Hurtado 1995: 135). The proposal sought to update the agrarian reform law of the 1950s. Among its many proposals was a demand for recognition of communal lands, cultural pluralism, and communal labor. These proposals essentially demanded that the state recognize and sanction the existence of indigenous modes of organizing, authority structures, customary law, and economic production at the local level rather than maintaining the fiction that the beneficiaries of land reform distribution were free agents that acted as individual peasants. In this sense, they rejected the homogenizing assumptions of existing state laws that dealt with residents in the countryside.

As part of this proposal, they wanted state reforms to develop and respect communal property rights, community organizations (which Cárdenas noted might be called sindicatos but are often ayllus by another name), communal political autonomy, and customary law (cf. Cárdenas 1985: 25–7).[51] Moreover, they demanded greater state services, particularly in education. While the proposal was submitted to Congress and to President Hernán Siles Suazo, in 1984, it was never brought to a vote.[52] Yet even if the proposal was not passed, it highlighted the importance of communal autonomy for all of Bolivia's indigenous movements – even to those groups that rejected the proposal as a whole.[53]

The ideas of communal autonomy and an indigenous national assembly were not dropped from the political agenda. These ideas were raised in

[51] The Congresses of Indigenous Authorities held in November 1986 and November 1988 also announced a commitment to strengthen indigenous authority structures and inter-community relations. See *Presencia*, November 26, 1986; *Hoy*, November 14, 1988; and *Presencia*, March 14, 1999. *Presencia* (April 7, 1990) reports on efforts to reconstitute the cabildo system in the Provincia de Aroma.

[52] Cárdenas (1985); Healy (1989: 20); Pinelo (1989: 244); Albó (1991: 316); Hurtado (1995); and Van Cott (2001: 194–5).

[53] "Encuesta a los partidos políticos sobre el proyecto de ley fundamental agraria." *Historia Boliviana: Revista Semanal*. Cochabamba, Bolivia, vols. 1–2 (1985): 29–44.

1988,[54] 1992,[55] 1994,[56] and 1996.[57] This pluricultural agenda eventually found some resonance during the administration of Gonzalo Sánchez de Lozada, 1993–1997 (a point discussed in Chapter 7). And it has been taken up full force by Felipe Quispe, the secretary general of the CSTUCB, as of this writing.

Second-Generation Movements

Neoliberal Reforms, the Valleys of Cochabamba, and the Cocaleros If the Kataristas were the first and most renowned indigenous movements in the region, they were later joined by other indigenous movements that emerged in the valleys (precisely those areas that did not first organize as Indian

[54] In 1988, a different version of the agrarian reform proposal resurfaced. In 1988, CSUTCB and CIDOB (the Amazonian indigenous federation discussed in Part II) formed joint committees to discuss the formation of *La Asamblea de Nacionalidades* (Assembly of Nationalities). The idea for the first assembly was first mentioned in the CSUTCB's *I Congreso Extraordinario*, where the importance of recognizing and organizing around communal power is mentioned several times over (Pinelo 1989: 83–9, 108). The assembly would have promoted the formal strengthening of local indigenous authority structures with a national institution that would have served as a forum for national level debates, discussion, and coordination among the local communities. While the initial idea was well received, it was never implemented – in part for fear of political manipulation or domination by one group (Ticona, Rojas, and Albó 1995: 209–10).

[55] For a discussion of the 1992 Assembly, see *Hoy* (October 13, 1992); *Ultima Hora* (October 13, 1992, October 14, 1992, October 15, 1992); *Presencia* (October 14, 1992, October 15, 1992, October 18, 1992); *La Razón* (October 14, 1992); and *Los Tiempos* (October 13, 1992, October 14, 1992, October 21, 1992). In 1992, the year coinciding with activities around/against the quincentennial of Columbus's arrival to the Americas and 500 years of indigenous resistance, the idea of forming an assembly of Indigenous Nations was floated again and an assembly was announced in mid-October. However the assembly confronted political divisions and significant internal debates that effectively suspended it.

[56] The CSUTCB's VI Congress in 1994 once again highlighted the importance of the *asamblea* as a political instrument: "We have to distinguish between unionism, which is an instrument of struggle, and our political instrument, which is the Assembly of Original Nations" (CSUTCB 1994: 31). This position was restated forcefully in the statutes that were published along with the documents from this conference (CSUTCB 1994: 92).

[57] The CSUTCB's VII Congress called for an *Asamblea de las Naciones Originarias y del Pueblo* – although the assembly is also referred to by three other names in the text (CSUTCB 1996: 15, 45–7, 71). While the discussion is short on details, the Congress promoted the idea of creating a political instrument that would both address class conflict and anticolonial struggles. In this sense, it would "articulate marxism, cosmovision, and liberation theology" (CSUCTB 1996: 69). Moreover it would set out to promote and achieve "COMMUNAL POWER based on the recuperation of territory, the defense of identity, and the support and development of production" (CSUTCB 1996: 71; also see 73–5).

movements in the 1960s and 1970s). In the 1980s and 1990s, a new round of indigenous organizing occurred among those who a) were adversely affected by a new round of state reforms, b) could build on preexisting networks and political associational space, and c) learned the *strategic* value of mobilizing along indigenous lines, as a result of the earlier successes of the Kataristas.

The turning point occurred in August 1985 when the government introduced the "New Economic Policy" (NEP, Decree 21060), colloquially referred to as "the Neoliberal Reforms." The NEP was designed to address hyperinflation that some report as having reached an unfathomable 25,000 percent in 1985,[58] budget deficits, balance of payments problems, and debt payments that totaled 70 percent of export revenues (Gamarra 1995: 18). Indeed, by 1985, the prices of Bolivia's major exports had also declined dramatically. To address this situation, the NEP essentially reversed many statist development policies and ruptured whatever remained of the corporatist pact founded by the MNR with organized sectors, including the peasantry. While this rupture had many antecedents, including various stabilization measures of the 1970s, during those earlier years the state had maintained the public commitment to active state involvement in economic development (Conaghan and Malloy 1994: 49). "Public sector investment and consumption... rose from 20 to 25 percent of GDP between 1974 and 1978" (Conaghan and Malloy 1994: 51). Having done this, the state could maintain the fiction that it was still committed to its organized corporatist base. The 1985 reforms shattered those images.[59] In that year, the state made no pretense about the peasant basis of the regime and actually dismantled several programs that had previously supported peasant communities. Among other things, the reforms removed price controls on and subsidies for agricultural products, petroleum and gas, and froze wages (Conaghan and Malloy 1994: 140, 144). The first of these severely

---

[58] Inflation figures for 1985 vary. Sachs and Morales (1988: 9) and Gamarra (1995: 18) report inflation reaching 25,000 percent in 1985. Pastor (1991) and Toranzo Roca (1996: 164) cite inflation rates of 8,000 percent for 1985. Arellano-López and Petras (1994) say 15,000 percent.

[59] This chapter largely focuses on those aspects of the NEP that ruptured the pact with the peasantry. For a more detailed discussion of the economic reforms, see Pastor (1991); Arellano-López and Petras (1994); Edwards (1995); Gamarra (1995); and Lustig (1995). For a discussion of the Emergency Social Fund designed to alleviate some of the hardships engendered by the NEP, see Graham (1992).

Table 5.3. *Evolution of Social Public Spending in Bolivia (1980–1989)* (*as percentage of GNP*)

	Education[a]	Ministry of Health[b]	Social Security[c]
1980	4.1	0.8	1.4
1981	2.9	0.5	1.2
1982	3.2	0.4	1.1
1983	3.4	0.4	0.8
1984	3.2	0.4	2.0
1985	3.3	0.4	1.0
1986	2.3	0.3	0.7
1987	2.6	0.5	N/A
1988	2.6	N/A	N/A

[a] Includes transfers from the central government to universities.
[b] National treasury funding of the Ministry of Social Welfare and Public Health; does not include either regional development corporation or municipal spending.
[c] Contribution of employees, employers, and government to social security system health plans.
Source: Morales (1994: 140). Based on data from World Bank.

challenged the corporatist agreement that the MNR had once made with the peasantry.

The decree froze wage rates for four months during a year when the annual inflation rate reached nearly 15,000 per cent, annulled all price controls, and reduced state food and fuel subsidies. This raised consumer prices by approximately 1,000 per cent. At the same time the Bolivian currency, the *peso*, was floated, with its value tied to that of the US dollar, and all exchange restrictions were removed. This resulted in an additional devaluation of the currency of about 100 per cent (Arellano-López and Petras 1994: 562).

Social services were cut in the initial two years of the NEP – measured as a proportion of social public spending to GNP (Morales 1994: 139). This was particularly notable in education and health (see Table 5.3). Morales (1994: 130) observes: "Although government programs that protect the most vulnerable social groups have not entirely disappeared, they have been greatly reduced." By 1988, however, there was a reported rise in social spending targeting the poor, some argue in response to World Bank pressures, which was confirmed by the World Bank (1996).

Healy (1989: 23) observes that the "CSUTCB's access to the Ministry of Agriculture and Peasant Affairs drastically changed." These measures were coupled with direct assaults on the labor federations. The government declared a state of siege, one of two during the Paz Zamora government (1989–1993). Moreover, the government harassed labor leaders, imprisoned some, and confined hundreds of others to remote places in the jungle (Conaghan and Malloy 1994: 193–5; Gamarra 1994: 205; Morales 1994: 145).

Simultaneously the state tried to set up a parallel official union federation and confederation. It called on peasant leaders active during the Military-Peasant Pact and deployed patronage to build support for the official union and to weaken the CSUTCB's constituency in the rural areas. This served to confuse people in the countryside, although its impact was not long lasting (Healy 1989: 23).

Among the most dramatic reforms was the closure of inefficient state mining enterprises. Tin mining had generated the highest (legal) contribution to foreign exchange. The closure ended in the dismissal of some 22,000–23,000 out of 28,000–30,000 workers at the state mining corporation, COMIBOL (Conaghan and Malloy 1994: 144; Healy 1997: 229). In several separate interviews, union leaders highlighted the importance of Decree 21060 (with no prompting from the author) to highlight how neoliberal reforms obliterated the historically important mining sector, liberalized agricultural prices, and liberalized trade – all of which had a detrimental impact on the rural sector.[60]

While the miners were not technically peasants, they did largely migrate from indigenous communities. With their dismissal, families lost a significant source of income. While some moved to urban areas, others returned to their communities of rural origin. Yet, interviewees told me that their communities were often incapable of absorbing them into the local economies. There was not enough land to go around and the land that was cultivated could not necessarily support the increase in numbers. Alejo Veliz also suggests that there were conflicts between the ex-miners and peasants in these communities, and the former were left with high levels of unemployment.[61] Moreover, according to Evo Morales, a good number of these ex-miners first returned to grow rice but found that with price liberalization, rice prices declined. Many ex-miners and other peasants therefore decided

---

[60] Román Loayza, interview, June 11, 1997; Alejo Veliz, interview, June 11, 1997; Nestor Bravo, interview, July 9, 1997; and Evo Morales, interview, July 30, 1997. See Nash (1992) for an account of the 1986 mining protest against these decrees.
[61] Alejo Veliz, interview, June 11, 1997.

to leave their communities of origin and move to the Chapare region to cultivate coca, a crop that promised good yields, international demand, and high prices.[62] Tin miners were known for labor radicalism. It is no surprise that this radicalism would carry over into the coca-growing communities in the Chapare.

Many indigenous ex-miners became politically active in the coca-growing regions in the Chapare. The Chapare offered the chance to either grow coca and/or to secure a job in the coca-paste processing pits. While exact figures do not exist, it is estimated that the number of those living in the Chapare more than doubled between 1984 and 1989 (Léons and Sanabria 1997: 14,18). Coca production skyrocketed in the years following the 1985 reforms. An estimated 250,000–300,000 people were involved in the coca industry (in one of its various stages of production and processing), an estimated 7 percent of the economically active population (Healy 1997: 229; Léons and Sanabria 1997: 18; Sanabria 1997: 172).

The first Andean Council for Coca Production was held in 1991. At its second council meeting in 1993, the assembly elected Evo Morales as president, who by the 1990s had become the undisputed leader of the emerging *cocalero* movement. The movement affiliated with the CSUTCB and has fought to valorize the coca leaf and to legalize its production and consumption. The growers claim that they are serving the indigenous community. Coca is a sacred leaf and is used both for ritual and for daily consumption. It is known to take the bite out of a cold night and to suppress hunger, both daily concerns for many indigenous men and women living in the highlands. They emphasize that while cocaine is processed from coca, that the two are distinct. A *New York Times* report on Morales indicates,

[o]nly a minority of the coca grown in the Chapare region, a main base of his support, winds up as cocaine, he says, arguing that most is used for traditional purposes. He says he is opposed to drug trafficking, but that the problem is one of demand. "The coca is not cocaine," he said (Juan Forero, *New York Times*, July 6, 2002).

The cocaleros have therefore, defended coca production as part of Indian culture and tradition – adopting some of the language used by the Kataristas in their earlier documents. They have woven an ethnic discourse about cultural rights and autonomy that has gained domestic and international attention. And in many ways, the growth of the movement has been bolstered

---

[62] Evo Morales, interview, July 30, 1997. Nash (1992: 277, 290) also reports that laid-off tin miners moved to Santa Cruz, Cochabamba, and the cocaine-producing regions in the Beni, the Chapare, and the Yungas.

by the very efforts to undermine it. Under pressure from the United States government, Bolivia has launched several unsuccessful attempts to destroy coca production in the Chapare – particularly in light of the ongoing debate over whether the coca produced in the Chapare primarily targets the indigenous market for coca or the export market for cocaine.

In this context, the cocaleros have grown in strength. They gained prominence within the CSUTCB in the 1990s, as illustrated by the election of Román Loayza as the Secretary General at the 1996 Congress of the peasant federation (Ticona 1996: 38).[63] They have gained greater access to the Ministry of Agriculture than any other peasant union since 1985 (Healy 1997).[64] And they have successfully fielded several political candidates in the formal electoral arena. In 1995, they succeeded in electing forty-seven concejales and ten mayors (Ticona 1996: 43). In the 1997 elections, the *Asamblea por la Soberanía de los Pueblos* (ASP), whose leaders came from the cocalero movement, unsuccesfully fielded Alejo Veliz for president but successfully fielded Evo Morales, Félix Sánchez, Néstor Gúzman, and CSUTCB president Román Loayza as national deputies for the term 1997–2002 (Urioste and Baldomar 1998: 157).[65] Morales has proven most visible in the legislature, building on and extending his national and international stature. In January 2002, he was expelled from the legislature on charges that he had instigated violence among the cocaleros. Weeks later he began campaigning for president, on the *Movemento al Socialismo* (MAS) ticket; in a field of eleven candidates, he came in second (which entitled him once again to assume a seat in the national legislature). Following the 2002 elections, his party, MAS became the second largest in the legislature. At the time of this writing, he continues to speak on behalf of the cocaleros, who continue to engage in mass protest.

---

[63] Reports published from CSUTCB's VI and VII Congresses (CSUTCB 1994 and 1996) also refer to the increasing power of the cocaleros within the CSUTCB.

[64] According to Evo Morales, the state has, however, consistently reneged on its commitments to include the cocaleros in decision making and in delivering alternative development projects to the communities. Evo Morales, interview, July 30, 1997.

[65] The ASP, founded in May 1995, self-consciously presented itself as an indigenous rights party – in particular mobilizing Quechua in the valleys of Cochabamba. Many of the ASP leaders were historically motivated by Guevarista principles of claim making and organizing. Unlike traditional Marxist organizing, however, the ASP expanded the idea of the people to include not only the proletariat but also indigenous people (Alejo Veliz, interview, July 18, 1997 and Evo Morales, interview, August 6, 1977). From this perspective, ASP was critical of contemporary democracy: "Democracy has been prostituted and invented. In practice, a true democracy does not exist" (Alejo Veliz, interview, July 18, 1997).

In short, the second-generation indigenous movement emerged to protest the harsh measures taken by the neoliberal citizenship regime. They did not necessarily emerge to defend local autonomy – as with the Kataristas before them – but soon came to talk about the needs and rights of their indigenous local communities in the Chapare. As such, they self-consciously started to talk about ethnicity as a key component of their political struggle. Strikingly, the second-generation movements assumed prominent positions in the very organization (CSUTCB) that the Kataristas founded. Their *contemporary* discourse around indigenous movements and local autonomy has even paralleled the Katarista discourse of the 1970s and 1980s. Perhaps it is not surprising then that Flores, one of the principal founders of the Katarista movement, remarked in 1997 that the ASP coincided with the ideals of the Kataristas and that the cocaleros were the only organized force in the contemporary period that had made gains for indigenous people.[66]

Movements to Defend Ayllus and Strengthen Local Autonomy The cocaleros were not the only ones to organize second-generation indigenous movements. Movements to defend ayllus and strengthen local autonomy emerged during the 1990s (Andolina, Radcliffe, and Laurie ms.; Ticona 1996). They included the *Federación de Ayllus del Sur de Oruro*, the *Federación de Ayllus Originarios del Norte de Potosí*, and the *Federación de Ayllus y Comunidades Originarias de la Provincia Ingavi*, among others. These movements self-consciously rejected the national organizational projects and strategies associated with CSUTCB and worked primarily at the local level to defend, nurture, and celebrate traditional indigenous authority structures. These efforts included the reaffirmation of the *ayllu*, indigenous identities, indigenous cultural values, communal organizations, or some combination thereof (Ticona 1996: 61–3). As part of this growing movement, several rural communities have relabeled their sindicatos (which were formed as part of the corporatist project) as ayllus.[67] The *Taller de Historia Oral Andina* (THOA) has also played an important role in working with local-level communities in this process.[68] Its radio programs and oral histories, in particular, have helped to strengthen and diffuse local narratives about historical origins and struggles. The goal in all cases has been to strengthen ayllus and local indigenous cultures.

[66] Jenaro Flores, interview, June 10, 1997.
[67] Ricardo Calla, interview, May 27, 1997.
[68] María Eugenia Choque Quispe, interview, May 21, 1997; Carlos Mamani, interviews, June 2, 1997 and June 16, 1997; and Stephenson (2002).

Other organizations have emerged, particularly among the youth, to promote local communities, local culture, and local leadership. *Integración de
Comunidades Aymaras de Bolivia* (ICAB) and *Aywi Aroma*, for example, identified the need to promote cultural identity, indigenous communal structures,
and alternative forms of development.[69] Rather than focusing on constructing a new national organization, they have attempted to work with NGOs
and other agencies to identify alternative ways of working at the *local* level
to achieve these goals. These incipient organizations, like many of the ayllu
movements, therefore have explicitly rejected the strategies and orienta-
tion of CSUTCB. In these cases, youth leaders have seen the CSUTCB as
too confrontational and too anti-statist with too little to show for their efforts. In interviews, leaders from these organizations observed that peasant
federations like CSUTCB had simply not delivered concrete goods to the
community. In this context, a new generation of young leaders has set out
to build something new, something more "organic," and something more
local.

NGOs and international development agencies have in several cases supported these local community efforts to strengthen the ayllu, local culture,
and local leadership. Examples include Semilla, Oxfam, the Inter-American
Foundation, and the Danish organization Ibis, among others. Indeed, in
the late 1980s, several NGOs expressed a new interest in the traditional authority structures and leaders in indigenous communities. They started to
organize workshops, seminars, and meetings to bring together traditional
indigenous leaders, create stronger ties among them, and promote greater
acceptance of these indigenous structures in society at large (Healy 1996:
256–7). The *Fondo Indígena*, a multilateral indigenous fund, also played a
role in supporting a new generation of indigenous leaders in their efforts to
chart out new ways of strengthening existing communities and promoting
alternative forms of development.

Several of these new organizations, particularly ICAB and Aywi Aroma,
turned to the Amazonian organizations for inspiration. As discussed in
the following section, the Amazonian organizations primarily deployed an
ethnic-based discourse (more than a class-based one), captured national attention with their marches, and negotiated with the state to secure some

---

[69] Community discussion with *Aywi Aroma* on July 10, 1997; community discussion with
representatives from Llojlla Chico, Llojlla Grande, and Llojlla Pampa on July 19, 1997;
Diomedes Layme Escalante, interviews, June 12, 1997, June 17, 1997, and July 9, 1997;
Liño Mamani, interview, July 9, 1997; and Belisario Mamani, interview, July 19, 1997.

measure of territorial autonomy. The youth hoped to learn how to negotiate with the state and other agencies to secure precisely this kind of local autonomy, pride, and future. While the future of these movements is an open question, it is clear that a process has been set in motion. The Kataristas opened the door to talk about indigenous culture and local autonomy; local ayllus and a new generation of leaders later reclaimed the right to promote their rights outside of the CSUTCB, and as of the time of this writing, the new leadership of the CSUTCB, particularly Felipe Quispe, have in turn incorporated the defense of the ayllu as part of their political mandate.[70]

From Local to Local: Defending Autonomy in the Andes

In short, indigenous movements first emerged in the Bolivian Andes to defend local autonomy against the erosion of corporatist citizenship regimes that took place with the Military-Peasant Pact of the 1960s. They emerged first in La Paz, where local indigenous authority structures had survived and were the target of state efforts to impose new leaders. In response, indigenous activists began to mobilize for change, with two competing approaches (and several internal factions). In this period of initial mobilization, the Kataristas proved most successful, precisely because they set out to mobilize local rural networks and to scale up their efforts during moments of political opening. They came to dominate Bolivia's main peasant federation and to assert its autonomy from the labor union. In turn, they influenced national political discourse, as they compelled politicians to discuss ethnic questions and to publicly debate how they could address indigenous needs and claims.

The success of the Kataristas in turn changed the landscape for future movements in Bolivia – who would draw on the "lessons" of their predecessors. Indeed, a second generation of movements capitalized on the Kataristas' successes and sought to minimize their weaknesses. The cocaleros saw the positive reception gained by the Kataristas and started to frame their struggle as one about indigenous rights. They banked on the perception that an ethnic struggle would resonate more powerfully than one for production alone. Hence they shifted their prior class-based rhetoric

---

[70] While in the late 1990s the CSUTCB started to modify its discourse to incorporate ayllus into the union structure, it remains uncertain what that discursive shift means in practice. Román Loayza, interviews, June 11, 1997 and June 19, 1997 and Ticona (1996: ch. IV).

to one about indigenous traditions and pride. Local youth and research groups, on the other hand, criticized the *contemporary* Katarista movement for not going far enough to protect, defend, and strengthen local indigenous communities. They praised the Kataristas for their pioneering work but criticized them for getting too caught up in the bureaucratic institutions associated with the CSUTCB. These second-generation organizations in turn have picked up the mantle of working with the local communities, in particular, the ayllus. As such, they have drawn inspiration from Amazonian indigenous organizations as well.

During the course of several interviews in 1995 and 1997, Jenaro Flores commented on the course of the indigenous movement: from its origins in defending local autonomy to its heyday in the national union movement and back to the need to strengthen local autonomy. For while he worked in the 1970s and 1980s to forge an indigenous movement through the Kataristas and then CSUTCB, he held up the second-generation movements as the future. He commended the cocaleros for their organization and effectiveness. Yet he also identified the need to strengthen indigenous authority structures against the onslaught of other political institutions. Remarkably in the late 1990s, both he and Constantino Lima, key founders of the Katarista and Indianista movements, respectively, had turned from building national organizations to strengthening and reviving local ones. At the time of my last interview with each, they were particularly active in their community of origin, where each aspired to consolidate a leadership position as an elder.

Part II: The Bolivian Amazon and CIDOB[71]

The Bolivian indigenous movement in the Amazon emerged in the 1980s and early 1990s, more than a decade after their Andean counterparts had forged the Katarista movement. Unlike the coca growers who also emerged relatively late, the Amazonian Indians did not replicate the organizational

---

[71] The Bolivian Amazon, as it is used in English, is a misnomer. In English, it is generally used to refer to the non-Andean regions that in fact encompass all of the eastern lowlands – including the tropical forests of the Amazon, the vast pastoral lands of Santa Cruz, and the dry desert-like areas of the Chaco. In Spanish, this entire region is generally referred to as the lowlands (las Tierras Bajas), including "el Oriente," el Chaco, and the Amazon. It comprises the departments of Beni, Santa Cruz, Pando as well as parts of La Paz, Tarija, and Cochabamba. In keeping with English usage, this book continues to use the term, the *Bolivian Amazon*, to refer to this broader concept of the East. See APCOB (1994: 3); Ticona, Rojas, and Albó (1995: 61); and Molina (1996b: 1).

model developed by the Kataristas. Whereas the latter had largely organized along lines that mimicked state-recognized boundaries – communities, provinces, departments – the Amazonian movement started off by organizing along ethnic community lines – regardless of whether ethnic lines coincided with municipal, departmental, or other boundaries.[72]

The Amazonian movement, however, would soon surpass the Kataristas both in mobilizational capacity and political capital. In a period of a few short years, they captured the political imagination of many Bolivians by successfully organizing indigenous marches, negotiating territorial autonomy in several regions, and participating actively in constitutional reforms. Hence, just as the Kataristas were losing their political position within the CSUTCB and within political circles (the election of Víctor Hugo Cárdenas, notwithstanding), Amazonian organizations were expanding their reach into society and their sway in formal politics.

While the later *timing* of this movement distinguishes it from the Andean movements in Bolivia and Ecuador, as well as from the Ecuadorian movement in the Amazon, the *explanation* of this movement's emergence, in fact is a similar one. Three factors (the changes in citizenship regimes that challenge local political autonomy, organizational networks, and political associational space) also proved important in the Bolivian Amazon. Where these three factors were present, indigenous communities found the motive, the opportunity, and the capacity to organize. The resulting Bolivian indigenous movements in the Amazon came to demand territorial autonomy; recognition of communal rights, indigenous authority, and juridical systems; respect for cultural diversity; and a more meaningful inclusion in the democracy that was built in the 1980s and 1990s. While Chapter 7 revisits this agenda, the rest of this chapter explains the emergence of this Amazonian movement.

At a Distance: Relative Political Autonomy

The indigenous population in the Bolivian Amazon is small. According to the 1994 Indigenous Census, the region claims an estimated 220,000 people – a number that includes thirty-six different indigenous peoples whose respective estimated populations range from 50 to 50,000 people (APCOB 1994: 3; Molina 1996b: 2) – with more than 90 percent living in

---

[72] Diego Iturralde and Sergio Delgado, interview, October 20, 1995.

Santa Cruz and the Beni.[73] This small population resides, however, in a vast area. Indeed, the Bolivian Amazon covers approximately two-thirds of the country's territory.[74]

Despite this vast expanse, the region has historically been marginalized from the twin projects of state building and economic markets.[75] Whereas the Bolivian state sought to incorporate the Andes through labor markets, land reforms, and state penetration, the Bolivian Amazon was more than a step removed from these processes, until the second half of the twentieth century. A rugged and demanding terrain coupled with a dispersed and low-density population made this region *relatively* uninviting to the colonial explorer, national administrator, and colonists.[76] Until the 1950s land reform and subsequent state development projects, the region was mapped but not politically administered in any meaningful way. The indigenous population therein has tended to live in "semi-permanently settled small communities (a few dozen families) [that] . . . periodically move depending on the season" (World Bank, 1996a: vol. I, 37). Of those communal systems of hunters, gatherers, and subsistence farmers in the Amazon, Eastern Lowlands, and the Chaco (i.e., those indigenous peoples living in the region): "Virtually 100 percent of members of this tenure system are extremely poor, among the poorest of the poor in the country. Little or no access to education, health, and other basic services severely . . . limits their chances of overcoming poverty" (World Bank, 1996b: vol. 2, 170).

The failure of the colonial and national states to penetrate this region meant that much of the Amazonian indigenous population escaped state efforts to create new indigenous communities and authority structures, demand tithes and taxes, and integrate them into new market structures. In short, Amazonian Indians maintained a significant degree of political, social, and cultural autonomy – particularly when compared to Indians in the Andes. While officially they were all subjects of the crown and later citizens

[73] There are thirty-nine distinct indigenous peoples in Bolivia, thirty-six of which live in the Amazonian region (Molina 1997: 28). Also see Murillo (1997).
[74] APCOB (1994: 3) and Ticona, Rojas, and Albó (1995: 61).
[75] Peasant organizers largely ignored this area as well (APCOB 1994: 23).
[76] Lehm (1994: 21) disputes the myth that indigenous territories were entirely isolated. At the end of the seventeenth century documentation exists of an exchange of goods, resources, and symbols – both between Amazonian communities; between Amazonian and Andean communities; and between Amazonian communities and Spanish settlements. She concludes that with the Jesuits' arrival, indigenous communities were put in enclosed spaces and, consequently, became more isolated from some of the groups with which they previously had contact.

of the state, practically speaking, Amazonian Indians were neither. This was particularly the case for those indigenous groups in the Amazon that were nomadic and deep in the Amazon – difficult for the state to track them down and to impose new structures, as it did in the Andes. Of the few remaining seminomadic peoples, there is no centralized authority or leader but several "strong men." Among the larger more sedentary indigenous groups, there are more institutionalized authority structures, although the exact name and terms of that authority vary from one group to the next (APCOB 1994: 14). In this context, indigenous identities were central to social and cultural life within and between Indian communities. However, ethnic cleavages were not politicized for much of the nineteenth and twentieth centuries.

The Motive, Space, and Networks

Given weak state penetration, control, and development of the Amazon, indigenous communities therein remained relatively autonomous from changes in state policy – although they were not entirely free of outside penetration.[77] This state of relative autonomy changed with the corporatist citizenship regimes that had incorporated indigenous peasants in the Andes. When the state promoted corporatist policies (i.e., land reform, agricultural subsidies, etc.) to incorporate and control Andean indigenous peasants (which inadvertently granted the latter greater local autonomy, as we have seen), it often did so at the expense of indigenous communities in the Amazon. Not only did the agrarian reform law disregard the interests of Amazonian Indians, it actually referred to them as wards of the

---

[77] In the absence of state penetration, adventurers/explorers, churches, and NGOs moved into the region. These waves of penetration, on the face of it, all challenged the local autonomy that indigenous groups had developed and maintained. This was perhaps nowhere more evident than with the waves of economic adventurers who sought riches in the Amazon – through the search for and exploration of minerals, logging of rich forests, cattle ranching, and the like. These initial wealth seekers were largely thwarted in their attempts during the colonial and national period (particularly in the tropical forests of the northern Amazon although less so in the lowlands of Santa Cruz) – due to inhospitable climates, deadly diseases, and poor infrastructure. So too they confronted indigenous groups that resisted this penetration into areas in which they had historically lived; but in the absence of the organizational networks between communities, this defense was sporadic and uncoordinated. Over time, however, these nonindigenous mavericks gained a greater toehold in the Amazon and increasingly displaced indigenous peoples from the lands that they had inhabited. While some indigenous families were pulled into the economic market, others took off for remote areas to maintain their autonomy from these marketeers.

state rather than capable and full-fledged citizens. Article 20 of the 1953 Land Reform, for example, declared that "[f]orest groups of the tropical and subtropical plain that find themselves in a savage state and that have a primitive form of organization, will remain under the protection of the State."[78] In the initial years following the land reform, this was tolerable in practice because the state actually made no effort to penetrate the area and subjugate the Amazonian communities as wards of the state. However, as the corporatist period continued (distributing lands, although with a decreasing commitment to this project), the state sought to capture the Amazon – both to defuse land pressures in the Andes and to promote grand scale development.

When the state initiated development projects to penetrate the Amazon with public and private forces, indigenous communities in the region began mobilizing to defend their autonomy from the state and to demand equal treatment before it. The 1966 Colonization Law, in particular, posed the most significant threats to Amazonian indigenous communities. Without regard for the indigenous peoples living in the Amazon, the state started to encourage Andean farmers and landholders to migrate east and colonize untitled areas. These migratory pressures into the Amazon increased with the 1966 Colonization Law. The law ostensibly protected indigenous peoples in the Amazon. Yet, despite a stated commitment to individual and collectively managed lands (as indicated in Article 92), the law continued to treat Amazonian Indians as wards of the state and declared their lands open to colonization.[79] In 1967, the state created a National Colonization Institute (*Instituto Nacional de Colonización*) and distributed lands in the Amazon to colonos and large landholders (World Bank, 1996b: vol. 2, 162).[80]

Between 1967 and 1993, some 3 to 5 million ha. were distributed to approximately 80,000 families in the Alto Beni Region of La Paz, Chapare in Cochabamba, and Northern Santa Cruz.... However, during the same period, the State also distributed some 25 to 30 million ha. of fiscal lands in non-hacienda regions (mostly Santa Cruz and Beni) by granting large allocations to reduced numbers

---

[78] Cited in Navia (1992: 10) and Vacaflor (1997: 18).

[79] Navia (1992: 10) and Vacaflor (1997: 19).

[80] See Murillo (1997: pt. II) for a statistical overview of the number of indigenous colonos from the highlands residing in the lowlands. Múñoz and Lavadenz (1997: 5) note that the process of land titling was not well planned or reliable – leading to corruption, arbitrariness, and "considerable overlapping of title and claims over land." Also see World Bank (1996: vol. I, 32) and Pacheco (1997: 4).

of individuals, leading to the emergence of junker-type corporate landholdings and large idle estates (also called neo-latifundia) (Múñoz and Lavadenz 1997: 3).

In Santa Cruz and the Beni, where these large landholdings were distributed in the highest numbers (and displaced indigenous peoples that had lived there), indigenous movements moved with the greatest force (Pacheco 1997: 5). The conflict with colonos would also become an important, although less pressing political issue.

By the 1980s, the option of fleeing the advance of outsiders became increasingly untenable as state reforms facilitated greater and faster penetration by these outside forces that, in turn, displaced Amazonian Indians from their land. In this context, economic penetration by loggers, ranchers, and even coca growers directly challenged local autonomy, catalyzing Amazonian Indians to organize in defense of their land and for territorial autonomy.

The Amazon, however, does not provide an auspicious terrain for organizing – not least because the distance between communities, the corresponding lack of communication, and the localization of identities have together posed significant obstacles to collective action. Hence, the initial capacity to organize among communities was dependent on and facilitated by the existence of transcommunity networks – which were present in some regions and not others. Unwittingly, churches left many of these networks in place. They sought to turn Indians into Christians. In the process, they left an infrastructure of transcommunity networks that subsequently enabled Indians to mobilize in order to defend their autonomy. Churches of various denominations took advantage of the state's historically weak presence in the Amazon to establish enclaves of political, social, economic, and, of course, religious control. In addition to establishing missions, proselytizing, and converting Indians to Christianity (in exchange for resources and later with the promise of salvation), churches imposed new ways of organizing indigenous peoples – forcing them to settle in communities (*reducciones*), at times harnessing their labor, and imposing new authority structures, cabildos, on indigenous communities. Speaking of the Chiquitanos, Guaraníes, and Mojeños, Almaraz (1998: 180) notes that "[t]he mission reducción, above all the Jesuit ones, have had a fundamental and definitive impact on these peoples' cultural identity, social organization, and attitude towards the rest of society."

Most scholars have accordingly and rightfully highlighted the ways in which churches undermined or at least distorted indigenous practices and

195

cultures in the Amazon. However, there was a range of consequences – with some cabildos falling under the control of outside forces, as in Guarayos, and others indigenizing the cabildos, as in Moxos.[81] As Block's study of Jesuit missions in Moxos finds: "the political structure of the Moxos missions confirmed traditional aboriginal leadership and gave them Spanish titles. The missionaries confirmed and legitimated the neophytes' choices but seldom overruled them" (Block 1994: 121). In a report commissioned by the indigenous group, CIDOB, the authors also concluded that:

Despite all of the pressures that the *Pueblos* suffer and of the State's imposition on the communities by the executive and through the arbitrary designation of authorities, the *pueblos* manage to maintain, within the interior of their communities, a minimum of traditional organization in their *cabildos, capitanías*, and *cacicazgos* (Grupo ip-Latina/CEDETI 1995: 6).

Hence, churches, like the union federations in the Bolivian Andes, sought to recreate new institutions. However, in many cases, indigenous communities subsequently used church networks and institutions as organizational resources to defend their territorial autonomy. The SIL provides such an example. The SIL focused its work in the Bolivian lowlands, where they assumed a parastatal role – particularly in the areas of literacy, bicultural education, leadership training, and radio communication.[82] They helped to create new communities (Castro Mantilla 1996: 94). In some cases, they even aided Indians in the effort to gain title to lands (Castro Mantilla 1996: 56–7). Castro Mantilla (1996: 99–100) suggests that those who attended SIL schools and programs had better skills and resources – including literacy, professional training, and knowledge of their rights, etc. Hence, churches (along with NGOs later in the twentieth century) unwittingly provided the *organizational* and *transcommunity networks* that were later used by indigenous groups to form indigenous movements in the 1980s and 1990s. This pattern parallels the one found for the Ecuadorian Amazon (see Chapter 4).

---

[81] Block (1994) and Ticona, Rojas, and Albó (1995: 73).

[82] See Castro Mantilla (1996). SIL in fact maintained that it was not a missionary organization but one that was largely concerned about linguistics and the integration of Indians into society (Castro Mantilla 1996: 50–1). In this spirit, various state ministries signed convenios with SIL from the 1950s–1960, including the *Ministerio de Asuntos Campesinos y Agropecuarios* (in 1954), the *Ministerio de Educación y Bellas Artes* (in 1961 and 1970), and the *Ministerio de Salud Pública* (in 1971) (Castro Mantilla 1996: 2, 29, 31). SIL maintained, however, strong ties with two missions, the *Misión Evangélica Nuevas Tribus* and the *Misión Evangélica Suiza*, which arrived in Bolivia in the 1940s.

NGOs for their part also played a key networking role in some parts of the Amazon. While NGOs played a minor role in the Ecuadorian Amazon, they played a central role in the Bolivian Amazon – first in Izozog and later in Mojos (the two centers of most prominent and active indigenous organizing in the Amazon). These organizations intentionally worked to provide and strengthen the networks and resources that would facilitate indigenous organizing – in some cases helping to reinforce networks that had already been left in place by church missions. In this sense, NGOs in Bolivia also provided the *networks* that supported the building and growth of indigenous movements in the region.[83]

The following narrative lays out how these elements (colonization as it challenged local autonomy and the networks left by churches and NGOs) came together to catalyze and support indigenous organizing in the region. In this discussion, the role of *political associational space* is, at first blush, less evident than it was in the Andes. There is little discussion of how political repression and authoritarian rule foreclosed political associational space for organizing and little analysis of how political liberalization provided important opportunities for mobilizing. Yet this should not be read as the decreased importance of political associational space for political organizing. As previously noted, fluctuations in political regimes were generally less apparent in the Amazon than in the more densely populated and administratively centralized Andes.[84] When repression ensued in the Andes, it did not usually find expression in the Amazon. When the state imposed states of siege on the country, there was no significant administrative structure to announce and/or uphold this policy in the Amazon. Consequently, the Amazon confronted a relatively constant political associational space – providing plenty of *opportunities* to organize. What was missing until the

---

[83] For an excellent overview of the role played by NGOs in creating networks, providing resources, and mobilizing support for indigenous communities, see Healy (1996).

[84] Indigenous leaders, such as José Guasebi, interview, October 26, 1995; Marcial Fabricano, interview, November 2, 1995; and Bonifacio Barrientos, interview, July 24, 1997 noted that they were not specifically affected by regime changes. When asked what precipitated the organization of indigenous peoples in Bolivia, Marcial Fabricano stated that "democracy had nothing to do with it." He noted that changes in democratic and authoritarian regimes at the national level had less impact on the Amazon than in the Andes. However, he did note in a June 13, 1997 interview that democracy did provide a more open environment for political organizing on a *national* level, even if democracy remained elitist and incomplete in practice. Ernesto Noe was the only interviewee (July 25, 1997) who noted that the period of military rule foreclosed options for organizing in the Amazon, as discussed in the section on CPIB.

1970s and 1980s was the *motive* to organize as Indians and the organizational *capacity* to do so. What follows is a brief description of a few important Amazonian indigenous movements and their subsequent formation of Bolivia's main Amazonian confederation.

Confederación de Indígenas del Oriente, Chaco y Amazonía de Bolivia (CIDOB)

The Central Indígena de Pueblos y Comunidades Indígenas del Oriente Boliviano (CIDOB) was founded in 1982 in the lowlands of Santa Cruz and the Chaco. By the 1990s, CIDOB had expanded its scope to become a confederation that included the entire Amazon, encompassing more localized indigenous organizations that had emerged in successive years and in its image. While challenges to local autonomy motivated leaders to organize, the existence of transcommunity networks (left by churches and NGOs) gave them the capacity to do so.

Indigenous organizing in this region began following changes in state law in the 1960s, as previously noted. State laws promulgated in the 1970s further facilitated the exploitation of indigenous lands. These included the *Ley Forestal, Ley Fauna y Vida Silvestre*, and the *Ley Mineral*, all of which granted concessions to exploit natural resources. With this new legislation, loggers and cattle ranchers moved more aggressively into the region, and additional rounds of colonization followed. These new rounds of colonization often surrounded indigenous communities and cut short their access to resources such as water, animals, and forest products (APCOB 1994: 20–1).

These reforms, therefore, directly impacted the geographic spaces in which indigenous peoples in the Amazon lived, compromising access to resources that are necessary for community survival. In this context, a new round of significant indigenous organizing emerged and culminated with the formation of CIDOB.

Organizing first occurred among the Izoceños-Guaraníes and was initiated and directed by Bonifacio Barrientos, the Capitán Grande of Alto and Bajo Izozog.[85] The Izoceños-Guaraníes had developed particularly strong intra- and intercommunal organizations prior to this time – including

---

[85] APCOB (1994: 10); Chirif and Castillo (1994: 11); and Marcial Fabricano, interviews, October 30, 1995 (La Paz) and November 2, 1995 (Santa Cruz). Fabricano discussed Barrientos in terms that Weber would quickly have identified as "charisma" – noting that he was born to work for the good of the people, he had a passion and a vision, was mystical, had authority, and had real relations with the people.

a periodic *Asamblea de Capitanes* attended by *capitanes* from various communities. Barrientos presided over this assembly as the *Capitán Grande*. Barrientos also developed a legendary reputation as a strong leader as a result of his unprecedented decision in the 1930s to march from Izozog to La Paz to demand community title for the Capitanía de Izozog, which he gained in 1947. In the 1980s, Bonifacio Barrientos therefore became a resource for the new generation of indigenous leaders interested in organizing to defend their lands from the new round of colonization. Yet whereas Barrientos conducted this struggle alone and on behalf of one indigenous group in the 1930s, he advised the newer generation to build alliances among indigenous groups in the region (APCOB 1994: 10).[86]

Barrientos began to contact different indigenous groups in the area, including the Guaraníes from the south, the Ayoreos, the Guarayos, and the Chiquitanos, between 1978–1982.[87] Prior to that date, communities were politically isolated and did not necessarily recognize the shared nature of their problems.[88] José Urañabi, who later became an indigenous leader in the Amazon (twice president of CIDOB) recounted that prior to his first meeting with other indigenous leaders, he had not realized that there were other indigenous groups with shared concerns; he thought that everyone was either Guarayu or white.[89] In this context, Barrientos started to call for communal meetings, assemblies, and local authorities.

---

[86] Bonifacio Barrientos held the position of Capitán Grande until 1984 when he handed the position to his son of the same name. The son indicated that he was elected in assembly in 1974 (Bonifacio Barrientos [the son], interview, July 25, 1997).

[87] In their first assembly in 1982, they founded the *Central Indígena de Pueblos y Comunidades Indígenas del Oriente Boliviano* and forged a common platform around autonomy, territory, economy, education, and health. The organization would come to encompass these groups and several others (Chirif and Castillo 1994: 11). Prior to this meeting in 1982, however, several smaller meetings took place. The first meeting among the Izozeños and Ayoréode took place in 1978. According to the testimonial record from that meeting, those present voiced concerns about uniting to acquire collective land titles and respect for their own authorities; subsidiary concerns also touched on health and education (CIDOB n.d.: 19–23). At the second meeting among the Chiriguano and Ayoréode in 1980, similar sentiments were expressed (CIDOB n.d.). They later started to meet with other indigenous groups in the region, including the Guarayos and Chiquitanos (see document by Alberto Chirif and Oscar Castillo 1994). "Analisis Estratégico CIDOB" cited in Grupo ip-Latina/CEDETI (1995: 11).

[88] Marcial Fabricano, interview, November 2, 1995 and José Urañabi, interview, July 2, 1997; Libermann and Godínez (1992: 31); APCOB (1994: 24); and Grupo ip-Latina/CEDETI (1995: 11).

[89] José Urañabi, interview, July 2, 1997.

This period of community organizing in the late 1970s initially coincided with military rule in Bolivia. Barrientos worked with military and civilian leaders alike to secure recognition and access to resources.[90] His ability to do so reflected not only his skill but also the underlying existence of political associational space in the Amazon, regardless of regime type. While there was more political associational space during democratic times, there was still space to organize in the Amazon during military times. "The change in governments has not affected anything because it has not affected us," stated Barrientos's son.[91] Urañabi noted, however, that there were some limitations imposed during military times, although they were not enforced. The military government "allowed" them to found CIDOB but did not allow them to call meetings; despite these restrictions, the state took no action to control the organization. With the democratic opening, freedom of expression was formally recognized, which subsequently made it easier to engage in dialogues about constitutional reform, educational reform, laws, etc.[92] Hence, political associational space existed during the military periods and was extended with the transition to democracy. As such, indigenous leaders began organizing across indigenous communities in the Amazon.

The founding meeting of CIDOB included representatives from the following indigenous groups, Izoceños-Guaraníes (who would later form the *Asamblea del Pueblo Guaraní* [APG] and the *Capitanía del Alto y Bajo Izozog* [CABI]), Ayoreos (who would later form the *Centro Ayoreo Nativo del Oriente Boliviano* [CANOB]), Guarayus (who would later form the *Central de Organizaciones de los Pueblos Nativos Guarayos* [COPNAG]), and Chiquitanos (who would later form the *Central Indígena de Comunidades Originarias de Lomerío* [CICOL] and the *Central Indígena de Comunidades de Concepción* [CICC]) (APCOB 1994: 24). CABI, CANOB, COPNAG, CICOL, and CICC would all become active organizational members of the confederation. The Izoceños in CIDOB hoped to export their model of intercommunal organization to other indigenous groups, including the Ayoreos and Chiquitanos.[93]

The founding story of CIDOB, however, cannot be disentangled from, or explained without noting, the important role of a group of anthropologists and sociologists in the NGO, *Apoyo para el Campesino-Indígena del*

[90] Bonifacio Barrientos (son), interview, July 25, 1997.
[91] Bonifacio Barrientos (son), interview, July 25, 1997.
[92] José Urañabi, interview, July 2, 1997.
[93] Graciela Zolezzi, interview, July 2, 1997.

Oriente Boliviano (APCOB).[94] The original founders of APCOB drew on experiences with and knowledge from the Peruvian experience, AIDESEP. According to Oscar Castillo, a Peruvian who worked at APCOB in the 1970s, APCOB did not want to create a hierarchical organization that imposed structures on indigenous communities, as had occurred in peasant union organizing in Peru and elsewhere. Rather, they wanted to work with the communities on the basis of preexisting political identities and structures.[95] APCOB saw itself engaging in a kind of research activism dedicated specifically to cultural issues such as the right to customary law and indigenous rights to territory – particularly as a space in which indigenous people could reproduce their sociocultural practices. Over the years, APCOB has focused on projects that address territorial demands, sociopolitical organization, gender, and culture.[96]

APCOB, which worked directly with the Capitanía de Izozog, encouraged those with whom they worked to create interethnic ties (APCOB 1994: 24). APCOB in turn helped to create links among indigenous communities, to help gain financial support, to facilitate invitations to international indigenous meetings, and to invite indigenous speakers from other countries to Bolivia. APCOB founded, for example, a Program on Interethnic Relations in 1982 that organized a bulletin, meetings, and trips to facilitate the process of interethnic contact.[97] In this regard, they helped to provide the intraorganizational resources to build the movement, information flows to keep it current, and the domestic and international contacts to position

---

[94] APCOB (1994: 24); Grupo ip-Latina/CEDETI (1995: 11); Diego Iturralde and Sergio Delgado, interviews, October 20, 1995; Marcial Fabricano, interview, October 30, 1995; Xavier Albó, interview, May 21, 1997; Angel Yandura and Bonifacio Barrientos, interview, July 2, 1997; Oscar Castillo, interview, July 25, 1997; and CIDOB (n.d.). Castillo observed that while APCOB played an integral role, it was neither necessary nor sufficient for the founding of CIDOB; he stated that "had APCOB not been there, others would have helped."

[95] Graciela Zolezzi, interview, July 2, 1997 and Oscar Castillo, interview, July 25, 1997. APCOB and CIPCA were two important NGOs in the region – each providing the networks for subsequent indigenous organizing. However, they used different organizing strategies at the local level and disagreed over the role that the capitanías should play. According to Oscar Castillo and Graciella Zolezzi, APCOB thought that they should work with the existing ethnic groups and their capitanes. CIPCA, on the other hand, initially promoted class-based, production-oriented, union-based associations. Healy (1996: 257) observes that CIPCA later agreed to work with the capitanía structure and helped them to organize the APG, a federation of capitanías that has undertaken small-scale development projects. Xavier Albó, interviews, May 21, 1997 and August 2, 1997.

[96] See APCOB (1996: 1–2) and Graciela Zolezzi, interview, July 2, 1997 and Oscar Castillo, interview, July 25, 1997.

[97] Oscar Castillo, interview, July 25, 1997.

the movement in a broader context.[98] At a testimonial from a 1981 meeting between Izozeños and Ayoréode, one speaker announced: "We are not manipulated/managed beyond our free will, we are not obligated to any patron, but we are here and we are the owners of our own free will. Why have we passed through this experience? It was due to the help of the anthropologists" (CIDOB n.d.: 35). But Urañabi also noted that while support from APCOB and other NGOs was important, it was not sufficient. The success of CIDOB depended on the skills of indigenous leaders (particularly Bonifacio Barrientos) to administer the organization, a skill without which the organization would have foundered.[99]

Following CIDOB's organizational successes, it more actively set out to help organize other organizations in the Amazon between 1985 and 1989, the *Central de Pueblos Indígenas del Beni* (CPIB) in the Beni being particuarly noteworthy among them (as discussed next).[100] CIDOB developed into a national confederation that represented more than thirty indigenous peoples in the following regions: Chaco (Departments of Santa Cruz, Tarija, and Cochabamba); Amazon (Departments of Pando and Beni); and Oriente (Department of Santa Cruz). The organization even had contacts with some indigenous groups in the highlands (APCOB 1994; Grupo ip-Latina/CEDETI 1995: 7, 11, 15).

CIDOB proposed in 1986 and 1988 the creation of a national assembly that would have brought together CIDOB and CSUTCB in the effort to create a national body. This would have been akin to the creation of CONAIE in Ecuador – with participation by both the highland and lowland indigenous organizations. The proposed assembly would have promoted the idea of a multiethnic and plurinational state in Bolivia – demanding greater local autonomy; indigenous territories; communal lands; natural resources; collective and individual rights; bilingual and multicultural education; and greater participation by women (Chirif and Castillo 1994: 13–14). These efforts did not come to fruition. Indigenous organizations in Bolivia have failed to forge a national confederation that works on behalf of indigenous peoples in the Amazon and Andes.

If CIDOB did not succeed in forging this national organization, it did make significant headway in the lowlands. With the creation of new

---

[98] International contacts shaped the conceptual frames used by some of the Bolivian Amazonian leaders. See CIDOB (n.d.: 4–6, 8, 14–18). Also based on interviews with José Urañabi, July 2, 1997 and Angel Yandura, July 28, 1997.

[99] José Urañabi, interview, July 2, 1997.

[100] See Chirif and Castillo (1994: 12).

indigenous organizations and the forging of linkages between existing various indigenous groups, CIDOB grew in regional scope and chose to relabel itself as a confederation. It kept the acronym but in 1989 changed its official name to the *Confederación Indígena del Oriente, Chaco y Amazonía de Bolivia.* In 1990, it acquired juridical standing. CIDOB became a coordinating body for autonomous departmental and regional organizations.[101]

CIDOB emerged as the spokesperson for indigenous organizations in the Amazon – particularly during the first Gonzalo Sánchez de Lozada administration (1993–1997). In its negotiations with Sánchez de Lozada, CIDOB demanded indigenous territory; organizational autonomy to decide the terms of political participation and development; the right to self-government; recognition of customary law and legal pluralism; and the right to cultural survival and development (APCOB 1994: 26; Grupo ip-Latina/CEDETI 1995: 12–14).[102] Of these, land access and territorial autonomy have remained the most central, for territorial recognition is understood as the very basis for survival and growth.

We have discovered that the first problem is land, territory. We believe that the fundamental base is territory; without mother earth we could not have education, there could be no health, there could be no *pueblo* with its own cultural identity, language, religion, etc. For the indigenous *pueblos* it's the fundamental base so that they will have life itself, so that there will be a guarantee for survival and population growth. That is what we seek; it's not as some sectors believe, that we want to establish another State within the State, that's not our objective, but rather it is to have a space because we are a family (Urañabi at 1991 conference, quoted in Libermann and Godínez 1992: 32).

---

[101] For a list of organizations affiliated with CIDOB, see APCOB (1994: 41–3) and Grupo ip-Latina/CEDETI (1995: 16–23).

[102] For an extended outline of CIDOB's agenda for the period 1995–1998, see Grupo ip-Latina/CEDETI 1995: 74–90). CIDOB has also developed and coordinated several other projects that include forest management projects; environmental protection; legal counseling; training projects; agricultural projects; women's health and development projects; and bilingual education, among others. These projects have developed in collaboration with several NGOs, most notably APCOB; *Asesoría Legal y de Asistencia Social* (ALAS); *Centro de Estudios Jurídicos e Investigación Social* (CEJIS); *Centro de Investigación, Diseño Artesenal y Comercialización Cooperativa* (CIDAC); CIDDEBENI; *Centro de Investigación y Manejo de Recursos Naturales Renovables* (CIMAR); CIPCA; and *Taller de Educación y Comunicación Guaraní* (Teko Guaraní). Funding has come from several international financial organizations, including *Servicio Holandés de Cooperación Técnica y Social* (SNV), *Misión de Cooperación Técnica Holandesa* (MCTH), *Institución Financiera de Holanda* (HIVOS), OXFAM-USA, *Inter-American Foundation* (IAF), Ibis, *Asistencia Técnica Alemana* (GTZ), and the Swiss Red Cross (APCOB 1994: 29–30, 27–37, 39); Grupo ip-Latina/CEDETI 1995: 10; and Xavier Albó, interview, May 21, 1997.

The organization, however, has also assumed an important role in calling for more democratic participation and respect for internationally recognized but domestically unfulfilled indigenous rights.[103] In this regard, while democratization did not necessarily create the explicit opportunities for organizing, its deficits and shortcomings have shaped subsequent agendas for inclusion.

We want to have a dialogue, demand these rights, converse, dialogue. *In this way we can, as we determine fit, make of this country an example for the rest of the countries of what it is to live in a democracy, genuinely in a participatory democracy, not in an imposed democracy*; that is to say, that the indigenous *pueblos* participate, that they make their voice heard, that the authorities listen to their demands.

There are many advances at the international level of indigenous rights, but internally these rights are not put into practice. That's why I say that the government, and we too, have to ensure that the laws that correspond to us are obeyed (in Libermann and Godínez 1992: 34, emphasis added).

In this regard, CIDOB has tied demands for territorial autonomy with demands for democratic inclusion, a point discussed at greater length in Chapter 7.

The Central de Pueblos Indígenas del Beni

While CIDOB emerged as the most significant regional organization in the Amazon, one of its regional affiliates became particularly important in its own right. CPIB took center stage in 1990. Challenging the idea that there were no Indians in the Amazon or, at best, that those living in the Amazon were savages and uncivilized, indigenous activists and their families set out from the lowlands of the Amazonian jungle to the highland capital of La Paz in a grueling 650 kilometer march called *La Marcha por el Territorio y la Dignidad*. They were demanding legal state recognition of indigenous territories, which was granted begrudgingly following the march.

CPIB emerged in the Upper Amazon in the department of Beni. Beni is home to at least fifteen indigenous populations, among which the Mojos are the largest group (CIDDEBENI 1988: 3; Molina 1997: 30).[104] While the Beni was relatively more incorporated into the Bolivian state than the

---

[103] Libermann and Godínez (1993) and CIDOB (n.d.: 14).
[104] The Beni is the second largest department in Bolivia. It claims 20 percent of the country's territorial surface although only 4.3 percent of the national population (Molina 1996b: 2; 1997: 29).

southern states of the Bolivian Amazon, the state's reach was uneven and weak, particularly when compared to the Bolivian Andes. Hence, despite a significant colonial history of Jesuit presence in the region – one which attempted to settle indigenous communities and impose a cabildo system – indigenous communities remained relatively autonomous, particularly those outside of the cities.[105] Even those that adopted the cabildo system (one that was responsible for the internal regulation and government of the communities – including rituals and festivals) came to indigenize that local governance structure (CIDDEBENI 1988: 11–12; CPIB n.d.: 2). Hence in many communities today the cabildo system remains and is seen as an indigenous form of governance (Block 1994 and Ticona, Rojas, and Albó 1995: 73).

This local form of autonomy in the Beni was challenged in the second half of the twentieth century by the land reform law and colonization programs that formed part of the corporatist citizenship regime. As already discussed for CIDOB, in the ensuing years, the state encouraged the migration of Andean peasants to the Amazon and distributed lands to these colonizers as well as to large ranchers – lands that had previously been used by Amazonian indigenous communities, but that were not legally titled by any state institution. Ranchers, in particular, took particular interest in the region as the rise in beef prices and the commercialization in beef cattle were also taking place (Jones 1990: 3–4). A land rush ensued as cattle ranchers sought to turn the Beni into a prime producer of cattle for Andean consumption. State titling overwhelmingly favored these ranchers and speculators. In turn, displaced indigenous communities fled these areas and were reduced to smaller and more remote areas (Jones 1990).

At the same time that the state promoted these development projects, it protected certain areas from development. In 1965 it created the *Parque Nacional Isiboro-Sécure* and in 1975 it created a *Reserva de Inmovilización Forestal* (Lehm 1996: 17, 20; Molina 1997). Nonetheless, the state did little to protect these areas and, in some cases, reversed this protective policy

---

[105] The Mojos historically were dispersed and itinerant populations that moved when resources dwindled (CIDDEBENI 1988: 4). The arrival of the Jesuits in the mid-seventeenth century led to the settlement of many Mojo families. The missions tried to concentrate as many as 2,000 people into one center. While they were relatively successful among the Mojos, they were much less so with the Chimanes, Yuracarés, Sirionós, Chocobos, and others (CPIB n.d.: 1). Most towns found today in the Beni were Jesuit missions dating from this period. See CIDDEBENI (1988: 3–6, 11–12); Jones (1990: 2–3); Block (1994); Ticona, Rojas, and Albó (1995: 73); and CPIB (n.d.: 1–2).

in the 1980s, in line with the neoliberal policies being implemented in the rest of the country. These economic policies (which opened up parts of the protected forests to the market) catalyzed the more aggressive arrival of the private sector into the southern and central part of the Beni (Molina 1997: 2).

In short, beginning in the late 1960s, but particularly in the 1980s, indigenous communities in the Beni confronted the ongoing threat of loggers, cattle ranchers, and colonos who occupied tracts of land considered by Amazonian Indians as open space for working, hunting, and residing. Alongside this state-sanctioned colonization occurred a wave of colonization by Andean Indians who had moved to the region to grow coca. This wave of colonization was particularly prevalent in the Parque Nacional Isiboro-Sécure, which has been the home to forty-seven Amazonian indigenous communities (over 4,500 residents) from three different indigenous groups (72 percent *mojeño-trinitario*, 19 percent *yuracarés*, and 9 percent *chimanes*) since precolonial times. The state presumably protected the rights of Amazonian communities in 1965 with the declaration of a national park in this region. However, the state had little capacity (and probably little political will) to defend the park's boundaries and protect the indigenous communities therein from the new wave of Andean colonos. The state's limited control of this area is illustrated by the fact that the park is situated on land that is being contested in an interdepartmental border dispute between the Beni and Cochabamba – with little state effort to resolve this issue and little state effort to protect the park. Since 1979, but particularly since the neoliberal reforms of the mid-1980s, Andean Indians committed to cultivating coca as a survival mechanism (as discussed in the Andean section) have migrated to the southern part of the park to colonize this area. Many of them have identified with the COB, CSUTCB, and the *Confederación de Colonizadores*. Remarkably, the number of Aymara and Quechua colonos from the Andes who now reside in the park exceeds the total number of Amazonian Indians residing there. In this regard, state policy was flouted and Amazonian indigenous communities were threatened by this growing sector of coca growers and later loggers (Lehm 1996: 17–18; Molina 1997: 6, 147–8, 151–2, 166, 168).

In the *Bosque de Chimanes*, a significant rise in land pressures also occurred in the 1980s. The Chimanes Forest is a particularly precious area as it claims "the largest mahogany reserve in Bolivia and one of the largest in South America" (Jones 1990: 4). With this in mind, it was declared a reserve (*Reserva de Inmovilización Forestal*). The reserve made commercial exploitation of natural resources illegal and unwittingly protected this area for indigenous communities residing therein. In late 1986, however, the state reversed this position by reclassifying 579,000 hectares as a forest in permanent production (*bosque de producción permanente*). This reclassification opened up the forest to "commercial timber extraction" and granted concessions in 1987 to Bolivian companies, with little consideration given to the indigenous peoples residing therein. Concessions totaled half of the forest (Jones 1990: 4; Lehm 1996: 18–20; Molina 1997: 88–91; and CPIB n.d.: 5). Within a year's time (1986 to 1987), the reported volume of mahogany extraction from the Beni more than doubled (Jones 1990: 4).

In this overall context of changing citizenship regimes and the attending waves of new settlers, indigenous communities from the Amazon were directly challenged. Those in the Bosque de Chimanes were threatened by loggers; the Sirionó were threatened by cattle ranchers; and those residing in the Parque Nacional Isiboro-Sécure were threatened by Andean colonos primarily cultivating coca (Molina 1997: 6). Not only were indigenous land spaces being challenged but so too were the autonomous spaces in which they lived. These pressures were perhaps most intense in the Chimanes Forest. Indigenous communities residing in the Bosque de Chimanes unsurprisingly voiced the need to defend their space and in 1987–1988 one finds the first demands in the Beni for indigenous territory, the right to use the natural resources therein, and the right to participate in decisions about the forest (Molina 1997: 97, 103; CPIB n.d.: 6).

However, the capacity to organize more broadly for territorial autonomy was stymied by two serious obstacles. Over time, the communities had developed different types of internal organizing structures. Those with a history of missions had developed cabildos; but those that had escaped this missionary control had maintained and developed other forms of local organization. Moreover, regardless of the types and diversity of internal organizations, the links between communities were weak in the twentieth century – for the links that the Jesuit missions had imposed on indigenous communities subsequently declined as indigenous communities, confronted with colonizers and explorers, retreated and dispersed into other areas.[106] Unlike the Andes, indigenous leaders interested in defending their communities could not draw on prior organizational networks left in place by strong peasant unions, since union organizing in the Beni had remained quite feeble.

[106] CIDDEBENI (1988: 5–6); Jones (1990: 2–3); Block (1994); and CPIB (n.d.: 2–3).

Confronted with weak transcommunity networks, indigenous organizing would emerge within an urban area among those who shared a common organizational structure and had prior organizing experience.[107] Because the urban areas were more integrated into the Bolivian state system than the rural areas in the Amazon, these indigenous activists did confront some fluctuation in political associational space – more than their Amazonian rural counterparts, although presumably less than their Andean counterparts. Indeed, Ernesto Noe, who became President of CPIB, claims that during the military regimes of Banzer and García Meza it was nearly impossible to organize – given that there were prohibitions on meetings of more than three people and brigades patrolled some of the communities – particularly in the Beni's departmental capital, Trinidad. "We began to organize when there was freedom to breathe, without fear of anything. We [mojeños] started to call meetings after the Banzer and García Meza governments."[108]

Several Mojeño leaders from the Cabildo Indigenal de Trinidad were in contact with CIDOB[109] and the *Servicio Nacional de Alfabetización Educación Popular* (SENALEP).[110] In March 1987, they organized *El Primer Encuentro de Autoridades Mojeñas* (the First Meeting of Mojeño Authorities). The *Mojeño* organizers had prior organizing experience in the *Cabildo Indígenal de Trinidad, Juntas Vecinales,* and/or peasant unions.[111] Gathering in Beni's capital city of Trinidad, they called a meeting to address the crisis within the cabildo system – which was vulnerable to manipulation

---

[107] See Molina (1997: Table 7) for a chronology of where and when meetings took place between 1987–1990.

[108] Ernesto Noe, interview, July 25, 1997.

[109] Marcial Fabricano, interviews, October 30, 1995 and November 2, 1995; Lorenzo Vare Chávez, interview, August 1, 1997; and Zuhlema Lehm, interview August 1, 1997. For newspaper coverage of this event, see *Presencia* March 7, 1987, March 12, 1987, and April 17, 1987. Marcial Fabricano stated in interviews on October 30, 1995 and November 2, 1995 that representatives from CIDOB were invited to and visited the Beni during this organizational stage. Lorenzo Vare Chávez, who had been the corregidor in Trinidad, noted, for example, that he, Ernesto Noe, and others from the Beni were invited to attend CIDOB's meeting with the Ayoreo in Santa Cruz, in 1987. When they returned from the meetings, they shared what had happened in Santa Cruz and started to organize.

[110] SENALEP was established by the *Unidad Democrática Popular* (UDP) government (1982–1985). SENALEP was committed to using indigenous languages to promote adult literacy and was actively engaged with NGOs, indigenous groups, and academics in the creation of literacy materials that had a strong ethnocultural focus. Their literacy materials were subsequently used by others (Healy 1996: 251).

[111] Ernesto Noe, interview, July 25, 1997 and Lorenzo Vare Chávez, interview, August 1, 1997.

by outsiders – in order to create greater internal and cultural unity among Mojeños, to create and solidify supra-local connections, and to unify administrative structures across communities. They set out to mobilize the cabildo structures that the Mojo communities shared and in April 1987, they created the *Central de Cabildos Indígenales Mojeños* (CCIM) in Trinidad.[112] At its initial stage, CCIM largely represented urban Indians and representatives from indigenous communities close to Trinidad (CIDDEBENI 1988: 12; Jones 1990: 4; Molina 1996b: 9; Molina 1997: 71; CPIB n.d.: 5). This initial stage of organizing was defensive, according to Molina (1996: 9). It sought to protect indigenous communal lands and practices from the loggers that were invading their areas. In a very short time, however, organizers started to talk about "territory," which assumed a broader and more proactive set of goals that extended beyond individual communities and voiced a more supra-local agenda. This required greater coordination between communities, a stronger cabildo system within each community, and a supra-local organization of cabildos to defend and secure the territorial spaces in which they had lived. As stated in a subsequent document:

> Indigenous territorial demands constitute the fundamental [basis] and the root of the process, development, and consolidation of the original [indigenous] people's movement of the Beni. From the beginning, indigenous demands have had a strong sense of demands centering around the recognition of collective lands; nonetheless, they have also set out demanding the right to education as well as respect for their culture and forms of organization (CPIB n.d.: 5).

The CCIM initially focused on organizing Mojeños from April 1987 to November 1989 (CIDDEBENI 1988: 13). However, threats to territorial integrity were not experienced by the Mojeños alone. In this context, CCIM identified the need to organize other ethnic groups or to help other ethnic groups in their organizing efforts – both for their individual demands and to unify what was perceived as a much broader struggle. CCIM started to work with indigenous leaders and organizations in the areas most threatened by loggers, cattle ranchers, and coca growers. They worked with the *Subcentral Indígena de San Ignacio* from the Bosque de Chimanes, the *caciques* among the Sirionó, and the Subcentral Indígena from the Parque

---

[112] Jones (1990: 4) suggests that the return of Jesuit parish priests in 1984 to Moxos also helped in this organizational process – creating eight Christian grassroots communities and raising awareness of indigenous issues.

Nacional Isiboro-Sécure. CCIM was particularly active in the Bosque de Chimanes and the Parque Nacional Isiboro-Sécure (Molina 1997: 75–9).[113] This transcommunity organizing required creating ties with groups that did not necessarily share a common language or set of traditions. It also required overcoming two organizational challenges: the fact that these communities often did not share the same missionary past and, therefore, did not have the same internal mode of organization (i.e., cabildos), and the fact that there were no prior links between these communities (Lehm 1996: 15–16). While CCIM assumed an energetic position vis-à-vis these tasks, it received important help from CIDOB; some state institutions (such as SENALEP); domestic NGOs (namely *Centro de Investigación y Documentación para el Desarrollo del Beni* [CIDDEBENI]) that provided technical assistance, training about indigenous rights, research, and documentation; and international organizations (such as Oxfam, IBIS, the ILO, among others) that provided training about development projects and (support in looking for) funding. They also received help from the Catholic Church. These organizations helped to provide the resources that enabled CCIM to create these links with and between indigenous authorities (and representatives) from disparate indigenous communities.[114] Indeed, Noe observes that after having received training and support from the ILO, they were better prepared to "go to each one of the communities, pueblo por pueblo" to organize the region.[115]

With this expanded base, CCIM became a broader interethnic regional organization and renamed itself as the *Central de Pueblos Indígenas del Beni* (CPIB) in 1989. CPIB, therefore, came to represent not only mojeños but indigenous *subcentrales* and councils of the Beni (Molina 1996a: 10–11; Romero and Sándoval 1996: Annex 1; Molina 1997: 78–9).

Faced with the increasing pressure from logging companies in the Bosque de Chimanes and from colonizers and cattle ranchers in the Isiboro-Sécure and Ibiato, territory emerged as the central and primary demand among the many ethnic communities living in the Bosque de Chimanes, among the Mojeños and Yuracarés in the Isiboro-Sécure Park in 1988, and among the *Sirionó* who wanted to reclaim lands taken from cattle

---

[113] See *Presencia*, July 31, 1988 and August 9, 1988.
[114] CIDDEBENI (1990); Molina (1996b: 9); Molina (1997: 46–7, 60–5, 78–9); Healy (2001: ch. 9); José Guasebi, interview, November 26, 1995; Ernesto Noe, interview, July 25, 1997; Lorenzo Vare Chávez, interview, August 1, 1997; Zuhlema Lehm, interview, August 1, 1997; CPIB (n.d.: 5–6).
[115] Ernesto Noe, interview, July 25, 1997.

ranchers (CPIB n.d.: 6),[116] and ultimately of CPIB as their representative organization (Molina 1996b: 11).

CCIM/CPIB's territorial demands have been articulated since 1987/1988 for the Bosque de Chimanes, since 1988 for the Isiboro-Sécure, and since 1989 for Ibiato.[117] It is important to note, however, that the process of indigenous organizing had transformed the ethnic basis for making the demands. Indigenous communities had scaled up their local ethnic demands into a broader indigenous agenda that transcended ethnic group particularities and proprietary demands. In particular, territorial demands in the Bosque de Chimanes and the Parque Nacional Isiboro-Sécure called for multiethnic territories that recognized the right of several indigenous groups to a given territory. They also recognized the right of indigenous groups outside of a given territory to come and use sacred places within the territory (Navia 1992 and 1996).

CCIM and later CPIB first planted their demands for territory at local levels of government. However, with each failed attempt, they racheted up their efforts to target the next level of government, eventually placing demands before national ministries and finally the Bolivian president.[118] In 1989, a government commission recommended that indigenous groups gain access to the forest fringe but that the center lands remain with the timber companies; this proposal was rejected by the indigenous movement (Jones 1990: 4). In February 1989, the national government issued the Resolución Suprema 205862, which stated the national need to address territorial demands in favor of Amazonian indigenous groups; however serious action was not forthcoming (Navia 1992: 5, 11; Lehm 1996: 21–3; Navia 1996: 7). Lehm (1996: 23) observes that while the decree was not implemented, it created an important precedent – recognizing for the first time the right of indigenous peoples to survive as such (rather than assimilate into national culture) and to do so on state-recognized territories. This created a political referent that would prove useful in subsequent discussions.

After several failed efforts to secure indigenous territories through these channels, CPIB decided to organize what would be called *La Marcha por el*

---

[116] For an excellent and concise overview of the historical context, organizing efforts, and consequences of each of these areas, see Lehm (1996).

[117] Marcial Fabricano Noé, one of CPIB's and later CIDOB's central leaders, discusses this organizing process in the Parque Isiboro-Sécure in Libermann and Godínez (1992: 35–6).

[118] See for example, *Presencia* (November 6, 1988; January 14, 1989; May 26, 1990; June 13, 1990) and *Hoy* (January 12, 1989).

Territorio y la Dignidad (the March for Territory and Dignity).[119] Fabricano and Guasebi suggested that while territory was articulated as a demand for communal space, dignity was a question of the rights of all individuals.[120] The march began with indigenous men, women, and children who set out from Trinidad, the capital of Beni, for La Paz, the capital of the country. While the participants were largely Mojeños from the Chimanes Forest, the Isiboro-Sécure Park, and other regions, the march did mobilize other ethnic groups within its ranks.[121] The marchers were demanding legal recognition of territorial autonomy and their indigenous authorities but also underscored the fact that they saw themselves as Bolivians who were committed to the nation-state. In other words, they wanted to carve out local autonomy but maintain adherence to the larger polity of which the proposed territory would remain a part (Jones 1990; Molina 1996a: 7–8; Molina 1997: 171–98; CPIB n.d.: 7).

The march culminated in September 1990 with President Paz Zamora issuing three executive decrees (22609, 22610, and 22611) that recognized indigenous territories (Jones 1990: 5; Navia 1992: 13).[122] The state had

---

[119] For newspaper accounts of the decisions leading up to the march and accounts of the march, see *El Diario* (January 7, 1989); *Los Tiempos* (January 5, 1989, August 11, 1989); *Presencia* (January 9, 1989, January 10, 1989, January 22, 1989, July 2, 1990, July 28, 1990, August 2, 1990, August 5, 1990, August 12, 1990, August 14, 1990, August 15, 1990, August 16, 1990, August 17, 1990, August 18, 1990); *El Día* (July 9, 1990); *Hoy* (August 11, 1999, August 17, 1990); *Ultima Hora* (August 12, 1990); and *El Mundo* (August 17, 1990, August 22, 1990).

[120] Marcial Fabricano, interviews, October 30, 1995 and November 2, 1995; José Guasebi, interview, October 26, 1995.

[121] Healy (2001: ch. 14) describes the march. According to Marcial Fabricano (interview November 2, 1995) 870 people left the Beni for La Paz, but they were joined en route. An estimated 1,000 people arrived in La Paz at the end of the march. Seventy humanitarian organizations comprised the *Coordinadora de Solidaridad con el Movimiento Indígena*, which supported the march. Among these the Catholic Church played a particularly important role in counseling the movement leaders and in mediating between the marchers and the government (Jones 1990: 2, 7). In a October 26, 1995 interview José Guasebi also noted the important mediating role often played by the Catholic Church during the march and negotiations. However, Lorenzo Vare Chávez was careful to note in an August 1, 1997 interview that churches were not helpful everywhere in the Beni. They were particularly important in Trinidad, but not necessarily in the surrounding communities.

[122] The indigenous proposal for the indigenous law is reprinted in Libermann and Godínez (1992: 65–73). The law was never passed as such, although elements of it were incorporated into political reforms undertaken during the first Gonzalo Sánchez de Lozada administration. During that administration, a commission worked on ways of making national and indigenous legal systems more compatible. The project was completed during the Banzer administration although its implementation was stalled (Van Cott 2000a: 213–18 and 2000b).

Table 5.4. *Indigenous Territories in Bolivia (1990–1992)*

Territory	Date Recognized	Land Mass (hectares)
Territorio Indígena Sirionó	1990	80,000
Territorio Indígena-Parque Nacional Isibore-Sécure	1990	1,100,00
Territorio Indígena Multiétnico	1990	355,000
Territorio Indígena Chimane	1990	392,000
Territorio Indígena Araona	1992	92,000
Reserva de la Biósfera-Territorio Indígena Pilón Lajas	1992	400,000
Territorio Indígena Yuqui	1992	115,000
Territorio Indígena Chiquitano	1992	24,634
TOTAL		2,558,634

Source: Navia (1992: 2)

unsuccessfully tried to divide the movement during the march (offering partial concessions to some groups over others). In particular, the administration did not want to concede the center of the Chimanes Forest and appeared willing to offer concessions in those areas where the state was the weakest (i.e., the Isiboro-Sécure National Park). The executive decrees, however, finally did concede to CPIB's demands – including the central part of the Chimanes Forest. A fourth decree also announced the establishment of a commission that would draft an indigenous law legally recognizing traditional indigenous authorities.[123]

The march was only the beginning of these negotiations. While the executive decree was politically significant, legally it was a weaker and more precarious action than legislation – precisely because it could simply be overturned or ignored by the following administration. Nonetheless, it set in motion a series of discussions and actions that marked the "right" of indigenous peoples to make territorial demands and also the capacity of the state to respond. By 1992, the state had recognized several territories, totaling over two and a half million hectares (see Table 5.4, Navia 1992: 2).[124]

The march and subsequent recognition of indigenous territories were significant turning points for the indigenous communities and leaders of

[123] Jones (1990: 5) and Molina (1997: 209–12).
[124] Paz Zamora further promoted indigenous issues in political circles by successfully inviting the Indigenous Peoples Fund to Bolivia and securing ratification of ILO Convention 169 during his administration. Van Cott (2000a: 130).

the Beni. First, the march served to raise national awareness of the plight of indigenous peoples in the Amazon; it was commonly stated in La Paz that prior to the march, Andean urbanites had no sense of what was happening in the Amazon. Second, the march strengthened a collective identity that revolved around self-defense and territorial rights.[125] Indeed, the march helped to solidify links within CPIB as it demonstrated its capacity not only to organize this demanding march but also to negotiate successfully with the state over territory.[126] The march helped to reinforce territorial demands as *the* central political issue for indigenous movements in the lowlands (Molina 1997: 5, 214). Third, the march created CPIB's cache within CIDOB.[127] Finally, with the presidential decrees, there were concrete (although contested) benefits for the indigenous communities of the Beni leading to a renewed round of organizing and training. CPIB organized courses, seminars, research, workshops, pamphlets, and the like to train indigenous men and women for the management of these territories – particularly in the areas of governance, planning, and borderguard protection (CPIB n.d.: 8–9). They also assumed responsibility for demarcating the territories recognized by the decrees, particularly given that the government dragged its heels in doing so (Molina 1996a: 14).

Internal organizing within the territories has also built on and transformed indigenous authority structures therein. As noted, CCIM and CPIB set out to link the traditional indigenous authorities with the aim of organizing the indigenous movement and making territorial demands. With the recognition of the territories, however, new layers of political reorganization have had to develop to allow for coordination between communities in the territory and between the territory and CPIB.[128]

These follow-up mechanisms were seen as crucial to the viability of the territories. Navia (1996: 11–15) reported that the territories faced several challenges that have worked against the consolidation of these legally recognized spaces.[129] By 1996, the state, for example, had exhibited an overall lack of political will – failing to demarcate the territories within the agreed upon period, neglecting to elaborate rules stipulated in the decrees,

---

[125] See *Grupo Técnico de Planificación* (1993) and CPIB and CIDDEBENI (1995: 47 and pt. V).
[126] See CPIB and CIDDEBENI (1995: 74–5).
[127] Marcial Fabricano, interview, October 30, 1995.
[128] See Libermann and Godínez (1992: 35–6) and Lehm (1996). Also, Zulehma Lehm, interview, August 1, 1997.
[129] See CPIB and CIDDEBENI (1995: 51–70) for an overview of problems confronted by fifteen subcentrales that comprise CPIB.

and doing little to prevent illegal logging in these areas.[130] Given limited resources, information, channels for dialogue between indigenous movements and state agencies, and lack of coordination between state channels, Navia concluded that the obstacles for the consolidation of recognized territories were serious indeed. In this context, loggers, cocaleros, and others continued to disregard territorial boundaries.

Regional Efforts to Demand Territorial Autonomy and Inclusion

CPIB and its parent organization, CIDOB, therefore organized actively around territorial claims. The demarcation of indigenous territories has provided the physical space in which indigenous peoples are working to maintain a dynamic balance between local autonomy and greater national political integration. The movement has demanded that the state recognize the right to greater incorporation into existing state institutions, the reform of political institutions to allow for more diverse representation and voice, and the recognition of legal pluralism (in particular the right to be treated fairly in Bolivian courts and the right of indigenous communities to follow their own traditional authorities and law). In this vein, José Guasebi stated in a 1997 interview that the demand for territory cannot be divorced from the "right to citizenship and the right to community. The constitution recognizes these rights, but there are no laws or institutions to actualize them."[131]

To institutionalize autonomy and inclusion, CIDOB started in 1986 to draft an indigenous law proposal to reflect these broader concerns.[132] The push for a wide-ranging indigenous agenda found echo and refrain in the administration of President Gonzalo Sánchez de Lozada and Vice President Víctor Hugo Cárdenas. The Gonzalo Sánchez de Lozada administration made some serious (if contested) overtures to the indigenous movements and passed significant reforms that opened up new political spaces for

---

[130] For complaints about failed compliance with the agreement, see *Los Tiempos* (March 17, 1991); *Presencia* (May 16, 1991; May 22, 1991; September 18, 1991; February 2, 1993; December 1, 1994; January 14, 1995; February 3, 1995; August 18, 1996; August 20, 1996; December 8, 1996); and *La Razón* (September 3, 1991).

[131] José Guasebi, interview, October 26, 1995.

[132] See *Los Tiempos* (August 14, 1991); *Presencia* (October 9, 1991); and *Ultima Hora* (October 27, 1991). For reports on indigenous movement pressure on the government to pass the indigenous law, see *Presencia* (January 21, 1993; January 31, 1993; April 8, 1993; and May 9, 1993).

negotiating with the state.[133] While the Andean organizations denounced these ties, the Amazonian Indians started to see important opportunities.[134] The administration implemented a series of institutional reforms that corresponded with some of the demands voiced by the indigenous movements – namely the demand for greater political participation and the demand for greater autonomy. Reforms included the creation of a Subsecretariat of Ethnic Affairs (SAE); constitutional reforms that recognized the multiethnic and pluricultural diversity of the Bolivian population as well as indigenous community lands; and the legislation of a municipalization and decentralization program in the much heralded Popular Participation Law. While these reforms represented significant advances, initially they were not unambiguously positive in the eyes of indigenous leaders. The issues of land and communal rights were now constitutional, but not yet fully realized.

Indeed, despite constitutional and administrative changes, CIDOB found state efforts lacking. In particular, the state did not explicitly pass a "Ley Indígena." CIDOB called for legislation that would grant legal weight to the executive decrees already passed in 1990 and successive years; would give greater authority to traditional indigenous leaders; and would grant greater access to state social and economic resources and support. Such legislation was not forthcoming. In this context, CIDOB decided to resurrect the march as a mobilizational and political tool (CIDOB 1996: 88–9; CPTI 1996: 79) – both to consolidate the existing territories and to demand new ones.

CSUTCB and the *Confederación Sindical de Colonizadores de Bolivia* (CSCB) joined CIDOB in its march for territory and expanded its goals to include a diverse set of demands. The ensuing march was the closest that

---

[133] For important discussions of these reforms, see Albó (1994); Ministerio de Desarrollo Humano (1996); Ticona (1996); Balslev (1997); Molina and Molina (1997); SAE (1997); Vacaflor (1997); Van Cott (2000a); and Booth et al. (forthcoming). Ramiro Molina, interview, October 24, 1995; Marcial Fabricano, interview, November 2, 1995; Iván Arias, interview, May 17, 1997; George Gray Molina, interview, June 4, 1997; David Murillo, Roberto Rozo, and Luis Antonio Rodríguez, interview, June 9, 1997; Alcides Vadillo, interview, June 11, 1997 and June 13, 1997; Angel Yandura and Bonifacio Barrientos, interview, July 2, 1997; Ricardo Calla, interview, July 4, 1997; Luz María Calvo, interview, July 9, 1997; and Bonifacio Barrientos, interview, July 25, 1997.

[134] The election of Víctor Hugo Cárdenas had a contradictory impact on the country's indigenous movements. While the Kataristas divided over his election – labeling him a traitor for having run with Gonzalo Sánchez de Lozada, the Amazonian movement saw an important opening in government (Grupo ip-Latina/CEDETI 1995: 7). Also see CSUTCB (1994: 36).

the various indigenous movements came to forging a national indigenous movement along the lines developed in Ecuador. According to CIDOB, the march started off with 2,000 people but culminated with 30,000 arriving in La Paz (CIDOB 1996: 89).[135] The march put forth the following demands: the titling of lands and territories held by indigenous peoples, peasants, and colonizadores; the incorporation of rural workers into the *Ley General del Trabajo*; the capacity to participate in politics without going through political parties; the creation of a development fund for indigenous peoples that would be administered by indigenous peoples; equal participation in the secretaries for economic and social development; the distribution of identity cards to all peoples; and a juridical definition of territory that would include control over natural resources and the distribution of lands therein. Despite initial efforts to join forces, the march ended in discord as the government negotiated the final terms of the *Ley de Instituto Nacional de Reforma Agraria* (Ley INRA) with CIDOB,[136] to the exclusion of CSUTCB and CSCB.

The Ley INRA was passed in October 1996. The new agrarian reform law was an unprecedented piece of legislation that recognized communal land rights for indigenous people living throughout the country. While the rest of Latin America was advocating the privatization of land markets, the Ley INRA provided mechanisms for the state to legally recognize indigenous communal lands in the form of *tierras comunitarias de origen* (TCOs) (Múñoz and Lavadenz 1997: 17–20; Vacaflor 1997). The law opened the door for indigenous people to petition INRA for territories of various sizes, an opportunity that Amazonian indigenous communities appeared best poised to take. With the recognition of TCOs, the law had essentially recognized spaces in which indigenous authorities could de facto

---

[135] See *La Razón* (August 5, 1996; August 28, 1996; September 6, 1996; September 11, 1996); *Presencia* (August 9, 1996; August 15, 1996; August 20, 1996; August 22, 1996; August 29 1996; September 1, 1996; September 7, 1996); *El Deber* (August 14, 1996; August 25, 1996); *Ultima Hora* (August 26, 1996; August 27, 1996); *Los Tiempos* (August 26, 1996; September 17, 1996); and *El Mundo* (August 30, 1996; September 1, 1996; September 8, 1996; September 11, 1996).

[136] For a report of the negotiations leading up to this agreement between the government and CIDOB, see *Hoy* (September 14, 1996) and *Presencia* (September 15, 1996). For a report on CSUTCB's distancing from Marcial Fabricano, who negotiated on behalf of CIDOB, see *Los Tiempos* (September 17, 1996; September 21, 1996). For a report on the colonizadores's distancing from Fabricano, see *El Mundo* (September 19, 1996). For a report on Fabricano's statement that he was not betraying these groups, see *Presencia* (September 20, 1996).

institutionalize their authority over the TCOs. By 2000, there were eighteen territories in the Beni, totaling about one-third of that department's land mass. Six of these territories had been titled through Executive Decrees, including those that had been recognized after the 1990 March by CPIB. Twelve of these territories were legally recognized but had not yet been surveyed and titled (Navia 2003: 189) (see Table 5.5). While the law was initially perceived as a way to respond to increasing demands for territory in the Amazon, it was not legally limited to this region. According to CIDOB (1996: 91–2), the Ley INRA in fact incorporated many of the ideas initially proposed in CIDOB's ideas for an indigenous law. In particular, it recognized the right of indigenous peoples to their original communal lands; the right to use natural resources located on their lands in a sustainable way; the titling of old and new territories; and so forth.

By the mid-1990s, therefore, CIDOB was indisputably a strong regional indigenous organization. It not only mobilized indigenous communities throughout the Bolivian Amazon, but it also came to negotiate successfully with governments in the 1990s. While it did not and could not control political outcomes, it was an important player in social movement circles and policy debates.

Conclusion: The Vagaries of Democracy

Bolivia's indigenous activists had illustrious success in forging regional movements that have introduced ethnic politics back into formal political debate. In response to a changing citizenship regime that challenged local autonomy, indigenous activists forged indigenous movements in the Andes and Amazon by drawing on transcommunity networks and political associational space. By doing so, they inserted ethnic demands into policy debates. While they have far from singlehandedly reshaped politics, they have put territorial autonomy, legal pluralism, land reform, and other indigenous issues on the political agenda. The unprecedented advance of these political reforms and new discourse are incontrovertible. Yet these successes have been tempered by the vagaries of Bolivian democracy. For the indigenous movements and associated policy reforms have not occurred free of a political field in which people and parties are maneuvering for advantage. Three processes served to weaken the initial indigenous movements and the associated reforms that they had supported.

First, the institutional success of the "indigenous reforms" has depended on the political will of Bolivian presidents to promote them and the

Table 5.5. *Beni: Land Area of Indigenous Territories (2000)*

No.	Indigenous Territory	Land Area (Hectares)	% of Total Land Area	Ethnic Group	Linguistic Family
	Titled by Supreme Decree	2,567,253.75	35.37%		
1	Chimane	401,322.81	5.53%	Chimanes	T'simane'
2	Multiétnico	343,262.45	4.73%	Trinitarios, Ignacianos, Yuracarés, Chimanes, Movimas	Multiétnico
3	Parque Nacional Isiboro–Sécure	1,236,296.33	17.03%	Trinitarios, Yuracarés, Chimanes	Multiétnico
4	Sirionó	62,903.44	0.87%	Sirionós	Tupi guarani
5	Pilón Lajas[a]	396,264.44	5.46%	Chimanes, Tacanas, Mosetenes	Multiétnico
6	Yuqui	127,204.28	1.75%	Yuquis	Tupi guarani
	Inmovilizados[b]	4,691,478.96	64.63%		
1	Baure	505,775.65	6.97%	Baures	Arawak
2	Itonama	1,227,362.95	16.91%	Itomanas	Itonama
3	Joaquiniano	345,507.37	4.76%	Joaquinianos	Multiétnico
4	Moré	81,974.08	1.13%	Morés	Chapakura
5	Cayubaba	651,839.61	8.98%	Cayubabas	Kayuvava
6	Chácobo/Pacahuara	510,895.20	7.04%	Chacobos, Pacahuaras	Pano
7	Cavineño	523,249.36	7.21%	Cavineños	Takana
8	Canichana	33,460.16	0.46%	Canichanas	Kanichana
9	Moxeño Ignaciano	98,388.90	1.36%	Moxeño-ignacianos	Arawak
10	Movima	27,219.23	0.37%	Movimas	Movima
11	Multiétnico 2[c]	441,470.60	6.08%	Esse Ejjas, Pacahuaras, Cavineños	Takana
12	Yuracaré	244,335.85	3.37%	Yuracarés	Yura
	TOTAL LAND AREA	7,258,732.71	100%		

[a] Land area shared with the Department of La Paz.
[b] Inmovilizados refers to a legal stage in which the demand for a TCO has been accepted and the land in question cannot be subject to further laws. However, prior to titling the land in question, it must first be surveyed and territorial boundaries must be clarified.
[c] Land area shared with the Department of Pando.

Source: CPTI-CTDOB (2000). Atlas de Territorios Indígenas en Bolivia. Situación de las Tierras Comunitarias de Origen (TCOs) y proceso de titulación. CTD/Plural eds. La Paz. Republished in Carlos Navia (2003). La cuestión indígena en el Beni. Reflexiones en la década de los 90s. A9 CIDDEBENI. Trinidad-Bolivia, pp. 205–6. Published with permission from author.

institutional capacity of the state to implement them. Following the wide-ranging reforms passed by the first Gonzalo Sánchez de Lozada adminis-tration, implementation was stymied by successive governments. General Hugo Banzer was elected as president in 1997. Despite receiving a distinct minority of the vote, he cobbled together an unwieldy coalition of disparate political forces. Banzer put the political reforms of the first administration of Gonzalo Sánchez de Lozada on the back burner. If Sánchez de Lozada reorganized the ministries and secretariats to create political spaces for re-form, Banzer reshuffled those same institutions in ways that demonstrated their decreased priority. Banzer fired key staff; reorganized secretariats (to signal the executive's declining support for many of Sánchez de Lozada's institutional reforms); and shifted key programs, such as the Law of Popu-lar Participation, away from an emphasis on local participation to poverty alleviation and away from the municipalities toward departmental political oversight (Van Cott 2000a: ch. 7). These changes indicated a minimal com-mitment to indigenous demands and agendas – including those that were legislated in the prior administration. Moreover, the great promise offered by the Ley INRA was dashed.[137] Van Cott (2000a: 217) reports that "[t]he distribution of indigenous-claimed land has come to a standstill. In Santa Cruz, in the first two years the agrarian reform has been in effect, not a single land title has been delivered to an indigenous community." The fate of the "indigenous agenda" of the 1990s is unclear as of the time of this writing. And while Gonzalo Sánchez de Lozada was elected as president again in 2002, he did not voice the same kind of popular commitment to ethnic demands. Indeed, by the end of 2003, he was forced from office, following multiclass and multiethnic street protests against him. In these demonstrations, indigenous movements played a lead role.

Political party competition posed a second obstacle for Bolivia's indige-nous movements. With the movements' successes came efforts by political parties to capture indigenous organizations. Efforts by left party activists to wrest control of the CSUTCB had detrimental consequences for the

---

[137] On the last day of the first Sánchez de Lozada administration, INRA issued a reglamento for the Ley INRA that worked against the rights outlined in the law (Almaraz 1998: 187–8). According to Almaraz, the reglamento created a long and expensive bureaucratic procedure for processing claims for TCOs that some saw as working against the spirit and intention of the law. Moreover, the reglamento made it extremely difficult for indigenous peoples to submit new petitions for TCOs. Hence, the subsequent administration of for-mer dictator and then President Hugo Banzer inherited a progressive law with restrictive implementation regulations.

Kataristas in the second half of the 1980s.[138] This kind of party competition was more apparent in Bolivia than in Ecuador. For while both have relatively weak party systems in the Latin American context (see Mainwaring and Scully 1995), Bolivia's parties have been more enduring and penetrating than their Ecuadorian counterparts. As such, political parties had greater capacity and experience in trying to capture civic organizations, such as the CSUTCB. This democratic competition at times weakened the Kataristas hold on the CSUTCB and their ability to shape the indigenous agenda therein.[139]

Finally, the lure of participating in electoral politics weakened these same movements. Indigenous activists in Bolivia, like their counterparts in Ecuador, eventually gravitated toward electoral politics. The Kataristas, for their part, divided over whether to enter the electoral fray, with whom to forge coalitions, and whether to run on other tickets (Hurtado 1986; Healy 1989: 24). By the end of the 1980s, the Kataristas had broken into in-fighting cliques. Víctor Hugo Cárdenas and Jenaro Flores, two of the key spokespersons for the Katarista movement, identified with different electoral parties, with the former tied to the *Movimiento Revolucionario Tupak Katari de Liberación Nacional* (MRTKL) and the latter forming a new party, the *Frente Unido de Liberación Katarista* (FULKA). Neither party did well in elections although Cárdenas was later elected as vice president on the ticket with Sánchez de Lozada (Hurtado 1986: 110–25, 145–7; Calla 1993: 19–20; Albó 1994: 60–1).

---

[138] As revealed at their national congresses, political parties successfully divided the peasant movement and, in turn, weakened the direct control that the Kataristas had once had on peasant politics. They managed to block several Katarista proposals to redesign institutions so as to take into account ethnic differences and authority structures (Hurtado 1986: 213–14; Rivera 1991: 22; Albó 1994: 60; Hurtado 1995: 137–9; and Jenaro Flores, interview, June 19, 1997). And finally, many have suggested that in this context, Jenaro Flores started to play partisan games and move away from his peasant base to maintain his leadership. By doing so, he lost credibility (Hurtado 1995: 138–41) and (Calla 1989: 47–52).

[139] In the CSUTCB's First Extraordinary Congress, these political divisions over the direction, purpose, and health of the union were also made apparent (see Calla 1989 and Ticona 1996: 22–4). At this Congress, Flores was ousted as *secretario ejecutivo*, a position that he had held since 1979. The rest of the National Executive Committee was also displaced – marking the end of the Katarista influence over the union (Calla 1989: 11). According to Calla, the CSUTCB has therefore moved from an organization dominated by the Kataristas (1979–1983), to one dominated by two parties (the Kataristas' MRTKL and the *Movimiento Campesino de Bases*) (1983–1987), to a more plural organization (Calla 1989: 12). In the 1990s, the Quechua cocaleros and ASP gained pride of place. In the 2000s, the Aymaran leader, Felipe Quispe, has promoted a new ethnic agenda within CSUTCB.

Electoral politics also weakened CIDOB. CIDOB had originally claimed that it did not want to engage in party politics. Indeed in a 1995 interview, Marcial Fabricano, then the President of CIDOB, stated that one of CIDOB's principal positions was to remain independent of partisan and religious politics.[140] Nonetheless, CIDOB did choose to participate formally in electoral politics just as CONAIE had in Ecuador. At the end of the day, several parties offered the vice presidency to Fabricano. CIDOB chose to ally with the *Movimiento Bolivia Libre* (MBL). The outcome of the elections was largely disastrous, however. National-level candidates fared poorly (as was expected) as did local-level candidates (which was unexpected). In other words, CIDOB's own communities did not vote for CIDOB leaders.[141] "The CIDOB-MBL ticket won less than 4 percent of the vote, garnering not a single representative" (Van Cott 2000a: 216). And many CIDOB-affiliated communities lamented the fact that their leadership was decreasingly in touch with the local levels that form the core of CIDOB.[142]

At the time of this writing the organizational fates of CIDOB in the Bolivian Amazon and the Kataristas in the Bolivian Andes are uncertain (particularly in the latter case). What remains clear, however, is that they have changed the field of play for other social movements and the state. For if this chapter has primarily argued a) that challenges to local autonomy, preexisting transcommunity networks, and political associational space provided the conditions for the first round of indigenous mobilization and b) that electoral competition has served to shake their unity/foundations, this chapter has also argued that c) time and sequence matter. The prior successes of the Andean and Amazonian indigenous movements have inspired a whole new generation of activists in the Andes – drawing on the organizational strategies and successes of the Kataristas and CIDOB. The cocalero movement has repeated the language and style of many of the Kataristas. And new ayllu movements and youth organizations have focused on the demands for territorial autonomy articulated by CIDOB. In

---

[140] Marcial Fabricano, interview, October 30, 1995.

[141] Prior to the elections, the newspapers reported on political divisions among CIDOB communities/organizations. See, for example, *Presencia* (February 19, 1997); *El Deber* (February 20, 1997); and *La Razón* (February 21, 1997).

[142] Community discussions conducted by Marcial Fabricano, José Urañabi, and Felicia Barrientos in late June 1997 in Camiri, Villamonte, and Monteagudo; CPIB (1997); reports in the press (*Presencia* [February 19, 1997]; *El Deber* [February 20, 1997 and March 7, 1997]; *La Razón* [February 21, 1997]; *Opinión* [February 26, 1997]; and *El Mundo* [March 7, 1997 and March 8, 1997]); and two anonymous 1997 interviews with consultants to CIDOB.

this regard, the next sequence is before us. Insofar as these new activists question the integrity of Bolivia's democracy and demand the autonomy of local communities, they parallel the Kataristas and CIDOB. But this new generation of indigenous activists will also emerge around new issues and will develop new agendas. There is no other way to interpret the emergence of second-generation indigenous movements among the cocaleros, the protests around water in Cochabamba in the early 2000s, the local-level effort to strengthen ayllus, and the decision by Evo Morales to run for president in 2002 in defense of the right of indigenous people to grow coca. Moreover, in the aftermath of Sánchez de Lozada's downfall in 2003, indigenous people have actively participated in national dialogues about constituent assemblies and economic development, hoping to shape institutional design and policy in a way that takes account of Bolivia's multiethnic population. In this regard, indigenous movements in Bolivia have had an enduring political impact. Indigenous mobilization and ethnic-based demands are now *part* of the national political lexicon, laws, and debates.

6

Peru

WEAK NATIONAL MOVEMENTS
AND SUBNATIONAL VARIATION

The current situation of indigenous people is of virtual abandonment and lack of legal protection.... In comparison with other sectors, indigenous participation, as individuals and as peoples, in the political activities of the country, is very limited (Américo Javier Aroca Medina 1999: 1–2).

In the 1780s, Tupak Amaru mobilized a widespread rebellion in the south of Peru. The indigenous leader intended to reassert Incan authority and indigenous autonomy. While the Spanish authorities put down the indigenous rebellion, its memory has grown as South America's most widespread and significant indigenous mobilization. Indigenous leaders throughout the Andes refer to this uprising, its lofty goals, and the possibility of power in numbers.

Two centuries later, widespread mobilizations once again emerged in the Peruvian countryside. Sendero Luminoso and the Tupak Amaru Revolutionary Movement (MRTA) organized guerilla movements that sought to topple the state. However, in marked contrast to the earlier period, these late-twentieth-century mobilizations were not committed to advancing indigenous identities or community autonomy. While these guerrilla movements mobilized in indigenous communities and occasionally incorporated indigenous symbols, these Marxist movements self-consciously mobilized along class lines, privileging class-based identities at the expense of indigenous ones.

Despite an oft-celebrated history of indigenous organizing and pattern of rural protest, Peru has experienced no comparable period of widespread indigenous movement organizing in the contemporary period. In this regard, Peru stands out as an anomaly, particularly when compared to the wave of indigenous movement formation in Ecuador, Bolivia, Mexico, Guatemala, and beyond. Why has Peru followed a different path? Why do we not find the same kinds of indigenous movements that have appeared in the rest of the region and that two centuries ago occurred in Peru? This is the central question addressed by this chapter.

In the spirit of observations made by McAdam, Tarrow, and Tilly (2001) and Stern (1987a and 1987b), I argue that we cannot explain Peru's "weak" indigenous mobilization from structural conditions alone. Peru, Ecuador, and Bolivia experienced many of the same structural historical changes that negatively affected indigenous communities. In each case, indigenous people confronted changes in citizenship regimes, among other things, that placed their communities in jeopardy. Peru differs, however, in terms of the weakness of transcommunity networks and political associational space. Where community ties were absent or weakened, indigenous mobilization did not emerge. By contrast, in those enclaves that escaped repression and sustained community ties, indigenous mobilization was possible and in fact, at the subnational level, started to emerge. This chapter supports this argument by making crossnational and subnational comparisons. Part I sketches out why we might have expected Peru to experience parallel indigenous movements, particularly given the characteristics it shares with the other case studies analyzed in this book. Part II then explains why national indigenous movements did not emerge in Peru – highlighting in particular the absence of political associational space and transcommunity networks. Part III concludes by looking below the surface. It identifies and explains two isolated and distinct examples of subnational variation – where changing citizenship regimes, political associational space, and transcommunity networks explained the emergence of discrete local movements.

Part I: Peru, Ecuador, and Bolivia: Most Similar Cases

Indigenous movements have not emerged on a national or even regional scale in contemporary Peru, as in Ecuador and Bolivia. This is a striking divergence in outcomes given significant parallels between Peru, Ecuador, and Bolivia. This section outlines how Peru, Ecuador, and Bolivia are most similar systems. After briefly reviewing common demographic and colonial characteristics, it turns to one of the main variables discussed in this book: changes from corporatist to neoliberal citizenship regimes.

Like Ecuador and Bolivia, Peru is situated in the Andean corridor and forms part of the Amazonian region. Like Ecuador and Bolivia, it has a significant indigenous population, with 35–40 percent of the Peruvian population estimated as indigenous.[1] Moreover, the country's indigenous people are diverse and dispersed in two distinct ecological and geographic zones: the Andes and Amazon. While the greatest percentage of indigenous people reside in the Andes (as in Ecuador and Bolivia), the greatest ethnic diversity exists in the Amazon (Dandler et al. 1998: 9; Valera 1998: 12; SETAI 1999).[2] Regardless of location, poverty levels are higher and delivery of social services is lower for Peru's indigenous peoples than the national average.[3] This correlation of indigenous ethnicity and poverty is high throughout Latin America. This demographic snapshot, of course, belies a complicated picture of identifying who counts as Indian and, therefore, how many Indians actually reside in Peru.[4]

Peru's similarities with Ecuador and Bolivia, however, are not limited to geography and demography. Peru has also experienced parallel political trajectories, starting with the colonial period. Indeed, colonial Peru extended along South America's Pacific coast and included what today we call Ecuador and Bolivia. As a consequence, the Peruvian colonial state enacted indigenous policies that shaped the constitution of indigenous communities throughout much of the Andean and Amazonian region – creating a politico-institutional parallel between Peru, Ecuador, and Bolivia. Throughout the region, we find colonial policies that enacted an early

---

[1] See Gonzales de Olarte (1994: 175–6) for a brief discussion of similarities shared by indigenous communities in Ecuador, Bolivia, and Peru.

[2] Accordingly, population density is higher in the Andes than in the Amazon, which claims 59 percent of the country's territory (Dandler et al. 1998: 9).

[3] See Psacharopoulos and Patrinos (1994); Gonzales de Olarte (1997); Escobal, Saavedra, and Torero (1998); Hentschel (1998); and Sheahan (1999: ch. 2).

[4] Counting "Indians" in Peru is no simple matter, as we saw in the Ecuadorian case. The 1993 census, for example, can lead to two separate conclusions, depending on the proxy used for indigenous identity. If one counts residents in "peasant communities" and "native communities," one finds that Peru's indigenous population is close to 35 percent of the national total – with the overwhelming majority of that population living in the Andes. This is the number used by Peru's *Secretaría Técnica de Asuntos Indígenas del Perú* (SETAI), which is part of the *Ministerio de Promoción de la Mujer y Desarrollo Humano* (PROMUDEH). However, in many countries, it is common to approximate indigenous identity by language use. If one counts those people who *only* speak an indigenous language (excluding those who are bilingual in Spanish and an indigenous language), then one concludes from this census that the indigenous population is only 19 percent of the national population. However, using language as a proxy for identity is a risky enterprise because the census categorizes bilingual speakers as Spanish speakers – which also is likely to underestimate indigenous populations. Finally, as with any census, indigenous families are likely to underreport indigenous language use, because it has often been interpreted as a marker of backwardness. This underreporting is exacerbated by the fact that the census takers were not comprehensive in surveying the Amazon. For a brief critique of the 1993 census, see Dandler et al. (1998: 10).

version of "corporatism," creating a separate ascriptive and legal category of Indians as well as concentrating and institutionalizing indigenous communities as separate and unequal spheres.[5] By creating the "Republic of Indians," the colonial state subordinated indigenous people *and* granted them an important element of community autonomy.[6] In the subsequent postcolonial period, Peru (along with Ecuador and Bolivia) reversed these policies and advanced so-called "liberal" policies that set out to incorporate, assimilate, and dominate indigenous peoples as "equal" individuals of the national "mestizo" republic – taking away their community claims for local autonomy and privilege.[7] This alternation between "corporatist" and "liberal" state policies provides a common historical background shared by Peru, Ecuador, and Bolivia (the three case countries analyzed closely

---

[5] Indigenous communities were not closed corporate communities, as once argued by an earlier generation of anthropologists. For a discussion of the complexity, character, conflicts, and changes within communities, see Bourque and Warren (1978a); Mallon (1983 and 1995); and Gonzales de Olarte (1994: 193).

[6] The Republic of Indians was predicated on the idea that there was a unitary category of peoples who would fall under colonial jurisdiction but who would have different rights than those granted to the Republics. By creating these Republics, the state essentially created a new category, "Indian," to refer to all indigenous peoples. It concentrated them into particular areas – thereby initiating a process of state building that undermined the more fluid boundaries and geographically discontinuous spaces governed by indigenous communities. It also made these communities all the more intelligible to the state, thereby enabling states to govern, control, and tax these communities. In turn, these communities became important sources of revenue, as communities were required to pay tribute to the colonial state. Indigenous chiefs and elders (and later alcaldes, rotating village leaders) continued to play a crucial role – governing these spaces and serving as interlocutors before the state. For a discussion of the Republic of Indians, see Remy (1994: 110–11); Mallon (1995); Thurner (1997: ch. 1, 149); and Yrigoyen (2002: 158–9), among others.

[7] With the nineteenth-century Liberal policies, the state ostensibly offered indigenous people proto-liberal rights with equal status and equal responsibilities as individual members of the Peruvian nation-state. Accordingly, the state extended suffrage rights to Indians, although there were always stipulations that in practice limited this right (See Mallon 1995: 181, 217–18). Moreover, throughout the century, the Peruvian state dismantled policies that had singled out Indians (and their communities and lands) as specific categories with specific rights and responsibilities. Hence, in 1824–1825, Bolívar decreed that land could only be held by individuals, thereby undermining the legal basis for maintaining the communal lands. This resulted in the privatization of landholdings and a loss of communal lands held by indigenous peoples during the colonial period (Smith 1989: 8; Klarén 2000: 146). In 1854, the state also ended policies that had defined indigenous communities as "Indian," that had extracted tribute from them, and that had prohibited the sale of communal lands (Remy 1994: 111). These policies were accompanied by "civilizing" programs of mestizaje (miscegenation). Historians of this period observe that there was a localization of politics – with local/regional power brokers providing the linkages between communities and the state (Remy 1994: 111; Mallon 1995: 17, 181; and Thurner 1997: 46–7, 140–3).

in Part II of this book) and has been richly explored by scholars of the period.[8] These political parallels extend into the twentieth century with the enactment of new kinds of corporatist and then neoliberal citizenship regimes. The rest of this section explores at greater length Peru's twentieth-century parallels with Ecuador and Bolivia. Despite most similar systems, these countries experienced a striking divergence in indigenous movement outcomes.

The Corporatist Citizenship Regime

Peru's corporatist period has its roots in the 1920 Constitution. The Leguía administration reversed many of the liberal tendencies of the nineteenth century by reinstating ethnic corporatist principles in the 1920 Consti-tution.[9] In particular, the constitution created the institutional and le-gal mechanisms for indigenous communities to gain legal recognition, to achieve juridical standing, and to act on behalf of indigenous peoples. The state therefore, granted, a kind of legal imprimatur that (re)institutionalized communities and gave them access to the state. It also created indigenist organizations that ostensibly served as interlocutors with indigenous com-munities.[10] In turn, the state assumed a more formidable role in governing and regulating the countryside.[11]

The 1920 Constitution not only redefined the relationship between in-digenous communities and the state, it also restored the right of indige-nous communities to communal landholdings. It thereby institutionalized the physical space within which indigenous communities would live and institutionalized their political identity before the state and market. As in

---

[8] See Bourque and Warren (1978a); Mallon (1983 and 1995); Gonzales de Olarte (1994); Remy (1994); Thurner (1997); and Yrigoyen (2002).

[9] For brief discussions of the 1920 constitution vis-à-vis indigenous rights, see Harding (1975); Mallon (1983: 232–5, 270–1); Smith (1989: 8); Remy (1994); and Yrigoyen (2002: 160–1).

[10] Leguía created several indigenist organizations, including the Bureau of Indian Affairs (*Sección de Asuntos Indígenas*) in 1921, the *Patronato de la Raza Indígena* in 1922, and the Roca Commission (to investigate land titles in Puno) (Harding 1975: 226 and Mallon 1983: 234). Additionally, the Leguía government hosted an Indian Congress in 1921, from which emerged the Comité Pro Derecho Indígena Tahuantisuyo (Tahuantinsuyo Committee in Favor of Indian Rights) (Mallon 1983: 234).

[11] Yrigoyen (2002: 160) discusses the 1924 Penal Codes, which continued to view indigenous peoples in the Andes and Amazon as "semi-civilized" and "savages," respectively.

Ecuador, this state policy catalyzed communities to register with the state.[12] It did not impose an organization on these communities, however, until 1969 (as discussed in the following text). Yet it would be naïve to read this period of community recognition as an unambiguous pro-Indian and pro-poor measure for the countryside. Leguía's populist rhetoric of the 1910s–1930s eventually gave way to more cautious political alliances and policy making. He took agrarian reform and servile rural/ethnic social relations off the political agenda and abolished indigenista organizations that were suggesting substantive changes.[13] Indeed, in this period, hacienda expansion continued and in many cases challenged the landholdings and labor practices of indigenous communities.[14] In short, the ethnic corporatist citizenship regime of the 1920s was discursively and legally consequential but in practice had a limited immediate impact. It provided the means to legalize the community as the interlocutor for indigenous peoples but did not translate into enduring modes of interest intermedation; nor did it secure landholdings for indigenous communities. In this regard, the 1920 Peruvian Constitution played a similar role to that of the Ley de Comunas in Ecuador, providing a legal precedent for communities, which would become consequential in subsequent years.

A full-fledged corporatist citizenship regime did not emerge as such, however, until the 1960s and 1970s. As in Ecuador, a populist military leader initiated a series of reforms that both privileged corporatist modes of interest intermediation and extended social rights in the form of communal land and social services. As with Ecuador and Bolivia's corporatist citizenship regimes of the twentieth century (but unlike past Peruvian experience), the corporatist policies privileged *class* rather than ethnic identities, concerns, and rights. So too as in Ecuador and Bolivia, Peru's class-based corporatist citizenship regime unwittingly secured the spaces within which indigenous peoples secured a certain degree of local autonomy, as elaborated next.

In 1968, General Juan Velasco Alvarado (1968–1975) initiated the coup that set this corporatist experiment in motion. Velasco assumed power in

---

[12] Remy (1994: 112) and Mallon (1983: 270–1).
[13] Mallon (1983: 235) and Stern (1998: 14).
[14] See Seligmann (1995: 45); Kay (1982: 144–5); and Mallon (1983: 235). In this period we find the radicalization of the labor movement and the emergence of more radical ideas about indigenous rights and the historic role for indigenous peoples in a revolutionary movement. José Carlos Mariátegui, in particular, articulated powerful and highly influential positions on indigenous peoples and their revolutionary role.

a context of extreme land inequalities and peasant mobilizations.[15] Indeed Peru's Gini Index was among the worst reported in a comparative study of fifty-four countries (McClintock 1981: 64–7). These structural conditions coincided with "guerrilla warfare in the southern highlands, syndical radicalism on the coast, and an overall growing peasant movement throughout the country" (Hunefeldt 1997: 109). Velasco argued that he would work against inequalities and for a more inclusive Peruvian nation. As part of this project, he occasionally engaged in strikingly egalitarian and symbolic public behavior: "when a peasant knelt before him to ask a favor during a highlands meeting, he asked the peasant to rise and then, when the peasant did not, knelt down with him."[16]

While the scope of the Velasco reforms was wide, this chapter focuses particularly on those reforms that restructured the countryside and ostensibly incorporated Indians into the Peruvian polity.[17] Of these, the most important was the land reform.[18] Velasco announced this reform on June 24, 1969 (the Day of the Indian). At a symbolic level, he chose to redesignate that day as the Day of the Peasant, symbolizing the administration's presumed commitment to move away from divisive ethnic categories and toward a more inclusive and unified Peruvian nation (Seligmann 1995: 58–9). This effort to project national unity was intimately and fundamentally tied to Velasco's belief that he could incorporate this sector into the polity and nation by making them equal citizens of Peru and that the way to

[15] See Bourque and Palmer (1975) and Handelman (1975) for a discussion of the rise in rural mobilization, in general, and see de la Cadena (2000: 185–91, 311) for a description of the rise in class-based organizing that occurred in Cusco. See McClintock (1981: 73); Gonzales de Olarte (1994: 45); and Hunefeldt (1997: 111, fn. 4) for data on Peru's unequal land distribution in the 1960s.

[16] McClintock (1981: 294–5).

[17] For a discussion of this period and its impact on the countryside, see Bourque and Palmer (1975); Cotler (1975); Webb (1975); McClintock (1981); Hunefeldt (1997); and Sheahan (1999), among many others. Velasco initiated many other reforms besides those discussed in the text – including the reorganization of industry and mining; the nationalization of fishing; the partial nationalization of banking; and the expansion of the state's role in the economy.

[18] This was not Peru's first land reform. For a general discussion of early reform measures, see Bourque and Palmer (1975); Harding (1975); Webb (1975); McClintock (1981: 71); and Alvarez Rodrich (1995). The preceding civilian government of Belaúnde initiated a significant but less ambitious land reform in 1964. According to Bourque and Palmer (1975: 197–8), Belaúnde's land reform largely benefited those who had occupied lands illegally – thereby legitimating what had already been done rather than launching a widespread process of redistribution.

do this was by restructuring rural relations. As Seligmann (1995: 3) states in her anthropological study of the land reform:

> The Velasco regime . . . tried to restructure ethnic relations. It assumed that once peasants had control over their land and labor, they would regain their dignity and, in a general sense, cease to be "Indians." . . . The [land] reform measures thus spelled out the path that Quechua peasants should follow if they wanted to receive the benefits of the reform *and* recognition as national citizens (Seligmann 1995: 3).

Accordingly, the Velasco government officially abandoned the term *Indian* and replaced it with two distinct references: *peasants* (campesinos) and *peasant communities* (comunidades campesinas)[19] when referring to the Andes and *native communities* (comunidades nativas) when referring to the Amazon.[20]

The land reform was radical in scope and distributed property to associative and cooperative enterprises referred to as SAISs (*Sociedades Agrícolas de Interés Social*, Agrarian Social Interest Societies) and CAPs (*Cooperativas Agrarias de Producción*, Agrarian Production Cooperatives), as discussed in the following text. As is so often the case, there is inconsistent data about how much land was distributed and to whom.[21] Yet if the exact amount of land redistributed and the exact number of beneficiaries is debated (at the margins), it is generally agreed that the reform as a whole decimated the large landowning class: "By 1977, there were virtually no more haciendas in Peru" (McClintock 1981: 60). Indeed, McClintock (1981: 60) suggests that reform in Peru had a more significant impact on large landowners than comparable reforms in Chile, Mexico, Bolivia, or Venezuela. And while other land reforms often left the most fertile lands in the hands of large (and efficient) landowners, in Peru these very lands were expropriated and redistributed (McClintock 1981: 62). Given that the largest haciendas and

---

[19] According to the III Censo Agropecuario conducted in 1994 (heretofore referred to as the 1994 Census), there are 5,860 peasant communities in the country. While these communities are found throughout the country, they are concentrated in the Andes, with more than half of them found in four departments: Puno, Cusco, Huancavelica, and Ayacucho (Valera 998: 11). Of these 5,860 peasant communities, 73.1 percent are titled.

[20] The 1994 Census also indicates that there are 1,192 comunidades nativas, which are basically located in the Amazon – with more than half of them in two departments alone, Loreto and Ucayali (Valera 1998: 11–12).

[21] Gonzales de Olarte (1994: 45) reports that the land reform redistributed 28.5 percent of arable lands (8.3 million hectares) to 359,600 families. Hunefeldt (1997: 109–10) reports that by 1980, 8.6 million hectares were distributed (39 percent of the land) to 390,684 peasants.

most fertile lands were found on the coast, the 1969 land reform responded by targeting and most intensively distributing lands in this region.[22] So too, the Agrarian Bank tended to extend the largest amounts of credit to the coast – even while the largest number of loans went to the Andes. It should be noted, however, that these loans increasingly benefited associations (rather than individuals) in the 1970s, for reasons that are discussed in the next section.[23]

The Velasco government complemented this radical land reform with the 1970 Statute on Peasant Communities.[24] The statute sought to redefine Indians as peasants, to reorganize the heretofore indigenous communities along cooperative lines, and to create sharper divisions between comuneros and those who worked in the broader market. In other words, the state once again tried to penetrate these communities, to undermine their ethnic identification, and to modernize them in ways that were compatible with a Western notion of progressive economic development and organization. While the statute privileged stronger class identification and organization, the intention was not to politicize class so much as to harness it and depoliticize it by institutionalizing it in these various organizations (Bourque and Palmer 1975: 189–90; Cotler 1975: 70).

> Under [this statute] . . . the cooperative concept was extended to the 2,337 recognized Indian communities and their 390,000 families. The statute establishes new membership criteria: only those comuneros who are full-time farmers and residents of the community may enjoy full membership. Secondly, the communities are to be reorganized along cooperative lines, with a new governing framework of administration and vigilance councils to supplant the old *junta comunal* and *personero*. In addition, the private holdings which prevail in the majority of communities are to be "restructured" into cooperatively owned land. . . . The community statute disregards such traditional community structures as the ayllu and varayoh; it restricts elected positions in the new cooperative to those who can read and write Spanish. In addition, it prevents comuneros from seeking employment and maintaining plots outside the community (Bourque and Palmer 1975: 189–90).

A significant number of these peasant communities gained legal access to community lands. By the 1990s, there were 35 million hectares of

---

[22] The state distributed 64.5 percent of agricultural and pastoral lands on the coast; by contrast, the state distributed 36.7% of agricultural and pastoral lands in the Andes (Gonzales de Olarte 1994: 47).

[23] Rodríguez-Seguí (1999a) based on information from the Banco Agrario del Perú (1970: 1; 1975: 47; 1980: 36; 1985: 29; and 1988: 31) and Palomino-Bujele (1993: 61–2).

[24] The following discussion of the 1970 statute draws on Bourque and Palmer (1975: 189–90; 204–5); McClintock (1981: 36–7); Remy (1994: 115); and Seligmann (1995: 60–2).

agricultural and pastoral lands, 24 million of which were community lands, with 18 million of them belonging to the peasant communities and the other 6 million belonging to native communities (Valero 1998: 37–9).

Alongside these efforts to redistribute land and reorganize the communities along class-based lines, the state sought to increase ties to the peasantry. They did so largely through the dissolution in 1972 of the *Sociedad Nacional Agraria* (SNA, the oligarchic association that had wielded important political power) and the creation of the *Sistema Nacional de Apoyo a la Movilización Nacional* (SINAMOS) and the *Confederación Nacional Agraria* (CNA).[25] According to CNA President Julio Cantalicio, the principal goal of the CNA was to defend lands and to convert them into cooperatives.[26] By creating these new organizations, Velasco essentially undermined the legitimacy and political power of existent peasant unions.

The state set out to impose organizational characteristics on the new agrarian associations; to define their objectives (to support the state); and to limit their involvement in party politics. SINAMOS, in turn, sought to mobilize various organizations as a means of generating support for the government and channeling participation into legal and state-sanctioned channels. Hence, SINAMOS included the CNA (McClintock 1981: 54–7). As an added incentive to take part in the CNA, the state indicated that only those agrarian associations that had registered with SINAMOS would be granted juridical standing (Cotler 1975: 71–2). While SINAMOS preached participation, it was hierarchical, tied to the military government, and therefore as much about control as about political mobilization.

Through these various measures, Velasco fostered peasant organizing and ties to the state. Hence we find that whereas 1,344 communities were registered in the 1972 *censo agropecuario*, that number increased in subsequent years to 3,030 in 1980, 3,672 in 1987, 4,811 in 1991, 4,976 in 1992, and 5,680 in 1994; that is a compound annual growth rate of 6.4 percent (INEI 1998: 43).

Hence, as in Ecuador and Bolivia, Velasco set out to reframe Indians as peasants, to institutionalize their ties to the land and their ties to the

---

[25] For discussions of SINAMOS and CNA, see Bourque and Palmer (1975: 191–2); Cotler (1975: 71–2); Harding (1975: 245); McClintock (1981: 37–8, 54–7, ch. 9); Seligmann (1995: 70–1); and Hunefeldt (1997: 111–12). Hunefeldt reports that the state also created the *Confederación Campesina del Perú* (CCP), which was also a vertical organization that sought to organize the peasantry in support of the state. However, it was less prominent than CNA.

[26] Julio Cantalicio, interview, August 20, 1997.

Table 6.1. *Peru: Number of Peasant and Native Communities, by Region and Department, 1997*

Department	Peasant Communities #	%	Native Communities #	%	Total Communities #	%
Andes/Sierra						
Puno	1,274	22.43			1,274	18.54
Cusco	927	16.32	47	3.94	974	14.17
Junín	414	7.29	203	17.03	617	8.98
Huancavelica	500	8.80			500	7.28
Ayacucho	454	7.99			454	6.61
Apurímac	438	7.71			438	6.37
Huánuco	241	4.24	11	0.92	252	3.67
Cajamarca	110	1.94	4	0.34	114	1.66
Arequipa	91	1.60			91	1.32
Coast						
Ancash	350	6.16			350	5.09
Lima	289	5.09			289	4.21
Piura	154	2.71			154	2.24
La Libertad	125	2.20			125	1.82
Moquegua	68	1.20			68	0.99
Tacna	48	0.85			48	0.70
Lambayeque	33	0.58			33	0.48
Ica	7	0.12			7	0.10
Tumbes	1	0.02			1	0.01
Amazon/Jungle						
Loreto	8	0.14	384	32.21	392	5.70
Amazonas	50	0.88	193	16.19	243	3.54
Ucayali			230	19.3	230	3.35
Pasco	96	1.69	85	7.13	181	2.63
Madre de Dios	1	0.02	23	1.93	24	0.35
San Martín	1	0.02	12	1.01	13	0.19
TOTAL	5,680	100	1.192	100	6,872	100

Source: Valera (1998: 13).

state, and to organize them in state-sanctioned and regulated organizations. As in Ecuador and Bolivia, efforts to regulate these communities and re-structure their internal organization were only partially successful. Even following the land reform, these communities continued to maintain tradi-tional systems of political authority. While the state imposed new forms of governance, these often became shells for prior systems of political authority (Gonzales de Olarte 1994: 186–8; Seligmann 1995: ch. 8; and INEI 1998: 43).

To be sure, since the 1969 agrarian reform, the internal functioning of the communities has been standardized, creating the administrative council and vigilance council as governing organizations of the communities. These norms permitted for a more fluid relationship between the communities and the state institutions, although internally the important decisions continue to be made according to custom, since the administrative council is in reality the ancient body of *varayocs* or *regidores* (Gonzales de Olarte 1994: 187).

In short, Peru's corporatist citizenship regime paralleled similar periods in Ecuador and Bolivia. It granted indigenous peoples formal autonomy from landlords, provided them with (or imposed on them) class-based corporatist modes of interest intermediation with the state, and granted them collective lands and credit, which unwittingly provided the space within which local autonomy was institutionalized. Hence, the class-based corporatist citizenship regime unintentionally enabled local *indigenous* communities to defend and develop local autonomy and authority systems – much as occurred in Bolivia and Ecuador.

The Neoliberal Citizenship Regime

The erosion of the corporatist citizenship regime eventually gave way to the institutionalization of a neoliberal citizenship regime, as in Ecuador and Bolivia. The erosion occurred during the military regime of General Francisco Morales Bermúdez. He launched a bloodless coup against Velasco in 1975 and initiated a move rightward. He cracked down on popular organizations and weakened or dismantled many of the corporatist policies and institutions that had privileged peasants. Morales Bermúdez's military administration, therefore, marked the end of the corporatist citizenship regime.

The institutionalization of a neoliberal citizenship regime, in turn, occurred in the 1980s and 1990s – beginning with the transition from military rule in 1979 and followed by the implementation of neoliberal economic policies. These momentous changes both privileged the role of the individual – in terms of primary modes of interest intermediation and in terms of rights. Hence, the transition from authoritarianism witnessed the return of political rights (namely the right to vote) and significantly extended the suffrage to illiterates (with important consequences for the indigenous

Table 6.2. *Peru's Central Government Expenditures by Economic Sector, as Percentage of GDP*

	1980	1981	1982	1983	1984	1985	1986	1987	1988	1989	1990	1991
Agriculture	3.7	3.7	2.7	2.5	0.9	1.8	2.0	2.3	1.2	1.7	1.2	1.0
Education	3.0	3.2	2.8	2.9	2.8	2.6	3.4	2.2	2.1	2.3	1.8	1.6
Health	1.1	1.1	0.9	1.0	1.0	1.0	1.0	0.8	0.7	0.6	0.6	0.5

Source: Gonzales de Olarte (1996: 39). Based on the *Compendio Estadística* 1993, Tomo III. INEI, Lima.

population). As in the rest of the region, the extension of political rights was soon followed by the retraction of many social rights – although the route was at times more circuitous in Peru than elsewhere.

For Peru's indigenous population, the most significant neoliberal reforms were those that challenged protected land markets and associated agricultural supports. Peruvian administrations (military and democratic alike) started to cut back on the delivery of social services and support for agriculture, education, and health (see Table 6.2). Public investment in agriculture stopped growing – first during the Morales Bermúdez military government (1975–1979) and second during Belaúnde's second administration (1980–1985) – although private investment increased slightly. Central government expenditures on agriculture, as a percentage of GDP dropped from a high in 1980 (3.7 percent) to a low in 1984 (0.9 percent). While there was an increase in expenditures in the middle of the 1980s (with a high of 2.3 percent in 1987), these expenditures never regained prior levels and subsequently dropped significantly, hovering around 1.0 and 1.2 percent in 1988, 1990, and 1991 (Gonzales de Olarte 1996: 39).

Belaúnde also oversaw a policy change to privatize cooperatives and dismantle the associative enterprises (Gonzales de Olarte 1994: 48; Hunefeldt 1997: 112). The administration sought more flexibility in land markets and thus granted peasant communities the right to sell or mortgage lands (Hunefeldt 1997: 112). Estimates indicate that as of 1986, 59.6 percent of cooperatives had been redistributed as individual parcels of land (Gonzales de Olarte 1994: 48). The state also decimated the subsidies programs (Hunefeldt 1997: 112). While the flexibilization of land markets freed peasants to do as they pleased with their lands, these policies appear to have most benefited richer peasants, who could purchase lands from their poorer neighbors in need of cash (Hunefeldt 1997: 112). These policies, which appeared to give peasants greater latitude, occurred during the 1982 drought, precisely when the poorer among them would have needed the greatest support. In this context, former landlords sought to reassert power in regions where earlier they had lost their lands (Hunefeldt 1997: 113).

The following administration of President Alan García implemented economic policies that ultimately challenged indigenous collective rights – although he initially started off on a populist note (Sheahan 1999: 68, 140–1).[27] García initially supported associative enterprises founded during the 1970s. Shortly thereafter, however, he did an about-face and supported the privatization of the CAPs and SAIS (Hunefeldt 1997: 113–14). By 1989, two-thirds of the associative enterprises were subdivided; most of this parcelization took place on the coast of Peru, where the most fertile lands are found (Hunefeldt 1997: 117–19).

The subsequent administration of Alberto Fujimori dealt the final blow to the corporatist citizenship regime created by Velasco's land reform and agricultural support policies.[28] While Fujimori promoted the clarification of land titles and temporarily taxed agricultural imports, he also fundamentally restructured land markets and agrarian markets (Sheahan 1999: 69). Fujimori liberalized land markets (enabling co-op members and communities to sell lands that were previously considered inalienable); eliminated most of the remaining price supports and subsidies to agriculture (including eliminating interest-free credits from the Banco Agraria); allowed

---

[27] García initiated massive credit programs, price supports, subsidies, a rise in public investment, a new land distribution program, and an exchange rate policy designed to stabilize production costs (McClintock 1989: 91–4; Hunefeldt 1997: 113–14; Rodríguez-Seguí 1999b; Sheahan 1999: 67–8). To emphasize the populist thrust of his administration, García also organized a series of conversations with indigenous leaders that were supposed to reach out to Andean and Amazonian communities. According to Aroca Medina, García would literally visit with leaders and write checks from the National Treasury for individual projects, items such as sewing machines, and the like. Aroca Medina notes that while the money often ended up in the pockets of leaders, communities ended up supporting García's populist measures (Américo Javier Aroca Medina, interview conducted by Maritza Rodríguez-Seguí, September 16, 1999).

[28] Fujimori had campaigned calling for a more slow-paced and gradual set of reforms than those promoted by his competitor – expressing concern for the lower and middle classes. Once he was elected, he implemented many of the drastic measures that his opponent had proposed during the campaign. See Gonzales de Olarte (1993); Roberts (1995); Kay (1996); and Stokes (1997).

larger landholdings to be exempt from expropriation; eliminated the Banco Agraria; and reduced expenses for infrastructure and social investment (Seligmann 1995: 73; Gonzales de Olarte 1996: 33 and ch. 2; Sheahan 1999: 69).

Of these reforms, the 1995 *Ley de Tierras* (Law 26505) was perhaps the most threatening for indigenous communities.[29] It privatized land markets by eliminating limits on landholdings and reversing the inviolability of community-held lands. While the law was largely implemented on modern and profitable agricultural ventures on the coast, campesino organizations expressed fear that community lands in the Andes would also be affected. Indeed, the fear of losing community-held lands was all the more pressing given that some communities had not completed the registration process, which is long and complicated.[30] Peasant organizations protested the reversal of prior laws and constitutional provisions that had protected these communally held lands.[31] Some have called for a legal guarantee of communally held lands. As Julio Cantalicio of the CNA observed, Fujimori's neoliberal politics, in particular Law 26505, "tried to go against the autonomy of peasant communities and the lands of peasant communities. It violates Law 24656 [and] it does not recognize the ILO's Convention 169."[32] These economic reforms clearly prioritized individual rights over collective ones, a pattern also found in Ecuador and Bolivia.

On the face of it, Fujimori's neoliberal reforms challenged local autonomy and therefore provided the very motive that catalyzed indigenous organizing in Ecuador and Bolivia. Indeed, during these years, indigenous communities suffered along many dimensions, including devastating

---

[29] See Gonzales de Olarte (1996: 79) and Manrique (1996).

[30] Only 2,000 of the 5,200 campesino communities that had been officially recognized possessed registered land titles by the mid-1990s. The law did not say how communities with unregistered or no land titles would be treated.

[31] The 1993 Peruvian Constitution overwhelmingly privileges the individual. However, the constitution does include some language that privileges collective and cultural rights. The document recognizes that Peru is a multiethnic, pluricultural, and multilingual country. Moreover, it recognizes the legal rights of peasant and native communities including juridical personality; cultural rights; the right to use indigenous language before public authorities; bilingual education; the right to customary law; among other things (Dandler et al. 1998: 7). Finally, and of particular relevance for the peasant organizations, Article 89 grants peasant communities organizational autonomy and labels their lands as imprescriptible (except when those lands are abandoned) (Gonzales de Olarte 1996: 77–9). The 1995 Ley de Tierras obviously disregarded the constitutionally recognized inviolability of communally held lands.

[32] Julio Cantalicio, interview, August 20, 1997. Also see Manrique (1996).

poverty levels. Even though agricultural output was growing in the 1990s, poverty levels remained higher in the mid-1990s than in 1985, with more than 50 percent of the population living below the poverty line (Gonzales de Olarte 1997: 31–2; Escobal, Saavedra, and Torero 1998: 85; Sheahan 1999: 69ff., 105, 165, 167). By any measure, indigenous people were the worst off – experiencing significantly higher poverty and extreme poverty rates than the nonindigenous population (Psacharapoulos and Patrinos 1994: 171; Hentschel 1998: 148; Sheahan 1999: 112). Fujimori did create social safety nets and social investment funds; however, these populist assistance programs were neither institutionalized, universal, nor integral to long-term development plans (Roberts 1995; Kay 1996). As such, they helped to soften the blow for some communities, which in some cases developed stronger clientelist ties to the state. However, for most indigenous communities these programs did not fundamentally address the underlying problems experienced in the aftermath of the neoliberal reforms.

In this overall context of policy shifts, state retreat, populist handouts, and rising poverty, a neoliberal citizenship regime was institutionalized, one that fundamentally challenged the community rights that the Velasco years had extended between 1968–1975. And by doing so, it challenged the inviolability of community lands, the prospects for sustaining community boundaries, and the power of autonomous community organizations.

In short, indigenous peoples in the Peruvian highlands have experienced parallel developments to those described previously in Ecuador and Bolivia. By the end of the twentieth century, they were neither totally assimilated nor autonomous, an in-between status that repeated a history of granting communal rights and then denying them. Colonial states institutionalized indigenous communities and granted a degree of political autonomy in exchange for tribute. Postcolonial administrations wavered between recognizing and undermining the legal and material basis for indigenous autonomy. By the end of the century, these communities were once again coming under attack as the neoliberal citizenship regime privatized land markets, reduced agricultural subsidies, and reversed the state's prior commitment to protect them as such. As in Bolivia and Ecuador, these economic reforms occurred at the same time that the promise of democratic political rights was extended, poorly protected though they were. For despite the turn toward democratic rule, it would be difficult to argue that indigenous peoples, as individuals, enjoyed or practiced the basic political rights associated with citizenship. Thurner (1997: 19), writing about an earlier period states: "Their ambivalent predicament vis-à-vis the Peruvian nation-state was to be separate in their integration, outside in their belonging." This predicament remains as true today in Peru as in the rest of the Andean region. Given the parallel challenge to local autonomy (plus the incomplete terms of democratization), why then did indigenous movements not also emerge in Peru?

Part II: No National Indigenous Movements: Explaining the Peruvian Anomaly

Given these similarities, it is particularly striking that national indigenous movements have not emerged in Peru alongside those in Bolivia and Ecuador. Indeed, Julio Cantalicio, the leader of the largest peasant confederation, the CNA, indicated in no uncertain terms that the association does not prioritize mobilization at all. Cantalicio stated that they were fighting to defend peasants and their right to the land. However, whereas before they would mobilize to promote their cause, he observed that now they do not. Instead they meet with other organizations to come up with alternative proposals. They started to adopt this strategy once Alan García assumed office. "Leaders have adopted a new role; they need to be more pragmatic. Now we do not enter in partisan politics.... What has not changed is our opposition vis-à-vis the government. But our opposition now takes the form of argument and proposals."[33] How does one explain why Peru has failed to mobilize along ethnic-based lines?

This section explains the obstacles to building an indigenous movement in Peru. Two factors are highlighted: the weakness of *transcommunity networks* and the lack of *political associational space*. To explain these developments, this section analyzes two successive periods. First, we revisit the corporatist citizenship regime and its impact. This section highlights that corporatist policies and organizations inserted distrust and tensions within and between communities rather than the cooperation and collaboration suggested by official rhetoric. While these developments did not foreclose possibilities for indigenous organizing, they certainly raised significant barriers to doing so. Second, and more importantly, the civil war in the 1980s and early 1990s had a devastating impact on both transcommunity networks and political associational space. Political violence essentially destroyed these elements, foreclosing opportunities for grand-scale organizing by and across indigenous communities.

[33] Julio Cantalicio, interview, August 20, 1997.

Revisiting Peru's Corporatist Citizenship Regime

Peru's corporatist citizenship regime fundamentally changed class relations in the Peruvian countryside – decimating the landed elite, distributing land in record numbers to peasants and rural workers, and actively organizing the countryside into corporatist organizations. This section enumerates these developments in light of the ensuing conflicts within and between communities. Rather than foster community ties and corporatist solidarity, as in Ecuador and Bolivia, Peru's corporatist policies often had the opposite impact – generating greater tension, distrust, and competition. As such, the corporatist citizenship regime did not substantially strengthen transcommunity networks or by extension substantially increase the *capacity* of indigenous people to organize, in marked contrast to the experiences in Ecuador and Bolivia.

General Velasco forged the corporatist citizenship regime in the countryside with the goal of building worker-owned enterprises and of fostering a cooperative spirit. He hoped to construct a series of local cooperatives that would be connected and coordinated by regional and national associations (Manrique 1996). Accordingly Velasco's land reform primarily distributed land to collective units such as cooperatives, agrarian societies, and peasant communities (see Table 6.3).[34]

The reform, however, did not distribute lands in a uniform way. Rather, the land reform provided for two different types of associations: CAP and SAIS. Both the CAPs and SAISs turned former workers into shareholders, workers, and managers (McClintock 1981: 34–5). However, the two types of cooperatives differed in important ways. The CAPs were most prevalent on the coast (where indigenous and peasant communities were scarce) and converted more modern sugar and cotton enterprises into cooperatives where the workers were the *sole* members of the enterprise. The SAISs, by contrast, were most prevalent in the highlands, where more feudal relations had been dominant and where indigenous communities were most numerous. The SAISs operated on lands expropriated from at least one ex-hacienda and were owned and managed by the ex-hacienda workers, surrounding peasant communities, and technicians. As such, its membership was more *diverse*.[35]

---

[34] For discussion of the land reform, see Cotler (1975); Harding (1975); Bourque and Warren (1978b); McClintock (1981); Kay (1982); Gonzales de Olarte (1994); Hunefeldt (1997); and Sheahan (1999: 63–7).

[35] Seligmann (1995: 59) indicates that the SAIS were more prevalent in the *central* highlands and the coast than in the southern highlands.

Table 6.3. *Estimated Distribution of Peruvian Peasants by Type of Agricultural Work (1977)*

	N	Thousands of Hectares	Total Farm Families	Families Benefiting from Reform	Percentage of Total Rural Farm Families
CAP	578	2,225	107,137	107,137	7
Peasant Groups[a]	798	1,586	43,945	43,945	3
SAIS	60	2,802	60,930	60,930	4
Peasant Communities	4,000	8,191	500,000	110,971	31
Private Farms	NA	8,000	600,000[b]	31,918	37
Eventuales	–	–	250,000	–	16
TOTAL	–	23,500	1,600,000	356,276[c]	

Notes: See Appendix 3 of McClintock (1981). McClintock cautions that except for the data on the CAPs, peasant groups, and SAISs, the figures are derived from census information that may not be reliable.

[a] This text does not elaborate on this category, which is briefly discussed in McClintock (1981) and Seligmann (1995: 62). It was created in 1976 (after Velasco was overthrown) to accommodate demands of a conglomeration of peasants who, for a variety of reasons, did not qualify as part of a peasant community.

[b] Approximately 20 percent of these farms are over 20 hectares, but under 100 hectares, and 75 percent are under 20 hectares.

[c] Figure includes 1,375 peasants in Social Property enterprises.

Source: McClintock (1981: 93).

The SAISs, however, did not assuage tensions in the highlands but, in fact, exacerbated some and created others. First, the SAISs did not prove to be productive enterprises.[36] Situated on former haciendas that often lacked modern equipment and appropriate infrastructure, they proved to be much less productive than the CAPs on the coast, which inherited modern enterprises in fertile lands. Consequently, while the situation of CAP workers tended to improve, that of the SAIS workers did not.[37] In other words, the SAISs did not change two basic and widespread problems: low productivity and poverty (Gonzales de Olarte 1994: 36). Manrique (1996) therefore

[36] Gonzales de Olarte (1994: 36); Manrique (1996); and Sheahan (1999: 64).

[37] The land reform coincided with other policies that weakened the productive capacity of agriculture. Kay (1982: 162) observes that Velasco introduced a foreign exchange policy that went further than before to encourage agricultural imports (this in turn disadvantaged agricultural exports); he extended price controls on agricultural products – benefiting consumers over producers. Moreover, he introduced agricultural subsidies for imported products.

observes that while some of the CAPs survived into the 1990s, the SAISs and other highland cooperatives "failed miserably." These economic failures exacerbated the problems outlined next.

A second critical issue revolved around who benefited from the land reform distribution. The land reform significantly restructured property relations but was less beneficial for indigenous communities than one might at first expect. This was so for several reasons. In the Andes, land was distributed as SAIS and, as such, included various sectors such as ex-hacienda workers and communities. The ex-hacienda workers, however, were the primary beneficiaries. They received individual share-outs while the communities did not; the latter benefited from infrastructural investments alone (Harding 1975: 247–8). As Bourque and Palmer (1975: 188) anticipated, and others confirmed, this created a host of tensions between the ex-hacienda workers and the comuneros. Not only did comuneros feel disadvantaged economically, but many also felt that the distribution of lands as SAIS had preempted communities from reclaiming lands that many had lost to haciendas over the years (Gonzales de Olarte 1994: 42). Writing in 1975, Harding observed:

Under the SAIS arrangement, the few permanent wage laborers form a service cooperative and are represented on the administrative councils along with members of the neighboring comunidades, which are made members of the SAIS collectively rather than individually. Any profits are shared between the laborers' cooperative and the comunidades, which receive their part in the form of infrastructural investments rather than individual share-outs. This is a source of resentment for the *comuneros*, and the wealthier ones, who own the most sheep, object to the exclusion of their animals from the pastures of the former haciendas, which are invariably alloted to the SAIS for the production of improved breeds by scientific stock management. *In effect, the comunidades have lost their battles for land against the haciendas as a result of the agrarian reform*, and the higher profits to be made from the scientific use of the pastures by the SAIS are not usually accepted by *comuneros* as valid arguments for the exclusion of their sheep. Similarly, former *colonos* are reluctant to vacate their parcels. . . . *Consequently, the SAISs have not been very successful so far in eliminating social conflicts, and lack of cooperation from members has made them economically unsuccessful in the case of many crop-producing SAISs* (Harding 1975: 247–8, emphasis added).

The comuneros came to resist the SAISs not only because they differentially benefited them but also because they represented state efforts to encroach on community autonomy: "Few peasant communities have been restructured because of the comuneros' hostility to the prospect of losing their autonomy by becoming integrated into the State co-operative model" (Kay 1982: 163).

If the SAISs differentially benefited those who formed part of it, it also differentially benefited the countryside as a whole. In fact, the SAIS model largely excluded the highland communities of the Andes because land was distributed first and foremost to permanent workers on the haciendas. "Nationally, only 6 percent of all legally recognized peasant communities participated as members in SAISs" (Hunefeldt 1997: 123).[38] Moreover, the land reform excluded temporary workers, many of whom heralded from various communities.[39] The land reform therefore served to further fragment the Peruvian peasantry, with tensions emerging between these diverse members. In this context nonbeneficiaries started to target other peasants rather than the state.[40]

A third conflict revolved around state efforts to control community organizations. The 1970 Peasant Statute, for example, set out to impose communal forms of governance (or communal cooperatives) on peasant communities not incorporated or restructured by the SAISs.[41] The statute was to create communal harmony through the establishment of cooperatives. The statute, however, gave birth to new political divisions. It created internal divisions over authority structures, favoring younger comuneros who could speak Spanish. In addition, by demarcating community boundaries, it created conflicts among communities over those boundaries. Communities also protested the terms of the initial proposal, which sought to restrict community membership by residency (despite the fact that many comuneros migrated during part of the year) and to restrict the holding of noncontiguous land plots (Bourque and Palmer 1975: 204–5). While some of these restrictions were relaxed, it is hard to gauge if community suspicions

---

[38] By the mid–late 1970s, the land reform had benefited 10–15 percent of farm families (Bourque and Palmer 1975: 203 and McClintock 1981: 62). Writing in 1994, Gonzales de Olarte (1994: 45) increased that figure to 37.4 percent of farming families; 38.3 percent of these beneficiaries were comuneros – although they tended to receive less than a hectare per family.

[39] See Kay (1982: 153–4) and Grindle (1986: 154–8) for a discussion of how the agrarian reform differentially affected different rural sectors – with the former hacienda workers making out the best, temporary workers being excluded, and communities receiving somewhat uneven benefits depending on the circumstance.

[40] Bourque and Warren (1978b: 12); McClintock (1981: 35–6, ch. 9); and Grindle (1986: 154–5).

[41] Bourque and Palmer (1975); Seligmann (1995: 60); and Manrique (1996).

subsided as well. Regardless, these government plans fueled opposition to unwanted state intervention.

These community – state tensions were not necessarily expressed as communal claims but were often articulated as individual demands. Bourque and Warren (1978b) observed three highland peasant communities in which there was resistance to (inadequate and at times incompetent) state efforts to impose cooperatives and communal-based enterprises; individualistic practices were more pervasive and communal practices less prevalent than had often been assumed.[42] Consequently, "the 'new Peruvian man' with a collectivist perspective and a corporatist solution to inequality never emerged in the peasant communities" (Bourque and Warren 1978b: 15). In this context, nonbeneficiaries started to call for the breakup of the cooperatives (Grindle 1986: 154–5). Beneficiaries of the associative enterprises often did the same (Hunefeldt 1997: 116–19).

Finally, the corporatist modes of interest intermediation (CNA and SINAMOS) did not successfully link communities and the state. The CNA was created by leftist advocates in the state who realized that the agrarian reform had not benefited the comuneros as much as ex-hacienda workers. The CNA failed, however, to mobilize in great numbers, even though it favored comunero representation over that of cooperative members and even though both the CNA and SINAMOS supported land invasions of unexpropriated haciendas (McClintock 1981: 262–8).

> Peasants viewed the CNA and its Agrarian Leagues as they had . . . previous federations. . . . Even as of 1977, majorities or near-majorities had not heard of the CNA (technically the pinnacle of the federation), although by that year most had heard of the Agrarian Leagues, the second-level component of the federation. . . . Peasants criticised the leagues for doing nothing in the community or cooperative or for only politicking (McClintock 1981: 281).

> [In other words] [t]he new federations established under Velasco failed to provide sufficient incentives for solidarity among Peruvian peasants. Neither the political federation, the CNA with its Agrarian Leagues, nor the larger-scale economic organizations, the central cooperatives, were able to modify the traditional skepticism of peasants toward institutions beyond their own enterprise or community (McClintock 1981: 284).

Indeed, because the CNA was launched at the end of Velasco's government, it did not succeed in mobilizing the peasant communities into a

---

[42] Bourque and Warren (1978b) argue that where peasant families had established ties to the coast they were less likely to support state initiatives for cooperatives and rigidly defined community boundaries.

unified organizational structure or in channeling their demands to the state. Communities tended to seek out their own autonomy from the state and resented outside efforts to regulate their internal functions. And because each cooperative was in competition with the next, there was little short-term incentive to join forces with other SAIS and CAPs (McClintock 1981: chs. 9–10; Kay 1982: 158–9). In short, "traditional peasant skepticism toward the national government endured. [Cooperative] [m]embers turned their new political solidarity into a weapon against what they considered government encroachment on 'their' self-managed cooperatives" (McClintock 1981: 314).

Overall, then, the corporatist citizenship regime left a legacy of weak transcommunity networks, thereby making it unlikely that indigenous communities in Peru would have the capacity to forge a regional or national indigenous movement. The uneven distribution of benefits from the land reform served to create tensions among those who took part in the cooperative associations and between beneficiaries and nonbeneficiaries. Rather than fostering a desire to promote and defend community rights, it often served to weaken social capital, to catalyze land invasions, and to engender demands for the privatization of communally held lands. Late efforts to reorganize the internal organization of the communities and to tie them into broader modes of interest intermediation were resisted as unwanted efforts at state intervention. In this regard, corporatist organizations failed to construct strong networks among communities. Consequently, Peru lacked the organizational capacity that transcommunity networks had provided indigenous people in Ecuador and Bolivia.

The Civil War: Destroying Political Associational Space and Transcommunity Networks

If the corporatist citizenship regime failed to provide the networks on which indigenous people could mobilize in Peru, the subsequent civil war actually destroyed networks and closed off political associational space.[43] The war was primarily fought against Sendero Luminoso (which took up arms in 1980) but was also fought against the smaller MRTA (which took up arms

---

[43] See McClintock (1989); Palmer (1994); Burt (1997); Degregori (1997); Basombrío (1998); Degregori (1998); del Pino (1998); Hinajosa (1998); Mallon (1998); Manrique (1998); and Stern (1998).

in 1984) (Obando 1998: 386).[44] The civil war thereby posed insurmountable obstacles for widespread organizing in the countryside and ultimately foreclosed the possibility altogether of organizing an indigenous movement in Peru.

Sendero Luminoso emerged as an all-consuming kind of military organization. It did not tolerate alternative forms of organization and set out to destroy independent associations and networks. Even community activists were assassinated by Sendero. In this context, existing organizations were snuffed out and leaders were often silenced. In other words, Sendero Luminoso essentially destroyed potential frameworks for legal organizing along ethnic lines – destroying the communication links for sharing experiences, for the rise in alternative leaders, and for the maintenance of organizations working on related issues.

These guerrilla movements are oftentimes portrayed as indigenous movements that launched a violent war to defend indigenous ways. And indeed, Sendero Luminoso set out to recruit among indigenous men and women – particularly from those who had migrated to the urban areas and among those who had attended the university in Ayacucho. However, Sendero Luminoso and MRTA did not promote ethnic claim making per se. Sendero Luminoso set out to undermine indigenous communal systems – often leading to resistance in the highland communities where these ethnic authority and governing systems were strongest.[45]

In this context of civil war, the military became much less concerned with maintaining a kind of inclusionary corporatism, as Stepan (1978) had discussed and became much more of a "Latin American style military."[46] That is to say, the Peruvian military started to conduct military operations against internal guerrilla forces. While the military formally operated under civilian rule, it developed a significant degree of institutional autonomy to regulate its own affairs and to "govern" the countryside. With the intensification of the civil war in the early 1980s, President Belaúnde declared states of emergency in various provinces – first in Ayacucho but later in other departments as well (Mauceri 1997: 34; Roberts and Peceny 1997: 195–7).

---

[44] Sendero Luminoso developed particular strength in areas where the agrarian reform had the weakest impact – although as McClintock (1989) and Wickham-Crowley (1992) have argued, this is not a complete explanation of the rise of Sendero Luminoso. Hunefeldt (1997: 120–1) notes that the agrarian reform did not really reach Ayacucho, Apurímac, and Andahuaylas, the region in which Sendero Luminoso began.

[45] See Degregori (1998) and del Pino (1998).

[46] See Rospiglosi (1995); Mauceri (1997); and Obando (1998).

And "by June 1989, all or part of nine departments were in a state of emergency. By July 1991 the state of emergency covered eighty-five provinces in sixteen of Peru's twenty-four departments, including over half the national population and 40 percent of the territory" (Roberts and Peceny 1997: 198).

The military became the governing authority (with political and administrative authority) in these emergency zones and displaced elected local officials (Mauceri 1997: 34; Roberts and Peceny 1997: 195–6). In other words, Peru was nominally a democracy but practically speaking was a country dominated by military forces – Sendero Luminoso on one side and the Peruvian military on the other. As both Mauceri (1997) and Roberts and Peceny (1997) report, civil liberties barely existed and Peru established a record of serious human rights abuses. These human rights violations were committed by several forces, including the military, insurgencies, drug traffickers, death squads, and civilian paramilitary patrols (rondas campesinas) (Roberts and Peceny 1997: 192). In this context of "civilian rule," there were few political opportunities to organize alternative civic organizations.

Despite rhetorical commitments to human rights by elected officials, the pattern of violations continued through the Belaúnde, García, and Fujimori administrations, none of which proved capable of devising a counterinsurgency strategy that was compatible with minimum standards of human rights, democratic accountability, or the rule of law (Roberts and Peceny 1997: 192).

... the military initiated a scorched-earth campaign in the southern highlands in 1983 and 1984, when military sweeps through indigenous communities resulted in a wave of forced disappearances and mass killings, along with massive dislocation of the local population (Roberts and Peceny 1997: 197).

Many communities sought to ward off the destruction and violence that came with this war. The creation of the *rondas campesinas* was one response. They emerged first (in the north) to defend these communities and later (in the south) as a paramilitary force. The paramilitary version of these organizations became particularly prevalent during the García and Fujimori administrations, which armed these paramilitary civil defense patrols and placed them under the local military (Roberts and Peceny 1997: 200–1). They constituted a local militarization of the Peruvian countryside, with an estimated 4,600 rural patrols in existence by 1992 (Roberts and Peceny 1997). In the context of this brutal civil war, Peru's "democracy" would prove highly problematic as the civilian government ceded power to the military (particularly in emergency zones); the rule of law and constitutional guarantees broke down; and representative institutions and autonomous forms of interest intermediation were emasculated (Roberts and Peceny 1997: 195). In short, little to no political associational space existed.

Sendero Luminoso lost much of its steam after its leader, Abimael Gúzman, was captured in 1992.[47] Thereafter, the government also captured several of the leaders of the MRTA. With these successful operations, the military seemed to decapitate the two movements and to put an end to the brutal civil war. In this regard, the unambiguous restrictions on organizing were lifted. However, the end of the civil war was not replaced by a period of unambiguous civil liberties or the extension of political associational space. Indeed, the government of Fujimori implemented an autogolpe (a coup against his own government) in 1992 that shut down the civilian courts and representative institutions and undermined constitutional rights and protections (Roberts and Peceny 1997: 202).[48] During Fujimori's term, presses were closed, political parties were weakened, and civil liberties were often trampled. The military in turn acted with increased power and impunity. Hence, while political violence fell from 1992 to 1993, the number of provinces under a state of emergency increased from fifty-two to sixty-six. "At the end of 1994, nearly half the population continued to live in emergency zones" (Roberts and Peceny 1997: 203).

Since 2000, when Fujimori was forced out of office, Peru's human rights record has improved. Interim-president Valentín Paniagua was credited with having promoted a greater respect for the rule of law, democratic institutions, and civil liberties. Alejandro Toledo, who was elected to office in 2001, has since resorted to states of emergency, although on a much smaller scale than during the height of the civil war. At the time of this writing, therefore, political associational space has expanded since the repressive years of the 1980s and early 1990s. However, the legacy of the civil war continues to constrain organizing; political associational space remains far from institutionalized; and the destruction of transcommunity networks has been long lasting.

In short, the Peruvian countryside proved to be a complicated place to organize. Indigenous people generally hesitated to self-identify pubicly as Indians (Bourque and Warren 1978a; Degregori 1995; Mallon 1995; and de la Cadena 2000). Moreover, the history of political incorporation,

---

[47] See Degregori (1997) for a discussion of Gúzman's capture.
[48] See Roberts (1995) and Roberts and Peceny (1997: 202–3).

community recognition, and land distribution had a destructive impact on the indigenous community networks – creating more tensions and conflict than one might have anticipated if one were to read through the lofty cooperative goals enunciated by the Velasco regime. Finally, the civil war destroyed the remaining political networks that had been left in place and closed off political associational space. In this context, indigenous leaders did not emerge and, if they had, would have been unable to organize a national indigenous movement. It is all the more striking then that incipient indigenous movements did emerge in two isolated regions of the country. The rest of this chapter takes up this subnational variation.

Part III: Explaining Subnational Variation

The picture thus far has assumed a somewhat homogeneous landscape – with the discussion focusing on the relationship between the state and indigenous communities in the Andean highlands. However, there is regional variation – both within the Andes (between the southern, central, and northern Sierra) and between the Andes and the Amazon. Indeed, in her sweeping comparative study of Peru and Mexico, Mallon (1995) concludes that the regional variation and fragmentation in Peru is profound. In this context of regional fragmentation, we find subnational variation. In the southern Andes and Amazon we find the maintenance of much stronger transcommunal networks and communal autonomy. So too we find that the war was least repressive in these regions. In other words, there are relatively greater social networks and political associational spaces in the Amazon and southern Andes. Extrapolating from the comparative argument developed in this book, one would therefore suspect that were an indigenous movement to emerge, it is in these regions that one might effectively find the seeds of an indigenous movement. This is precisely what the research unearthed, as witnessed by regionally contained movements: first in the Amazonian region and second in the southern department of Puno.

The Amazon

If Peru has thus far proven inauspicious for organizing indigenous movements on a national scale, the Amazon has provided a regional enclave for indigenous organizing. Dandler et al. (1998: 74) report that 85 percent of Amazonian Indians are affiliated with some kind of organization, with the majority belonging to some form of ethnic federation – with claims for territorial autonomy and self-determination. While some of these organizations were founded to defend against colonizers, others first started off as marketing organizations. They all became, however, organizations that focused on defending lands and territories; and on achieving the right to bicultural education and health (Dandler et al. 1998: 13). And these isolated organizations eventually scaled up into broader interethnic organizations.

The process of scaling up eventually culminated in the founding of the *Coordinadora de Comunidades Nativas de la Selva* (the Coordinating Committee of Native Communities of the Jungle) in 1979, which was renamed AIDESEP (the Interethnic Association of Development for the Peruvian Jungle) in 1980. As the name suggests, the association brought together different ethnic groups in the Amazon. AIDESEP represented several federations and in turn set out to strengthen local and regional initiatives designed to title lands, promote bilingual education, improve health, and enhance production projects. By 1998, there were fifty-nine federations in the Amazon with representation from sixty-five different indigenous groups. Together, these federations spoke on behalf of 93 percent of all *titled* indigenous communities in the Amazon (although it is important to recall that not all communities were either indigenous and/or titled) (Dandler et al. 1998: 14). Of these fifty-nine federations, forty-two affiliated with AIDESEP (Dandler et al. 1998: 14).

Why have these indigenous movements emerged in the Amazon? To make sense of this pocket of indigenous organizing, we need to highlight three factors: 1) The centrality of autonomy issues: Amazonian indigenous peoples had maintained autonomy from the state for most of Peru's history. Peru's corporatist citizenship regime served to institutionalize that autonomy and to secure some spaces within which indigenous communities could function and access the state. Simultaneous and subsequent state reforms, however, challenged that autonomy and motivated indigenous peoples to organize to defend their rights. 2) The church and NGOs created networks that subsequently provided the infrastructure and capacity for organizing. 3) The civil war was less pervasive in many parts of the Amazon than in the Andes – although it did have a very destructive impact in some communities. The Amazon, therefore, experienced greater political associational space, as a whole, than the rest of the country. This section highlights these points.

Autonomy   Indigenous communities in the Peruvian Amazon have always maintained a relatively high level of autonomy from the state and a corresponding strong identity as Indians of particular ethnic groups.[49] As in Ecuador and Bolivia, the Amazon remained a largely uncharted and unincorporated space where indigenous peoples lived in relatively autonomous circumstances. The state has weakly penetrated these areas and the market has been much less developed. In this context, community autonomy and ethnic differences have remained much more significant in these regions than elsewhere in the country. Indigenous peoples maintain ethnic markers such as the Ashaninka, Amuesha, and so forth, whereas Andean Indians are likely only to disintiguish, if they do, between the Aymara and the Quechua (Remy 1994: 109–10).

Until the last third of the twentieth century, the state essentially relinquished control of the Amazon to the churches, highlighting the state's relative absence in this part of the country. The churches in turn tried to govern these spaces at the same time that explorers tried to tap into the economic resources. The state signed a contract with the SIL to move into the Amazon and promote assimilation through bible translation, bicultural language training, and other forms of education (Grupo de Trabajo 1995: 35–6). César Sarasara, president of the *Conferación de Nacionalidades de la Amazonía Peruana* (CONAP), noted that the state essentially abandoned any idea that it actually governed the Amazon and delivered this role to the churches.[50]

The Velasco military government (1968–1975) changed the course of Amazonian–state relations. The state more actively sought to regulate the region and in that process institutionalized a new kind of community autonomy. With the 1974 *Ley de Comunidades Nativas* (the Law of Native Communities), the military government required communities to register with the state to gain political recognition and official title to lands.[51]

---

[49] The Peruvian state passed three laws at the turn of the twentieth century that ostensibly affected Amazonian lands. The *Ley de Inmigración y Colonización* (1893), the *Ley Orgánica de las Tierras de Montaña* (1889), and the *Ley General de Tierras de Montaña* (1909). The latter was not overturned until 1974 when the state denied that Amazonian lands were indigenous lands (unless a title or contract could be presented) and declared that all Amazonian lands were state lands and could be distributed at the state's initiative (Grupo de Trabajo 1995: 33–4).

[50] César Sarasara, interview, August 20, 1997.

[51] As part of this incorporation process, SINAMOS and other federations started to organize in the Amazon, although they had a less active presence here than in the Andes (Grupo de Trabajo 1995: 40; Evaristo Nukjuag, interview, August 18, 1997).

It also imposed a standardized form of communal organization – with communal authorities and an assembly (Valera 1998: 30). As such, this law provided a formula for anchoring Amazonian Indians to particular locales (thereby changing the ways of itinerant Amazonian indigenous peoples).

The decree not only legalized, standardized, and concentrated communities in a given site, but it also created a link with the state and provided the *legal* instruments for communities to claim lands, including the forests that they had always used and upon which they had always relied.[52] Indeed, forests and rivers, which were previously shared by indigenous peoples, were allocated as collective properties of distinct communities (Dandler et al. 1998: 21). The law recognized and granted communal land. The law secured these spaces by making them inalienable, unmortgageable, and imprescriptable. Moreover, indigenous authorities were granted jurisdiction over these spaces – recognizing the jurisdiction of customary law over areas of civil dispute that took place within a given community (Aroca Medina 1999: 3).[53] Finally the communities were made exempt from paying taxes (Dandler et al. 1998: 21).

The 1974 law therefore provided significant material and political incentives for indigenous people in the Amazon to settle down into communities, a point repeated in interviews with two key indigenous leaders, Evaristo Nukjuag and Gil Inoach.[54] Nukjuag observes that prior to the law, indigenous families occasionally settled down in places where schools had been set up. But it was the 1974 law, he noted, that really created a process of "nuclearization" whereby indigenous families settled down, formed communities (particularly near bilingual schools), and requested titles to

[52] Indigenous peoples started to use the native community law as a resource for organizing and securing the spaces within which indigenous peoples could reside and sustain political, cultural, and economic practices. The law enabled them to title individual communities but did not give them the legal basis for securing larger tracts of lands for indigenous peoples. The strategy, therefore, was to secure titling for each community in question. Hence, while in Ecuador the strategy has been to demand state recognition of large tracts of indigenous territory, in Peru the strategy has been to use the law to demarcate different indigenous communities (Gil Inoach, interview, August 20, 1997 and Evaristo Nukjjuag, interview, August 20, 1997).

[53] Gil Inoach, interview, August 19, 1997 and Aroca Medina (1999: 3) also observe that a 1978 Decreto Ley (22175) maintains in native communities the jurisdiction of customary law over internal conflicts, provided that legal decisions do not threaten the fundamental rights of an individual.

[54] Evaristo Nukjuag, interviews, August 18, 1997 and August 20, 1997; and Gil Inoach, interview, August 19, 1997.

the lands on which they had settled.[55] From that point on, one could start to talk about indigenous communities in the Amazon. As such, the state situated these native communities in particular locales, disregarding the fact that these peoples had previously occupied and lived in much broader spaces than those recognized and allocated by the state (Aroca 1989: 120; Grupo de Trabajo 1995: 37–8; Gray 1997: 77–9).

On balance, therefore, the 1974 law essentially created the contemporary "native community" as a regularized construct (Ballón 1987; Gray 1997: 86; Dandler et al. 1998: 78) – without trying to turn them into cooperative federations as intended in the Andean regions. While in some cases, comunidades nativas in the Amazon were simply new structures within which older forms of organization survived, in most others, these communities were formed anew (extending community boundaries beyond kinship ties). In this regard, the law served to create and institutionalize new ethnic boundaries. It imposed the idea of a sedentary community with Western forms of authority and governance. Gil Inoach observes that it also scaled up community boundaries from the family as the unit to a more extended group of families residing in the same area. He notes that this process often seemed set to displace traditional authorities (elders, shamans, chiefs, etc.) and to impose new laws and forms of governance.[56] Gray (1997) and Dandler et al. (1998) indicate, however, that these new governing institutions existed de jure but not always de facto. As with the ayllus in Bolivia, communities often elected these new officials but continued to defer to older systems of representation, participation, and authority. And it is in this context that a new round of indigenous leaders in the 1970s started to emerge. For as Sarasara succinctly stated: "All of this [Velasco's state reforms that organized communities along western lines; Summer Institute of Linguistics evangelizing that trained future community leaders; and the rise in NGOs working in the area with particular communities] centralized the native community. All weight was given to the native community."[57] Under these circumstances, there were great incentives to forge native communities and to identify as such.

The Challenge to Local Autonomy Under these circumstances, what then catalyzed the indigenous communities in the Amazon to organize

---

[55] Evaristo Nukjuag, interview, August 18, 1997.
[56] Gil Inoach, interview, August 19, 1997.
[57] César Sarasara, interview, August 20, 1997.

indigenous federations? The central point of departure has to do with state reforms that simultaneously and subsequently challenged community autonomy, in general, and threatened indigenous lands, in particular. As stated by an indigenous working group, *El Grupo de Trabajo* (1995: 21): "The indigenous Amazonian movement emerges, as in the Andean case, precisely when the invasion of lands and the plunder of resources became intolerable." They continue: "In this manner, territory, identity, language, sovereignty, culture, and their own form of regulating relations with nature, between themselves, and with other people, was converted into the movement's political platform" (Grupo de Trabajo 1995: 23). The reference to "intolerable" levels highlights that the challenge to community autonomy (understood as territory, identity, language, sovereignty, culture, and self-governance) had been ongoing but reached a new plateau in the late 1960s and 1970s when the local indigenous organizations started to emerge. As we will see, the incipient indigenous organizations emerged in response to the challenge to local autonomy (and prior to the 1974 community law), but they would scale up as federations only once native communities had been put into place, in accord with the 1974 law. To make sense of this sequencing, this chapter next highlights the pattern of public and private challenges to Amazonian indigenous autonomy.

As in Ecuador and Bolivia, the state promoted colonization programs in the Amazon.[58] In the early twentieth century, the state discovered petroleum in the Amazonian jungle and encouraged oil exploration in the 1920s and 1930s (Grupo de Trajabo 1995: 34; Dandler et al. 1998: 31–50).[59] This discovery initiated a more active period of colonization and infrastructure creation (Grupo de Trabajo 1995: 35). While this process of colonization was initiated by Prado in the 1920s, it was accelerated by Belaúnde in the 1960s and created a certain disequilibrium in this region

---

[58] See Santos-Granero and Barclay (1998) for a detailed discussion of colonization in the selva central. They note (1998: 12) that the area was occupied in various waves: missionary settlement (1635–1742), indigenous reconquest (1742–1847), pioneer settlement (1847–1947), and mass settlement (1947–1990). This chapter focuses on the last of these.

[59] See Dandler et al. (1998: 31–50) for a discussion of oil exploration in the Amazon and its consequences. Oil exploration dates back to 1911 but was significantly promoted first by the military government of President Odría. President Velasco nationalized several oil installations and refineries, which led to the retreat of several foreign oil companies. Velasco, however, did promote oil exploration during the 1970s. During the second government of Belaúnde the state once again promoted foreign investment. In all cases, the state has promoted limited protection of indigenous peoples and their lands, with deleterious consequences for indigenous communities and the environment.

(Grupo de Trabajo 1995: 35–7). In general, the state assumed that Amazonian lands were *baldíos* (abandoned/unoccupied) and therefore state property. In this context, colonos could petition for these lands. Apart from a not-very-well-known decree in 1956, there were no laws on the books that protected Amazonian Indian claims to these lands (Smith 1996: 88). The consequence was more rapid population growth (from the 1940s on particularly in the 1960s) in the Amazon than in the rest of the country, in large part due to migration flows. Migration flows, however, disproportionately tended toward the *selva alta* over the *selva baja* (Aramburú 1989: 128–32). The population more than quintupled in the Amazon from 428,597 in 1940 to 1,912,395 in 1981 – increasing more than sixfold in the selva alta and more than threefold in the selva baja (Aramburú 1989: 142). Integrally tied to these migration flows was an increasing challenge to the physical spaces in which native communities had lived.

Velasco encouraged these migration flows toward the Amazon. While he passed measures to register, regulate, and protect native communities in 1974, he also promoted colonization programs in the Amazon starting in 1969. A significant process of colonization by Andean migrants took place and loggers started to move into the area at a more rapid pace – gaining title to lands previously used by indigenous peoples, who considered them as part of indigenous community patrimony (Grupo de Trabajo 1995: 37, 39).

The challenge to native communities only accelerated during the subsequent administrations. In 1978 the Morales Bermúdez government backpedaled from the 1974 Ley de Comunidades Nativas and stated that communal lands that were largely forest lands were actually the property of the state. The comuneros could use them but they could not claim ownership of them (Grupo de Trabajo 1995: 39; Dandler et al. 1998: 22). The 1979 Constitution, which marked the return to civilian rule, recognized native communities but moved away from the inalienability of their lands by indicating the conditions under which they could now sell their communal lands (Grupo de Trabajo 1995: 41).[60] The 1992 Decreto Legislativo No. 02, *Ley de Promoción y Desarrollo Agrario*, further aggravated indigenous autonomy in this region by promoting development projects that were intended to attract capitalist investment but largely catalyzed loggers and the rural

[60] The 1984 Civil Code also granted community rights to stable indigenous communities, which by extension denied these same rights to itinerant groups (a large number in the Amazon) (Grupo de Trabajo 1995: 41).

poor to move into the Amazon (Grupo de Trabajo 1995: 41–3). Nukjuag notes that in these years, one finds the increasing penetration of colonizers who were occupying territories that indigenous peoples considered theirs. In this context, indigenous communities became more preoccupied with demarcating and titling communities and lands.[61]

The 1993 Constitution weakened these communities further. It reversed the inalienability and nonmortgageability of native community lands and weakened the imprescriptibility of communal lands by indicating that where lands were "abandoned," it was legal to claim those lands and buy them from the state (Grupo de Trabajo 1995: 61–9; Gray 1997: 79–80; Dandler et al. 1998: 21).[62] Indeed, the 1993 Constitution completely undermined one of the fundamental bases for claiming and sustaining indigenous community autonomy in the Amazon. The new constitution weakened indigenous claims to territory, created legal insecurity about the viability and sustainability of communal land, and increased competition for control of this space and its resources. With the economic crisis of the 1980s, moreover, the national state essentially abandoned the area to regional governments (Grupo de Trabajo 1995: 44; Dandler et al. 1998: 21).

This formal state retreat only compounded what had informally been a problematic institutional context for indigenous peoples in the Amazon. State offices designed to advance or defend the interests of indigenous peoples were often few in number, incapable of carrying out their responsibilities, and hesitant to uphold constitutional provisions or to extend social services. According to a report published by the state's autonomous organ, the *Defensoría del Pueblo*, the state administration has not always followed constitutional provisions that recognize indigenous peoples – particularly those in the Amazon (Yáñez 1998: 9–23). In this context, indigenous peoples in the Amazon have been "juridically vulnerable" (Yáñez 1998: 77, 80). Moreover, the state's weak presence in the Amazon has resulted in the paltry extension of social services and state protection (Yáñez 1998: 84). "In the context described, one could affirm that indigenous peoples

---

[61] Evaristo Nukjuag, interview, August 20, 1997.

[62] This reform fundamentally went against the commitment made publicly by Fujimori in 1990 when he announced that an important task of his government "would be the authentic recognition, guarantee and defense of the territorial, political, cultural, economic and human rights of the aboriginal peoples of the Amazon" (reported in Mendoza 1993: 533). It also goes against the government report to the Instituto Indigenista Interamericano in 1993, the same year in which these constitutional reforms were passed (Mendoza 1993: 534).

and communities of the Amazon live in a situation of legal abandonment" (Yáñez 1998: 85). As Aroca Medina, the head of the Special Program of Native Communities (which is part of the Defensoría del Pueblo), stated so succinctly,

... [T]he most vulnerable social sector is the sector of native communities in the jungle. If one reviews their situation a little one sees that the majority of them are communities that maintain a strong element of self-identification as Indians; they have had a series of disillusionments with the state, because it has not wanted to recognize them; strange people invade their communities; and in a certain manner they are the ones that suffer the most from discrimination by state functionaries (interview, Aroca Medina, September 16, 1999, conducted by Maritza Rodríguez-Seguí).

Indeed, while Aroca Medina estimates that in 1999 there were some 1,400 native communities, only 900 were recognized. Of these, only about 620 had land titles and of those only around 500 had actually achieved the final stage of inscription in the public register, "which is when one finally arrives at having a certain security about the lands that one occupies."[63]

Hence, from the late 1960s on (and particularly by the end of the 1990s), indigenous peoples in the Amazon were living in an increasingly precarious position; in many cases they were recognized as communities but were also experiencing weakened communal rights; there were increasing challenges from colonos; and there were incompetent public officials often unwilling to advance the constitutional rights of native communities. In this growing wave of uncertainty, indigenous leaders decided to take action.[64]

Mobilizing Networks In the late 1960s and 1970s, indigenous peoples in the Amazon therefore started to discuss the need to organize in defense of their lands, livelihood, and future. The question was how to bridge physical and social distances between peoples living in the Amazon. As we also found in Bolivia and Ecuador, churches unwittingly bridged these distances. The SIL, for example, operated bilingual education programs in Peru from 1945 on (Drysdale and Meyers 1975: 274). In a lengthy interview, Evaristo Nukjuag highlighted the role that the Summer Institute of Linguistics had played in unintentionally preparing himself and other indigenous boys

---

[63] Américo Javier Aroca Medina, interview, September 16, 1999.
[64] See documents in Grupo de Trabajo (1995, passim) for a discussion of how state reforms challenge local autonomy. See particularly page 181 for a discussion of the uneven reach of the state and the weakness of the rule of law in the Amazon. For a particularly concise enumeration of demands, see 175–89.

as leaders of their communities. Nukjuag played a primary role in founding the *Consejo de Aguaruna-Huambisa* in the late 1970s and later in founding AIDESEP and COICA. Sarasara and Inoach, who now belong to competing organizations, also underscored the key role that churches, in particular the Summer Institute of Linguistics, played in promoting bilingual educational programs in the Amazon. While the mission was evangelical, the outcome was to preserve indigenous languages in the face of colonizing efforts that often undermined indigenous communities. The Summer Institute of Linguistics' presence, therefore, helped to train indigenous boys (who became conversant in their own languages and Spanish) who later would emerge as leaders in their communities and beyond.[65] As in Ecuador and Bolivia, the provision of these tools occurred in the context of an evangelizing and paternalistic mission that also set out to undermine indigenous religions and to subject them to an evangelical morality. But these schools ultimately also served to provide future leaders with the skills and networks that they later used to start organizing on behalf of indigenous peoples.[66]

International NGOs and academics subsequently played a conscious and active role in bridging distances between communities and in providing forums for indigenous communities to meet and work toward common goals (Smith 1996). Smith (1996: 89), who observed and took part in this process among the Amuesha in the *selva central*, observes:

For three years, between 1966 and 1969, I worked with the teachers of the Amuesha school and with some of the leaders to develop the notion of community as a place of residence, as a political strategy for the defense of natural resources and of land, as a secure place for the life [and survival] of indigenous culture, and as a legal entity [necessary for making claims] for a territorial title or to achieve bureaucratic or legal actions. These were crucial years: in 1969, 20 Amuesha poblados, together with an equal number of sedentary Ashaninka poblaciones, called themselves "communities," formalizing a new leadership structure, establishing territorial boundaries, taking actions to demand the right to legal property over the land, and in some cases, expelling abusive colonos. After two years of careful preparation, the two new Amuesha communities sent representatives, primarily elders as well as school

---

[65] Evaristo Nukjuag, interview, August 18, 1997; Gil Inoach, interview, August 19, 1997; and César Sarasara, interview, August 20, 1997. Sarasara observes that whereas Catholic schools tended to only teach Spanish, the Summer Institute of Linguistics stood out for having taught both Spanish and indigenous languages.

[66] In interviews with Evaristo Nukjuag, August 18, 1997; Gil Inoach, August 19, 1997; and César Sarasara, August 19, 1997; they all noted the importance of the Summer Institute of Linguistics in unintentionally forming new leaders.

teachers, to a conference in the community of Miraflores (Oxapampa) in July of 1969. . . . *The topic on everyone's mind, that which came out in every conversation, was that of land and its resources: how to protect them in the face of the incessant invasion by colonos.* Those that met wrote a letter to the President of Peru, demanding that the government pay more attention to their situation and grant them titles for communal property for lands sufficiently sized to guarantee their physical and cultural reproduction as a people (Smith 196: 89–90, emphasis added).

Hence, local-level organizations emerged in these years to carve out and defend local autonomy – against a field of new state reforms, colonization, and development schemes. Starting in 1969, organizations started to emerge in the selva central (the Yáneshas founded the *Congreso de Comunidades Amueshas* in 1969 and the Asháninkas organized the *Central de Comunidades Nativas de la Selva Central* in 1970), in the Amazonía Norte (Chapi-Shiwag and Achuarti Ijumdramu in 1969), in the Amazonía Nor-andina (*Organización de Comunidades Aguarunas del Alto Marañón*), and elsewhere (Dandler et al. 1998: 12–13, esp. app., Table A-1).

Indigenous federations started to form in the 1970s, including *la Central de Comunidades Campa de la Selva Central* (CECONSEC), *el Congreso Campa del Pinchis* (later known as ANAP), and *el Consejo Aguaruna-Huambisa del Alto Marañón* (Smith 1996: 94).

In 1979, several federations came together to found the organization (ultimately renamed AIDESEP in 1980) that first claimed to represent these separate ethnic federations. As with all founding stories, there is not exact agreement about the origins of the organization. Nukjuag recalls that leaders from the various Amazonian organizations kept on meeting coincidentally in Lima at state ministries where they went to discuss the issues facing their respective communities. They would talk while waiting to meet with public officials and over time started to realize that they were duplicating efforts and should join forces.[67] They eventually turned to the NGO, *Centro de Investigación y Promoción Amazónica* (CIPA), for help.[68] CIPA supported these meetings by extending resources, office space, technical support, and so forth.[69] Through these meetings in the late 1970s, they increasingly came to agreement and decided to form a single organization to work on behalf

---

[67] Evaristo Nukjuag, interview, August 18, 1997.

[68] Smith (1996) notes that these same NGOs at times had divisive and deleterious consequences.

[69] CIPA's role was described by Evaristo Nujkuag in an interview on August 18, 1997. According to Nujkuag, many of those who worked at CIPA had worked prior to that for

of the indigenous organizations. Smith (1996) also highlights the role of Peruvian professionals in creating networks among communities, although he recounts a different (albeit not necessarily incompatible) narrative. He states that Peruvian professionals observed the detention of Paraguayan anthropologists who had worked with indigenous communities. The former sought to prevent such an eventuality in Peru and decided to meet regularly to that end. They invited several indigenous leaders from the Amazon and, thereby, created links among communities and ethnic federations. In particular, indigenous leaders from among the Amuesha, Aguaruna-Huambisa, the Asháninka, and Shipibo-Conibo met for the first time and subsequently started to meet regularly, hold courses and meetings, and raise funds. According to Smith, this group met every four months for several years running. Participation by indigenous leaders increased and eventually they sought to exclude the nonindigenous professionals from these meetings.[70]

At the end of 1979, several indigenous organizations founded a new confederation, *Consejo de Comunidades Nativas de la Selva Peruana* (CO-CONASEP), which was renamed the following year as AIDESEP. While the organization brought together the Congreso Amuesha,[71] the Congreso del Río Pichís, CECONSEC, an incipient alliance among the Shipibo-Conibo, and the Consejo Aguaruna-Huambisa, the latter dominated the

SINAMOS. CIPA had worked in the communities and was involved in overseeing many projects.

[70] One indigenous leader tells of the increasing frustration with and lack of confidence in CIPA, which refused to share financial details related to projects on which they all worked. This frustration led to a division with CIPA in 1980 (anonymous interview, August 18, 1997).

[71] Confronted with land invasions that threatened the integrity of these communities and drawing on networks provided by teachers, the communities of Amuesha started to organize conferences that led to the founding of the Congreso de las Comunidades Amuesha. Drawing on the 1974 law previously discussed, the Congress of Amuesha Communities was able to gain legal recognition and titling for twenty-four out of twenty-seven communities (Smith 1996: 90). Smith (1996: 91–4) indicates that the growth of these organizations was not unambiguously an exercise in popular will and democratic provenance. Indeed, these organizations also became vehicles for leaders to establish political strongholds and gain material advantage above and beyond the interests of their reputed base. This was all the more so in the 1980s as international organizations made financial resources more available. Moreover, some political parties maneuvered to penetrate these organizations, which had divisive consequences for indigenous communities and the confederations in which they took part.

organization through the late 1980s (Smith 1996: 95–7).[72] Each of these narratives, despite differences, highlights the primary role that intellectuals and/or NGOs played in providing the networks that enabled indigenous communities to meet, organize, and promote their causes.

The question, however, was how to actualize these networks among disparate and dispersed communities. As discussed next, indigenous peoples in the Amazon confronted a relatively larger political opportunity to organize than their counterparts throughout much of the Peruvian Andes.

Political Associational Space   The Peruvian Amazon has always confronted greater political associational spaces than the Andes, a point that parallels the regional differences found in Ecuador and Bolivia. As noted, the state was relatively absent for much of the twentieth century, despite scattered efforts to explore and harness the region.

With Velasco's overthrow in 1975 and, more importantly, the outbreak of civil war during the civilian administrations of the 1980s and 1990s, this political associational space was quashed in some important regions of the Amazon. The violence and impact of the civil war was most severe amongst the Asháninka of the selva central. In this part of the Amazon, a type of power vacuum developed in which the two guerrilla movements, Sendero Luminoso and MRTA, successfully maneuvered to establish a stronghold. Sendero Luminoso set out to gain control of the selva central, a strategic area in which the Asháninka live.[73] At the same time that the guerrillas were moving in, drug traffickers were trying to make inroads. The state and paramilitary forces also tried to recapture control of this area. The war in fact had a very destructive impact on the Asháninka living in this region – dividing communities over support; human rights abuses; migration; and so forth (Grupo de Trabajo 1995: 45; Manrique 1998: 217; and Dandler et al. 1998: 51–68). As stated by the Asháninka leader, Mino

---

[72] This process of unification, however, was not unencumbered. Internal divisions gave way to the founding of CONAP in 1987 – founded largely by the Amuesha (Smith 1996: 96, 98–9, 123).

[73] See Manrique (1998: 212–18) for a brief discussion of the central selva, Sendero Luminoso, and drug trafficking. These observations coincide with comments made in an anonymous August 1997 interview with an indigenous activist (Grupo de Trabajo 1995: 44–5; SAIIC 1995; Dandler et al. 1998: 51–68; and Yáñez 1998: 109–24). For a discussion of Sendero Luminoso and the Alto Huallaga, see Villanueva (1989). For a discussion of how the war placed the Asháninka in a situation of emergency and how the Asháninka responded with the formation of different organizations, see *Comisión de Emergencia Asháninka* (1995).

Eusebio Castro: "The guerrilla groups Shining Path (Sendero Luminoso) and the Tupak Amaru Revolutionary Movement (MRTA) have also violated Indigenous rights. They have oppressed us and killed bilingual teachers and leaders."[74]

The violence has destroyed numerous Asháninka settlements and has forced a vast migration. An estimated one-fifth of the population of the macroethnic group has been displaced as a result of the war. The social structure of the native societies has suffered grave damage; animosities that date to ancestral epochs have been reinvigorated. But the Asháninka have not been victims only of the actions of the insurgent forces; there have also been multiple denunciations of human rights violations committed by the counterinsurgency forces. Such abuses were favored by ethnic and racial prejudices that cast conscripts from the sierra and the coast as superior to the jungle "savages" or *chunchos*, by the relative impunity with which soldiers may act against the local inhabitants, and by the Asháninkas' chronic conditions as "suspicious" due to their lack of documents. From the point of view of official Peru, thousands of these inhabitants of the Amazon do not even have legal existence; they are not inscribed in civil registers and therefore are not citizens. The legal limbo in which many Asháninka live excludes them from rights which, at least formally, are enjoyed by legally recognized citizens. Part of the Asháninka tragedy, in their relationship with both Shining Path and the counterinsurgency forces, has its origins in this juridical nonexistence. From a formal point of view, it is difficult to prove the violation of rights of people who, according to law, do not exist (Manrique 1998: 217–18).

In short, the civil war seriously foreclosed the ability of the Asháninka to remain organized as an active movement during these years.

However, it would be wrong to generalize from this tragic violence that the civil war had an equal effect throughout the Amazon. In fact, it did not. For the civil war did not reach (or equally affect) all parts of the Amazon. Organizing, unsurprisingly, was most effective in those areas where the civil war was least strong. The Grupo de Trabajo (1995: 45) reports that indigenous organizations started to make inroads not in these contested areas of the selva central (where the civil war was raging) but in the selva baja (where they continued to organize for and received a sizeable number of land titles).

In short, political associational space was necessary, although not sufficient for indigenous organizing. It was relatively present prior to the civil war and, therefore, one finds grassroots organizing throughout the Amazon in these years – as local indigenous communities drew on networks to defend

[74] SAIIC (1995).

their local autonomy. With the outbreak of the civil war, some political associational spaces closed down, particularly among the Asháninka – with attending consequences for the indigenous communities and movements that were repressed in the process. The political violence associated with the civil war, however, did not universally and equally affect all parts of the Amazon. Where political associational space remained relatively open, and Amazonian indigenous leaders were at greater liberty to speak out, organize, and travel, they took the opportunity and worked to scale up their local organizations into regional federations, as discussed next.

The Emergence of the Regional Confederations The emergence and growth of indigenous federations in the Amazon, therefore, occurred precisely in those areas where we find the following factors:

- The institutionalization of indigenous communities reinforced by the 1974 Law of Native Communities;
- The politicization of those communities as a result of colonization and development programs that threatened the material and political autonomy of these communities;
- The relative persistence of political associational space in some communities despite the outbreak of violent civil war; and
- The networks established by professionals, schools, and NGOs that provided organizational capacity.

It is in this context that we find the emergence of AIDESEP in 1980. AIDESEP has primarily defended indigenous lands, territory, and natural resources; as well as demanded recognition of the right to self-determinination (including the right to practice indigenous cultures, language and education, and to claim the protection of human and political rights).[75] It has organized around several axes, including territory and natural resources; economy and alternative development; indigenous health; indigenous and civil rights; and education and culture. Smith (1996: 100) remarks that among these, the first and last have emerged as the most important in their work. These goals have become particularly salient in the face of various colonization programs, exploration projects, and state reforms that challenge the territorial basis within which indigenous peoples have

---

[75] See Grupo de Trabajo (1995) and AIDESEP's Web page, www.aidesep.org.pe.

maintained political, economic, and cultural autonomy in the Amazon.[76] One of AIDESEP's presidents, Gil Inoach, observed in an interview that it is not possible to defend these rights through armed struggle. He noted: "Peru is living in a period of laws. To defend our rights, we need to fight with words. But for this strategy to have any impact, we have to organize."[77]

The power and success of AIDESEP, however, has been uneven. Internal conflicts divided the federations that once formed part of AIDESEP and resulted in the founding of a competitive indigenous organization, CONAP.[78] Some scholars saw these divisions as the result of too much NGO meddling, which heightened and perhaps even fostered divisions among indigenous peoples.[79]

The internal divisions in AIDESEP extended beyond the conflict with CONAP. Inoach, then president of AIDESEP, reflected on AIDESEP's internal problems in 1997. He noted then that AIDESEP had been in crisis for at least four years. The crisis included financial concerns about solvency and accountability as well as institutional problems that included caudillismo, the related centralization of power, the distancing from the organizational base, and poor leadership. These problems had occurred, some argued, at the expense of the communities. Inoach noted that others were saying that when AIDESEP was weaker, the bases became stronger.[80] Inoach set out as president to strengthen the communities, to work in and with local governments, and to focus on microregions.

Despite these problems, AIDESEP and CONAP set out to mediate between their constitutive organizations and state institutions. They each fundamentally work to advance and defend indigenous rights in the Amazon. CONAP, for example, seeks to defend indigenous cultures; to defend the environment; to oversee negotiations with outside companies; to secure the political rights of traditional organizations; to defend territories; to strengthen the idea of nationalities; and to promote training. In a CONAP (n.d.) document declaring its principles, the organization stated: "The

---

[76] See Grupo del Trabajo (1995: 59–189) for examples of AIDESEP's protests against state reforms.

[77] Gil Inoach, interview, August 19, 1997, Lima, Peru.

[78] César Sarasara, president of CONAP, interview, August 20, 1997 and Aroca Medina, interview, by Maritza Rodríguez-Seguí, September 16, 1999.

[79] In some cases, NGOs exacerbated divisions within AIDESEP and helped to promote CONAP, according to Smith (1996); Evaristo Nukjuag, interview, August 18, 1997; Gil Inoach, interview, August 19, 1997; and Dandler et al. (1998: 15, 19).

[80] Gil Inoach, interview, August 19, 1997.

AUTONOMY to organize ourselves and to administer ourselves as the [Peruvian] State's own constitution gives us is the fundamental principle that will allow us to achieve THE HISTORIC PROJECT OF SELF-DEVELOPMENT, self-determination, and self-management, and as such, we reject all efforts to return to paternalistic indigenist policies or to the corporatist interventions, either by the state or by any other national or international institution" (emphasis in original). CONAP has also opposed government constitutional reforms (Articles 88 and 89) and Law 26505, which are seen as threatening the autonomy of indigenous peoples and their capacity to protect their territories. So too it has called for constitutional reforms to reinstate the inalienability, unmortgageability, and imprescriptability of their territories and lands (CONAP 1995 and 1997).

The emergence of these organizations has shifted relations with the state and ultimately forced state officials to acknowledge and occasionally negotiate with these organizations, if only at arms length. During the Fujimori administration, the government signed compacts with several indigenous organizations and acknowledged (although did not necessarily act upon) the co-demands for political inclusion as equals and for collective rights as Indians.[81] Américo Javier Aroca Medina noted that in fact the majority of issues that were brought before the Special Program for Native Communities (part of the Defensoría del Pueblo) are initiated by AIDESEP and CONAP. "Between the two, they practically represent all of the federations and communities in the Peruvian selva. Therefore they are the ones that channel complaints and request the intervention of the Defensoría."[82] "The majority of them [complaints] are about land titling for native communities; problems related to legal recognition; problems of access to justice, the detention of natives who are in different penal facilities for different crimes; problems that they have had with other persons, with colonos; for access to natural and forest resources; or their relationship with oil companies that are conducting exploration in the forest; or with logging companies."[83] Aroca Medina noted that one of the fundamental problems that his office found was that functionaries do not know the law as it relates to indigenous peoples.

AIDESEP and CONAP have also worked with state institutions to try to pass an indigenous law. As Aroca Medina described it, the proposals have

---

[81] See Mendoza (1993: 532–3).
[82] Aroca Medina, interview, by Maritza Rodríguez-Seguí, September 16, 1999.
[83] Aroca Medina, interview, by Maritza Rodríguez-Seguí, September 16, 1999.

tended to push for recognition of rights as indigenous communities and as citizens of Peru. This has included the right to indigenous customary law; the right to take part in decisions that affect the communities; and legal recognition of their organizations as indigenous. This process has been complicated and stalled, however, by the conflicts between congressional representatives and indigenous organizations over who should author and present the law before Congress.[84]

At the time of this writing, AIDESEP and CONAP confront the new political administration of Toledo, who assumed office following the crisis and collapse of the Fujimori administration. Toledo made much of his indigenous heritage during his presidential campaigns. After taking office, Toledo and his wife, Eliane Karp, formed the National Commission of Indigenous, Amazonian, and Afroperuvian Peoples (CONAPA) ostensibly to advance indigenous rights in particular and ethnic rights in general. Less than two years into his administration, however, indigenous organizations distanced themselves from Toledo and signed a declaration on August 14, 2003 stating that they would no longer work with CONAPA, which had failed to create adequate channels of consultation and representation. So too it had failed to advance substantive political or legal reforms on behalf of indigenous rights (Martin 2003; Martin and Greene 2004). As such, Peru's indigenous organizations continue to face an uphill battle. Thus far they have not been able to sustain a unified front, and they do not have consistent, proactive, and reliable political support within the state.

Puno

The emergence of indigenous movements in the Amazon was not replicated (at least not on the same scale) in the Andes. As so many scholars have noted, indigenous movements have largely failed to emerge among peasants living in this part of the country. Puno, however, seems to be the subnational exception to the Andean rule. In the 1980s, Puno became home to a small regionally based indigenous organization, the Unión de Comunidades Aymaras, UNCA.

Why did an indigenous movement emerge in this southern Peruvian department but not elsewhere in the Peruvian Andes? This section highlights that Puno maintained political associational space and transcommunity networks, two factors that were destroyed elsewhere by the civil war between the Peruvian state and Sendero Luminoso. Indeed, the South (and

---

[84] Aroca Medina, interview, by Maritza Rodríguez-Seguí, September 16, 1999.

Puno, in particular) remained relatively distant from the ravages of the war – less fighting, less repression, and less patrolling. Hence, while Sendero gained cadre and the civil war became more brutal in the central Andean region, Sendero never succeeded in establishing a significant base in Puno (McClintock 1989: 95; Rénique 1998) – even if the area was contested in the 1990s. Networks remained in place among communities, and leaders mobilized these networks to resist the state reforms that challenged local autonomy. It is in this context that Aymara activists founded UNCA, an indigenous organization that privileges and promotes indigenous identities and related political and socioeconomic issues. For as Aroca Medina stated in a 1999 interview: "Following the Velasco period, which privileged class, the use of the term 'Indian' was seen as 'pejorative.' Those who today fully identify as Indians are those who live in the jungle. The peasant communities, no [they don't identify as Indians]. There is however a recent movement, above all among the Aymara, and influenced by Bolivia, that self-identifies as pueblos originarios. The rest [of the peasant communities in the Andes] don't. The rest do not accept being called Indian."[85] Aroca Medina is referring to UNCA. This final section sets out to explain why and how UNCA emerged – in contrast to the rest of the Peruvian Andes.

The Subnational Context   Puno has always been far removed from the center of political and economic power in Peru. It is the southernmost department in Peru. Its significant Aymara population bridges the border with Bolivia – with attending splits in loyalties to the nation-state and the transnational ethnic community. While the Aymara constitute an estimated 6 percent of the Peruvian population, they constitute a much higher percentage of the department of Puno – particularly in the southernmost part of the department (Cruz 1993: 544).[86]

Puno stands out, however, not only because of its significant Aymara population but also because of the particularly significant impact of the corporatist citizenship regime on community organization. More families were incorporated into the agrarian reform–related SAIS enterprises in Puno than elsewhere in Peru. Twenty-three SAISs were established in Puno

[85] Aroca Medina, interview, by Maritza Rodríguez-Seguí, September 16, 1999.
[86] Aymaras are located in Peru, Bolivia, Chile, and Argentina. While exact data is lacking, it is estimated that Aymaras are approximately 6 percent of the Peruvian population; 38 percent of the Bolivian population; 0.33 percent of the Chilean population; and 0.014 percent of the Argentine population (Cruz Alanguía 1993: 544).

Table 6.4. *Distribution of SAIS in Peru*
by Department (1971–1988)

Department	# of SAIS
Puno	23
La Libertad	13
Ancash	8
Junín	6
Cajamarca	2
Cusco	2
Arequipa	2
Huancavelica	1
Tacna	1
TOTAL	58

Source: Hunefeldt (1997: 122, fn. 16).

out of a total of fifty-eight (Hunefeldt 1997: 122; see Table 6.4). Moreover, while peasants claimed only 19.5 percent of the department lands prior to the agrarian reform, they nominally claimed 30.4 percent of department lands after the reform (Hunefeldt 1997: 122).[87] Indeed, peasant communities in Puno received 11.7 percent of all the lands distributed nationally to these communities (Hunefeldt 1997: 122).

The greater number of SAIS and landholdings also corresponds with a higher number of recognized peasant communities.[88] Statistically speaking, we find a large number of peasant communities in Puno, relative to the national average. "Of a total of 3,312 recognized peasant communities in 1986...487 [were] in Puno" (Hunefeldt 1997: 122, fn. 15). Of a total of

---

[87] Peasant communities constitute a greater share of agricultural and pastoral units in Apurímac (81.9 percent), Huancavelica (75.09 percent), Cusco (69.87 percent), and Pasco (67.85 percent) than in Puno (less than 60 percent) (Valera 1998: 29).

[88] In Puno, as elsewhere, there was a gap between the number of peasant communities that were recognized and the SAIS that were established. These associative enterprises often managed the most fertile land in the region. Yet, there was low participation of these communities in the SAISs and CAPs that were established (Hunefeldt 1997: 122–3). Consequently, conflicts often emerged between these new cooperative ventures and the peasant communities. Land invasions took place (Hunefeldt 1997: 123, fn. 18). And indigenous communities started to contest the associative enterprises (Rénique 1998: 310). According to Rénique, the communities often viewed the SAISs as little more than the contemporary incarnation of the haciendas that once existed.

5,680 peasant communities recognized in 1994, 1,274 (or 22 percent) were in Puno (Valera 1998: 11–13).[89]

Moreover, Puno claimed, by the 1990s, the highest percentage of community-owned lands (12.95 percent of the national total). Within community confines, it is the community in Puno that decides how lands are to be used – communally or individually; it is the community that divides up lands when they are to be parceled out; and it is the comuneros who are both the subjects and objects of these decisions. In this regard, while the boundaries, operation, and identification of the community have shifted over time, the community has remained an ongoing reference point.

While community organizations set out to register with the state, it appears that the transformation of existent cooperative associations also resulted in the rise in individual land use (Rénique 1998; Valera 1998: 49). In other words, with disproportionate registration of peasant communities in Puno, there was also an accompanying (and perhaps rising) pattern of noncommunal farming and noncommunity identification.[90] Notably, Puno also exhibited the highest percentage of individually held lands within those communities,[91] and large numbers of *"comuneros"* identifying as *"propietarios"* (individual property owners who form part of a community) rather than as *"comuneros natos"* (community members, first and foremost) (Valera 1998: 21–3, 38, 53). That said, communal cultivation of agricultural lands remains higher in Puno than most other departments in contemporary Peru.[92]

Puno had relatively more developed community structures (and increasing individual land use) than in the Central Sierra. This was not necessarily true when compared to other departments in the south of Peru. Indeed, some other southern departments also maintained strong communal identifications and strong communal work traditions. To explain why local indigenous movements emerge in Puno (and not elsewhere in the Peruvian Andes), we turn next to subnational variations in

[89] The five departments that claim the highest percentage of the country's peasant communities included Puno (22 percent), followed by Cusco (16 percent), Huancavelica (9 percent), Ayacucho (8 percent), and Apurímac (8 percent) (Valera 1998: 11–13).

[90] Gonzales de Olarte (1994); Hunefeldt (1997: 122); and Valera (1998).

[91] In Puno, more than a fifth (21.89 percent) of community lands are held individually. The next closest percentage is found in Cusco with 12.99 percent and Huancavelica with 6.61 percent (Valera 1998: 37, 89).

[92] Communally cultivated agricultural lands constitute 20.87 percent of agricultural lands in Apurímac, 16.25 percent in Cusco, and 14.43 percent in Puno – with lower numbers for other departments (Valera 1998: 55).

political associational space (opportunities) and transcommunity networks (capacities).

Movement Emergence   UNCA was founded in Puno in the 1980s – in the southernmost part of that department.[93] UNCA built on and created links among the communal organizations that had formed in the prior decades – particularly during the corporatist and neoliberal citizenship regimes. Indeed, Puno had more developed networks than those found in other regions – particularly given the comparatively weak presence of the civil war in the region.[94] Rénique (1998: 308, 310–11) finds that by the 1980s, the progressive church, peasant organizations, and political parties had a more sustained and developed presence in the countryside than that found in other provinces.

During the Velasco years, the state had helped to build up significant associations – including the CAPs, *asociaciones integrales*, and later the *multicomunales*. This organizational basis served as the foundation for the formation of UNCA in the early 1980s. Bonifacio Cruz, who was one of the founders of UNCA and its first president (1984–1993) indicated that the Velasco years created a "favorable opening" by initiating the land reform (that liquidated the oligarchy and distributed land) and by creating an organizing experience for the youth. "Velasco generated a political space that was rather favorable ... It allowed us to organize."[95] While Cruz started to organize after Velasco was overthrown, he did so in the organizations that Velasco set in motion – including the organization to get legal standing for his community and in the agrarian leagues. By the early 1980s he had become president of a district Agrarian League and the Provincial Agrarian League in Puno.[96]

The opportunity to organize in Puno, however, reflected the comparatively greater political associational space in this part of Peru. Even though the civil war reached its height in the 1980s, Puno was comparatively

---

[93] This discussion of UNCA is based on interviews with Bonifacio Cruz (June 22, 1997; July 9, 1997; August 14, 1997) and José Pinelo (July 8, 1997) as well as two group interviews with the 1997 Consejo Directivo and a collective discussion with UNCA community members in Desaguadero (both on August 22, 1997).

[94] Cruz notes that while the civil war did not directly paralyze their work (because the war did not penetrate Puno as it did other Andean regions), it did hinder their ability to coordinate with others outside of Puno. Bonifacio Cruz, interviews, July 9, 1997 and August 14, 1997.

[95] Bonifacio Cruz, interview, August 14, 1997.

[96] Bonifacio Cruz, interview, July 9, 1997.

spared – with less repression and a more open political environment for organizing. And even though repression did occur, particularly in the early 1990s, it remained localized in the northernmost part of the department of Puno.[97]

The indigenous organizing that did occur in the Andes, therefore, took place in the southernmost part of Puno. This organizing did not expand much beyond this area but was confined to an Aymara area near the Bolivian border, where Sendero Luminoso and the military had a relatively weak presence.

UNCA emerged in this organizational context and in response to a climactic disaster. Cruz recalls that there was a severe drought in 1983 that led, according to Cruz, to an 80 percent loss in agricultural production. This coincided with the Latin American–wide economic crisis that devastated the economies of the region and later triggered the turn to neoliberal citizenship regimes. In this time of serious need, the limitations of the local peasant organizations became apparent to him and others. He recalls that the provincial agrarian league was solid, but he could not make the same claim of the League as a whole.

When the Agrarian League demonstrated its weakness in confronting the drought, we saw that it could not respond to the drought, production issues, and the state. Moreover, left parties were infiltrating the league and a conflict ensued with them. We decided that we are Aymara, with a pre-Hispanic and pre-Incan history. Why don't we rescue our identity. We are different than others – from the Quechua and from those living in the cities. We need another form of organizing that can respect a different logic in line with our cosmovision. This was our intent. But it was not possible to express these ideas openly. Given the laws, we did not express them openly but they formed part of our daily lives and organizations. We decided to open up spaces as Aymaras and Peruvians. As Aymaras, we have rights. Before there was a kind of marginalization and discrediting of Indians. One went along feeling marginalized and oppressed. This was a form of subsistence. But at heart, our Aymara identity is an important part of who we are. It is important to uncover this and to say that we are Aymara (Bonifacio Cruz, interview, July 9, 1997).

Moreover, the political parties expressed minimal interest in helping to solve these problems. Rénique (1998) also highlights that tension between communities and the associative enterprises escalated in the context of the

---

[97] Sendero Luminoso started to make some inroads in northern Puno in the 1990s as peasant organizations and political parties were internally divided over illegal occupations and taking up arms (Rénique 1998).

dismantling of agrarian assistance programs, declining economic conditions, and the drought that struck the country in the early 1980s.

At this point, Cruz and others started to question the union structure, which seemed more capable of responding to sectoral than to community-wide concerns. This led them to consider organizing along community lines that emphasized their Aymara identity. This commitment became even starker in the late 1980s and 1990s as state reforms increasingly challenged community autonomy. "Almost all of the achievements of years past have been erased by this [Fujimori's] government. . . . Consequently [with the privatization of land markets], the communities are not as autonomous as they once were," stated Cruz.[98]

In this context, several peasant leaders in the Agrarian Leagues called on 150 community leaders; 120 of them consulted with their communities and returned with official certificates (*actas*) that supported the idea of organizing along new lines – rooted in the Aymara community rather than a class-based conception of the peasantry. While this decision in practice seemed like a change of names alone – as the units were often the same communities and the leaders the same people – it was interpreted as integral to the promotion of a different type of mission: the "integral development" of the Aymara community rather than only production concerns for the peasantry. UNCA subsequently undertook new projects such as those promoting the integral development of children, education, health and nutrition, and fostering pride in Aymara identity.[99]

This public affirmation and expression of indigenous identity was a striking reversal of the policies and practices advocated since the time of Velasco. When asked what UNCA's principal objective was, Cruz stated that it was to "revalorize Aymara identity. . . . After that, we need to strengthen our communal and multicommunal organizations." It was only after having stated the need to promote Aymara identity and communal organizations that he elaborated on particular projects that address agricultural production, infrastructure, and services.[100] However, the pursuit of an Aymara identity was not purely tied to cultural needs but was also wielded as a political tool. When asked why indigenous identity was so central and why it had been adopted as the basis for organizing, Bonifacio Cruz stated that it was a contemporary reality, a form of local empowerment vis-à-vis the state,

[98] Bonifacio Cruz, interview, August 14, 1997.
[99] Bonifacio Cruz, interviews, July 9, 1997 and August 14, 1997.
[100] Bonifacio Cruz, interview, August 14, 1997,

and a form of accessing government resources. It was not seen as a means of sustaining traditional forms of governance, which had already been lost over decades.[101]

In UNCA we understand identity as something of our own, as something innate.... We don't want to rescue traditional forms. Traditional forms are a reference for affirming our identity. But we can't re-take these models now. Rather, identity is a form of access. We don't want to rescue traditional forms of governance.... We want to be equal while recognizing our differences. We want more professionals, we want equal access to education, and we want representatives in government.... But to be a leader, one has to have discovered one's identity and to have practiced it publicly. We don't pressure the people to follow particular rules.... It is important to have freedom of expression (Bonifacio Cruz, interview, July 9, 1997).

Hence Aymara identity is not necessarily instantiated in traditional authority structures but in the more contemporary idea of indigenous communities. While many recognize that these communities are relatively new institutions (at least in their present form, as recognized by the state), they have become the spatial expression of Aymara identity. Hence, UNCA has organized by community and has set out to strengthen the institutions that allow these communities to organize, select leaders, and provide for themselves. The idea has been to complement or infuse these relatively new institutions with "Aymara values."[102] In practice, this entails selecting leaders from the community rather than accepting the designation of leaders from outside. It also means the application of communal justice – based on a fusion of Aymara community norms and Peruvian law. The goals then have been to promote culture *and* create a formal set of institutions that can govern local relations.

This language is not so dissimilar from that found and used in Ecuador and Bolivia. However, while UNCA leaders indicate that UNCA formed after indigenous organizations emerged abroad and around the same time as the Amazonian organizations were founded in Peru, Cruz suggests that they had no real idea of what was happening elsewhere. Coordination between organizations occurred later – not to form organizations but to promote common goals.[103]

---

[101] Bonifacio Cruz, interview, July 9, 1997.
[102] Bonifacio Cruz, interview, August 14, 1997.
[103] Bonifacio Cruz, interview, August 14, 1997.

Cruz's account of UNCA's origins and goals broadly paralleled comments made during a 1997 collective discussion with community members (although community members tended to focus more on the contemporary demands for autonomy, resources, and inclusion, rather than on the specific origins and first goals of the organization). In these community discussions, there was a prevailing sense of abandonment by the government, particularly since the 1980s.[104] One man said: "The government has practically forgotten us." Another man said: "The indigenous sector is marginalized. The government neglects it." In general, there was a sense that democracy had either not really come and/or had passed them by.

There is no true democracy. I don't see it. More than anything, there is more corruption. It lands in the hands of the top leaders. Because of all this, UNCA was organized. Hopefully Indians will gain some rights.[105]

We are between a rock and a hard place. The climate is difficult. The government does not take us into account and does not respect the Aymara people. There isn't support for the peasant communities, which have to look for their own way out. There are laws but they do not favor the communities. The support that exists is politicized.... The Aymara culture has knowledge, values, and wisdom. But no one takes this into account.[106]

The government wants to privatize the rural areas. We are not going to have access. Health is not going to come to these heights [the Andean region can reach as high as 6,700 meters above sea level]. Our language is not valorized . . . whereas before we had access to credit from the Banco del Crédito, now we don't. Organizations have declined in strength. We need to organize to defend our human rights, women's rights, and children's rights.[107]

When asked to define UNCA's main objective, one community leader said: "UNCA is here primarily to make us respect our own Aymara culture and then to seek out economic development for all the Aymara people." And when asked how that differed from the Agrarian Leagues that had previously organized there, one leader said: "We have recently found a way to valorize our Aymara identity. Although there were agrarian leagues, they primarily organized around here. They were interested in unions and politics.

---

[104] Collective discussion with about twenty members of UNCA in Desaguadero, Peru on August 22, 1997.

[105] Anonymous participant in collective discussion among UNCA members in Desaguadero, Peru, August 22, 1997.

[106] Anonymous participant in collective discussion among UNCA members in Desaguadero, Peru, August 22, 1997.

[107] Anonymous participant in collective discussion among UNCA members in Desaguadero, Peru, August 22, 1997.

Today we are also interested in our culture." Then another stated that the agrarian leagues in fact had been grafted on top of preexisting ayllus but that the agrarian leagues had not delivered. All of the participants seemed to agree that the agrarian leagues had come at the expense of cultural pride.

With this as a background, UNCA essentially followed two stages of work. In its initial incarnation, UNCA organized around microprojects. The directorship worked actively to develop short-term (1–6 month) programs to present to the government. At one point they were juggling around forty microprojects. Conflicts emerged in the leadership, however, between Bonifacio Cruz (president from 1984–1993) and some members of the technical team who organized against Cruz in 1993.[108] A broader opposition formed and started to work more actively with the communities (which had started to lose faith in UNCA, according to an August 22, 1997 interview with the *Consejo Directivo*).

The communities called a 1993 assembly. By all accounts, the assembly represented a turning point. It saved UNCA from demise and reoriented its work. In this second stage, UNCA's new Consejo Directivo decided to stop organizing around/for short-term projects and to develop programs targeting Aymara people as a whole. In other words, they decided to develop more programmatic objectives. And they decided to change the balance of forces on the board – with 80 percent coming from the communities and 20 percent from the technical team.[109] By 1997, UNCA claimed to work with 250 communities, with eighteen multicomunales, and in three provinces.[110] On August 21, 1997, they outlined the overall desire to develop integrated programs for education, agricultural production, and the like in a meeting with about twenty-five community leaders and the board. As the board noted the following evening (August 22, 1997), the Agrarian Leagues and CNA are political organizations that have waned in strength. UNCA was formed to fill that void – to promote the community needs without devolving into

---

[108] The opposition from the technical team claimed that Cruz had centralized power and did not consult or take into account the advice of others. This led to an internal conflict and splintering over the direction of UNCA – including whether or not it should be an NGO or a movement organization. This point was made both by UNCA's Consejo Directivo on August 22, 1997 and by Bonifacio Cruz on August 14, 1997.

[109] The 1997 Consejo Directivo of UNCA suggested that prior to 1993, the organization was largely dominated by professionals and técnicos who had a limited relationship with their base. Consejo Directivo of UNCA, interview, August 22, 1997.

[110] Based on collective interview, UNCA's Consejo Directivo, August 22, 1997.

partisan politics. According to Pinelo, by 1995 UNCA had developed an impressive organization with concrete and strong ties to its members' communities.[111]

UNCA's origin story highlights the conjunction of three factors:

1. The corporatist citizenship regime (in particular, the Velasco land reforms) provided land and structured communities in ways subsequently challenged by the neoliberal citizenship regime of the 1980s and 1990s. With the drought in the early 1980s, these challenges became all the more stark.
2. Puno stood out for having strong community associations – again a legacy of the corporatist citizenship regime. In this context, Aymara activists were able to build on corporatist networks to forge a new indigenous association.
3. The ability of these communities to scale up was based on the relatively significant political associational space in Puno (particularly when compared to other parts of the Peruvian Andes). Sendero Luminoso failed to organize in Puno – at least to the same degree found in other regions. Unlike other areas, the military was able to keep Sendero Luminoso out but was not able to impose its own structure through the rondas campesinas.

In this context, UNCA emerged as an indigenous organization committed to making ethnic-based claims for collective autonomy and democratic inclusion.

Conclusion

Peru has followed, thus far, a different trajectory than the rest of the region. Unlike most other Latin American countries, Peru has not experienced the emergence of powerful national or even regional indigenous organizations. This chapter has primarily focused on explaining the striking absence of indigenous movements in Peru despite broad political, geographic, demographic, and historical similarities with Ecuador and Bolivia. It has done so by highlighting that while eroding corporatist citizenship regimes and drastic neoliberal citizenship regimes have challenged the local autonomy of indigenous communities, nationally speaking these same communities

---

[111] José Pinelo was sent by the Fondo Indígena (based in La Paz) to evaluate UNCA for a 1995 project assessment. José Pinelo, interview, July 8, 1997.

have not been able to draw on transcommunity networks and political associational space, which were severely curtailed during the civil war of the 1980s and 1990s.

These broad national patterns in Peru, however, do coexist with some subnational variation. In two regions of Peru where political associational space was comparatively deeper and networks were still present, indigenous communities were able to mobilize against state reforms that challenged local autonomy. The examples of AIDESEP and CONAP in the Amazon and UNCA in the Andes are telling. They provide further evidence that where three variables (political associational space, networks, and changing citizenship regimes that challenge local autonomy) did concatenate, indigenous movements have emerged. But the three organizations also highlight that where these broad conditions do not obtain nationally (as is the case in Peru), it is enormously difficult for local movements to scale up into significant and consequential regional and national movements. In geographically contained contexts, such Peruvian organizations have had a weaker mobilizational capacity and political impact than their counterparts in other countries. Indeed, Aroca Medina remarks that the salience of the "indigenous question" in political circles is less a function of the organizing efforts of these organizations and more a consequence of the pressures placed by international agencies. In this regard, the subnational indigenous organizations in Peru are noteworthy but weak indigenous movements that have thus far neither been able to scale up nor to influence policy debates and outcomes. Were Peru to experience greater and sustained political associational space for organizing and networking, the winds might indeed shift for Peru's indigenous organizations.

PART III

Conclusion

7

<hr>

Democracy and the Postliberal Challenge in Latin America

Latin American democracies are facing unprecedented challenges and opportunities. Indigenous people are stepping forward to demand new rights, seek equal protection, and articulate bold proposals for change. These are remarkable developments in a region where ethnic cleavages were once universally described as weak and indigenous people were described as politically irrelevant, at best, and anachronistic, at worst. By the end of the twentieth century, indigenous movements had grown in numbers and strength throughout much of Latin America. Indigenous activists, elected officials, and spokespersons are increasingly commonplace in protests, discussions, and deliberations over policy. In turn, politicians of all types have been forced to contend with multiculturalism, pluriethnicity, and multilingualism – in some cases reformulating constitutions, legislation, and ministerial charges to incorporate more inclusive language about diverse ethnic and racial populations. These unprecedented developments call out for an explanation.

This book has focused on explaining the contemporary and uneven emergence of Latin American indigenous movements – addressing both why indigenous identities have become *politically* salient in the contemporary period and why they have translated into significant political organizations in some places and not others. After briefly revisiting the argument developed in Parts I and II of this book, this chapter introduces a new question: what is the broader relevance of these movements for Latin American democracies?

In particular, this chapter poses the question: what political relevance do these contemporary indigenous movements have for the study of democracy and for the third-wave democracies that are now in place? This concluding

This chapter draws, in part, on Yashar (1999).

281

chapter takes up this issue by analyzing two sides of this question. On the one hand, this chapter analyzes how indigenous movements, by posing a postliberal challenge, are contesting the contemporary terms of democratic citizenship in the region. On the other hand, this chapter analyzes how the new democracies in the region have, in turn, challenged the unity and integrity of the movements that are in place. These two questions lead to the same conclusion: that democratic politics is very much in flux. For if the postliberal challenge reflects the uneven institutionalization of liberal rights in the new democracies, so too a weak showing by indigenous movements in electoral politics forms part of a broader "crisis" of political parties and representation in the region as a whole. Both the postliberal challenge and the contemporary crisis of representation compel us to analyze the fragility of democratic politics in light of the uneven reach of the state and its bearing on society.

Restating the Argument

At its most general, this book argues that state institutions and policies profoundly shape identity politics. They seek to forge national citizens, to define the terms of interest intermediation, and to channel the expression of identity into particular institutions and locales. The rich literature on nationalism has long made this claim. This book extends this argument by noting that citizenship regimes in general have also attempted to refashion identities and affiliations. They have defined who is a citizen, how citizens should interact with the state, and what rights citizens might claim. Indeed, citizenship regimes – during democratic and authoritarian regimes – have profoundly attempted to shape and regularize the terms of state–society relations and, as such, have imposed certain identities on those that fall within its institutional domain.

States, however, are neither omnipotent nor omnipresent. In the developing world, in particular, the "capacity" to implement policies, enforce the rule of law, and define public allegiance are open to debate and certainly subject to question and scrutiny. While in some cases, this disparity between state projects and societal identification is openly (even violently) contested, in many others this gap has existed below the proverbial surface. In many countries, we find that ethnic communities have outwardly accepted national identities, all the while maintaining local communities with distinct identities, governance structures, and cultural allegiances. Most surprisingly of all, in some cases, local communities have been able to maintain these local traditions by harnessing state policies that were designed for other purposes.

The politicization of ethnic identities, therefore, is likely to occur where state policies challenge the material and political foundations necessary for local community autonomy. Indeed, this is the core and underlying argument of this book. While this argument self-consciously speaks to the developing world – in particular those countries with significant, varied, and somewhat autonomous rural populations – it also resonates in those European countries where the state's reach has remained in question, as in Northern Ireland and the Basque country. This core argument, however, can take many empirical guises because the content, configuration, and sequencing of state–society relations and citizenship regimes (and therefore the spaces for local autonomy) have taken different forms in different parts of the world. To explain where and when ethnic cleavages are therefore politicized, one must analyze the empirical record of state–society relations to specify the content and consequences of changing citizenship regimes.

To advance this overall argument in the context of Latin America, this book first focused on the five cases with the region's largest indigenous populations and then used a most similar systems design to probe three cases – Ecuador, Bolivia, and Peru. These last three countries share common histories, demography, and political trajectories but have experienced divergent histories of indigenous movement organizing in the late twentieth century. The comparative historical analysis unearthed the following pattern. Shifting *citizenship regimes* fundamentally affected the politicization of ethnic cleavages. Contrary to what one would expect from the social science literature, corporatist citizenship regimes at mid-century unwittingly provided relatively secure local spaces in which indigenous communities and governance structures survived. Consequently, while corporatist citizenship regimes were designed to turn Indians into national peasants, they in practice sheltered these same indigenous communities – thereby depoliticizing ethnic cleavages. The subsequent erosion of corporatist citizenship regimes (and their eventual replacement by neoliberal ones) in turn politicized these same cleavages by challenging this de facto local autonomy and, consequently, the viability and integrity of local indigenous communities. These twentieth-century changes in citizenship regimes were common to all of the countries studied in this book and to Latin America, as a whole. These changes provided the common motive for the first wave of indigenous organizing in Latin America in the last third of the twentieth century.

However, the call to defend autonomy (regardless of the motives) is not enough to explain where activists could actually scale up and organize regional and national movements. Only where communities could draw on existing *transcommunity networks* and *political associational space* did they develop the capacity and opportunity to mobilize regional and national indigenous movements (refer to Tables 3.1 and 3.2). These final two variables provide the analytic leverage to explain when and where indigenous activists could scale up their demands to forge indigenous movements on a regional and national scale. The two strongest indigenous movements emerged in Ecuador and Bolivia and in each case, activists took advantage of transcommunity networks and political associational space throughout the country. Peru, which has experienced relatively weak (some would say nonexistent) indigenous movements had no widespread set of transcommunity networks and space. To the contrary, the civil war simultaneously foreclosed most political associational space and destroyed preexisting transcommunity networks in the country.

Part II primarily developed this tripartite argument about changing citizenship regimes, transcommunity networks, and political associational space by looking at national cases. However, the case studies also provided the opportunity to probe subnational variations. The last two variables, in particular, varied geographically across subnational regions. Hence, one finds that first-generation indigenous movements emerged in those geographic spaces where networks and political associational space were both present. This geographic pattern emerged in Ecuador and Bolivia (where movements were strongest). But even more striking, it has occurred in Peruvian enclaves. For while nationally speaking Peruvian networks and political associational space were weak at best, Chapter 6 noted two enclaves where both variables (transcommunity networks and political associational space) were comparatively stronger than in the rest of the country. In these two enclaves, indigenous movements started to take form, although these movements have been localized and constrained.

Timing and sequence emerged as another secondary theme in the case studies presented in Part II. For while the tripartite argument appears rather robust when explaining first-generation indigenous movements, its explanatory punch diminishes once first-generation movements are in place. With the emergence of successful indigenous movements in Bolivia and Ecuador, the social movement landscape changed. Not only have new indigenous movements drawn on and transformed existent models, but the first-generation movements have come to expand their agendas. Once formed, these indigenous movements have come to take on more than the defense of their collective rights – as one would expect if one analyzed the origins of the movements alone. They have *also* come to demand inclusion and equal treatment as individuals in the democracies that are now in place.[1] As such, these movements are challenging the homogenizing impulse of both the corporatist and neoliberal citizenship regimes, which had promoted the collective and individual, respectively. They are pushing us to reconsider and revamp citizenship regimes in Latin America.

The Postliberal Challenge

Indigenous movements have come to challenge contemporary political agendas in multiple ways. In one sense, these movements have formed part of a broader social movement effort to restore the social rights once associated with corporatist citizenship regimes and to advance the political and civil rights associated with neoliberal citizenship regimes. In Ecuador and Bolivia, in particular, indigenous movements have spearheaded these society-wide protests. But in a deeper sense, Latin America's indigenous movements are pushing forth a *new* postliberal challenge that calls on states to incorporate *heterogeneous* notions of *who* is a citizen, *how* citizenship is mediated, and *where* authority is vested. In answering each of these questions, they are calling on Latin American polities to recognize and institutionalize a more differentiated set of citizenship regimes that can accommodate the claims of the individual alongside claims for the collective.[2] As such, they are fundamentally rethinking the homogenizing and liberal precepts of contemporary citizenship regimes *and* the state.

Viewed as a whole, the postliberal challenge compels us to consider the coexistence of multiple national identities associated with national citizenship, multiple modes of interest intermediation, and multiple

---

[1] In this regard, the agenda charted (for collective autonomy and individual equality) cannot simply be deduced from what causes the movements, although neither is it wholly divorced from it. Agendas are strategic positions that balance between collective memories (which are socially constructed but are understood as historic fact) and the contemporary context (which shapes who is targeted). In turn, they can change over time and can reconstitute the identities of movements in the process. For discussions of the tension between memory and strategy, see Rappaport (1990); Uehling (2000: 262); McAdam, Tarrow, and Tilly (2001); and Radcliffe (2001: 28–9).

[2] These proposals parallel some of the theoretical arguments for a differentiated form of citizenship, as articulated by Young (1995), and multicultural citizenship, as articulated by Kymlicka (1995).

institutional sites formally vested with political power and jurisdiction. For indigenous movements challenge the idea that there is one overarching political culture (be it national or civic) for each state, that there is one unit of societal representation, and that there is one kind of state that can or should regulate state–society relations. These challenges are more akin to the multicultural challenges found in the advanced industrial democracies than the ethnic conflicts found in other parts of the developing and post-Soviet world. In this regard, the postliberal challenge elaborated in the following text elucidates the ways in which indigenous movements are pushing the democratic envelope in a multicultural direction. To this we now turn.

Challenging National Homogeneity: Redrawing the Nation-State, Recognizing a Diverse Citizenry

In the modern world, talk about citizenship sometimes presupposes, as a background assumption, an idealized (and misleading) conception of the nation-state as an administratively centralized, culturally homogenous form of political community in which citizenship is treated primarily as a legal status that is universal, equal, and democratic. In this idealized conception, the nation-state is the only locus of political community that really matters and citizenship just means membership in a nation-state (Carens 2000: 161).[3]

Indigenous movements in Latin America are effectively challenging prevailing cultural norms of *who* is and can be a citizen. As Chapter 2 highlighted, Latin American countries have extended citizenship on the basis of *jus soli* (granting membership on the basis of birth in a given territory). This principle of citizenship might initially suggest that Latin American states have not equated citizenship with the nation (at least not in the essentialist sense presumed by the principle of *jus sanguinis*). However, this would be a superficial reading of a more nuanced political history. For Latin American regimes found other ways to restrict citizenship along ethnic lines and to identify citizenship with national projects.

Indeed, Latin American rulers have *not* historically embraced and accepted their ethnically diverse populations as full members or citizens of

---

[3] Carens (2000) presents a different although compatible way of angling into the multiple memberships that define citizenship. Both the postliberal challenge discussed here and in Carens (2000) argue that citizenship cannot be reduced to a formalistic and homogenous definition, but must take into account the multiple and changing practices that one finds in different contexts.

the polity. Rhetoric aside, the history of ethnic relations in Latin America has been one of violence, subordination, marginalization, and assimilation.[4] In all cases, Latin American states have historically delimited the principle of *jus soli* by restricting citizenship along Aristotelian lines (literacy, property, gender) – a measure that commonly excluded indigenous peoples from practicing full citizenship rights. And when those restrictions were (slowly) lifted in the twentieth century, Latin American politicians found other ways of identifying citizenship with the nation. Throughout the region, state officials and intellectuals of all political stripes advocated assimilation policies, hoping to construct a unified nation based on mestizaje and "whitening." Most politicians and scholars assumed that the existing state was legitimate and that what needed fixing was the construction and identification of primary identities – be they around the mestizo nation and/or class.

As part of this national project, Latin American governments promoted corporatist citizenship regimes, as discussed at length in Part II of this book, that were designed to turn Indians into *national* peasants. Latin American politicians complemented these incorporating measures with educational programs and Indian Institutes to promote assimilation.[5] These policies were designed in places such as Mexico, Guatemala, Peru, and Bolivia to incorporate people perceived as backward into the ranks of a new and presumably more civilized nation.[6] States encouraged indigenous men and women to discard any public display of indigenous identity, encouraged the adoption of mestizo identities, and, consequently, encouraged miscegenation to "whiten" the population. According to positions articulated

[4] Military expeditions against the indigenous population were particularly brutal in Uruguay, Argentina, and Chile and, to a lesser degree, in Brazil (Stavenhagen 1988: 29 and Maybury-Lewis 1991). These same countries, like many others in Latin America, enacted legislation to attract European immigration, arguing that this would improve the racial composition and, therefore, the economic and political prospects of the new states. Latin American nation-states treated indigenous peoples as heathens, a threat to security, an impediment to economic development, and a source of cheap, if not free, labor. The various states enacted corresponding, if at times internally contradictory, policies to address these fears, perceptions, and goals. They killed those perceived as a threat to an emerging nation-state, isolated and/or denied the existence of those in remote areas, coerced populations for their labor, and/or promoted a policy of assimilation.

[5] Latin American regimes created Indian Institutes to study indigenous populations – much as one would analyze national folklore – and to produce the mechanisms to assimilate them into the national (read *modern mestizo*) population. While Brazil formed an Indian office in 1910, other Latin American countries founded these offices in the 1930s and 1940s (Stavenhagen 1988: 105 and Maybury-Lewis 1991).

[6] See Mallon (1992); Stavenhagen (1992); and Wade (1997).

by state officials and intellectuals, mestizaje allowed for social mobility as one's ethnic status changed from indigenous (other) to mestizo (us); this process presumably depoliticized ethnic cleavages.

In short, nineteenth- and twentieth-century politicians in Latin America engaged in nation-building projects that sought to create national unity – a policy that legitimated both the assimilation of indigenous peoples and attacks on indigenous communal lands. With the principle of *jus soli*, they advocated a citizenship that would be accorded to all those residing in a given territory. Where nationals did not exist, they would forge them; if not in this generation, then the next. These nation-building projects were more than ideological exercises. They were codified in national constitutions in the nineteenth and twentieth centuries and shaped political behavior toward indigenous peoples.

Against this backdrop, indigenous men and women would seem to disappear, responding passively to the incursion of new states (as well as markets and clerics) whose very purpose to undermine the political structures, economies, and cosmologies of indigenous groups remains unchallenged. Yet, these assumptions regarding the passivity and obsolescence of indigenous peoples have been repeatedly challenged, particularly over the last two decades of the twentieth century.

Indeed, the Latin American indigenous movements that have emerged at the end of the twentieth century have come to challenge these projects of nation building and assimilation that were associated with nineteenth-century Liberal parties and that have been inscribed in Latin American constitutions since then. For while many indigenous men and women outwardly assimilated into mestizo culture (leading to an official decline in the absolute numbers of self-identified indigenous peoples), self-identified indigenous communities have survived – albeit as with all communities, they have changed over time. The challenge is more than a question of demography and numbers. It is a question of organized resistance and agenda setting. With the third wave of democratization, indigenous movements in Ecuador, Bolivia, Mexico, Guatemala, Colombia, and Brazil have demanded constitutional reforms recognizing the *multiethnic and plurinational composition of their countries*. These demands highlight the endurance of many ethnic communities (even while the content of those identities has surely changed) despite nation-building projects. Moreover, the emergence of indigenous movements and their denunciation of assimilationist policies challenge the conception in Latin America that a mestizo nation does or should correspond to the existing state. Indeed, indigenous movements want to expand the idea of the *nation* to reflect a more ethnically and culturally heterogeneous citizenry.

As part of this effort, indigenous movements have appealed to norms, laws, and organizations operating in the international arena.[7] In particular, indigenous movements have lobbied Latin American states to ratify ILO Convention 169 on Indigenous and Tribal Peoples in Independent Countries. Convention 169 outlines the rights of indigenous peoples and the responsibilities of multiethnic states toward them. At a minimum, it calls on states to recognize ethnic heterogeneity where they had previously advanced nationalist aspirations of mestizo homogeneity. The following Latin American states have ratified ILO Convention 169: Mexico (1990), Bolivia (1991), Colombia (1991), Costa Rica (1993), Paraguay (1993), Peru (1994), Honduras (1995), Guatemala (1996), Ecuador (1998), Argentina (2000), Brazil (2002), Venezuela (2002), and Dominica (2002).[8] Ratification provides a mechanism for advocating constitutional reforms to accommodate ethnically diverse populations; it should not necessarily be seen as a prelude to secession.

While these Latin American states have yet to live up to the terms of the convention, they have discussed constitutional amendments that recognize the multiethnic and pluricultural makeup of each country, as in Colombia (1991), Mexico (1992), Peru (1993), Bolivia (1994), and Ecuador (1998).[9] These reforms are an important symbolic victory for indigenous peoples who have worked to change myths of national unity and to promote a new basis for understanding political identities and membership. Indeed, the constitutional recognition of ethnic heterogeneity in some Latin American states has opened up possibilities to discuss and debate other kinds of democratic institutions that can accommodate a diverse citizenry – including debates about decentralization, legal pluralism, federalism, consociationalism, electoral systems, and the like. "It has become clearer that what began as demands for specific rights and compensatory measures has turned into a new view of the nation and the state" (Stavenhagen 2002: 41).

---

[7] Wilmer (1993) and Brysk (1994, 1996, and 2000).

[8] As of August 2004, seventeen countries had ratified Convention 169, including Denmark, Fiji, the Netherlands, and Norway. See http://www.ilo.org/ilolex/english/convdisp1.htm.

[9] Dandler (1996); Van Cott (2000a: 265–8); and Yrigoyen (2000). In a striking May 1999 Guatemalan referendum the voting population (18 percent of the eligible electorate) *rejected* proposed reforms to amend the constitution and acknowledge the multiethnic composition of the country (as outlined in the 1996 Guatemalan peace accords).

Challenging Homogeneous Units of Representation: Advancing Multiple Modes of Interest Intermediation

... [R]epresentation mediates between individual and state by the way in which it aggregates citizen preferences for the purposes of responsiveness. No matter how individualistic the premises of a political system, all political representation is group representation, insofar as legislators represent constituencies and constituencies are defined by some shared characteristic, that is, as a group (Williams 1998: 25).

The demand for multicultural recognition is the first step toward making claims that indigenous cultures cannot be reduced to individual identities and rights, as liberal theory and neoliberal citizenship regimes would have it, but in fact also rest on primary and collective sets of identities, organizations, and rights, as communitarians would presume. Accordingly, indigenous movements have challenged the effort to homogenize and individualize the appropriate unit of political representation and interest intermediation. They want to be recognized as individuals and collectivities.

As we have seen, Latin American regimes have tended to assume unit homogeneity. Whereas Latin American regimes once privileged corporatist forms of interest intermediation – a point elaborated throughout this book – they now privilege individuals as the primary unit. Latin American politicians of the 1980s and 1990s have contended that the central political unit is and should be the individual. The individual chooses to vote, to join political parties, to participate in organizations, and to hold government accountable. In short, the individual is the foundational unit of rights and responsibilities in a polity presumed to be moving toward a more liberal democracy. Policy makers have voiced concern about equalizing treatment before a state that engaged in indiscriminate repression and torture and, to that end, advocate paying closer attention to the rule of law. In a context where dissidents were killed or jailed, indigenous people were excluded and/or repressed, and regions were controlled by local bosses, the call for a universalizing set of norms and institutions to protect individuals is an important normative step toward deepening democracy.

Given the democratizing intentions of the third wave, it is striking that indigenous movements in the region are *cautious* about the drive to promote the individual as the primary political unit of democracy. The constitutions of Latin America, in fact, do not directly and explicitly discriminate against Indians as individuals. However, legislation has historically often treated Indians as wards of the state. For example, despite comparatively liberal

Brazilian legislation, indigenous men and women have been discussed in statutes referring to legal minors and the juridically handicapped.[10] "In 1988, Brazil's constitutional reform shifted Indians from a tutelary and assimilationist regime to an enfranchised and protected minority group" (Brysk 2000: 260). But this is not the kind of legal outcome sought by the overwhelming number of indigenous movements. For as stated by Pedro Balcúmez, a Mayan Indian leader with the Consejo de Organizaciones Maya: "We do not want protection but effective participation in society and the economy."[11]

Even where legal equality is granted, equal treatment often remains a distant hope. Stavenhagen (1988: 23, 95 and 2002: 36) notes that while the constitutions of many Latin American countries have stipulated the juridical equality of its citizens, that in fact, the human rights of indigenous men and women are not universally respected. Where the dominant political discourse suggests the advance of individual rights, indigenous communities often see, at best, no change at all and, at worst, an infringement on indigenous autonomy and resources. Because indigenous communities have rarely experienced the full complement of civil and political rights associated with liberal democracy, they have little reason to believe that the contemporary wave of democratization will necessarily fulfill these promises now. As stated boldly by CONAIE, Ecuador's largest and most prominent indigenous movement: "In Ecuador the fundamental principles of democracy – equality, liberty, fraternity, and social peace – have not been achieved."[12] Throughout the region indigenous leaders have made similar points. They recount the ways in which individuals' rights have been dismissed – in voting booths, courts, and schools – and argue that the state should do more to uphold and protect their individual rights.[13]

Hence, despite a neoliberal discourse of individual civil and political rights, states remain incapable of protecting them.[14] The state's inability to secure individual rights makes many indigenous communities even more

---

[10] See Stavenhagen (1988: 344–5) and Maybury-Lewis (1991: 218–26).
[11] Latin American Weekly Reports, February 2, 1993.
[12] CONAIE (n.d.: 6).
[13] Based on more than a dozen anonymous small-group discussions conducted by the author in Ecuador, Bolivia, and Peru during the course of 1997, and repeated in most 1995–1997 interviews with indigenous leaders in Ecuador, Bolivia, Peru, Guatemala, and Mexico.
[14] Stavenhagen and Iturralde (1990); Torres Galarza (1995); and Dandler (1996).

wary of the restrictions that neoliberal citizenship regimes would place on the inalienable *community rights* and de facto *local autonomy* that they had secured during the prior corporatist citizenship regime. And as communitarians have long argued, individual rights at times cannot be pursued absent a prior respect for collective ones (see Chapter 2). This is, at the very least, the perspective advocated in documents and discourse emanating from Latin American indigenous movements. In his work on federalism, Stepan (1999) also notes,

> In multinational polities . . . some groups may be able to participate fully as individual citizens only if they acquire, as a group, the right to have schooling, mass media, and religious or even legal structures that correspond to their language and culture. Some of these rights may be described as group-specific collective rights. Many thinkers in the liberal tradition assume that all rights are individual and universal and view any deviation from individualism and universalism with suspicion, but this assumption is open to question (Stepan 1999: 31).

> . . . [W]hile individual rights are universal, it is simply bad history to argue that in actual democracies all rights have been universal. Frequently, the struggle to reconcile the imperatives of political integration with the legitimate imperatives of cultural difference has led countries to award certain minorities group-specific rights, such as those given to French-speaking Quebec in Canada, to cultural councils in Belgium and to Muslim family courts in India. The key point is that it is the obligation of the democratic state to ensure that no group-specific right violates individual or universal rights (Stepan 1999: 32).

In this context, contemporary indigenous movements have brought into sharp relief the tense interplay between the contemporary celebration of the individual and indigenous community practices. Indigenous movements generally argue that the individual should not be the only unit of representation, nor should it be privileged. They demand that the state uphold equal rights and responsibilities for Indians as individuals and in this sense are calling for the fulfillment of liberal ideals. But they argue as well that the state should recognize indigenous communities as a historically prior and autonomous sphere of political rights, jurisdiction, and autonomy. These demands range from the call for community or supracommunity autonomy to the call for designated representation in legislatures, ministries, state offices, and constituent assemblies.[15] The demand is not to identify these communities as historic relics confined to *local* politics but as contemporary,

---

[15] For a discussion of representation in constituent assemblies and representation designated by constitutions, see Andolina (1997) and Van Cott (2001). For a discussion of representation in state ministries and state agencies, see Lucero (2002).

capable, and representative units that can both take care of local politics *and* act before and within the state.

If we look at a series of indigenous movements in Ecuador (CONAIE), Bolivia (CIDOB and CSUTCB), Mexico (EZLN), Guatemala (COMG), and Peru (AIDESEP), we find that their strategies have differed. In some cases they have taken up arms (Mexico); in others they have organized marches for recognition (Ecuador and Bolivia); in others they have negotiated directly with the government for new laws that recognize communities (Mexico, Guatemala, and Bolivia); and in others they have used existing administrative laws that map out local political units to secure a de facto space in which indigenous communities can indirectly act as a political unit (Peru). But despite these differences, we find each movement demanding that the state simultaneously protect members' individual civil and political rights *and* recognize indigenous communities as a political unit. This position is forcefully articulated in several movement documents,[16] as well as in interviews with leaders from each of the movements.[17]

Challenging Homogeneous and Unitary States:
The Where(withal) of Political Authority

One important obstacle to the project of aboriginal self-government has been the hegemony of the unitary model of citizenship, the widespread view that any form of differentiated citizenship would be incompatible with the inclusion of aboriginal people in a Canadian political community in which they were full citizens and all citizens were treated equally (Carens 2000: 177).

Many indigenous movements have also come to challenge basic normative assumptions about the desirability of universal administrative boundaries within the state. These administrative designs assume neutrality, fairness, and equality. But the *experiences* of indigenous peoples have been anything but that. Rejecting state-formation projects that have sought to centralize or decentralize political institutions according to a single blueprint, indigenous movements throughout the region have demanded that the state recognize

[16] COMG (1995); Servicios del Pueblo Mixe, A.C. (1996); and CONAIE (n.d.: 11–12).
[17] These statements were made in 1997 interviews (listed in the bibliography) with indigenous leaders: from Peru, with Evaristo Nukguaj and Bonifacio Cruz Alanguía; from Bolivia, with Marcial Fabricano and Román Loayza; and from Ecuador, with Luis Macas, Leonardo Viteri, César Cerda, and Valerio Grefa. Similar statements were made in an interview in the United States with Guatemalans Manuela Alvarado, Alberto Mazariegos, and Juanita Bazibal Tujal, May 3, 1998.

administrative boundaries that are unique to indigenous peoples. In this regard, it is not enough to promote municipalization, decentralization, and accountability as a means of increasing the representation, accountability, and transparency of local governments. Indeed, indigenous movements have increasingly demanded that the state recognize territorial boundaries (even, or particularly, where they cut across municipal or provincial boundaries) in which social relations are regulated by indigenous authority systems and customary law. These movements have articulated these demands as autonomy claims. In other words, they are arguing that a differentiated citizenship should coincide with differentiated administrative boundaries.[18] These multiple sites of administration would theoretically accommodate political allegiance to the state (national law) and local communities (customary law). Remarkably, new constitutions in Colombia (1991), Peru (1993), Bolivia (1994), and Ecuador (1998) have gone a long way toward recognizing (although not necessarily implementing the recognition of) indigenous laws and norms, indigenous authorities and authority systems, and jurisdictional functions (Van Cott 2000a and 2002; Yrigoyen 2000).

Demands for territorial autonomy have been particularly significant in the Amazon. As states have actively promoted development and governance in the Amazonian region, they have challenged the physical spaces in which indigenous communities lived – catalyzing a move by the latter to defend their local spaces (including the right to work and govern that land). Challenging national stereotypes of the Amazon as virgin territory and national patrimony, indigenous communities and organizations have launched discussions about indigenous territories. Indeed, indigenous organizations in the Amazon have been surprisingly successful at negotiating various forms of autonomy, as noted in Chapters 4 and 5. In Ecuador, for example, OPIP placed territorial demands on the political map with a thirteen-day, two-thousand-person march from Puyo to Quito in 1992. The government eventually conceded nineteen different territorial blocs that totaled 138 legally recognized communities and 1,115,475 hectares.[19] In Bolivia the main Amazonian indigenous organizations also won territorial

---

[18] References to country-specific demands for differentiated administrative boundaries follow. For a comparative overview of the current state of legal pluralism and autonomy regimes, see Assies and Hoekema (1994); Dandler (1996); Smith (1999); and Van Cott (2000a: ch. 9) and (2001).

[19] Leonardo Viteri, interview, March 6, 1997; Gonzalo Ortiz Crespo, interview, March 11, 1997; and César Cerda, interview, May 6, 1997. Also see Selverston (1994: 146 and 2001: 45). See Chapter 4 for further elaboration.

autonomy.[20] Demands were first articulated during the 1990 March for Territory and Dignity, organized by CPIB. The president responded by issuing presidential decrees that recognized four indigenous territories. In 1996 the government passed a new agrarian reform that provided indigenous communities with the legal basis for appealing for territorial recognition and by August 1997 the state had recognized seven distinct territories totaling 2.6 million hectares.[21] And in 1998, the Bolivian government created a program to title ten million hectares of indigenous lands (Plant 2002: 217). However, the Banzer administration (1997–2002) delayed the process of titling these lands (Van Cott 2002: 56). And third-party colonist and forestry concessions have also slowed this process down (Plant 2002: 209). Demands for territorial autonomy in Bolivia have been complemented by efforts to establish indigenous districts. With the 1994 Bolivian Law of Popular Participation (largely a municipalization and decentralization law), indigenous communities gained the right to request indigenous districts – albeit with mixed results.[22] In the 1991 Colombian Constituent Assembly, moreover, indigenous peoples also negotiated reforms that granted territorial autonomy.[23] The 1991 Colombian Constitution referred to indigenous lands as *territorial entities* in Article 286. According to this article, existing political authority structures assume governing capacity, including criminal and civil jurisdiction, in these territories. The territories are responsible for determining their own development strategy and for administering public resources as if they were municipalities. We also find states recognizing some version of autonomy regimes (reserves) in the Amazonian Basin in Brazil (Brysk 2000: 201). While concessions of territorial autonomy in each country have confronted serious obstacles in implementation (Plant 2002: 209), they constitute a significant symbolic and legal precedent for indigenous movements as a whole.

[20] Interviews conducted with indigenous leaders Marcial Fabricano, November 2, 1995 and June 13, 1997 and Ernesto Noe July, 25, 1997; with researchers Zulehma Lehm, August 1, 1997, and Wilder Molina, July 29, 1997; and with lawyer Carlos Romero Bonifaz July 1, 1997. See Libermann and Godínez (1992); Navia Ribera (1996); Molina (1997); and Van Cott (2000a and 2000c).

[21] Interviews conducted with Isabel Lavadenz, former national director of the Bolivian National Institute of Agrarian Reform, on August 4, 1997 and August 5, 1997, and Jorge Múñoz, researcher at UDAPSO, on May 31, 1997. See also Múñoz and Lavadenz (1997). See Chapter 5 for further elaboration.

[22] Alcides Vadillo, interview, June 11, 1997; Luz María Calvo, interview, July 9, 1997; and George Gray Molina, interview, June 4, 1997. Also see Balslev (1997: 35–41, 53–8, 86).

[23] Clavero (1994: 187–9) and Van Cott (2000a and 2000c).

Beyond the Amazon as well, there are now demands for state recognition of indigenous communities as politically autonomous units, further challenging the hegemonic idea of administrative homogeneity. In Nicaragua, Miskito Indians fought a civil war to secure autonomy from the Sandinista regime (Hale 1994). In Bolivia, in particular, there has been a push to recognize, reconstitute, and/or register ayllus (communal kinship organizations) that dot the Andean countryside.[24] In Ecuador this public discussion moved forward considerably with the 1998 Constitution that created *"Circunscripciones Territoriales Indígenas y Negras,"* (Indigenous and Black Territorial Circumscriptions) although legislative action is still required at the time of this writing to turn this constitutional opening into a reality. Moreover, indigenous movements and NGOs in Ecuador have engaged in dialogue and initiated projects to strengthen and/or reconstitute systems of elders.[25] Mexico and Guatemala have seen separate efforts to negotiate or proclaim autonomy for the Mayan populations residing on either side of the border.[26] In Mexico, the EZLN demanded that the state recognize the autonomy of indigenous communities, which was incorporated into the accords of San Andrés (signed in 1996). The accords were not implemented, however. Thereafter, the Zapatistas organized a historic march from the state of Chiapas to Mexico City and restated their autonomy demands before the Mexican legislature in early 2001. The legislature subsequently did pass a law, which was denounced by the EZLN as devoid of any effective autonomy for indigenous communities. Finally, Guatemala signed a historic 1995 Accord on Identity and Rights of Indigenous Peoples and a 1996 Peace Accord that granted autonomy to indigenous communities; this has, however, not been implemented in any meaningful way, at the time of this writing. Indeed, Stavenhagen (2002: 34–5) concludes that many of the autonomous agreements remain ill-defined and weakly implemented.

Hence, indigenous movements throughout the Americas are claiming their right to new administrative spheres that have a certain degree of

---

[24] María Eugenia Choque Quispe, interview, May 21, 1997; Carlos Mamani, interview, June 16, 1997; Constantino Lima, interview, June 17, 1997; Ramón Conde, interview, June 25, 1997; and Ricardo Calla, interview, July 4, 1997. See Molina and Arias (1996) and Albó and Ayllu Sartañani (manuscript).

[25] Luis Maldonado, interview, March 12, 1997; José María Cabascango, interview, March 19, 1997; and Luis Macas, interview, May 6, 1997.

[26] For examples of autonomy debates in Mexico and Guatemala, see *Acuerdo sobre identitad y derechos de los pueblos indígenas* (Guatemala: 1995); *Ojarasca* (1995); the 1996 Guatemalan Peace Accords (Guatemala: 1997); the 1995 Guatemalan Accord on Identity and Rights of Indigenous Peoples; Díaz-Polanco (1997); Sieder (1998); and Burguete (2000).

political autonomy at the local level. This is more than just a call for more land, although that is certainly a *core* and *necessary* component of the demand. Rather, it is a demand that the state recognize indigenous political jurisdiction over that land, including the right of indigenous legal systems and authorities to process and adjudicate claims. In this regard, diversified state structures would coincide with some form of legal pluralism.

These calls might support federalism and/or decentralization but cannot necessarily be reduced to either one or the other.[27] Federalism and decentralization are generally designed to grant greater local sovereignty over local issues; federalism and decentralization tend to assume an important degree of administrative homogeneity.[28] Each assumes that an entire country will be defined by federal and/or municipal administrative boundaries. Each administrative unit (whether the state and/or the municipality) ideally governs with the same understanding of the dividing line between federal/national and local jurisdiction. Many indigenous organizations support this idea insofar as it provides additional entry points for participation as both electors and elected. And indeed, with decentralization, the level of indigenous participation in elections has grown; in Bolivia, for example, the number of elected indigenous officials has increased noticeably.[29]

Demands for local autonomy, however, actually challenge the administrative homogeneity entailed in decentralization and classic types of federalism. Indigenous organizations assert that their collective identity – which is historically prior to the formation of each Latin American state – entitles them to special jurisdictions that crosscut, transcend, and are distinct from homogenous state administrative boundaries. They want not only more local autonomy but also more expansive jurisdiction for Indian communities – an arrangement that would not necessarily be accorded nonindigenous communities. Hence, regardless of whether a country is defined by federal units, indigenous movements are demanding that the state recognize political and juridical spaces that are primarily occupied and administered by indigenous communities. These proposals would in fact result in a more

---

[27] For the differences between territorial autonomy, federalism, and decentralization, see Lapidoth (1997: 50–2).

[28] Stepan (1999) notes that contrary to common perceptions, there are in fact two types of federalism: symmetric and asymmetric federalism. The latter could conceivably accommodate the types of autonomy demands being put forth by indigenous movements insofar as it grants "different competencies and group-specific rights to some states" (1999: 21).

[29] See Ministerio de Desarrollo Humano, Secretaría Nacional de Participación Popular (1997).

multilayered conception of the polity, the state, and its citizens, one that would promote inclusion and autonomy simultaneously.

These are not demands for secession but for institutional pluralism in multiethnic settings. Nonetheless, demands for recognition as a people have raised legal eyebrows, for fear that recognition as a people is the first step toward secession and/or a threat to the power of the national state. This might be the case among a few groups; but it appears to be uncommon. Miguel Sucuquí, a Mayan organizer in the governing board of CERJ, a largely indigenous human rights organization in Guatemala, said,

> So our most immediate task is organization and unification, and this must be done on the basis of our culture and our traditions. With that unification, we Mayans would have an enormous capacity to build our own life within the Guatemalan state. *We are not forming a state within another state* – we want that to be well understood. But were there freedom of organization, of expression, of religion, the Mayan people could unite, strengthen ourselves, and create the proper institutional expressions for sustaining our lives as a people.[30]

In short, indigenous movements are posing a new postliberal challenge. They are challenging the homogenizing assumptions that suggest that individuals unambiguously constitute the primary political unit and that administrative boundaries and jurisdictions should be uniformly defined throughout a country. They call instead for more differentiated forms of citizenship and political boundaries, ones that grant individuals rights as citizens but that also grant collective rights and political autonomy. Finally, in calling for the constitutional recognition of pluriethnic and multicultural states, they challenge the idea that the state (democratic or otherwise) should correspond to a presumed homogeneous nation. In this regard, they challenge claims of ethnonational homogeneity and assert the political salience of ethnic diversity. By advocating a differentiated kind of citizenship regime, they are pushing to redefine democratic institutions in dramatic ways. And where states have already incorporated these claims formally into constitutions, legislation, and statutes, they are working to implement and enforce these changes so that they are more than symbolic achievements.[31]

While these legal advances are surely important in themselves, the open question is how the new legislation will be implemented and how Indian communities will

---

[30] Reported in *Report on Guatamala* (September 1993), emphasis added.

[31] See Brysk (2000: ch. 6) and Van Cott (2000a: ch. 9) for a discussion of constitutional changes and policy reforms that have advanced indigenous rights. Both authors report that policy changes have not easily translated into implementation.

benefit. The answer is not clear. Complaints are increasingly heard that the new laws are not being implemented as they should be, or that secondary legislation has not been adopted after general principles were laid down in the new constitutions (Stavenhagen 2002: 33–4).

Lest we conclude that these are political battles peculiar to Latin America, we should cast a comparative glance once again around the world. For we see that postliberal challenges emerge as a subtype of the multicultural struggles found in other "immigrant" countries in the United States, Canada, New Zealand, and Australia. In all of these cases, we find that indigenous peoples are demanding not only the right to be citizens of their respective countries but also the right to local autonomy. Insofar as the postliberal agenda formally seeks to secure collective and individual rights, it is both a historically rooted and future-oriented project. It is historically rooted insofar as indigenous movements seek to recapture the collective right to identity, respect for their communities, and the right to some autonomy that was understood as once theirs. It is forward looking insofar as it seeks to complement these demands with the right to form part of the existing liberal polities – with equal individual rights before and in the state.

Here is where political agenda setting meets the unknown. For it remains unclear how to harmonize these different systems in a coherent, democratic, and sustainable way. Scholars of multiculturalism have analyzed this dilemma within political theory, as discussed in Chapter 2. Empirically speaking, however, they have not found an institutional mechanism to consistently accommodate the norms of such diverse paradigms of citizenship and governance. This is nowhere more apparent than when we analyze the question of local autonomy. Local autonomy can increase the possibility for local participation. It could also tend toward illiberal politics at the local level. The recognition of local autonomy could provide traditional authorities with the means to carve out their own fiefdoms with few outside checks on the exercise of that power – thereby inhibiting the democratization of local life within indigenous communities. Moreover, defending local autonomy and traditional indigenous practices could disadvantage certain groups within indigenous society – limiting their voice, access to resources, and individual autonomy. Gender relations are particularly relevant in this regard. Women have historically been excluded from public political spheres, where the male head of household often speaks for the family unit, where women are often denied equal access to education and social services, and where battered women often have had little legal recourse within the community.

Local autonomy does not necessarily advance gender equality and might work against it. Consequently, the postliberal challenge could simultaneously increase local autonomy (a liberal good) and decrease local tolerance (an illiberal outcome).

Given the fundamental challenges that the postliberal agenda poses, it is perhaps all the more remarkable then that the recent politicization of ethnic cleavages in Latin America has not unleashed ethnic conflict but has led to an explicit effort to accommodate a diverse ethnic population in a more plural form of democracy.

The Democratic/Electoral Challenge: The Siren's Call?

As I complete this book, indigenous movements have primarily articulated this postliberal agenda through social movement politics – in the streets, in protests, in documents, and in international fora. And they have achieved some notable political successes, as summarized previously and discussed in Part II of this book – including the negotiation of territorial autonomy, bicultural education, a chance to help run state offices, and a voice in public debates. In other words, key demands have found their way into policy (although rarely solely because of indigenous mobilization) – even when indigenous movements eschewed party politics, electoral campaigns, and the like.

With their mobilizational successes, however, several indigenous leaders have rethought their exclusive mobilizational strategy. Many have moved into electoral politics. That is to say, they have chosen to run for office, form political parties, and engage in partisan alliances. This is a striking development because so many indigenous leaders initially rejected the idea of taking part in the electoral process, as discussed for Ecuador and Bolivia. Nonetheless, as indigenous movements, in both of these countries and elsewhere, achieved political successes, they have rethought this position. With increasing overtures by existing political parties (concerned to harness a mobilized indigenous constituency), and with electoral reforms in many countries that decreased barriers to entry (Van Cott 2003), it also became more pressing and feasible to enter the electoral races. In this context, by the end of the 1990s, indigenous leaders were participating in executive, legislative, and local-level races.

There have been notable electoral success stories here. First and foremost among them was the election in 1993 of Víctor Hugo Cárdenas as vice-president of Bolivia. But important indigenous leaders were also elected to legislatures and local offices in Bolivia, Ecuador, Guatemala, Colombia, Venezuela, Brazil, and beyond.[32] As seen in prior chapters, a significant part of the historic leadership in Ecuador's CONAIE has taken part in elections and since 1996 has successfully fielded several candidates, including Luis Macas, Miguel Lluco, Nina Pacari, among others. So too, their leadership won 10 percent of the seats in the Constituent Assembly (1997–1998). And Brysk (2000: 255) reports local electoral successes following the 1996 election: "almost a dozen indigenous mayors and scores of council members have assumed power in some regions." In Bolivia, as well, we have seen significant electoral gains, particularly by indigenous leaders in the CSUTCB, in general, and the coca movement, in particular – with Evo Morales making it to the runoff in the 2003 presidential election and his party gaining seats in the legislature. With the Bolivian law of popular participation, one also found a dramatic rise in the number of indigenous local counselors – at least 464 in 1997 (29 percent of the total) (Albó 2002: 82). The 1997 elections also resulted in nine indigenous-campesino deputies (Albó 2002: 95).

These successful electoral campaigns, however, have not all translated into the growth and strength of indigenous movements as a whole. For despite early optimism and fanfare, electoral participation has posed some (perhaps short-term) challenges to the existing indigenous movements – just as the broader literature on social movements and democracy would caution. Political parties, interactions with state officials, and reform policies can undermine movement organizations that were once vibrant organizers of protest – as their struggles are subsumed or displaced by these formal institutions and sites of political negotiation, as noted by Piven and Cloward (1979) and Tarrow (1998). Accordingly, Latin American social movements have historically voiced concern about the destructive impact that political parties and alliances with state officials can have on movement autonomy and integrity.[33]

In general, it appears that political party activity is always potentially divisive of social movements at the local and community level in Latin America. . . . In addition to different agendas and different roles, the sad fact is that party militancy and divisions often exacerbate the factionalism which tends to infect social movements (Foweraker 1995: 84).

[32] For Ecuador and Bolivia, refer to Chapters 4 and 5. For a discussion of indigenous participation in political parties and elections, see Van Cott (2003).

[33] See Canel (1992); Escobar and Alvarez (1992); Hellman (1992); Schneider (1992); and Foweraker (1995: ch. 4).

At this early stage in the game, it would be foolhardy to draw conclusions about the fate of Latin America's indigenous movements and their decision to take part in elections. Moreover, we should be wary of simple generalizations about Latin American indigenous movements as a whole given varied national contexts, including different histories with democracy, clientelism, party systems, electoral rules, and the like. As Eckstein (2001) has stated,

> The relationship between democratization and social movements is, in essence, historically contingent. If and when political parties get the upper hand, social movements tend to lose their vitality; however, if they do not or before they do, political parties and social movements may nurture each other (Eckstein 2001: 398).

This contingency requires a greater span of time in which to observe these relationships. For democracy, in general, and electoral participation, in particular, can pose both opportunities and constraints for social movements, in ways aptly delineated by Eckstein (2001: 398–400).

That said, a few cautionary observations are in order because electoral participation (taken to mean the decision to run in elections) can pose serious challenges to the unity and integrity of social movements. Four dynamics are highlighted, the last of which is likely to pose the most severe challenge to Latin America's indigenous movements. Examples are drawn from material presented in Part II of this book, although the broader dynamic does not seem to be limited to these cases.

First, as indigenous leaders are elected and appointed as political officials (bringing an advisory staff along with them) they often leave indigenous movements with less experienced leadership to take their place. For relatively young movements, this can be a particular problem. While this would not necessarily be a problem if movements were better institutionalized, in the short run it has challenged movements to identify new actors who can assume the leadership of these movements and to institutionalize the mechanisms for doing so. This challenge was particularly noteworthy in Ecuador as the key executive leadership (which had visibly dominated the movement since the 1980s) chose to run for seats in the legislature, beginning in 1996. When Luis Macas, Nina Pacari, Jose María Cabascango, Miguel Lluco, and others left the CONAIE leadership, Ecuador's national indigenous confederation was placed in a position of identifying leaders who could manage the confederation *and* command the loyalty of its diverse constituency. Antonio Vargas was elected in an extremely contentious process. While Vargas subsequently made a name for himself as the new president of the movement, key actions have been severely questioned and have, at least in the short term, weakened the power and influence of the movement. Vargas led CONAIE when it decided to form an alliance with the military to overthrow the constitutionally elected government of Jamil Mahuad in January 2000. Not only did participation in the coup raise questions about the democratic credentials and credibility of Vargas's leadership, but it also led to cuts in external aid to the movement as a whole (Lucero 2001). Moreover, the fact that CONAIE was quickly sidelined in the aftermath of the coup raised questions about Vargas's political skill. It is unclear if more experienced leaders would have made similar choices. But it is commonly suggested otherwise. In other words, movements that have been identified with a small circle of leaders confront (short-term) obstacles when that leadership chooses to move into party politics.

Second, those indigenous movement leaders who are elected to political office confront a Herculean task. Given their small numbers, it is nearly impossible for them to deliver on major demands once made as movement leaders; for obviously, legislative action requires numbers – it cannot just be mandated once in office. In this context, elected indigenous leaders are confronted with what appears to be a choice between a) maintaining their ideological purity and hence appearing ineffective (because they cannot achieve concrete goals) or b) working to deliver on some issues through legislative compromise, logrolling, and coalition building (potentially appearing to betray the ideals of the movement).[34] The ability to navigate these two extremes is no easy task – particularly in a context of prevailing economic crisis, weak party systems, and patronage politics. This in turn can have negative consequences for the movement from which these leaders emerged.

The process of co-optation into the machine of "politics as normal" is a powerful danger as indigenous senators and representatives get sucked into the power play of dispensing patronage in exchange for votes. There is also the related threat of fragmentation as factions divide over control of votes and resources and over alliances with mainstream political parties (Wade 1997: 17).

The Bolivian case is telling in this regard. Víctor Hugo Cárdenas (one of the original Kataristas) was elected as Bolivia's first indigenous vice president. While he achieved national and international kudos for his role in creating greater spaces for indigenous voices and advances in important legislation, he was widely critiqued by the Kataristas in the Andes for betraying the ideals of the movement. While this criticism stemmed in part

---

[34] Also see Albó 2002: 98.

from older debates and divisions within Katarismo, it was not limited to this. Indeed, Cárdenas ended up working most closely with CIDOB from the Amazon (with whom he developed cordial and productive relations) rather than CSUTCB from the Andes (with whom relations were conflictual). The Ecuadorean case is also suggestive on this score. We find that CONAIE had an impressive first showing in 1996. Just two years later, however, CONAIE witnessed a decline in electoral support from 10 to 5 percent of the congressional seats (Mijeski and Beck 1998: 12). The reasons for this decline in support are up for debate. But at the very least, this data unequivocally indicates that one cannot assume that indigenous electoral participation translates into constant and ongoing support. Thus far, we have no indication that this is the case. To the contrary, indigenous officials confront even more difficult tasks: not only crystallizing their electoral constituency in a national context of weak parties, apathetic electorates and economic downturn, but maintaining their image as political warriors for the indigenous movement from which they emerged.

Third, highly respected leaders of indigenous movements are not necessarily embraced as ideal elected officials, particularly in better-established political party systems. In other words, we cannot assume that ethnic identification translates into votes for those who share an ethnic background. There are clear success stories, particularly in the case of Ecuador and Guatemala, where indigenous leaders participated in systems with weak party systems and short-lived political parties. As in Ecuador, nationally recognized indigenous leaders in Guatemala were elected to the national legislature – as with Rosalina Tuyuc, among others. However, in cases where there was a "comparatively" stronger and older party system, as in Bolivia, we find a more checkered history.[35] Indigenous activists in CSUTCB from Bolivia's coca-growing region have won legislative races in the 1990s; and their leader, Evo Morales, placed second in the 2003 presidential elections, as noted. However, these seem to be exceptions, rather than the rule in Bolivia. Indeed, Bolivia's movements in the Andes (CSUTCB) and Amazon (CIDOB) suffered miserable failures when they *first* entered the electoral arena; this was true of races at both the executive and legislative levels.[36] These electoral

---

[35] Bolivia has a weak party system, as noted by Mainwaring and Scully (1995). However, compared to Ecuador, Guatemala, and Peru, its system has been relatively more institutionalized.

[36] For a discussion of the Kataristas and their experiences in forming several parties and taking part in elections, see Hurtado (1986: 110–25, 145–7); Calla (1993: 19–20); Albó (1994: 60–1); and Healy (n.d.: 24). For a discussion of CIDOB's electoral defeat and internal

failures followed on the heels of remarkable movement successes in mobilizing indigenous people and negotiating favorable policy outcomes with the government in place. Not only did the CSUTCB and CIDOB leadership perform poorly in national elections in both cases (as was largely expected), but they also performed miserably at the legislative level as well (which was unexpected). At the very least, indigenous candidates thought that they would do well in their home districts. Yet in the 1997 elections, CIDOB (which allied with the MBL) did not manage to elect a single legislative candidate. Hypotheses about these failed showings also abound – including the failure of the leadership to consult with their base and the internal racism that leads many indigenous people to question if their own leaders will and can perform adequately in the formal "white" world of electoral politics.[37] Either way, the simple fact is that one cannot predict indigenous electoral successes from indigenous movement success. The case of Bolivia is an important reminder of this, as discussed in Chapter 5.[38] And in the short-term again, these disastrous electoral showings weakened indigenous movements, which came to question their political choice to enter elections and the failed outcome having done so.

Fourth, as indigenous leaders engage in partisan politics, indigenous movements are more likely to fall prey to partisan competition, thereby exposing themselves to the kinds of political cleavages that can divide movements. As with the third observation, this is particularly problematic in cases with relatively stronger political party systems.[39] This kind of partisan competition is likely to happen anyway in a competitive electoral system. But as indigenous leaders search for partisan affiliations or coalitions, they accelerate latent partisan divides within a given movement. As long as indigenous movements did not take a formal political stance, it was possible for the same movement to house multiple partisan affiliations. Where and when movements formally decided to forge and/or ally with a given party, however, these political divides were made manifest. This dynamic was illustrated by indigenous movements that consciously chose not to take a partisan stand to avoid divisions within the

divisions, see CPIB (1997). These patterns were also observed in two anonymous 1997 interviews with consultants to CIDOB.

[37] The author traveled with members of CIDOB in a postelection four-day tour and observed various community discussions (June 27–30, 1997).

[38] Indigenous representation at the municipal level did increase following the law of popular participation (Albó 1997a). However, the data does not reveal how many of those local-level leaders were tied to or identified with the indigenous movement.

[39] Albó (2002: 57) makes a similar point.

movement (as with UNCA in Peru and CONAIE in Ecuador prior to 1996) and by movements that engaged directly in elections and confronted internal infighting (as with CSUTCB and CIDOB in Bolivia, and CONAIE following its decision to take part in elections in 1996).[40] Indeed, in the aftermath of CIDOB's failed 1997 electoral run, various community members lamented CIDOB's decision to run, because it made manifest intra-CIDOB partisan differences that had previously been latent. As such, it served to further divide some local communities.[41] So too CSUTCB has been wracked by partisan divides since the 1980s.[42] And as Albó notes (2002: 96) indigenous peasants who were elected as Bolivian national deputies have been divided by partisan politics as well.

Concluding with Democracy

In short, democracy has not only extended political associational space but also tested the indigenous movements that have chosen to take part in the game of representative democracy and electoral politics. This is an observation that is as relevant for the indigenous movements of the region as it is for other political-social movements in Latin America and beyond. The Worker's Party in Brazil, Causa R in Venezuela, and the Greens throughout Europe, for example, have all witnessed serious challenges to the unity and integrity of their movements following the decision to enter electoral races.

This challenge is particularly severe in Latin America given what is commonly seen as a crisis of democratic representation and institutions – particularly in the countries discussed in this book. While this crisis is, in

---

[40] The case studies have generated one other important hypothesis about the relationship between elections and the scale of movements. It appears that sequencing and organizational fields matter. Where regional organizations entered electoral politics prior to forming *national* movements, it seemed extremely unlikely that they would be able to transcend internal divides, scale up, and forge national movements – for they became internally divided along partisan lines; this was the case in Bolivia. Where, however, regional organizations chose not to enter partisan politics, the possibilities of scaling up into a national confederation were more open, as ultimately occurred in Ecuador. Lucero (2002) arrived at a similar conclusion in his comparative work on Ecuador and Bolivia. Yet, regardless of which sequence was followed, this book also suggests that in *all cases*, once movements entered electoral politics, partisan competition weakened the unity of the movements, at least in the short term.

[41] Based on collective interviews led by CIDOB with community members (June 27–30, 1997).

[42] Calla (1989; 11–12); Hurtado (1995); Ticona (1996: 44–6); and Jenaro Flores, interviews, October 24, 1995 and June 10, 1997.

part, a function of weak competitive party systems in the five countries discussed at greatest length in this book,[43] it is perhaps more profoundly a function of the weak reach of the state and the corresponding mistrust of political institutions in the region as a whole.[44] Given weak institutions and low trust, even laudable political reforms have been compromised by the inability of the state to implement them, the resistance of authoritarian social forces, and the weak ability and presence of the state (in particular in the countryside). Accordingly, indigenous movements and leaders confront particularly high hurdles to gaining office, maintaining their positions, and effecting widespread and long-standing political reforms.

It is in this context then that efforts to organize within civil and political society are so striking – even if at times they appear quixotic. For while electoral politics has created some political turbulence (at least in the short run) for Latin America's indigenous movements, the counterfactual must be posed: would indigenous movements be more effective in promoting the postliberal challenge absent an effort to engage directly with political parties, to take part in the legislature, and the like? The educated guess is *no*. While particular indigenous movements and indigenous political officials might not survive the short term, it is clear that their mobilization in *both* realms has solidified indigenous peoples as political actors whose interests are now part of the national dialogue. Other political parties must at least take a stance on some of the issues associated with the postliberal agenda.

While we cannot be so sanguine about the degree to which the postliberal challenge will or will not be institutionalized, we can be certain that it has highlighted that indigenous peoples are *part of* the citizenry and electorate and that their political issues (diverse as they are) must at least form part of the political dialogue about what democracy is, can, and should be. Hence, as with the civil rights movement in the United States, one cannot see Latin America's indigenous movements as an absolute success – when measured against the survival of the movement and the ability to achieve

---

[43] Mainwaring and Scully (1995) observe that Ecuador, Bolivia, and Peru (and I would add Guatemala) have inchoate party systems. They are neither institutionalized nor stable. Mexico, by contrast has had (until recently) a hegemonic party system – preventing effective and meaningful forms of competitive democratic participation. Scholars of these cases commonly refer to a crisis of representation – particularly in the Andean cases.

[44] When Latin Americans were asked in 2001 if they had confidence in the following institutions – the president, the judiciary, the national congress, and political parties – Latinobarómetro reported that the percentage of those responding in the affirmative was in the single digits (Lagos 2003: 145).

all of its stated goals. But nor can one imagine calling it a failure. Far from it. The civil rights movement in the United States fundamentally changed the national terms of identifying, debating, and promoting diverse interests that had until then largely been sidelined. The same can be said of Latin America's indigenous movements and their postliberal agenda. With the politicization of ethnic cleavages, the organization of indigenous movements, and their entry into partisan debates, Latin American societies have started, however haltingly, to confront competing visions of how to accommodate a multiethnic citizenry in a democratic polity. In this sense, the democratic challenge in Latin America is not simply one of creating more stable institutions, but also and more fundamentally of redesigning those institutions in ways that can incorporate and respect diverse ethnic communities. It is an open question as to whether these states will be successful in their efforts to recognize individual and communal rights in an ideologically meaningful, practically feasible, and enduring way. What is indisputable, however, is that indigenous movements have brought these issues to the table, fostering a new set of deliberations about the practice and meaning of democracy.

Bibliography

Adrianzén, Alberto et al. 1993. *Democracia, etnicidad y violencia política en los países andinos*. Lima: Instituto de Estudios Peruanos and Instituto Francés de Estudios Andinos.

Aguinaga, Consuelo. 1991. *Ecuador: Mapa de necesidades básicas insatisfechas*. Quito: INEC.

Albó, Xavier. 2002. "Bolivia: From Indian and Campesino Leaders to Councillors and Parliamentary Deputies." In Rachel Sieder, ed., *Multiculturalism in Latin America: Indigenous Rights, Diversity and Democracy*. New York: Palgrave Macmillan.

———. 1997a. "Alcaldes concejales campesinos/indígenas: La lógica tras las cifras." *Indígenas en el poder local*. República de Bolivia, Ministerio de Desarrollo Humano, Secretaría Nacional de Participación Popular. La Paz: Talleres de Editorial Offset Boliviana Ltda. "ERBOL."

———. 1997b. "Los Derechos de le los Indios en Bolivia." Conferencia en la Noche Parlamentaria. La Paz, Hotel Raddison, February 26, 1997, pp. 18–37.

———. 1996. "La búsqueda desde adentro: Calidoscopio de auto-imágenes en el debate étnico-boliviano." *Primer Artículo* Año 1, no. 1 (Jan.–Mar.): 5–21.

———. 1994. "And from Kataristas to MNRistas? The Surprising and Bold Alliance between Aymaras and Neoliberals in Bolivia." In Donna Lee Van Cott, ed., *Indigenous Peoples and Democracy in Latin America*. New York: St. Martin's Press in association with the InterAmerican Dialogue, pp. 55–81.

———. 1991. "El retorno del indio." *Revista Andina*. Año 9, no. 2 (Dec.): 299–331.

———. 1984a. "Etnicidad y clase en la gran rebelión Aymara/Quechua, Kataris, Amarus y Bases 1780–1781." In Fernando Calderón and Jorge Dandler, eds., *Bolivia: La fuerza histórica del campesinado: Movimientos campesinos y etnicidad*. United Nations Research Institute for Social Development and Centro de Estudios de la Realidad Económica y Social. Cochabamba, Bolivia: Artes Gráficas "El Buitre," pp. 51–118.

———. 1984b. "Bases étnicas y sociales para la participación Aymara." In Fernando Calderón and Jorge Dandler, eds., *Bolivia: La fuerza histórica del campesinado: Movimientos campesinos y etnicidad.* United Nations Research Institute for Social Development and Centro de Estudios de la Realidad Económica y Social. Cochabamba, Bolivia: Artes Gráficas "El Buitre," pp. 401–43.

—————. 1983. *Bodas de plata? o requiem por una reforma agraria.* La Paz: Centro de Investigación y Promoción del Campesinado.

Albó, Xavier and Ayllu Sartañani. Manuscript. "Participación popular en tierra de ayllus." In David Booth, ed., *Popular Participation: Democratising the State in Rural Bolivia.*

Almaraz, Alejandro. 1998. "Bolivia: Los pueblos indígenas de la Amazonía." In Carlos Iván Degregori, ed., *Comunidades: Tierra, instituciones, identidad.* Lima: Diakonía-CEPES-Araiwa.

Almeida, Ileana et al. 1992. *Indios: Una reflexión sobre el levantamiento indígena de 1990.* 2nd ed. Quito: ILDIS, Ediciones Abya-Yala.

Almeida, José et al. 1993. *Sismo étnico en el Ecuador: varias perspectivas.* Quito: Ediciones Abya-Yala and CEDIME.

Almeida, Patricio and Rebeca Almeida. 1988. *Estadísticas Económicas Históricas, 1948–1983.* Quito: Banco Central del Ecuador.

Altimir, Oscar. 1998. "Inequality, Employment, and Poverty in Latin America: An Overview." In Víctor E. Tokman and Guillermo O'Donnell, eds., *Poverty and Inequality in Latin America: Issues and New Challenges.* Notre Dame, IN: University of Notre Dame Press, pp. 3–35.

Alvarez Rodrich, Augusto. 1995. "Del Estado empresario al Estado regulador." In Julio Cotler, ed., *Perú 1964–1994: Economía, Sociedad, y Política.* Lima: Instituto de Estudios Peruanos, pp. 69–91.

Alvarez, Sonia and Arturo Escobar. 1992. "Conclusion: Theoretical and Political Horizons of Change in Contemporary Latin American Social Movements." In Arturo Escobar and Sonia Alvarez, eds., *The Making of Social Movements in Latin America.* Boulder, CO: Westview Press.

Ames, Barry. 1999. "Approaches to the Study of Institutions in Latin American Politics." *Latin American Research Review* 34, no. 1: 221–36.

Anderson, Benedict. 1991. *Imagined Communities: Reflections on the Origin and Spread of Nationalism.* London: Verso.

Andolina, Robert James. 1999. "Colonial Legacies and Plurinational Imaginaries: Indigenous Movement Politics in Ecuador and Bolivia." Ph.D. Diss., University of Minnesota.

—————. 1998. "CONAIE (and others) on the Ambiguous Spaces of Democracy: Positioning for the 1997–8 Asamblea Nacional Constituyente in Ecuador." Presented at XXI International Congress of Latin American Studies Association, Palmer House Hilton Hotel, Chicago, Sept. 24–26, 1998.

Andolina, Robert, Sarah A. Radcliffe, and Nina Laurie. n.d. Manuscript. "Development and Culture: Transnational Identity-Making in Latin America."

Antezana Salvatierra, Alejandro Vladimir. 1992. *Estructura agraria en el siglo XIX: Legislación agraria y transformación de la realidad rural de Bolivia.* La Paz: Centro de Información para el Desarrollo.

Bibliography

APCOB (Apoyo para el Campesino-Indígena del Oriente Boliviano). 1996. *Políticas y lineamientos para el trabajo con pueblos indígenas.* Santa Cruz, Bolivia: Editora el País.
———. 1994. *Población indígena en las tierras bajas de Bolivia.* Santa Cruz, Bolivia: APCOB.
APG. 1991. Manuscript. "Mensaje del Capitán Grande del Alto y Bajo Izozog, Bonifacio Barrientos Cuellar." IX Congreso del CIDOB, Oct. 21–26, Santa Cruz, Bolivia.
Aramburú, Carlos E. 1989. "Cambios poblacionales y económicos en la Amazonía peruana: notas para discutir." In Carlos Contreras et al., *Comunidades campesinas y nativas: Normatividad y desarrollo.* Lima: Fundación Friedrich Naumann, pp. 127–45.
Arcia, Gustavo and Angel Saltos. 1995. *Análisis de la crisis educativa en Ecuador: Bases para un consenso.* Quito: Fundación Ecuador, USAID, RTI.
Arellano-López, Sonia and James F. Petras. 1994. "Non-Governmental Organizations and Poverty Alleviation in Bolivia." *Development and Change* 25: 555–68.
Aroca Medina, Américo Javier. 1999. "El papel de la justicia en la resolución de conflictos multiétnicos: El caso peruano." Paper presented at conference on Latin America sponsored by the Institute of Federalism at the University of Fribourg.
———. 1989. "Problemas de tierras de las comunidades nativas." In Carlos Contreras et al., eds., *Comunidades campesinas y nativas: Normatividad y desarrollo.* Lima: Fundación Friedrich Naumann, pp. 117–25.
Artículo Primero: Revista de Debate Social y Jurídico. 1996. Año 1, no. 2, (Oct.–Dec.). Santa Cruz, Bolivia.
Assies, W. J. and A. J. Hoekema, eds. 1994. *Indigenous Peoples' Experiences with Self-Government.* Copenhagen, Amsterdam: IWGIA, University of Amsterdam.
Ayllu Sartañäni. 1995. *Perspectivas de decentralización en Karankas: La visión comunaria.* La Paz: PROADE and ILDIS.
Ballón, Francisco. 1989. "Recursos naturales y comunidades nativas: legislación y política." In Carlos Contreras et al., eds., *Comunidades campesinas y nativas: Normatividad y desarrollo.* Lima: Fundación Friedrich Naumann, pp. 103–9.
———. 1987. "Política de la supervivencia: Las Organizaciones de los pueblos indígenas de la amazonía peruana." *Apuntes* 20, no. 1: 105–19.
Balslev, Anne. 1997. *Distritos municipales indígenas en Bolivia: Las Primeras experiencias en el Chaco.* La Paz: Subsecretaría de Asuntos Etnicos.
Banco Agrario del Perú. 1988. *Estadísticas de préstamos ejecutados.* Ejercicio. Lima.
———. 1985. *Estadísticas de préstamos ejecutados.* Ejercicio. Lima.
———. 1980. *Estadísticas de préstamos ejecutados.* Ejercicio. Lima.
———. 1975. *Estadísticas de préstamos ejecutados.* Ejercicio. Lima.
———. 1970. *Estadísticas de préstamos ejecutados.* Ejercicio. Lima.
Barre, Marie-Chantal. 1983. *Ideologías indigenistas y movimientos indios.* Mexico: Siglo Veintiuno Editores.
Barsky, Osvaldo. 1984. *La reforma agraria ecuatoriana.* Quito: Corporación Editora Nacional.

Barth, Frederik. 1969. "Introduction." In Frederik Barth, ed., *Ethnic Groups and Boundaries: The Social Organization of Cultural Difference.* Boston: Little Brown and Company, pp. 9–38.

Basombrío Iglesias, Carlos. 1998. "Sendero Luminoso and Human Rights: A Perverse Logic that Captured the Country." In Steve J. Stern, ed., *Shining and Other Paths: War and Society in Peru, 1980–1995.* Durham, NC: Duke University Press.

Bastos, Santiago and Manuela Camus. 1995a. *Abriendo Caminos: Las organizaciones mayas desde el Nobel hasta el acuerdo de derechos indígenas.* Guatemala: FLACSO.

————. 1993b. *Quebrando el Silencio: Organizaciones del Pueblo Maya y sus Demandas (1986–1992),* 2nd ed. (Guatemala: FLACSO).

Bates, Robert. 1974. "Ethnic Competition and Modernization in Contemporary Africa." *Comparative Political Studies* 6 (Jan.).

Bates, Robert and Barry Weingast. 1995. "A New Comparative Politics: Integrating Rational Choice and Interpretivist Perspectives." Paper presented at the 1995 Annual Meetings of the American Political Science Association, Aug. 31–Sept. 3.

Bates, Robert H., Rui J. P. de Figueiredo, Jr., and Barry R. Weingast. 1998. "The Politics of Interpretation: Rationality, Culture, and Transition." *Politics and Society* 26, no. 4.

Bebbington, Anthony, Galo Ramón, Hernán Carrasco, Víctor Hugo Torres, Lourdes Peralvo, and Jorge Trujillo. 1992. *Actores de una década ganada: Tribus, comunidades y campesinos en la modernidad.* Quito: Comunidec.

Becker, David. 1999. "Latin America: Beyond Democratic Consolidation." *Journal of Democracy* 10, no. 2 (Apr.): 138–51.

Beiner, Ronald, ed. 1995. *Theorizing Citizenship.* Albany: State University of New York Press.

Benalcázar R. René. 1989. *Análisis del desarrollo económico del Ecuador.* Quito: Ediciones Banco Central del Ecuador.

Benjamin, Thomas. 1996. *A Rich Land, A Poor People: Politics and Society in Modern Chiapas.* Albuquerque: University of New Mexico.

Berman, Sheri. 1997. "Civil Society and the Collapse of the Weimar Republic." *World Politics* 49, no. 3: 401–29.

Betancourt, Ana Cecilia and Hernán Rodríguez. 1994. "After the Constitution: Indigenous Proposals for Territorial Demarcation in Colombia." *Abya Yala News.* Journal of the South and Meso-American Indian Information Center. Vol. 8, 1–2 (Summer).

Black, Chad. 1998. "The 1990 Indian Uprising in Ecuador: Culture, Ethnicity, and Post-Marxist Social Praxis." Presented at XXI International Congress of Latin American Studies Association, Palmer House Hilton Hotel, Chicago, Sept. 24–26.

Block, David. 1994. *Mission Culture on the Upper Amazon: Native Tradition, Jesuit Enterprise, and Secular Policy in Moxos, 1660–1880.* Lincoln: University of Nebraska Press.

Bolivia, República de; Ministerio de Desarrollo Humano, Secretaría Nacional de Participación Popular. 1997. *Indígenas en el poder local.* La Paz: Talleres de Editorial Offset Boliviana Ltda. "ERBOL."

Bibliography

Bolivia, República de; Ministerio de Desarrollo Humano. 1994. *Mapa de Pobreza: Una Guía para la Acción Social.* 2nd ed. La Paz: Stilo IndustriA GráficA.

Bonilla, Heraclio. 1987. "The Indian Peasantry and 'Peru' during the War with Chile." In Steve J. Stern, ed., *Resistance, Rebellion, and Consciousness in the Andean Peasant World, 18th to 20th Centuries.* Madison: University of Wisconsin Press, pp. 219–31.

Booth, David et al., *Popular Participation: Democratising the State in Rural Bolivia.* Report to Sida, Commissioned through Development Studies Unit, Department of Social Anthropology, Stockholm University.

Bottasso, Juan. 1993. *Los Salesianos y la amazonia.* Quito: Abya-Yala.

Bourque, Susan C. and David Scott Palmer. 1975. "Transforming the Rural Sector: Government Policy and Peasant Response." In Abraham F. Lowenthal, ed., *The Peruvian Experiment: Continuity and Change under Military Rule.* Princeton: Princeton University Press, pp. 179–219.

Bourque, Susan C. and Kay B. Warren. 1978a. "Denial and Reaffirmation of Ethnic Identities: A Comparative Examination of Guatemalan and Peruvian Communities." University of Massachusetts, Amherst, Program in Latin American Studies, Occasional Paper Series, No. 8.

_____. 1978b. "Political Participation and the Revolution: Lessons From Rural Peru." Washington, DC: The Wilson Center: Latin American Program, Working Paper, No. 25.

Bourricaud, Francois. 1975. "Indian, Mestizo, and Cholo as Symbols in the Peruvian System of Stratification." In Nathan Glazer and Daniel P. Moynihan, eds., *Ethnicity: Theory and Experience.* Cambridge, MA: Harvard University Press, pp. 351–87.

Brass, Tom. 1983. "Agrarian Reform and the Struggle for Labour-Power: A Peruvian Case Study." *The Journal of Development Studies* 19, no. 3 (Apr.): 368–89.

Breuilly, John. 1993. *Nationalism and the State.* 2nd ed. Chicago: University of Chicago Press.

Browman, David L. and Ronald A. Schwarz, eds. 1979. *Peasants, Primitives, and Proletariats: The Struggle for Identity in South America.* The Hague: Mouton Publishers.

Brown, Michael F. 1993. "Facing the State, Facing the World: Amazonia's Native Leaders and the New Politics of Identity." *L'Homme* 126–8 (Apr.–Dec.): 307–26.

Brubaker, Rogers. 1992. *Citizenship and Nationhood in France and Germany.* Cambridge: Harvard University Press.

Brysk, Alison. 2000. *From Tribal Village to Global Village: Indian Rights and International Relations in Latin America.* Stanford: Stanford University Press.

_____. 1996. "Turning Weakness into Strength: The Internationalization of Indian Rights." *Latin American Perspectives* 23, no. 2: 38–57.

_____. 1994. "Acting Globally: Indian Rights and International Politics in Latin America." In Donna Lee Van Cott, ed., *Indigenous Peoples and Democracy in Latin America.* New York: St. Martin's Press.

Brysk, Alison and Carol Wise. 1995. "Economic Adjustment and Ethnic Conflict in Bolivia, Peru, and Mexico." Washington, DC: Woodrow Wilson International Center for Scholars: Latin American Program, Working Paper, No. 216.

Buechler, Hans C. and Judith-Maria Buechler. 1977. "Conduct and Code: An Analysis of Market Syndicates and Social Revolution in La Paz, Bolivia." In June Nash, Juan Corradi, and Hobart Spalding, Jr., eds., *Ideology and Social Change in Latin America*. New York: Gordon and Breach, pp. 174–84.

Burback, Roger and Peter Rossett. 1994. "Chiapas and the Crisis of Mexican Agriculture." Oakland: Institute for Food and Development Policy, Policy Brief No. 1.

Burguete Cal y Mayor, Aracely, ed. 2000. *Indigenous Autonomy in Mexico*. Copenhagen: IWGIA Document No. 94.

Burke, Pamela. 1997. "The Globalization of Contentious Politics: The Case of Amazonian Indigenous Rights in Ecuador." Paper Presented at the Annual American Political Science Association Conference, Washington, DC, August 28–31.

Burt, Jo-Marie. 1997. "Political Violence and the Grassroots in Lima, Peru." In Douglas Chalmers et al., eds., *The New Politics of Inequality in Latin America*. New York: Oxford University Press.

Caballero, José María and Elena Alvarez. 1980. *Aspectos cuantitativos de la reforma agraria (1969–1979)*. Lima: Instituto de Estudios Peruanos.

Calderón, Fernando and Jorge Dandler, eds. 1984a. *Bolivia: La fuerza histórica del campesinado: Movimientos campesinos y etnicidad*. United Nations Research Institute for Social Development and Centro de Estudios de la Realidad Económica y Social. Cochabamba, Bolivia: Artes Gráficas "El Buitre."

———. 1984b. "Movimientos Campesinos y Estado en Bolivia." In Fernando Calderón and Jorge Dandler, eds., *Bolivia: La fuerza histórica del campesinado: Movimientos campesinos y etnicidad*. United Nations Research Institute for Social Development and Centro de Estudios de la Realidad Económica y Social. Cochabamba, Bolivia: Artes Gráficas "El Buitre," pp. 15–50.

Calla Ortega, Ricardo. 1993. "*Hallu hayllisa huti*. Identificación étnica y procesos políticos en Bolivia (1973–1991)." Alberto Adrianzén et al. *Democracia, etnicidad y violencia política en los países andinos*. Lima: IEP ediciones and Instituto Francés de Estudios Andinos, pp. 56–81.

———. 1989. "Apuntes para una lectura crítica de los documentos del I Congreso Extraordinaria de la CSUTCB." In Ricardo Calla, José Enrique Pinelo, and Miguel Urioste, *CSUTCB: Debate sobre documentos y asamblea de nacionalidades*. La Paz: CEDLA (Centro Laboral de Estudios para el Desarrollo Laboral y Agrario).

Cameron, Maxwell A. and Philip Mauceri. 1997. "Conclusion: Threads in the Peruivan Labyrinth." In Maxwell A. Cameron and Philip Mauceri, eds., *The Peruvian Labyrinth: Politics, Society, Economy*. University Park.: Pennsylvania State University Press, pp. 223–43.

Canel, Eduardo. 1992. "Democratization and the Decline of Urban Social Movements in Uruguay: A Political-Institutional Account." In Arturo Escobar and Sonia Alvarez, eds., *The Making of Social Movements in Latin America*. Boulder, CO: Westview Press, pp. 276–90.

Bibliography

Cárdenas, Víctor Hugo. 1997. "Los pueblos indígenas y la democracia en Bolivia: algunas reflexiones." Conferencia en la Noche Parlamentaria. La Paz, Hotel Raddison, February 26, 1997, pp. 1–17.

———. 1989. "De Cerca con Víctor Hugo Cárdenas." *De Cerca.* Interview, March 20, 1989. Canal 2 Telesistema Boliviano, La Paz, pp. 382–99.

———. 1985. "La ley agraria fundamental, algunas notas sobre su orígen, protagonistas y fundamentos." *Historia Boliviana: Revista Semanal.* Cochabamba, Bolivia. Vols. 1–2: 19–27.

Carens, Joseph H. 2000. *Culture, Citizenship, and Community: A Contextual Exploration of Justice as Evenhandedness.* New York: Oxford University Press.

Carrasco M., Hernán. 1994. "Población Indígena, Población Mestiza y Democratización de los Poderes Locales en Chimborazo." In Centro Latinoamericano de Demografía (CELADE), Confederación Indígena del Oriente Boliviano (CIDOB), Fondo de Población de las Naciones Unidas (FNUAP), Instituto de Cooperación Iberoamericano (ICI), eds., *Estudios sociodemográficos de pueblos indígenas.* Santiago de Chile: Centro Latinoamericano de Demografía (CELADE), pp. 479–504.

———. 1993. "Democratización de los Poderes Locales y Levantamiento Indígena." In Jose Almeida et al., eds., *Sismo étnico en el Ecuador: varias perspectivas.* Quito: Ediciones Abya-Yala and CEDIME.

Castañeda, Jorge G. 1993. *Utopia Unarmed: The Latin American Left after the Cold War.* New York: Knopf.

Castro Mantilla, María Dolores. 1996. "El Trabajo del ILV en Bolivia, 1954–1980 (Informe Final)." Subsecretaría de Asuntos Etnicos. Secretaría Nacional de Asuntos Etnicos de Género y Generacionales. Ministerio de Desarrollo Humano. La Paz (July).

Chalmers, Douglas, et al. 1997. *The New Politics of Inequality in Latin America.* New York: Oxford University Press.

Chase Smith, Richard. 1984. "A Search for Unity within Diversity: Peasant Unions, Ethnic Federations, and Indianist Movements in the Andean Republics." *Cultural Survival Quarterly* no. 4 (Dec.): 6–13.

Chesterman, John and Brian Galligan. 1997. *Citizens without Rights: Aborigenes and Australian Citizenship.* New York: Cambridge University Press.

Chiodi, Francesco, Luca Citarella, Massimo Amadio, and Madeleine Zuñiga. 1990. *La Educación Indígena en América Latina: México, Guatemala, Ecuador, Perú, Bolivia.* Vols. I and II, Francesco Chiodi, ed. Copublished in Quito: PEBI (MEC-GTZ), Abya–Yala, and in Santiago: UNESCO/OREALC.

Chirif, Alberto and Oscar Castillo. 1994. "Análisis Estratégico CIDOB: Documento Final." Santa Cruz, Trinidad, and Iquitos, Bolivia.

Chojnacki, Ruth J. 1995. "Indigenous Apostles: Notes on Maya Catechists Working the Word and Working the Land in Highland Chiapas." Paper presented at the 1995 Annual Meeting of the Latin American Studies Association, Washington, DC, Sept. 28–30.

CIDDEBENI. 1998. *Pueblos indígenas y movimiento regional en el Beni.* Trinidad, El Beni, Bolivia: CIDDEBENI, Publicación no. 9, Nov. 1988.

————. 1990. "Conclusiones de seminario – taller: Los derechos indígenas." Beni, Bolivia: CIDDEBENI, Publicación no. 17, Feb. 1990.

CIDOB. 1996. "La Marcha indígena y el papel de CIDOB: Un Balance necesario." *Artículo Primero: Revista de Debate Social y Jurídico* Año 1, no. 2 (Oct.–Dec.). Santa Cruz, Bolivia.

————. 1982. "Primer encuentro de poblaciones indígenas del oriente boliviano ixoxeño y ava guaraní, chiquitano, mataca, guarayo y ayoréode," Santa Cruz, Bolivia. Oct. 1–3.

CIPCA. 1997. "Reflexión acerca de la situación actual de la Asamblea del Pueblo Guaraní (visión de CIPCA). Handout.

Clarke, Paul Barry. 1994. "Citizen Human." In Paul Barry Clarke, ed., *Citizenship*. London: Pluto Press, pp. 3–33.

Clavero, Bartolomé. 1994. *Derecho indígena y cultura constitucional en América*. Mexico: Siglo Veintiuno.

Cohen, Jean L. 1985. "Strategy or Identity: New Theoretical Paradigms and Contemporary Social Movements." *Social Research* 52, no. 4 (Winter): 663–716.

Cojti, Demetrio. 1996. "The Politics of Maya Revindication." In E. Fischer and R. Mckenna Brown, eds., *Maya Cultural Activism in Guatemala*. Austin: University of Texas Press, pp. 19–50.

Collier, David. 1995. "Trajectory of a Concept: 'Corporatism' in the Study of Latin American Politics." In Peter H. Smith, ed., *Latin America in Comparative Perspective: New Approaches to Methods and Analysis*. Boulder, CO: Westview Press.

Collier, David and Ruth Berins Collier. 1991. *Shaping the Political Arena: Critical Junctures, the Labor Movement, and Regime Dynamics*. Princeton: Princeton University Press.

Collier, George A. and Elizabeth Lowery Quaratiello. 1994. *Basta! Land and the Zapatista Rebellion in Chiapas*. Oakland: The Institute for Food and Development Policy.

Colyer, Dale. 1990. "Agriculture and the Public Sector." In Morris D. Whitaker and Dale Colyer, eds., *Agriculture and Economic Survival: The Role of Agriculture in Ecuador's Development*. Boulder, CO: Westview Press, pp. 267–99.

COMG. 1995. *Construyendo un futuro para nuestro pasado: Derechos del Pueblo maya y el proceso de paz*. Guatemala City: Editorial Cholsamaj.

Comisión de Emergencia Asháninka. 1995. *Voz Indígena Ashaninka: Edición Especial de la Comisión de Emergencia Asháninka*. Lima.

Conaghan, Catherine M. and James M. Malloy. 1994. *Unsettling Statecraft: Democracy and Neoliberalism in the Central Andes*. Pittsburgh: University of Pittsburgh Press.

CONAP. 1997. "Declaración de la Confederación de Nacionalidades Amazónicas del Perú ante la Conmemoración de su X Aniversario de la Constitución 16 de marzo, 1987–1997: Nacionalidades indígenas amazónicas un pasado viviente: nuevos desafíos hacia el siglo XXI." Lima.

————. 1995. "Reivindicaciones fundamentales del proyecto político de la Confederación de Nacionalidades Amazónicas del Perú: Por la Reafirmación histórico de la defensa de nuestro territorio, por la vida y el desarollo indígena amazónico." Lima.

Bibliography

——— . n.d. "Declaración de la Principios de la Confederación de Nacionalidades Amazónicas del Perú-CONAP." Lima.

Confederación de Organizaciones Indígenas del Ecuador (CONAIE). 1989. *Las Nacionalidades indígenas en el Ecuador: Nuestro proceso organizativo*. Quito: Ediciones Tinkui.

——— . n.d. *Proyecto político de la CONAIE*. Quito: CONAIE.

Contreras, Carlos et al. 1989. *Comunidades campesinas y nativas: Normatividad y desarrollo*. Lima: Fundación Friedrich Naumann.

Contreras, Jesus, ed. 1988. *Identidad étnica y movimientos indios: La Cara india, la cruz del 92*. Madrid: Editorial Revolución, S.A.L.

Cooke, Jacob E., ed. 1961. *The Federalist*. Middletown, CT: Wesleyan University Press.

Corkhill, David and David Cubitt. 1988. *Ecuador: Fragile Democracy*. London: Latin America Bureau.

Cotler, Julio. 1975. "The New Mode of Political Domination in Peru." In Abraham F. Lowenthal, ed., *The Peruvian Experiment: Continuity and Change under Military Rule*. Princeton: Princeton University Press, pp. 44–78.

——— . 1970. "Traditional Haciendas and Communities in a Context of Political Mobilization in Peru." In Rodolfo Stavenhagen, ed., *Agrarian Problems and Peasant Movements in Latin America*. Garden City, NY: Anchor Books, Doubleday and Company Inc., pp. 533–58.

Cotler, Julio and Felipe Portocarrero. 1969. "Peru: Peasant Organizations." In Henry A. Landsberger, ed., *Latin American Peasant Movements*. Ithaca, NY: Cornell University Press.

CPIB (Central de Pueblos Indígenas del Beni). 1997. "Central de Pueblos Indígenas del Beni: Evaluación Política." Transcript of June 1997 Meeting in Trinidad, Beni, Bolivia.

CPIB. n.d. Manuscript. "Movimientos y territorios indígenas en el Beni: Resúmen histórico, 1987–1995."

CPIB and CMIB (Central de Mujeres Indígenas del Beni). Feb. 1996. "Resolución de la V Reunión Cabildo Consultivo."

CPIB and CIDDEBENI (Centro de Investigación y Documentación para el Desarrollo del Beni). 1995. *Hacia una propuesta indígena de decentralización del Estado*. La Paz: PROADE and ILDIS.

CPIB, CIDDEBENI, and PROADE. 1994. Manuscript. "Hacia una propuesta indígena de decentralización del Estado." Trinidad, Bolivia.

CPTI (Centro de Planificación Territorial Indígena de la CIDOB). 1996. "Los territorios indígenas en Bolivia: Una aproximación a su situación actual." *Artículo Primero: Revista de Debate Social y Jurídico* Año 1, no. 2 (Oct.–Dec.). Santa Cruz, Bolivia.

Cruz Alanguía, Bonifacio. 1993. "Perú: Informe de los indígenas." *Anuario Indigenista* xxxii (Dec.). Mexico: Instituto Indigenista Interamericano, pp. 543–6.

CSUTCB. 1996. *VII congreso CSUTCB, Santa Cruz, 29 de marzo al 3 de abril de 1996: Documentos y resoluciones*. La Paz: CEDOIN.

——— . 1994. *VI congreso CSUTCB, Cochabamba, del 27 de enero al 2 de febrero de 1994: Documentos y resoluciones*. La Paz: CEDOIN.

317

Cuadros, Diego, ed. 1991. *La Revuelta de las nacionalidades*. La Paz: Unión Nacional de Instituciones para el Trabajo de Acción Social.

Cusicanqui, Silvia Rivera. 1984. *Oprimidos pero no vencidos: Luchas del campesinado aymara y qhechwa de Bolivia, 1900–1980*. La Paz: HISBOL-CSUTCB.

Dalder, Hans. 1973. "The Consociational Democracy Theme." *World Politics* 26 (Oct.): 604–21.

Dandler, Jorge. With collaboration by Antonio González Urday et al. 1998. *Pueblos Indígenas de la Amazonía Peruana y Desarrollo Sostenible*. Documento de Trabajo 68. Lima: Oficina Internacional del Trabajo (ILO) (Oficina de Area y Equipo Técnico Multidisciplinario para los Países del Area Andina).

Dandler, Jorge E. 1996. "Indigenous Peoples and the Rule of Law in Latin America: Do They Have a Chance?" Paper prepared for the academic workshop on the Rule of Law and the Underprivileged in Latin America, Helen Kellogg Institute for International Studies, University of Notre Dame, November 9–11, 1996.

—————. 1984. "La 'Ch'ampa Guerra de Cochabamba: Un proceso de digregación política." In Fernando Calderón and Jorge Dandler, eds., *Bolivia: La Fuerza histórica del campesinado: Movimientos campesinos y etnicidad*. United Nations Research Institute for Social Development and Centro de Estudios de la Realidad Económica y Social. Cochabamba, Bolivia: Artes Gráficas "El Buitre."

Davenport, Christian. n.d. Manuscript. "Human Rights and the Promise of Democratic Pacification." University of Maryland.

Davenport, Christian and David Armstrong. 2002. Manuscript. "Democracy and the Violation of Human Rights: A Statistical Analysis of the Third Wave." University of Maryland.

Davis, Shelton. 2002. "Indigenous Peoples, Poverty and Participatory Development: The Experiences of the World Bank in Latin America." In Rachel Sieder, ed., *Multiculturalism in Latin America: Indigenous Rights, Diversity and Democracy*. New York: Palgrave Macmillan.

Davis, Shelton and William Partridge. 1994. "Promoting the Development of Indigenous People in Latin America." *Finance and Development* 31, no. 1 (Mar.): 38–40.

Davis, Shelton H. and Harry Anthony Patrinos. 1996. "Investing in Latin America's Indigenous Peoples: The Human and Social Capital Dimensions." Written for the Nordic Council of Ministers "Seminar on Indigenous Peoples Production and Trade." Copenhagen, Jan. 15–17.

de Janvry, Alain, et al. 1994. "Ecuador." In Alain de Janvry et al., *The Political Feasibility of Adjustment in Ecuador and Venezuela*. Paris: OECD.

de la Cadena, Marisol. 2000. *Indigenous Mestizos: The Politics of Race and Culture in Cuzco, Peru, 1919–1991*. Durham, NC: Duke University Press.

—————. 1998. "From Race to Class: Insurgent Intellectuals *de provincia* in Peru, 1910–1970." In Steve J. Stern, ed., *Shining and Other Paths: War and Society in Peru, 1980–1995*. Durham, NC: Duke University Press.

de la Cruz, Rodrigo. 1993. "Aportes del derecho consuetudinario a la reforma jurídica del Estado." In Alberto Wray et al., *Derecho, pueblos indígenas y reforma del Estado*. Quito: Ediciones Abya-Yala, pp. 71–123.

Bibliography

Degler, Carl N. 1971. *Neither Black nor White: Slavery and Race Relations in Brazil and the United States*. Madison: University of Wisconsin Press.

Degregori, Carlos Iván. 1998. "Harvesting Storms: Peasant *Rondas* and the Defeat of Sendero Luminoso in Ayachucho." In Steve J. Stern, ed., *Shining and Other Paths: War and Society in Peru, 1980–1995*. Durham, NC: Duke University Press.

———. 1997. "After the Fall of Abimael Guzmán: The Limits of Sendero Luminoso." In Maxwell A. Cameron and Philip Mauceri, eds., *The Peruvian Labyrinth: Politics, Society, Economy*. University Park: Pennsylvania State University Press, pp. 179–91.

———. 1995. "El estudio del otro: cambios en los análisis sobre etnicidad en el Perú." In Julio Cotler, ed., *Perú 1964–1994: Economía, Sociedad, y Política*. Lima: Instituto de Estudios Peruanos, pp. 303–32.

———. 1993. "Identidad étnica. Movimientos sociales y participación política en el Perú." In Alberto Adrianzén et al., *Democracia, etnicidad y violencia política en los países andinos*. Lima: Instituto de Estudios Peruanos and Instituto Francés de Estudios Andinos, pp. 113–33.

Del Pino, Ponciano. 1998. "Family, Culture, and 'Revolution': Everyday Life with Sendero Luminoso." In Steve J. Stern, ed., *Shining and Other Paths: War and Society in Peru, 1980–1995*. Durham, NC: Duke University Press.

Deutsch, Karl Wolfgang. 1953. *Nationalism and Social Communication: An Inquiry into the Foundations of Nationality*. Published jointly by the Technology Press of the Massachusetts Institute of Technology, Cambridge, MA and Wiley, New York.

Diamond, Larry. 1993. "Civil Society and the Construction of Democracy." Remarks delivered at Harvard University (Dec. 7).

———. 1987. "Ethnicity and Ethnic Conflict." *The Journal of Modern African Studies* 25, no. 1: 117–28.

Díaz-Polanco, Héctor. 1997. *La rebelión zapatista y la autonomía*. Mexico: Siglo Veintiuno Editores.

DRP. 1996. "Diagnóstico Rural Participativo en la Provincia de Pastaza/Región Amazónica Ecuatoriana." Puyo, Pastaza, Ecuador (Dec.).

Drysdale, Robert S. and Robert G. Meyers. "Continuity and Change; Peruvian Education." In Abraham F. Lowenthal, ed., *The Peruvian Experiment: Continuity and Change under Military Rule*. Princeton: Princeton University Press, pp. 254–301.

Dunkerley, James. 1984. *Rebellion in the Veins: Political Struggle in Bolivia, 1952–1982*. London: Verso.

Eckstein, Susan. 2001. "Where Have All the Movements Gone: Latin American Social Movements at the Millenium." In Susan Eckstein, ed., *Power and Popular Protest: Latin American Social Movements*. Updated and expanded version. Berkeley: University of California Press, pp. 351–406.

———. 1989. *Power and Popular Protest: Latin American Social Movements*. Berkeley: University of California.

———. 1983. "Transformation of a 'Revolution from Below' – Bolivia and International Capital." *Comparative Studies in Society and History* 25, no. 1 (Jan.): 105–35.

Edwards, Sebastian. 1995. *Crisis and Reform in Latin America: From Despair to Hope.* Oxford: Oxford University Press.

Eisinger, Peter K. 1973. "The Conditions of Protest Behavior in American Cities." *American Political Science Review* 67, no. 1 (Mar.): 11–28.

Escobal, J. J. Saavedra and M. Torero (Grupo de Análisis para al Desarrollo. GRADE). 1998. "Los Activos de los Pobres en el Perú." *Diálogo sobre experiencias y retos de la lucha contra la pobreza: Análisis y plenarias.* Tomo I, Primer Foro. Ica: Perú. Published by the Comité Organizador del Foro, Oct. 27–28.

Escobar, Arturo and Sonia Alvarez, eds. 1992. *The Making of Social Movements in Latin America.* Boulder, CO: Westview Press.

Esman, Milton J. and Itamar Rabinovitch. 1988. *Ethnicity, Pluralism, and the State in the Middle East.* Ithaca, NY and London: Cornell University Press.

Espinosa, Simón. 1992. "El papel de la iglesia católica en el movimiento indígena." In Almeida, Ileana et al., *Indios: Una reflexion sobre el levantamiento indígena de 1990.* 2nd ed. Quito: ILDIS, Ediciones Abya-Yala, pp. 179–220.

Evans, Sara M. and Harry C. Boyte. 1986. *Free Spaces: The Sources of Democratic Change in America.* New York: Harper and Row Publishers.

Favre, Henri. 1988. "Capitalismo y etnicidad: La Política indigenista de Perú." *Indianidad, etnocidio, indigenismo en América Latina.* Mexico: Instituto Indigenista.

Fearon, James D. "Commitment Problems and the Spread of Ethnic Conflict." In David A. Lake and Donald Rothchild, eds., *International Spread of Ethnic Conflict.* Princeton: Princeton University Press, pp. 107–26.

Fearon, James D. and David D. Laitin. 2000. "Violence and the Social Construction of Ethnic Identity." *International Organization* 45, no. 4 (Autumn).

———. 1996. "Explaining Interethnic Cooperation." *American Political Science Review* 90, no. 4 (Dec.): 715–21.

Federación Indígena y Campesina de Imbabura (FICI). 1994. "Imbabura Runacunapac Jatun Tantanacuipac Camachic Ley Orgánica de la Federación Indígena y Campesina de Imbabura." Document dated May 15, 1994.

Figueroa, Adolfo. 1995. "Peru: Social Policies and Economic Adjustment in the 1980s." In Nora Lustig, ed., *Coping with Austerity: Poverty and Inequality in Latin America.* Washington DC: The Brookings Institution, pp. 375–99.

Flores C., Gonzalo. 1984. "Estado, políticas agrarias y luchas campesinas: Revisión de una década en Bolivia." In Fernando Calderón and Jorge Dandler, eds., *Bolivia: La Fuerza histórica del campesinado: Movimientos campesinos y etnicidad.* United Nations Research Institute for Social Development and Centro de Estudios de la Realidad Económica y Social. Cochabamba, Bolivia: Artes Gráficas "El Buitre," pp. 445–545.

Floyd, Charlene. 1995. "Catalysts of Democracy: Maya Catechists as Political Actors in Chiapas." Paper presented at the 1995 Annual Meeting of the Latin American Studies Association, Washington, DC, Sept. 28–30.

FOIN. n.d. Manuscript. "FOIN: La lucha de los Napo Runas."

Fondo Indígena. n.d. *Bolivia.* Diagnóstico.

Fontaine, Pierre Michel. 1985. *Race, Class, and Power in Brazil.* Los Angeles: Center for Afro-American Studies, University of California.

Bibliography

Forero, Juan. "From Llama Trails to the Corridors of Power." *The New York Times.* July 6, 2002, A4.

Foster, Robert J. 1991. "Making National Cultures in the Global Ecumene." *Annual Review of Anthropology* 20: 235–60.

Foucault, Michel. 1980. *Power/Knowledge.* New York: Pantheon Books.

Foweraker, Joe. 1995. *Theorizing Social Movements.* London: Pluto Press.

Foweraker, Joe and Todd Landman. 1997. *Citizenship Rights and Social Movements: A Comparative and Statistical Analysis.* Oxford: Oxford University Press.

Fox, Jonathan. 1994a. "The Difficult Transition from Clientelism to Citizenship: Lessons from Mexico." *World Politics* 46, no. 2 (Jan.): 151–84.

_____. 1994b. "Latin America's Emerging Local Politics." *Journal of Democracy* 5, no. 2 (Apr.): 105–16.

_____. 1994c. "The Roots of Chiapas." *The Boston Review* 19, no. 2 (Apr./May): 24–7.

Fox, Jonathan, ed. 1990. "The Challenge of Rural Democratisation: Perspectives from Latin America and the Philippines." *Journal of Development Studies* (special issue) 26 (July).

Gamarra, Eduardo A. 1995. "Democracia, reformas económicas y gobernabilidad en Bolivia." Santiago de Chile: Comisión Económica para América Latina y el Caribe, Naciones Unidas, Serie Reformas de Política Pública 36.

_____. 1994. "Crafting Political Support for Stabilization: Political Pacts and the New Economic Policy in Bolivia." In William C. Smith, Carlos H. Acuña, and Eduardo A. Gamarra, eds., *Democracy, Markets, and Structural Reform in Latin America.* New Brunswick, NJ: Transaction Publishers, pp. 105–27.

Gavilanes del Castillo, Luís Ma. 1995. *El FEPP: Llamada, Pulso, y Desafío: El Caminar de XXV años del "Fondo Populorum Progressio" desde la inspiración cristiano de su fundador Monseñor Cándido Rada.* Quito: Fondo Ecuatoriano Populorum Progressio.

Geertz, Clifford. 1963. "The Integrative Revolution: Primordial Sentiments and Civil Politics in the New States." In *Old Societies and New States: The Quest for Modernity in Asia and Africa.* New York: Free Press of Glencoe.

Gellner, Ernest. 1983. *Nations and Nationalism.* Oxford: Blackwell.

Gibson, Edward L. 1997. "The Populist Road to Market Reform: Policy and Electoral Coalitions in Mexico and Argentina." *World Politics* 49, no. 3 (Apr.): 339–70.

Gill, Lesley. 1985. "La Reforma agraria y el desarrollo del capitalismo en Santa Cruz, Bolivia (1952–1980)." *Historia Boliviana: Revista Semanal.* Cochabamba, Bolivia. Vols. 1–2: 67–85.

Godoy, Ricardo. 1990. *Mining and Agriculture in Highland Bolivia: Ecology, History, and Commerce among the Jukumanis.* Tucson: The University of Arizona Press.

Golte, Jurgen. 1995. "Nuevos actores y culturas antiguas." In Julio Cotler, ed., *Perú 1964–1994: Economía, Sociedad, y Política.* Lima: Instituto de Estudios Peruanos, pp. 135–48.

Gonzales, Tirso A. 1996. "Arriando las banderas de la soberanía. Campesinado, semillas nativas, derechos de propiedad y ONGs en Latinoamérica: El Caso del

Perú, 1940–1993." In Stefano Varese, ed., *Pueblos indios, soberanía y globalismo*. Quito: Ediciones Abya-Yala, pp. 295–359.

Gonzales de Olarte, Efraín. 1997. *The Distribution of Welfare in Peru in 1985–1986*. Lima: Instituto de Estudios Peruanos.

————. 1996. *El Ajuste estructural y los campesinos*. Lima: Instituto de Estudios Peruanos; Ayuda en Acción–Perú; Action Aid–UK.

————. 1995. "Transformación sin desarrollo: Perú 1964–1994." In Julio Cotler, ed., *Perú 1964–1994: Economía, Sociedad, y Política*. Lima: Instituto de Estudios Peruanos, pp. 42–68.

————. 1994. *En las fronteras del mercado: Economía política del campesinado en el Perú*. Lima: Instituto de Estudios Peruanos.

————. 1993. "Economic Stabilization and Structural Adjustment Under Fujimori." *Journal of Interamerican Studies and World Affairs* 35, no. 2 (Summer): 51–80.

Gootenberg, Paul. 1991. "Population and Ethnicity in Early Republican Peru: Some Revisions." *Latin American Research Review*, pp. 109–55.

Graham, Carol. 1992. "The Politics of Protecting the Poor During Adjustment: Bolivia's Emergency Social Fund." *World Development* 20, no. 9: 1233–51.

Graham, Richard, ed. 1990. *The Idea of Race in Latin America, 1870–1940*. Austin: University of Texas Press.

Granovetter, Mark. 1995. *Getting a Job: A Study of Contacts and Careers*. 2nd ed. Chicago: University of Chicago Press.

————. 1985. "Economic Action and Social Structure: The Problem of Embeddedness." *American Journal of Sociology* 91, no. 3 (Nov.): 481–510. Reprinted in Mark Granovetter. 1995. *Getting a Job: A Study of Contacts and Careers*. 2nd ed. Chicago: University of Chicago Press, pp. 211–40.

Gray, Andrew. 1997. *Indigenous Rights and Development: Self-Determination in an Amazonian Community*. Providence, RI: Bergahn Books.

Grindle, Merilee L. 1986. *State and Countryside: Development Policy and Agrarian Politics in Latin America*. Baltimore: The Johns Hopkins University Press.

Groch, Sharon. 2001. "Free Spaces: Creating Oppositional Consciousness in the Disability Right's Movement." In Jane Mansbridge and Aldon Morris, eds., *Oppositional Consciousness: The Subjective Roots of Social Protest*. Chicago: University of Chicago Press, pp. 65–98.

Grupo de Trabajo "Racimos de Ungurahui." 1995. *Territorios indígenas y la nueva legislación agraria en el Perú*. Lima: Grupo Internacional de Trabajo Sobre Asuntos Indígenas and "Racimos de Ungurahui."

Grupo-ip-Latina/CEDETI. 1995. *Asesoramiento en fortalecimiento organizativo-institucional de la CIDOB: Informe Final Version II*. Santa Cruz: CIDOB y Agencias.

Grupo Técnico de Planificación TIM. 1993. *Qué es nuestro Territorio?* Trinidad, Beni, Bolivia: CIDDEBENI.

Guatemala. 1997. *Acuerdos de Paz*. Signed December 29, 1996. Guatemala: Universidad Rafael Landívar and Misión de Verificación de las Naciones Unidas.

Bibliography

———. 1995. *Acuerdo sobre identidad y derechos de los pueblos indígenas*. Signed March 31, 1995. Guatemala: Editorial Cholsamaj.

Guerrero, Andrés. 1995. "Équateur: discourse et représentation politique des indigènes" Problèmes d'Amérique Latine no. 19 (Oct.–Dec.): 51–74.

———. 1993. "De sujetos indios a ciudadanos-étnicos: De la manifestación de 1961 al levantamiento de 1990." In Alberto Adrianzén et al., eds., *Democracia, etnicidad y violencia política en los países andinos*. Lima: Instituto de Estudios Peruanos (IEP) and Instituto Francés de Estudios Andinos, pp. 83–101.

Guidry, John A., Michael D. Kennedy, and Mayer N. Zald, eds., 2000. *Globalizations and Social Movements: Culture, Power, and the Transnational Public Sphere*. Ann Arbor: University of Michigan Press.

Gurr, Ted Robert. 2000. *Peoples Versus States: Minorities at Risk in the New Century*. Washington, DC: United States Institute of Peace Press.

Gurr, Ted Robert with Barbara Harff, Monty G. Marshall, and James R. Scarritt. 1993. *Minorities at Risk: A Global View of Ethnopolitical Conflicts*. Washington, DC: United States Institute of Peace Press.

Gutmann, Amy, ed. 1994. *Multiculturalism: Examining the Politics of Recognition*. Princeton: Princeton University Press.

Hagopian, Frances. 1996a. *Traditional Politics and Regime Change in Brazil*. New York: Cambridge University Press.

———. 1996b. "Traditional Power Structures and Democratic Governance in Latin America." In Jorge I. Domínguez and Abraham F. Lowenthal, eds., *Constructing Democratic Governance: Latin America and the Caribbean in the 1990s – Themes and Issues*. Baltimore: Johns Hopkins University Press, 64–86.

Hale, Charles R. 1994. *Resistance and Contradiction: Miskitu Indians and the Nicaraguan State, 1894–1987*. Stanford: Stanford University Press.

Hanchard, Michael. 1994. *Orpheus and Power: The Movimento Negro of Rio de Janeiro and Sao Paulo, 1945–1988*. Princeton: Princeton University Press.

Handelman, Howard. 1975. *Struggle in the Andes: Peasant Political Mobilization in Peru*. Austin: University of Texas Press.

Hannum, Hurst. 1993. "Rethinking Self-Determination." *Virginia Journal of International Law* 34, no. 1 (Fall): 1–70.

Hardin, Russell. 1995. *One for All: The Logic of Group Conflict*. Princeton: Princeton University Press.

Harding, Colin. 1975. "Land Reform and Social Conflict in Peru." In Abraham F. Lowenthal, ed., *The Peruvian Experiment: Continuity and Change under Military Rule*. Princeton: Princeton University Press, pp. 220–53.

Harty, Siobhan. 2001. "The Institutional Foundations of Substate National Movements." *Comparative Politics* 33, no. 2 (Jan.): 191–210.

Harvey, Neil. 1998. *The Chiapas Rebellion: The Struggle for Land and Democracy*. Durham, NC: Duke University Press.

———. 1996. "Impact of Reforms to Article 27 on Chiapas: Peasant Resistance in the Neoliberal Sphere." In Laura Randall, ed., *Reforming Mexico's Agrarian Reform*. Armonk, NY: M. E. Sharpe.

Harvey, Neil, Luis Navarro Hernández, and Jeffrey Rubin. 1994. *Transformation of Rural Mexico*, no. 5. La Jolla, CA: Center for U.S.-Mexican Studies.

Healy, Kevin. 2001. *Llamas, Weavings, and Organic Chocolate: Multicultural Grassroots Development in the Andes and Amazon of Bolivia*. South Bend, IN: University of Notre Dame Press.

————. 1997. "The Coca-Cocaine Issue in Bolivia: A Political Resource for All Seasons." In Madeline Barbara Léons and Harry Sanabria, eds., *Coca, Cocaine, and the Bolivian Reality*. Albany: State University of New York Press, pp. 227–41.

————. 1996. "Ethnodevelopment of Indigenous Bolivian Communities: Emerging Paradigms." In Alan L. Kolata, ed., *Tiwanaku and its Hinterland: Archaeology and Paleoecology of an Andean Civilization*. Washington and London: Smithsonian Institution Press, pp. 241–313.

————. 1992. "Allies and Opposition Groups to the 1990 Political Mobilizations in Ecuador and Bolivia." Presented at the XVII International Congress of the Latin American Studies Association, Sept. 24–27, Los Angeles.

————. 1991. "Political Ascent of Bolivia's Peasant Coca Leaf Producers." *Journal of Interamerican Studies and World Affairs* 33, no. 1 (Spring): 87–122.

————. 1989. "The Political Activism of the Bolivian Sindicatos in the New Democratic Order of the 1980s." Columbia and NYU Latin American, Caribbean and Iberian Occasional Papers, no. 6.

Heater, Derek. 1999. *What Is Citizenship?* Cambridge: Polity Press.

Heath, Dwight B. 1955. "Land Reform in Bolivia." *Inter-American Economic Affairs* 12, no. 4: 3–27.

Held, David, ed. 1993. *Prospects for Democracy: North, South, East, West*. Stanford: Stanford University Press.

Hellman, Judith. 1992. "The Study of New Social Movements in Latin America and the Question of Autonomy." In Arturo Escobar and Sonia Alvarez, eds., *The Making of Social Movements in Latin America*. Boulder, CO: Westview Press, pp. 51–61.

Hendricks, Janet W. 1996. "Poder y conocimiento: Discurso y transformación ideológica entre los Shuar." In Fernando Santos Granero, ed., *Globalización y cambio en la amazonía indígena*. Vol. 1. Quito: Ediciones Abya-Yala, pp. 131–82.

Hentschel, Jesco. 1998. "Perú: Pobreza y desarrollo social, 1994–1997." *Diálogo sobre experiencias y retos de la lucha contra la pobreza: Análisis y plenarias*. Tomo I. Primero Foro. Ica, Peru, published by the Comité Organizador del Foro, Oct. 27–28.

Herbst, Jeffrey. 2000. *States and Power in Africa: Comparative Lessons in Authority and Control*. Princeton: Princeton University Press.

Hinajosa, Iván. 1998. "On Poor Relations and the Nouveau Riche: Shining Path and the Radical Peruvian Left." In Steve J. Stern, ed., *Shining and Other Paths: War and Society in Peru, 1980–1995*. Durham, NC: Duke University Press.

Hobsbawm, E. J. 1990. *Nations and Nationalism since 1780: Programme, Myth Reality*. Cambridge and New York: Cambridge University Press.

Bibliography

Hobsbawm, Eric and Terence Ranger, eds. 1983. *The Invention of Tradition.* Cambridge and New York: Cambridge University Press.

Honig, Bonnie. 2001. *Democracy and the Foreigner.* Princeton: Princeton University Press.

Horowitz, Donald L. 1993. "Democracy in Divided Societies: The Challenge of Ethnic Conflict." *Journal of Democracy* 4, no. 4 (Oct.): 18–38.

———. 1985. *Ethnic Groups in Conflict.* Berkeley, Los Angeles, and London: University of California Press.

Huber, Evelyne and Frank Safford, eds. 1995. *Agrarian Structure and Political Power: Landlord and Peasant in the Making of Latin America.* Pittsburgh: University of Pittsburgh Press.

Hunefeldt, Christine. 1997. "The Rural Landscape and Changing Political Awareness: Enterprises, Agrarian Producers, and Peasant Communities, 1969–1994." In Maxwell A. Cameron and Philip Mauceri, eds., *The Peruvian Labyrinth: Polity, Society, Economy.* University Park: Pennsylvania State University Press, pp. 197–33.

Huntington, Samuel P. 1986. "The Change to Change." In Roy C. Macridis and Bernard E. Brown, eds., *Comparative Politics: Notes and Readings.* Chicago: Dorsey Press.

———. 1968. *Political Order in Changing Societies.* New Haven: Yale University Press.

Huntington, Samuel P. and Jorge I. Domínguez. 1975. "Political Development." In Fred I. Greenstein and Nelson W. Polsby, eds., *Handbook of Political Science 3*, pp. 1–114.

Hurtado Mercado, Javier. 1995. "Comportamientos políticos del campesinado 1978/1995." *Opiniones y análisis* (May) La Paz, pp. 127–54.

———. 1986. *El Katarismo.* La Paz: Instituto de historia social boliviana, Hisbol.

Hurtado, Osvaldo. 1980. *Political Power in Ecuador.* Nick D. Mills, Jr., trans., Albuquerque: University of New Mexico Press.

Ibarra, Alicia. 1992. *Los indígenas y el estado en el Ecuador.* Quito: Ediciones Abya-Yala.

INEI/UNFPA. 1994. *Perú: Mapa de necesidades básicas insatisfechas de los hogares a nivel distrital.* Tomo I (a nivel nacional, departamental y provincial). Dirección Técnica de Demografía y Estudios Sociales. Lima.

Instituto Cuánto. 1998. "Encuesta nacional sobre medición de niveles de vida (ENNIV)." Encuesta realizada por Instituto Cuánto con el auspicio del BID, USAID, UNICEF, Telefónica del Perú, Embajada de Holanda, COSUDE, GRADE, y Cementos de Lima. Lima.

Instituto Nacional de Estadística (INE). 1981. *Censo Nacional VIII de Población y III de Vivienda.* Lima.

Instituto Nacional de Estadística e Informática (INEI). 1998. *Perú en mapas: Estructura y dinámicas del espacio agropecuario.* III Censo Nacional Agropecuario 1994. Lima.

———. 1994a. "Perú: Comunidades Indígenas de la Amazonía: 1993." Basado en INEI-Censo Nacional de Población y Vivienda 1993. Lima.

———. 1994b. "Perú: Resultados Definitivos Perfil Socio Demográfico." Lima.

———. 1993. Censo Nacional XIX de Población y IV Vivienda. Lima.

———. 1984. Encuesta Nacional de Hogares Rurales. Lima.

Instituto de Planificación. 1961. Censo Nacional VI de Población y I de Vivienda. Lima.

International Labour Office (ILO). 1953. "Indigenous Peoples: Living and Working Conditions of Aboriginal Populations in Independent Countries." Published in the United Kingdom for the ILO by Staples Press Limited, London.

Isaacs, Harold R. 1975. "Basic Group Identity: The Idols of the Tribe." In Nathan Glazer and Daniel P. Moynihan, eds., *Ethnicity: Theory and Experience*. Cambridge, MA: Harvard University Press.

Iturralde, Diego. 1993. "Usos de la ley y usos de la costumbre: La reinvidicación del derecho indígena a la modernización." In Alberto Wray et al. eds., *Derecho, pueblos indígenas y reforma del Estado*. Quito: Ediciones Abya-Yala, pp. 125–50.

Janoski, Thomas. 1998. *Citizenship and Civil Society: A Framework of Rights and Obligations in Liberal, Traditional, and Social Democratic Regimes*. Cambridge, MA: Cambridge University Press.

Jara, Lily. 1997. "Ecuador Database Compiled for This Book. Includes Analytical Statement; Demography on Indigenous People; Land Distribution; Access to Credit; Education Health; and Poverty." Quito: Ecuador.

Jelin, Elizabeth. 1996. "Citizenship Revisited: Solidarity, Responsibility, and Rights." In Elizabeth Jelin and Eric Hershberg, eds., *Constructing Democracy: Human Rights, Citizenship, and Society in Latin America*. Boulder, CO: Westview Press, pp. 101–19.

Jelin, Elizabeth and Eric Hershberg, eds., 1996. *Constructing Democracy: Human Rights, Citizenship, and Society in Latin America*. Boulder, CO: Westview Press.

Jenson, Jane and Susan D. Phillips. 1996. "Regime Shift: New Citizenship Practices in Canada." *International Journal of Canadian Studies* 14 (Fall).

Jones, James. 1994. "A Native Movement and March in Eastern Bolivia: Rationale and Response." *Development Anthropology Network: Bulletin of the Institute for Development Anthropology* 8, no. 2 (Fall 1990): 1–8.

Jorgensen, Steen, Margaret Grosh, and Mark Schacter. 1992. *Bolivia's Answer to Poverty, Economic Crisis, and Adjustment: The Emergency Social Fund*. Washington, DC: The World Bank.

Joseph, Gilbert M. and Daniel Nugent, eds. 1994. *Everyday Forms of State Formation: Revolution and the Negotiation of Rule in Modern Mexico*. Durham, NC: Duke University Press.

Kay, Bruce H. 1996. "'Fujipopulism' and the Liberal State in Peru, 1990–1995." *Journal of Interamerican Studies and World Affairs* 38, no. 4: 55–98.

Kay, Cristóbal. 1982. "Achievements and Contradictions of the Peruvian Agrarian Reform." *The Journal of Development Studies* 18, no. 2 (Jan.): 141–70.

Keck, Margaret E. and Kathryn Sikkink. 1998. *Activists Beyond Borders: Advocacy Networks in International Politics*. Ithaca, NY: Cornell University Press.

Bibliography

Kimmerling, Judith. 1996. *El derecho del tambor: Derechos humanos y ambientales en los campos petroleros de la amazonía ecuatoriana.* Quito: Abya-Yala.
————. 1993. *Crudo amazónico.* Quito: Abya-Yala.
Klarén, Peter Flindell. 2000. *Peru: Society and Nationhood in the Andes.* New York: Oxford University Press.
Klein, Herbert S. 1992. *Bolivia: The Evolution of a Multi-Ethnic Society.* New York: Oxford University Press.
Korovkin, Tanya. 1997. "Taming Capitalism: The Evolution of the Indigenous Peasant Economy in Northern Ecuador." *Latin American Research Review* 32, no. 3: 89–110.
————. 1993. "Los Indígenas, Los Campesinos y el Estado: El Crecimiento del Movimiento Comunitario en la Sierra Ecuatoriana." FLACSO (sede Ecuador) Documentos de Trabajo no. 11.
Kymlicka, Will. 1995. *Multicultural Citizenship.* Oxford: Oxford University Press.
Kymlicka, Will, ed., 1995. *The Rights of Minority Cultures.* Oxford: Oxford University Press.
Kymlicka, Will and Wayne Norman. 1995. "Return of the Citizen: A Survey of Recent Work on Citizenship Theory." In Ronald Beiner, ed., *Theorizing Citizenship.* Albany: State University of New York Press, pp. 283–322.
Laclau, Ernesto and Chantal Mouffe. 1985. *Hegemony and Socialist Strategy: Towards a Radical Democratic Politics.* London: Verso.
Lagos, Maria L. 1994. *Autonomy and Power: The Dynamics of Class and Culture in Rural Bolivia.* Philadelphia: University of Pennsylvania Press.
Lagos, Marta. 2003. "Public Opinion." In Jorge I. Domínguez and Michael Shifter, eds., *Constructing Democratic Governance.* 2nd ed. Baltimore: Johns Hopkins University Press.
Laitin, David D. 1998. *Identity in Formation: The Russian Speaking Populations in the Near-Abroad.* Ithaca, NY: Cornell University Press.
————. 1986. *Hegemony and Culture: Politics and Religious Change among the Yoruba.* Chicago: University of Chicago Press.
Langer, Erik D. and Robert H. Jackson. 1988. "Colonial and Republican Missions Compared: The Cases of Alta California and Southeastern Bolivia." *Comparative Study of Society and History:* 286–311.
Lapidoth, Ruth. 1997. *Autonomy: Flexible Solutions to Ethnic Conflict.* Washington, DC: United States Institute of Peace Press.
Lapp, Nancy. 1994. "Expansion of Suffrage and the Timing of Land Reform in Latin America." Paper prepared for the 18th International Congress of the Latin American Studies Association, Atlanta, Mar. 10–12.
Larrea, Carlos. 1992. "The Mirage of Development: Oil, Employment, and Poverty in Ecuador (1972–1990)." Ph.D. Diss., Graduate Program in Social and Political Thought. York University, North York, Ontario.
Larrea, Carlos, et al. 1996. *Geografía de la Pobreza en el Ecuador.* Quito: Secretaría Técnica del Frente Social.
Larson, Brooke. 1998. *Cochabamba, 1550–1900: Colonialism and Agrarian Transformation in Bolivia.* Expanded ed. Durham, NC: Duke University Press.

Laurie, Nina, Robert Andolina, and Sarah Radcliffe. 2002. "The Excluded 'Indigenous'? The Implications of Multi-Ethnic Policies for Water Reform in Bolivia." In Rachel Sieder, ed., *Multiculturalism in Latin America: Indigenous Rights, Diversity and Democracy*. New York: Palgrave Macmillan.

Lavaud, Jean Pierre. 1984. "Los campesinos frente al estado." In Fernando Calderón and Jorge Dandler, eds., *Bolivia: La fuerza histórica del campesinado: Movimientos campesinos y etnicidad*. United Nations Research Institute for Social Development and Centro de Estudios de la Realidad Económica y Social. Cochabamba, Bolivia: Artes Gráficas "El Buitre," pp. 273–308.

Le Bot, Yvon. 1988. "Extranjeros en nuestro propio pais el movimiento indígena en Bolivia durante los años 70." In *Indianidad, etnocidio, indigenismo en América Latina*. Instituto Indigenista Interamericano and Centre d'Etudes Mexicaines et Centroamericaines.

Lehm Ardaya, Zulema. 1996. "Territorios indígenas en el departamento del Beni: Un balance general 1987–1996." *Artículo Primero: Revista de Debate Social y Jurídico* Año 1, no. 2 (Oct.–Dec.). Santa Cruz de la Sierra, Bolivia.

————. 1994. "Mitos y realidades de los territorios indígenas." *Nayonne (Huella de Todos): Boletín de información y análisis regional* Año 4, no. 15 (Mar.–Apr.) (published in Trinidad: CIDDEBENI): pp. 21–3.

Léons, Madeline Barbara and Harry Sanabria. 1997. "Coca and Cocaine in Bolivia: Reality and Policy Illusion." In Madeline Barbara Léons and Harry Sanabria, eds., *Coca, Cocaine, and the Bolivian Reality*. Albany: State University of New York Press.

León Trujillo, Jorge. 1994. *De campesinos a ciudadanos diferentes: El levantamiento indígena*. Quito: CEDIME.

Libermann, Kitula and Armando Godínez, eds. 1992. *Territorio y dignidad: Pueblos indígenas y medio ambiente en Bolivia*. La Paz: ILDIS and Caracas: Editorial Nueva Sociedad.

Lijphart, Arend. 1977. *Democracy in Plural Societies: A Comparative Exploration*. New Haven: Yale University Press.

Linz, Juan J. and Alfred Stepan. 1996. *Problems of Democratic Transition and Consolidation: Southern Europe, South America, and Post-Communist Europe*. Baltimore: Johns Hopkins University Press.

Lipset, Seymour Martin and Stein Rokkan. 1967. "Cleavage Structures, Party Systems, and Voter Alignments: An Introduction." In Lipset and Rokkan, eds., *Party Systems and Voter Alignments: Cross-National Perspectives*. New York: Free Press.

Lu, Flora. 1998. "The Impacts of Oil Development on the Diet, Work and Social Relations of a Huaorani Community in Ecuador." Presented at XXI International Congress of Latin American Studies Association, Palmer House Hilton Hotel, Chicago, Sept. 24–26.

Lucero, José Antonio. 2003. "Locating the 'Indian Problem': Community, Nationality, and Contradiction in Ecuadorian Indigenous Politics." *Latin American Perspectives* 30, no. 1 (Jan.): 23–48.

Bibliography

————. 2002. "Arts of Unification: Political Representation and Indigenous Movements in Bolivia and Ecuador." Ph.D. Diss., Princeton University.

————. 2001. "High Anxiety in the Andes: Crisis and Contention in Ecuador." *Journal of Democracy* 12, no. 2 (Apr.): 59–73.

Luque, Juan. 1998. "An Emergent Ecuadorian Quichua Foundation: Conservation Planning in Grassroots Development." Presented at XXI International Congress of Latin American Studies Association, Palmer House Hilton Hotel, Chicago, Sept. 24–26.

Lustig, Nora. 1995. *Coping with Austerity: Poverty and Inequality in Latin America.* Washington, DC: Brookings Institute.

Macas, Luis. 1995. "La ley agraria y el proceso de movilización por la vida." In Ramón Torres Galarza, ed., *Derechos de los Pueblos Indígenas: Situación Jurídica y Políticas de Estado.* Quito: Abya-Yala, CONAIE, CEPLAES, pp. 29–37.

————. 1994. "Comentarios." In Jorge León Trujillo, *De campesinos a ciudadanos diferentes: El levantamiento indígena.* Quito: CEDIME, pp. 175–8.

————. 1992. "El levantamiento indígena visto por sus protagonistas." In Almeida, Ileana et al., eds, *Indios: Una reflexión sobre el levantamiento indígena de 1990.* 2nd ed. Quito: ILDIS, Ediciones Abya-Yala, pp. 17–36.

Macedo, Stephen. 1990. *Liberal Virtues: Citizenship, Virtue, and Community in Liberal Constitutionalism.* Oxford: Clarendon Press.

MacIsaac, Donna J. and Marry Anthony Patrinos. 1995. "Labour Market Discrimination Against Indigenous People in Peru." *The Journal of Development Studies* 32, no. 2 (Dec.): 218–33.

Mainwaring, Scott, Guillermo O'Donnell, and J. Samuel Valenzuela, eds., 1992. *Issues in Democratic Consolidation: The New South American Democracies in Comparative Perspective.* Notre Dame: University of Notre Dame Press.

Mainwaring, Scott and Timothy R. Scully. 1995. "Introduction: Party Systems in Latin America." In Scott Mainwaring and Timothy R. Scully, eds., *Building Democratic Institutions: Party Systems in Latin America.* Stanford: Stanford University Press, 1–34.

Mainwaring, Scott and Matthew Soberg Shugart, eds. 1997. *Presidentialism and Democracy in Latin America.* Cambridge: Cambridge University Press.

Maldonado, Luis. 1996. "Desarrollo y fortalecimiento de los gobiernos comunitarios (Propuesta para una reestructuración del Movimiento Indígena)." *Imbacocha Boletín* 3 (Nov.), Otavalo, Ecuador.

Mallon, Florencia. 1998. "Chronicle of a Path Foretold? Velasco's Revolution, Vanguardia Revolucionaria, and 'Shining Omens' in the Indigenous Communities of Andahuaylas." In Steve J. Stern, ed., *Shining and Other Paths: War and Society in Peru, 1980–1995.* Durham, NC: Duke University Press.

————. 1995. *Peasant and Nation: The Making of Postcolonial Mexico and Peru.* Berkeley: University of California Press.

————. 1992. "Indian Communities, Political Cultures, and the State in Latin America, 1780–1990." *Journal of Latin American Studies* 24, Quincentenary Supp., pp. 35–53.

————. 1983. *The Defense of Community in Peru's Central Highlands: Peasant Struggle and Capitalist Transition, 1860–1940*. Princeton: Princeton University Press.

Malloy, James. 1970. *Bolivia: The Uncompleted Revolution*. Pittsburgh: University of Pittsburgh Press.

Malloy, James M. ed. 1977. *Authoritarianism and Corporatism in Latin America*. Pittsburgh: University of Pittsburgh Press.

Malloy, James and Eduardo Gamarra. 1988. *Revolution and Reaction: Bolivia, 1964–1985*. New Brunswick, NJ: Transaction Books.

Mann, Michael. 1986. *The Sources of Social Power: The Rise of Classes and Nation-States, 1760–1914*. Vol. II. Cambridge: Cambridge University Press.

Manrique, Nelson. 1998. "The War for the Central Sierra." In Steve J. Stern, ed., *Shining and Other Paths: War and Society in Peru, 1980–1995*. Durham, NC: Duke University Press.

————. 1996. "The Two Faces of Fujimori's Rural Policy." *Report on the Americas*. NACLA (July/Aug.).

Marshall, T. H. 1963. "Citizenship and Social Class." *Class, Citizenship, and Social Development*. Garden City, NY: Doubleday.

Martin, Zachary. 2003. "Peruvian Indigenous Organizations Declare CONAPA Defunct." *Cultural Survival Weekly Indigenous News* (October 1). Online version at www.culturalsurvival.org.

Martin, Zachary and Shane Green. 2004. "Dr. Juan Ossio, Defender of Indigenous People?" *Cultural Survival Weekly Indigenous News*. Letter to the editor. Online version at http://www.culturalsurvival.org/publications/news/editor4.cfm.

Marx, Anthony W. 1998. *Making Race and Nation: A Comparison of South Africa, the United States, and Brazil*. Cambridge: Cambridge University Press.

Marx, Karl. 1972. "On the Jewish Question." In Robert C. Tucker, ed., *The Marx-Engels Reader*. 2nd ed. New York: W. W. Norton and Company.

Matos Mar, José and José M. Mejía. 1980. *Reforma agraria: Logros y contradicciones, 1968–1979*. Lima: Instituto de Estudios Peruanos.

Mattiace, Shannan. 1997. "¡Zapata Vive! The EZLN, Indian Politics and the Autonomy Movement in Mexico." In George A. Collier and Lynn Stephen, special eds., *Journal of Latin American Anthropology* 3, no. 1: 32–71.

Mauceri, Philip. 1997. "The Transitions to 'Democracy' and the Failures of Institution Building." In Maxwell A. Cameron and Philip Mauceri, eds., *The Peruvian Labyrinth: Polity, Society, Economy*. University Park: Pennsylvania State University Press, pp. 13–36.

Maybury-Lewis, David. 1991. "Becoming Indian in Lowland South America." In Greg Urban and Joel Sherzer, eds., *Nation-States and Indians in Latin America*. Austin: University of Texas Press, pp. 207–35.

Mayer, Enrique. 1996. "Reflexiones sobre los derechos individuales y colectivos: Los derechos étnicos." In Elizabeth Jelín and Eric Hershberg, eds., *Construir la democracia: Derechos humanos, ciudadanía y sociedad en América Latina*. Caracas: Nueva Sociedad.

Mayer, Enrique and Elio Masferrer. 1979. "La Población Indígena en América en 1978." *América Indígena* 39, no. 2.

Bibliography

Mayor Ana María. 1996. "Detrás de nosotros estamos ustedes." In *EZLN: Crónicas intergalácticas. Primer Encuentro Intercontinental por la Humanidad y contra el Neoliberalismo.* Chiapas, Mexico.

Mayorga, René Antonio. 1988. "La Democracia en Bolivia: ¿Consolidación o desestabilizacion?" *Pensamiento Iberoamericano* no. 14 (July–Dec.): 21–45.

McAdam, Doug. 1996. "Conceptual origins, current problems, future directions." In Doug McAdam, John D. McCarthy, Mayer N. Zald, eds., *Comparative Perspectives on Social Movements: Political Opportunities, Mobilizing Structures, and Cultural Framings.* Cambridge: Cambridge University Press.

———. 1988. *Freedom Summer.* New York: Oxford University Press.

———. 1982. *Political Process and the Development of Black Insurgency, 1930–1970.* Chicago: University of Chicago Press.

McAdam, Doug, John D. McCarthy, and Mayer N. Zald, eds. 1996. *Comparative Perspectives on Social Movements: Political Opportunities, Mobilizing Structures, and Cultural Framings.* Cambridge: Cambridge University Press.

McAdam, Doug, Sidney Tarrow, and Charles Tilly. 2001. *Dynamics of Contention.* New York: Cambridge University Press.

McClintock, Cynthia. 1989. "Peru's Sendeo Luminoso Rebellion: Origins and Trajectories." In Susan Eckstein, ed., *Power and Protest: Latin American Social Movements.* Berkeley: University of California Press, pp. 61–101.

———. 1981. *Peasant Cooperatives and Political Change in Peru.* Princeton: Princeton University Press.

Melucci, Alberto. 1989. *Nomads of the Present: Social Movements and Individual Needs in Contemporary Society.* Philadelphia: Temple University Press.

Mendoza, Eduardo. 1993. "Peru: Informe de la Representación Gubernamental." *Anuario Indigenista* xxxii (Dec.). Mexico: Instituto Indigenista Interamericano, pp. 527–43.

Migdal, Joel S. 2001. *State in Society: Studying How States and Societies Transform and Constitute One Another.* New York: Cambridge University Press.

———. 1998. *Strong Societies and Weak States: State-Society Relations and State Capabilities in the Third World.* Princeton: Princeton University Press.

Migdal, Joel, Atul Kohli, and Vivienne Shue, eds., 1994. *State Power and Social Forces: Domination and Transformation in the Third World.* New York: Cambridge University Press.

Mijeski, Kenneth J. and Scott H. Beck. 1998. "Mainstreaming the Indigenous Movement in Ecuador: The Electoral Strategy." Presented at XXI International Congress of Latin American Studies Association, Palmer House Hilton Hotel, Chicago, Sept. 24–26.

Ministerio de Agricultura y Ganadería (MAG), Junta Nacional de Planificación (JUNAPLA), Instituto Ecuatoriano de Reforma Agraria y Colonización (IERAC). n.d. *Evaluación de la Reforma Agraria Ecuatoriana (ERA) 1964–1976.* Quito.

Ministerio de Asuntos Campesinos y Agropecuarios, Instituto Indigenista Boliviano. 1993. *Política en favor de los pueblos indígenas.* Informe de gestión, 1989–1993. La Paz, July.

Ministerio de Desarrollo Humano, Secretaría Nacional de Participación Popular. 1997. *Indígenas en el poder local.* La Paz: Talleres de Editorial Offset Boliviana.

————. 1996. *Apre(he)ndiendo la Participación Popular: Análisis y reflexiones sobre el modelo boliviano de descentralización.* La Paz: Editorial Offset Boliviana Ltda.

Ministerio de Hacienda y Comercio-Dirección Nacional de Estadísticas (MHC). 1940. *Censo Nacional de Población y Ocupación.* Lima.

Molina, George Gray and Carlos Hugo Molina. 1997. "Popular Participation and Decentralization in Bolivia: Building Accountability from the Grassroots." Paper prepared for the Harvard Institute for International Development (HIID), Cambridge, MA.

Molina Rivero, Ramiro and Jimena Portugal Loayza. 1995. *Consulta de base a los ayllus del Norte de Potosí y Sur de Oruro.* La Paz: PROADE and ILDIS.

Molina, Sergio and Iván Arias. 1996. *De la nación clandestina a la participación popular.* La Paz: Centro de Documentación e Información, CEDOIN.

Molina, Wilder M. 1997. "El movimiento social indígena del Beni en el contexto del proceso de consolidación de la movilización intercomunal hasta la Marcha por el Territoria y la Dignidad (1987–1990)." Centro de Documentación para el Desarrollo del Beni, Trinidad, Bolivia.

————. 1996a. "Las luchas indígenas en el Beni: Organización, movilización e institucionalización." Trinidad, El Beni, Bolivia: CIDDEBENI, Publicación no. 37.

————. 1996b. "Las luchas indígenas en el Beni: Resultados y efectos políticos." Trinidad, El Beni, Bolivia: CIDDEBENI, Publicación no. 38.

Moore Jr., Barrington. 1966. *Social Origins of Dictatorship and Democracy: Lord and Peasant in the Making of the Modern World.* Boston: Beacon Press.

Morales, Juan Antonio. 1994. "Democracy, Economic Liberalism, and Structural Reforms in Bolivia." In William C. Smith, Carlos H. Acuña, and Eduardo A. Gamarra, eds., *Democracy, Markets, and Structural Reform in Latin America.* New Brunswick, NJ: Transaction Publishers, pp. 129–48.

Morley, Samuel A. 1995. *Poverty and Inequality in Latin America: The Impact of Adjustment and Recovery in the 1980s.* Baltimore and London: Johns Hopkins University Press.

Mornissen, Judith. 1995. *Legislación Boliviana y Pueblos Indígenas: Inventario y analisis en la perspectiva de las demandas indígenas.* Santa Cruz, Bolivia: CEJIS.

Morris, Aldon and Naomi Braine. 2001. "Social Movements and Oppositional Consciousness." In Jane Mansbridge and Aldon Morris, eds., *Oppositional Consciousness: The Subjective Roots of Social Protest.* Chicago: University of Chicago Press, pp. 20–37.

Múñoz, Jorge A. and Isabel Lavadenz. 1997. "Reforming the Agrarian Reform in Bolivia." Paper prepared for the Harvard Institute for International Development, Cambridge, MA and UDAPSO, Bolivia.

Muratorio, Blanca. 1996. "Trabajando para la Shell: Resistencia cultural a la proletarianización en la amazonía ecuatoriana." In Fernando Santos Granero, ed., *Globalización y cambio en la amazonía indígena.* Vol. 1. Quito: Ediciones Abya-Yala, pp. 371–95.

Bibliography

Murillo, David, ed. 1997. *Población indígena y sección municipal*. La Paz: Ministerio de Desarrollo Humano, SNAEGG, SAE, PNUD.

Nagengast, Carole and Michael Kearney. 1990. "Mixtec Ethnicity: Social Identity, Political Consciousness, and Political Activism." *Latin American Research Review* 25, no. 2: 61–91.

Napolitano, Valentina and Xochitl Leyva Solano, eds. 1998. *Encuentros antropológicos: Politics, Identity, and Mobility in Mexican Society*. London: Institute of Latin American Studies.

Nash, June. 1992. "Interpreting social movements: Bolivian resistance to economic conditions imposed by the International Monetary Fund." *American Ethnologist* 19, no. 2 (May): 275–93.

———. 1989. "Cultural Resistance and Class Consciousness in Bolivian Tin-Mining Communities." In Susan Eckstein, ed., *Power and Popular Protest: Latin American Social Movements*. Berkeley: University of California Press.

Navarro, Maryssa. 1998. "The Personal is Political: Las Madres de Plaza de Mayo." In Susan Eckstein, ed., *Power and Popular Protest: Latin American Social Movements*. Berkeley: University of California Press.

Navia Ribera, Carlos. 2003. *La cuestión indígena en el Beni. Reflexiones en la década de los 90s*. Trinidad, Bolivia: CIDDEBENI.

———. 1996. "Reconocimiento, demarcación y control de territorios indígenas: Situación y experiencias en Bolivia." Working Paper no. 34. Trinidad, El Beni, Bolivia: Centro de Investigación y Documentación para el Desarrollo del Beni (CIDDEBENI).

———. 1992. "Esquemas para entender la cuestión territorial indígena en el Beni." Trinidad, el Beni, Bolivia, CIDDEBENI (Oct.).

Nelson, Diane. 1999. *A Finger in the Wound: Body Politics in Quincentennial Guatemala*. Berkeley: University of California Press.

Nelson, Joan. 1990. "Politics and Economic Crisis: A Comparative Study of Chile, Peru, and Colombia." In Joan M. Nelson, ed., *Economic Crisis and Policy Choice: The Politics of Adjustment in the Third World*. Princeton: Princeton University Press, pp. 113–67.

Newman, Saul. 1991. "Does Modernization Breed Ethnic Political Conflict?" *World Politics* 43, no. 3 (Apr.): 451–78.

Nickson, R. Andrew. 1995. *Local Government in Latin America*. Boulder, CO: Lynne Rienner.

Nobles, Melissa. 2000. *Shades of Citizenship: Race and the Census in Modern Politics*. Stanford: Stanford University Press.

North American Congress on Latin America (NACLA). 1992. "The Black Americas, 1492–1992." *Report on the Americas* 25 (Feb.).

———. 1991. *Report on the Americas: The First Nations, 1492–1992* 25, no. 3 (Dec.).

Obando, Enrique. 1998. "Civil-Military Relations in Peru, 1980–1996: How to Control and Coopt the Military (and the consequences of doing so)." In Steve J. Stern, ed., *Shining and Other Paths: War and Society in Peru, 1980–1995*. Durham, NC: Duke University Press.

O'Donnell, Guillermo. 2001. "Democracy, Law and Comparative Politics." *Studies in Comparative and International Development* 36, no. 1 (Spring): 7–36.

——. 1998. "Horizontal Accountability in New Democracies." *Journal of Democracy* 9, no. 3 (July): 112–26.

——. 1996. "Illusions about Democratic Consolidation." *Journal of Democracy* 7, no. 2 (Apr.): 34–51.

——. 1994. "Delegative Democracy?" *Journal of Democracy* 15, no. 1 (Jan.): 55–69.

——. 1993. "On the State, Democratization and Some Conceptual Problems: A Latin American View with Glances at Some Postcommunist Countries." *World Development* 21, no. 8 (Aug.): 1355–69.

——. 1979. "Tensions in the Bureaucratic-Authoritarian State and the Question of Democracy." In David Collier, ed., *The New Authoritarianism in Latin America*. Princeton: Princeton University Press, pp. 285–318.

Oficina Nacional de Estadística y Censos (ONEC). Censo Nacional VII de Población y II de Vivienda 1972. Lima.

Ojarasca no. 45 (Aug.–Nov. 1995) Mexico.

Olson, Mancur. 1965. *The Logic of Collective Action*. Cambridge, MA: Harvard University Press.

Organización Nacional Agraria. 1990. *La agricultura peruana: Veinte años después de la reforma agraria*. Documento elaborado bajo la responsabilidad de la Gerencia Técnica de la ONA. Lima.

Ortiz Crespo, Gonzalo. 1992 "El problema indígena y el gobierno." In Almeida, Ileana et al. *Indios: Una reflexion sobre el levantamiento indígena de 1990*. 2nd ed. Quito: ILDIS, Ediciones Abya-Yala, pp. 99–178.

Pacari, Nina. 1996. "Ecuador Taking on the Neoliberal Agenda." *NACLA Report on the Americas* 29 no. 5: 23–30.

Pachano, Simón. 1996. *Democracia sin sociedad*. Quito: ILDIS.

Pacheco, B. Pablo. 1997. "Políticas de tierra y desarrollo rural." Serie 6, Aportes al Debate Electoral. La Paz: CEDLA (Centro de Estudios para el desarrollo laboral y agrario), May 18.

Pallares, Amalia Veronika. 1997. "From Peasant Struggles to Indian Resistance: Political Identity in Highland Ecuador 1964–1992." Ph.D. Diss., University of Texas at Austin.

Palmer, David Scott, ed. 1994. *The Shining Path of Peru*. 2nd ed., New York: St. Martin's Press.

Palomino-Bujele, Luis. 1993. *Dos décadas de crédito agrario*. Universidad de Lima, Facultad de Economía. Centro de Investigaciones Económicos y Sociales. Lima.

Paredes, Carlos E. and Jeffrey D. Sachs. 1991. *Peru's Path to Recovery: A Plan for Economic Stabilization and Growth*. Washington, DC: The Brookings Institution.

Pastor, Manuel. 1991. "Bolivia: Hyperinflation, Stabilisation, and Beyond." *The Journal of Development Studies*, 27, no. 2 (Jan.): 211–37.

Pearce, Andrew. 1984. "Campesinado y revolución: El caso de Bolivia." In Fernando Calderón and Jorge Dandler, eds., *Bolivia: La fuerza histórica del campesinado: Movimientos campesinos y etnicidad*. United Nations Research Institute for Social

Bibliography

Development and Centro de Estudios de la Realidad Económica y Social. Cochabamba, Bolivia: Artes Gráficas "El Buitre," pp. 309–58.

Peña, Milagros. 1995. *Theologies and Liberation in Peru: The Role of Ideas in Social Movements*. Philadelphia: Temple University Press.

Pinelo, José Enrique. 1989. "Asamblea de Nacionalidades." In Ricardo, Calla Ortega, José Enrique Pinelo, and Miguel Urioste Fernández de Córdova, *CSUTCB: Debate sobre documentos y asamblea de nacionalidades*. La Paz: CEDLA (Centro Laboral de Estudios para el Desarrollo Laboral y Agrario).

Piven, Frances Fox and Richard A. Cloward. 1979. *Poor People's Movements: Why They Succeed, How They Fail*. New York: Vintage.

Plant, Roger. 2002. "Latin America's Multiculturalism: Economic and Agrarian Dimensions." In Rachel Sieder, ed., *Multiculturalism in Latin America: Indigenous Rights, Diversity and Democracy*. New York: Palgrave Macmillan.

Platt, Tristan. 1982. *Estado boliviano y ayllu andino: Tierra y tributo en el norte de Potosí*. Lima: Instituto de Estudios Peruanos.

Podolny, Joel M. and Karen L. Page. 1998. "Network Forms of Organization." *Annual Review of Sociology* 24: 57–76.

PROMUDEH (Ministerio de Promoción de la Mujer y del Desarrollo Humano). "Perú: Comunidades Indígenas de la Amazonía, 1993." Gerencia de Gestión Administrativa, Unidad de Informática y Sistemas. Lima. Jan. 1999.

Psacharopoulos, George and Harry A. Patrinos, eds. 1994. *Indigenous People and Poverty in Latin America: An Empirical Analysis*. World Bank Regional and Sectoral Studies. Washington, DC: World Bank.

Putnam, Robert D. 1993. *Making Democracy Work: Civic Traditions in Modern Italy*. Princeton: Princeton University Press.

Rabushka, Alvin and Kenneth A. Shepsle. 1972. *Politics in Plural Societies: A Theory of Democratic Instability*. Columbus, OH: Charles E. Merrill Publishing Company.

Racines, Francisco. 1993. "De la establilización monetaria al ajuste estructural: Impactos sociales y alternativas de desarrollo." In J. Baldiva, F. Racines, and I. Mendoza. *Ajuste estructural en los Andes: Impactos sociales y desarrollo*. Quito: Ediciones Abya-Yala and CECI-Andes, pp. 59–130.

Radcliffe, Sarah A. 2001. "Development, the State, and Transnational Political Connections: State and Subject Formations in Latin America." *Global Networks* 1, no. 1: 19–36.

Ramón, Galo. 1994. "Comentario." In Jorge León Trujillo. *De campesinos a ciudadanos diferentes: El levantamiento indígena*. Quito: CEDIME, pp. 179–81.

———. 1990. "El problema de la tierra en el Ecuador." *Diario Hoy*. September 23, 1990, p. A1.

Ramos, Hugo and Lindon Robison. 1990. "Credit and Credit Policies." In Morris D. Whitaker and Dale Colyer, eds., *Agriculture and Economic Survival: The Role of Agriculture in Ecuador's Development*. Boulder, CO: Westview Press. pp. 225–45.

Rappaport, Joanne. 1990. *The Politics of Memory: Native Historical Interpretation in the Colombian Andes*. New York: Cambridge University Press.

Remy, María Isabel. 1995. "Historia y discurso social. El debate de la identidad nacional." In Julio Cotler, ed., *Perú 1964–1994: Economía, Sociedad, y Política*. Lima: Instituto de Estudios Peruanos, pp. 275–92.

335

——— . 1994. "The Indigenous Population and the Construction of Democracy in Peru." In Donna Lee Van Cott, ed., *Indigenous Peoples and Democracy in Latin America*. New York: St. Martin's Press in association with the Inter-American Dialogue, pp. 107–30.

Rénique, José Luis. 1998. "Apogee and Crisis of a 'Third Path': *Mariateguismo*, 'People's War,' and Counterinsurgency in Puno, 1987–1994." In Steve J. Stern, ed., *Shining and Other Paths: War and Society in Peru, 1980–1995*. Durham, NC: Duke University Press.

Rivera Cusicanqui, Silvia. 1991. "Aymara Past, Aymara Future." *Report on the Americas* 25, no. 3 (Dec. 1991): 18–23.

——— . 1990. "Democracia liberal y democracia de ayllu: el caso de Norte del Potosí, Bolivia." In Carlos F. Toranzo Roca, ed., *El difícil camino hacia la democracia*. La Paz: ILDIS, 1990.

——— . 1987. *Oppressed but not Defeated: Peasant Struggles among the Aymara and the Qhechwa in Bolivia, 1900–1980*. Geneva: United Nations Research Institute for Social Development.

Rivera Cusicanqui, Silvia with Ramón Conde and Felipe Santos. 1992. *Ayllus y Proyectos de desarrollo en el norte de Potosí*. La Paz: Ediciones Aruwiyiri.

Roberts, Kenneth M. 1995. "Neoliberalism and the Transformation of Populism in Latin America." *World Politics* 48 no. 1 (Oct.): 82 (35).

Roberts, Kenneth and Mark Peceny. 1997. "Human Rights and United States Policy Toward Peru." In Maxwell A. Cameron and Philip Mauceri, eds., *The Peruvian Labyrinth: Politics, Society, Economy*. University Park: Pennsylvania State University Press, pp. 192–222.

Rodríguez-Seguí, Maritza. 1999a. Unpublished longitudinal database compiled for this book. Includes Data on Indigenous Peoples; Credit, Poverty, and Land Distribution.

——— . 1999b. Manuscript. "Structural Adjustment, Agricultural Production and Welfare among the Indigenous People in the Peruvian Highlands." Princeton University.

Rodrik, Dani. 1997. *Has Globalization Gone Too Far?* Washington, DC: Institute for International Economics.

Romero Bonifaz, Carlos and Sándoval Romero, Filemón. 1996. "Los pueblos indígenas y la participación popular." Trinidad: Centro de Estudios Jurídicos e Investigación Social – CEJIS.

Rosero, Fernando. 1991. *Levantamiento indígena: Tierra y precios*. 2nd ed. Quito: CEDIS.

Rospigliosi, Fernando. 1995. "Fuerzas Armadas, corporativismo y autoritarismo: ¿Qué ha cambiado en tres décadas?" In Julio Cotler, ed., *Perú 1964–1994: Economía, Sociedad, y Política*. Lima: Instituto de Estudios Peruanos, pp. 215–36.

Rustow, Dankwart. 1970. "Transitions to Democracy: Toward a Dynamic Model." *Comparative Politics* 2, no. 3 (Apr.): 337–63.

Rubio-Marín, Ruth. 2000. *Immigration as Democratic Challenge: Citizenship and Inclusion in Germany and the United States*. Cambridge: Cambridge University Press.

Rubin, Jeffrey W. 1997. *Decentering the Regime: Ethnicity, Radicalism, and Democracy in Juchitán Mexico*. Durham, NC: Duke University Press.

Bibliography

Ruiz, Lucy M. 1992. "Pueblos indígenas y etnicidad en la amazonía." In Almeida, Ileana et al., eds., *Indios: Una reflexion sobre el levantamiento indígena de 1990*. 2nd ed. Quito: ILDIS, Ediciones Abya-Yala, pp. 449–98.

Ruiz, Lucy, ed. 1993. *Amazonía: Escenarios y conflictos*. Quito: CEDIME and Ediciones Abya-Yala.

Rus, Jan. 1994. "The 'Comunidad Revolucionaria Institucional': The Subversion of Native Government in Highland Chiapas, 1936–1968." In Gilbert M. Joseph and Daniel Nugent, eds., *Everyday Forms of State Formation: Revolution and the Negotiation of Rule in Modern Mexico*. Durham, NC: Duke University Press, pp. 265–300.

Sachs, Jeffrey and Juan Antonio Morales. 1988. *Bolivia: 1952–1986*. San Francisco: International Center for Economic Growth affiliated with the Institute for Contemporary Studies.

SAIIC (South and Meso American Indian Rights Center). 1995. "Interview with Mino Eusebio Castro." *Abya Yala News* 9, no. 1 (Spring) (as posted on SAIIC home page, http://www.igc.apc.org/saiic/saiic.html).

Sanabria, Harry. 1997. "The Discourse and Practice of Repression and Resistance in the Chapare." In Madeline Barbara Léons and Harry Sanabria, eds., *Coca, Cocaine, and the Bolivian Reality*. Albany: State University of New York Press, pp. 169–94.

Sánchez-Parga, José. 1996. *Población y Pobreza Indígena*. Quito: Centro Andina de Acción Popular (CAAP).

Santana, Roberto. 1995. *Ciudadanos en la etnicidad: Los indios en los política o la política de los indios*. Quito: Ediciones Abya-Yala.

Santos-Granero, Fernando, ed. 1996. *Globalización y cambio en la amazonía indígena*. Quito: FLACSO and Ediciones Abya-Yala.

Santos-Granero, Fernando and Federica Barclay. 1998. *Selva Central: History, Economy, and Land Use in Peruvian Amazon*. Washington, DC: Smithsonian Institution Press.

Sawyer, Suzana. 1996. "Indigenous Initiatives and Petroleum Politics in the Ecuadorian Amazon." *Cultural Survival Quarterly* 20, no. 1 (Spring): 26–30.

Schattsneider, E. E. 1975. *The Semisovereign People: A Realist's View of Democracy in America*. Hinsdale, IL: The Dryden Press.

Schemo, Diane. "Ecuadorians Want Texaco to Clear Toxic Residue," *The New York Times*, February 1, 1998, A12.

Schmitter, Philippe C. 1993. "The Consolidation of Democracy and Representation of Social Groups." *American Behavioral Scientist* 35 (Mar.–June).

Schneider, Ben Ross. 1995. "Democratic Consolidations: Some Broad Comparisons and Sweeping Arguments." *Latin American Research Review* 30, no. 2.

Schneider, Cathy. 1992. "Radical Opposition Parties and Squatter Movements in Pinochet's Chile." In Arturo Escobar and Sonia Alvarez, eds., *The Making of Social Movements in Latin America*. Boulder, CO: Westview Press.

Scott, James C. 1998. *Seeing Like a State: How Certain Schemes to Improve the Human Condition Have Failed*. New Haven: Yale University Press.

———. 1990. *Domination and the Arts of Resistance: Hidden Transcripts*. New Haven: Yale University Press.

Bibliography

———. 1985. *Weapons of the Weak: Everyday Forms of Peasant Resistance.* New Haven: Yale University Press.

Scully, Timothy R. 1992. *Rethinking the Center: Party Politics in Nineteenth and Twentieth-Century Chile.* Stanford: Stanford University Press.

Secretaría de Asuntos Indígenas (SETAI). 1999. "Datos Básicos sobre las poblaciónes indígenas del Perú." Lima (SETAI-DRL/07-09-99).

Seligmann, Linda J. 1995. *Between Reform and Revolution: Political Struggles in the Peruvian Andes, 1969–1991.* Stanford: Stanford University Press.

Selverston, Melina H. 1997. "The Politics of Identity Reconstruction: Indians and Democracy in Ecuador." In Douglas Chalmers et al., eds., *The New Politics of Inequality in Latin America: Rethinking Participation.* Oxford: Oxford University Press, pp. 170–91.

———. 1994. "The Politics of Culture: Indigenous Peoples and the State in Ecuador." In Donna Lee Van Cott, ed., *Indigenous Peoples and Democracy in Latin America.* New York: St. Martin's Press in association with the Inter-American Dialogue, pp. 131–52.

Selverston-Scher, Melina. 2001. *Ethnopolitics in Ecuador: Indigenous Rights and the Strengthening of Democracy.* Coral Gable, FL: North-South Center Press.

Servicios del Pueblo Mixe, A. C. 1996. "Autonomía, una forma concreta de ejercicio del derecho a la libre determinación y sus alcances." *Chiapas 2.* Mexico City: Ediciones ERA, S. A. de C.V.

Shafir, Gershon. 1998. "Introduction: The Evolving Tradition of Citizenship." In Gershon Shafir, ed., *The Citizenship Debates: A Reader.* Minneapolis: University of Minnesota Press, pp. 1–28.

Shapiro, Ian. 1993. "Democratic Innovation: South Africa in Comparative Context." *World Politics* 46 (Oct.): 121–50.

Shapiro, Ian and Will Kymlicka, eds. 1997. *Ethnicity and Group Rights* 39, Yearbook of the American Society for Political and Legal Philosophy. New York: New York University Press.

Sheahan, John. 1999. *Searching for a Better Society: The Peruvian Economy from 1950.* University Park: Pennsylvania State University Press.

Shklar, Judith N. 1991. *American Citizenship: The Quest for Inclusion.* Cambridge, MA: Harvard University Press.

Sieder, Rachel. 2002. "Recognising Indigenous Law and the Politics of State Formation in Mesoamerica." In Rachel Sieder, ed., *Multiculturalism in Latin America: Indigenous Rights, Diversity and Democracy.* New York: Palgrave Macmillan.

Sieder, Rachael, ed. 1998. *Guatemala After the Peace Accords.* London: Institute of Latin American Studies, University of London.

Silva Charvet, Paula. 1986. *Gamonalismo y lucha campesina: Estudio de la sobrevivencia y disolución de un sector terrateniente: el caso de la provincia de Chimborazo: 1940–1979.* Quito: Ediciones Abya-Yala.

Skœpol, Theda. 1979. *States and Social Revolutions: A Comparative Analysis of France, Russia, and China.* Cambridge: Cambridge University Press.

Smith, Carol A. 1990. *Guatemalan Indians and the State, 1540 to 1988.* Austin: University of Texas Press.

Bibliography

————. 1987. "Culture and Community: The Language of Class in Guatemala." In *The Year Left: An American Socialist Yearbook*. London: Verso, pp. 197–217.

Smith, Gavin. 1989. *Livelihood and Resistance: Peasants and the Politics of Land in Peru*. Berkeley: University of California Press.

Smith, Michael Addison. 1999. Manuscript. "Indigenous Law and the Nation States of the Latin American Region." University of Texas, School of Law and the Mexican Center, April 20.

Smith, Richard Chase. 1996. "La política de la diversidad COICA y las federaciones étnicas de la Amazonía." In Stefano Varese, ed., *Pueblos indios, soberanía y globalismo*. Quito: Ediciones Abya-Yala, pp. 81–126.

————. 1985. "A Search for Unity Within Diversity: Peasant Unions, Ethnic Federations, and Indianist Movements in the Andean Republics." In Theodore MacDonald, ed., *Native Peoples and Economic Development*. Issue 16. Cambridge, MA: Cultural Survival, Inc., pp. 5–38.

Snyder, Jack. 2000. *From Voting to Violence: Democratization and Nationalist Conflict*. New York: Columbia University Press.

Solón, Pablo. 1997. *Horizontes sin tierra? Análisis crítico de la Ley INRA*. La Paz: CEDOIN.

————. 1995. *La tierra prometida: Un aporte al debate sobre las modificaciones a la legislación agraria*. La Paz: CEDOIN.

Soysal, Yasemin Nuhoğlu. 1994. *Limits of Citizenship: Migrants and Postnational Membership in Europe*. Chicago: University of Chicago Press.

Spedding, Alison L. 1997. "Cocataki, Taki-Coca: Trade, Traffic, and Organized Peasant Resistance in the Yungas of La Paz." In Madeline Barbara Léons and Harry Sanabria, eds., *Coca, Cocaine, and the Bolivian Reality*. Albany: State University of New York Press, pp. 117–38.

Stack, John. 1986. *The Primordial Challenge: Ethnicity in the Contemporary World*. New York: Greenwood Press.

Starn, Orin. 1999. *Nightwatch: The Politics of Protest in the Andes*. Durham, NC and London: Duke University Press.

————. 1998. "Villagers at Arms: War and Counterrevolution in the Central-South Andes." In Steve J. Stern, ed., *Shining and Other Paths: War and Society in Peru, 1980–1995*. Durham, NC: Duke University Press.

————. 1992. "'I Dreamed of Foxes and Hawks': Reflections on Peasant Protest, New Social Movements and the Rondas Campesinas of Northern Peru." In Arturo Escobar and Sonia Alvarez, eds., *The Making of Social Movements in Latin America: Identity, Strategy, and Democracy*. Boulder, CO: Westview.

————. 1991. "Missing the Revolution: Anthropologists and the War in Peru." *Cultural Anthropology* 6, no. 3: 63–91.

Statistical Abstract of Latin America. 2001. Vol. 37.

Statistical Abstract of Latin America. 1993. Vol. 30, pt. I.

Stavenhagen, Rodolfo. 2002. "Indigenous Peoples and the State in Latin America: An Ongoing Debate." In Rachel Sieder, ed., *Multiculturalism in Latin America: Indigenous Rights, Diversity and Democracy*. New York: Palgrave Macmillan.

———. 1996. "Los derechos indígenas: Algunos problemas conceptuales." In Eric Hershberg and Elizabeth Jelín, eds., *Construir la democracia: Derechos humanos, ciudadanía y sociedad en América Latina*. Caracas: Nueva Sociedad.

———. 1992. "Challenging the Nation-State in Latin America." *Journal of International Affairs* 45, no. 2 (Winter): 421–40.

———. 1990. *The Ethnic Question: Conflicts, Development, and Human Rights*. Tokyo, Japan: United Nations University Press.

———. 1988. *Derecho indígena y derechos humanos en América Latina*. Mexico: El Colegio de Mexico, Instituto Interamericano de Derechos Humanos.

Stavenhagen, Rodolfo and Diego Ituralde, eds. 1990. *Entre la ley y la costumbre: El derecho consuetudinario indígena en América Latina*. Mexico City: Instituto Indigenista Interamericano; San José, Costa Rica: Instituto Interamericano de Derechos Humanos.

Stepan, Alfred. 1999. "Federalism and Democracy: Beyond the U.S. Model." *Journal of Democracy* 10, no. 4 (Oct.): 19–34.

———. 1978. *State and Society: Peru in Comparative Perspective*. Princeton: Princeton University Press.

Stepan, Alfred and Cindy Skach. 1993. "Constitutional Frameworks and Democratic Consolidation: Parliamentarism versus Presidentialism?" *World Politics* 46, no. 1 (Oct.): 1–22.

Stephen, Lynn. 1997. "Redefined Nationalism in Building a Movement for Indigenous Autonomy in Southern Mexico." *Journal of Latin American Anthropology* 3, no. 1: 72–101.

———. 1996. "The Creation and Re-creation of Ethnicity: Lessons from the Zapotec and Mixtec of Oaxaca." *Latin American Perspectives* 23, no. 2 (Spring): 17–37.

Stephenson, Marcia. 2002. "Forging an Indigenous Counterrepublic Sphere: The Taller de Historia Oral Andina in Bolivia." *Latin American Research Review* 37, no. 2: 99–118.

Stern, Steve J. 1992. "Paradigms of Conquest: History, Historiography, and Politics." *Journal of Latin American Studies* 24: 1–34. Quincentenary Supp.

———. 1987a. "New Approaches to the Study of Peasant Rebellion and Consciousness: Implications of the Andean Experience." In Steve J. Stern, ed., *Resistance, Rebellion, and Consciousness in the Andean Peasant World, 18th to 20th Centuries*. Madison: University of Wisconsin Press, pp. 3–28.

———. 1987b. "The Age of Andean Insurrection, 1742–1782: A Reappraisal." In Steve J. Stern, ed., *Resistance, Rebellion, and Consciousness in the Andean Peasant World, 18th to 20th Centuries*. Madison: University of Wisconsin Press, pp. 34–93.

Stern, Steve J., ed. 1998. *Shining and Other Paths: War and Society in Peru, 1980–1995*. Durham, NC: Duke University Press.

Stokes, Susan. 1997. "Democratic Accountability and Policy Change: Economic Policy in Fujimori's Peru." *Comparative Politics* 29, no. 2 (Jan.): 209–26.

Stoll, David. 1990. *Is Latin America Turning Protestant?: The Politics of Evangelical Growth*. Berkeley: University of California Press.

Bibliography

Ströbele-Gregor, Juliana. 1996. "Culture and Political Practice of the Aymara and Quechua in Bolivia: Autonomous Forms of Modernity in the Andes." *Latin American Perspectives* 23, no. 2 (Spring): 72–91.

Stoner-Weiss, Kathryn. Forthcoming. *Resisting the State: Reform and Retrenchment in Post-Soviet Russia.* Cambridge University Press.

Subsecretaría de Asuntos Etnicos (SAE). 1997. "Apoyo al desarrollo de los pueblos indígenas." La Paz, Feb. 22.

Tarrow, Sidney. 1998. *Power in Movement: Social Movements, Collective Action and Politics.* 2nd ed. New York: Cambridge University Press.

———. 1996. "Making Social Science Work Across Space and Time: A Critical Reflection on Robert Putnam's Making Democracy Work." *American Political Science Review* 90, no. 2 (June): 389–97.

Taylor, Anne-Christiane. 1996. "La riqueza de Dios: Los Achuar y las misiones." In Fernando Santos Granero, ed., *Globalización y cambio en la amazonía indígena.* Vol. 1. Quito: Ediciones Abya-Yala, pp. 219–59.

Thoumi, Francisco and Merilee Grindle. 1992. *La política de la economía del ajuste: La actual experiencia ecuatoriana.* Quito: FLACSO.

Thurner, Mark. 1997. *From Two Republics to One Divided: Contradictions of Postcolonial Nationmaking in Andean Peru.* Durham, NC: Duke University Press.

Ticona, Esteban Alejo. 1996. *CSUTCB: Trayectoria y desafíos.* La Paz: CEDOIN.

Ticona A., Esteban, Gonzalo Rojas O., and Xavier Albó C. 1995. *Votos y wiphalas: Campesinos y pueblos orginarios en democracia.* La Paz: Fundación Milenio and CIPCA.

Tilly, Charles. 2002. Manuscript. "Repression, Mobilization, and Explanation." Columbia University, Sept. 1.

———. 1999. "Why Worry about Citizenship." In Michael Hanagan and Charles Tilly, eds., *Extending Citizenship: Reconfiguring States.* Lanham, MD: Rowman and Littlefield, pp. 247–59.

———. 1990. *Coercion, Capital, and European States, AD. 990–1990.* Cambridge, MA: Blackwell Publishers.

———. 1984. "Social Movements and National Politics." In Charles Bright and Susan Harding, eds., *Statemaking and Social Movements.* Ann Arbor: The University of Michigan Press, pp. 297–317.

———. 1975. *The Formation of National States in Western Europe.* Princeton: Princeton University Press.

Toranza Roca, Carlos F. 1996. "Bolivia: Crisis, Structural Adjustment and Democracy." In Alex E. Fernández Jilberto and André Mommen, eds., *Liberalization in the Developing World: Institutional and Economic Changes in Latin America, Africa, and Asia.* London and New York: Routledge.

Torres Galarza, Ramón. 1995. "Régimen constitucional y derechos de los pueblos indígenas." In Ramón Torres Galarza, ed., *Derechos de los Pueblos Indígenas: Situación Jurídica y Políticas de Estado.* Quito: Abya-Yala, CONAIE, CEPLAES, pp. 45–60.

Touraine, Alain. 1988. *The Return of the Actor: Social Theory in Postindustrial Society.* Minneapolis: University of Minnesota Press.

Treakle, Kay. 1990. "Ecuador: Structural Adjustment and Indigenous and Environmentalist Resistance." In Jonathan A. Fox and David L. Brown, eds., *The Struggle for Accountability: The World Bank, NGOs, and Grassroots Movements.* Cambridge, MA: MIT Press, pp. 219–64.

Trujillo, Jorge León. 1994. *De campesinos a ciudadanos diferentes: El levantamiento indígena.* Quito: Cedime and Abya-Yala.

Turner, Bryan S. 1990. "Outline of a Theory of Citizenship." *Sociology* 24, no. 2 (May): 189–217.

Uehling, Greta. 2000. "Social Memory as Collective Action: The Crimean Tatar National Movement." In Guidry et al., eds., *Globalizations and Social Movements: Culture, Power, and the Transnational Public Sphere.* Ann Arbor: The University of Michigan Press, pp. 260–87.

Urban, Greg. 1991. "The Semiotics of State-Indian Linguistic Relationships: Peru, Paraguay, and Brazil." In Greg Urban and Joel Sherzer, eds., *Nation-States and Indians in Latin America.* Austin: University of Texas Press, pp. 307–30.

Urban, Greg and Joel Sherzer. 1991. *Nation-States and Indians in Latin America.* Austin: University of Texas Press.

Urioste Fernández de Córdova, Miguel. 1992. *Fortalecer las comunidades: Una utopía subversiva, democrática . . . y posible.* La Paz: AIPE/PROCOM/TIERRA.

———. 1989. "Provocaciones para continuar la discusión." In Ricardo Calla Ortega, José Enrique Pinelo, and Miguel Urioste Fernández de Córdova, eds., *CSUTCB: Debate sobre documentos y asamblea de nacionalidades.* La Paz: CEDLA (Centro Laboral de Estudios para el Desarrollo Laboral y Agrario).

Urioste Fernández de Córdova, Miguel and Luis Baldomar. 1998. "Bolivia campesina en 1997." In Carlos Iván Degregori, ed., *Comunidades: Tierra, instituciones, identidad.* Lima: Diakonía-CEPES-Araiwa.

U.S. Department of State, Department of State Dispatch, Colombia Human Rights Practice in 1993.

Vacaflor Gonzales, Jorge Luis, ed. 1997. *Legislación Indígena, Compilación 1991–1997.* La Paz: Vicepresidente de la República de Bolivia, OIT, and Fondo para el Dearrollo de los Pueblos Indígenas de América Latina y el Caribe.

Valera Moreno, Guillermo. 1998. *Las comunidades en el Perú: Una visión nacional desde las series departamentales.* Lima: Instituto Rural del Perú; Coordinadora Rural.

———. 1997. "Las comunidades en el Perú: Una aproximación estadística." Instituto Rural del Perú. Document. Lima.

Van Cott, Donna Lee. Manuscript. "From Movements to Parties: The Evolution of Ethnic Politics in Latin America."

———. 2003. "Institutional Change and Ethnic Parties in South America." *Latin American Politics and Society* 45, no. 2 (Summer): 1–39.

———. 2002. "Constitutional Reform in the Andes: Redefining Indigenous-State Relations." In Rachel Sieder, ed., *Multiculturalism in Latin America: Indigenous Rights, Diversity and Democracy.* New York: Palgrave Macmillan.

———. 2001. "Explaining Ethnic Autonomy Regimes in Latin America." *Studies in Comparative and International Development* 35, no. 4 (Winter): 30–58.

Bibliography

_____. 2000a. _The Friendly Liquidation of the Past: The Politics of Diversity in Latin America_. Pittsburgh: University of Pittsburgh Press.

_____. 2000b. "Indigenous Populations and Party Systems in Latin America. Theoretical Reflections on the Bolivian Case." _Party Politics_ 6 (2): 155–74.

_____. 2000c. "A Political Analysis of Legal Pluralism in Bolivia and Colombia." _Journal of Latin American Studies_ 32, 1 (Feb.): 207–34.

_____. 1994. _Indigenous Peoples and Democracy in Latin America_. New York: St. Martin's Press in association with the Inter-American Dialogue.

van den Berghe, Pierre L. 1981. _The Ethnic Phenomenon_. New York: Elsevier.

_____. 1979. "Ethnicity and Class in Highland Peru." In David L. Browman and Ronald A. Schwarz, eds., _Peasants, Primitives, and Proletariats: The Struggle for Identity in South America_. The Hague: Mouton Publishers.

Varese, Stefano. 1991. "Think Locally, Act Globally." _Report on the Americas_ XXV, no. 3 (Dec.).

Varshney, Ashutosh. 2002. _Ethnic Conflict and Civic Life: Hindus and Muslims in India_. New Haven: Yale University Press.

_____. 1995. "Ethnic Conflict and Rational Choice: A Theoretical Engagement." Working Paper no. 95–11. Cambridge, MA: Center for International Affairs, Harvard University.

Villanueva Arévalo, César. 1989. "Problemática de la violencia y el narcotráfico en la región de la selva." In Carlos Contreras et al., _Comunidades campesinas y nativas: Normatividad y desarrollo_. Lima: Fundación Friedrich Naumann, pp. 147–64.

von Mettenheim, Kurt and James Malloy. 1998. "Introduction." In Kurt von Mettenheim and James Malloy, eds., _Deepening Democracy in Latin America_. Pittsburgh: University of Pittsburgh Press.

Wade, Peter. 1997. _Race and Ethnicity in Latin America_. London: Pluto Press.

Walzer, Michael. 1993. "Exclusion, Injustice, and the Democratic State." _Dissent_ Winter, pp. 55–64.

_____. 1983. _Spheres of Justice: A Defense of Pluralism and Equality_. New York: Basic Books.

Warren, Kay B. 1998. _Indigenous Movements and Their Critics: Pan-Maya Activism in Guatemala_. Princeton: Princeton University Press.

Webb, R. and Llamas, T. Grupo de Análisis de Política Agrícola. 1987. "Aspectos metodológicos y macroeconómicos." _Los hogares rurales en el Perú: Importancia y articulación en el desarrollo agrario_. Proyecto PADI-Ministerio de Agricultura: Fundación Friedrich Ebert. Lima. (Análisis de la Encuesta de Hogares Rurales-INEI, 1984).

Webb, Richard. 1975. "Government Policy and the Distribution of Income in Peru, 1963–1973." In Abraham F. Lowenthal, ed., _The Peruvian Experiment: Continuity and Change under Military Rule_. Princeton: Princeton University Press, pp. 79–127.

Weber, Eugen. 1976. _Peasants into Frenchmen: The Modernization of Rural France, 1870–1914_. Stanford: Stanford University Press.

Weber, Max. 1946. "Politics as a Vocation." In H. H. Gerth and C. Wright Mills, ed. and trans., *From Max Weber: Essays in Sociology*. New York: Oxford University Press.

Weeks, David. 1947. Land Tenure in Bolivia. Paper No. 120. Giannini Foundation of Agricultural Economics, University of California, August.

Weyland, Kurt. 1999. "Neoliberal Populism in Latin America and Eastern Europe." *Comparative Politics* 31, no. 4 (July): 379–402.

Whitaker, Morris and Duty Greene. 1990. "Development Policy and Agriculture." In Morris D. Whitaker and Dale Colyer, eds., *Agriculture and Economic Survival: The Role of Agriculture in Ecuador's Development*. Boulder, CO: Westview Press, pp. 21–42.

Whitten, Jr., Norman E. 1979. "Jungle Quechua Ethnicity: An Ecuadorian Case Study." In David L. Browman and Ronald A. Schwarz, eds. *Peasants, Primitives, and Proletariats: The Struggle for Identity in South America*. The Hague: Mouton Publishers.

Wickham-Crowley, Timothy P. 1992. *Guerrillas and Revolution in Latin America: A Comparative Study of Insurgents and Regimes since 1956*. Princeton: Princeton University Press.

Wiener, Antje. 1999. "From Special to Specialized Rights: The Politics of Citizenship and Identity in the European Union." In Michael Hanagan and Charles Tilly, eds., *Extending Citizenship: Reconfiguring States*. Lanham, MD: Rowman and Littlefield, pp. 195–227.

Wilkie, James W., Carlos Alberto Contreras, and Katherine Komisaruk, eds. 1995. *Statistical Abstract of Latin America*, vol. 31. Los Angeles: UCLA Latin American Center Publications, University of California.

Williams, Melissa S. 1998. *Voice, Trust, and Memory: Marginalized Groups and the Failings of Liberal Representation*. Princeton: Princeton University Press.

Wilmer, Franke. 1993. *The Indigenous Voice in World Politics*. Thousand Oaks, CA: Sage Press.

Winant, Howard, 1992. "Rethinking Race in Brazil," *Journal of Latin American Studies* 24, no. 1 (Feb.): 173–92;

Wise, Carol. 1997. "State Policy and Social Conflict in Peru." In Maxwell A. Cameron and Philip Mauceri, eds. *The Peruvian Labyrinth: Polity, Society, Economy*. University Park: Pennsylvania State University Press, pp. 70–103.

Wolf, Eric. 1957. "Closed Corporate Peasant Communities in Mesoamerica and Central Java," *Southwestern Journal of Anthropology* 13: 1–18.

Womack, Jr., John, ed. 1999. *Rebellion in Chiapas: An Historical Reader*. New York: New Press; distributed by W. W. Norton and Company, Inc.

World Bank. 1996a. *Bolivia: Poverty, Equity, and Income: Selected Policies for Expanding Opportunities for the Poor. Volume I: The Main Report*. Washington, DC, February 22, 1996.

———. 1996b. *Bolivia: Poverty, Equity, and Income: Selected Policies for Expanding Opportunities for the Poor. Volume II: Background Papers*. Washington, DC, February 22, 1996.

Bibliography

———. 1995a. *Ecuador: Poverty Report. Volume 1. Components of a Poverty Reduction Strategy*. Washington, DC.

———. 1995b. *Ecuador Poverty Report: Volume 2: Working Papers*. Washington, DC.

Wray, Alberto. 1993. "El problema indígena y la reforma del estado." In Alberto Wray et al., eds. *Derecho, pueblos indígenous y reforma del Estado*. Quito: Ediciones Abya-Yala, pp. 11–69.

Yáñez, Carlos, ed. 1998. *Nosotros y los otros: Avances de la afirmación de los derechos de los pueblos indígenas amazónicos*. Lima: Defensoría del Pueblos, Adjuntía para los Derechos Humanos, Programa Especial de Comunidades Natívas.

Yashar, Deborah J. 2002. "Globalization and Collective Action: A Review Essay." *Comparative Politics* 34 (April).

———. 1999. "Democracy, Indigenous Movements, and the Postliberal Challenge in Latin America." *World Politics* 52 (Oct.): 76–104.

———. 1998. "Contesting Citizenship: Indigenous Movements and Democracy in Latin America." *Comparative Politics* 31, no. 1 (Oct.): 23–42.

———. 1997a. *Demanding Democracy: Reform and Reaction in Costa Rica and Guatemala, 1870s–1950s*. Stanford: Stanford University Press.

———. 1997b. "The Quetzal is Red: Political Liberalization, Participation, and Violence in Guatemala." In Douglas Chalmers et al., eds., *The New Politics of Inequality in Latin America: Rethinking Participation*. Oxford: Oxford University Press.

Young, Crawford. 1976. *The Politics of Cultural Pluralism*. Madison: University of Wisconsin Press.

Young, Iris Marion. 2000. *Inclusion and Democracy*. Oxford: Oxford University Press.

———. 1995. "Polity and Group Difference: A Critique of the Ideal of Universal Citizenship." Reprinted in Ronald Beiner, ed., *Theorizing Citizenship*. Albany: State University of New York Press, pp. 175–208.

Younger, Stephen D., Mauricio Villafuerte, and Lily Jara. 1997. *Incidencia distributiva del gasto público y funciones de demanda en el Ecuador: Educación, salud y crédito agrícola*. Quito: Boletín Estadístico.

Yrigoyen Fajardo, Raquel. 2002. "Peru: Pluralist Constitution, Monist Judiciary – A Post-Reform Assessment." In Rachel Sieder, ed., *Multiculturalism in Latin America: Indigenous Rights, Diversity and Democracy*. New York: Palgrave Macmillan.

———. 2002. "The Constitutional Recognition of Indigenous Law in the Andean Countries." In Willem Assies, Gemma van der Haar, and Andres Hoekema, eds., *The Challenge of Diversity: Indigenous Peoples and Reform of the State in Latin America*. Amsterdam: Thela Thesis.

Zamosc, Leon. 1995. *Estadística de las áreas de predominio étnico de la sierra ecuatoriana: Población rural, indicadores cantonales y organizaciones de base*. Quito: Ediciones Abya-Yala.

———. 1994. "Agrarian Protest and the Indian Movement in the Ecuadorian Highlands." *Latin American Research Review* 29, no. 3: 37–68.

Bolivian Newspapers Consulted at CEDOIN

El Deber   (Santa Cruz)
El Día   (Santa Cruz)
El Diario   (La Paz)
El Mundo   (Santa Cruz)
Hoy   (La Paz)
Opinión   (Cochamba)
Presencia   (La Paz)
La Razón   (La Paz)
Los Tiempos (Cochabamba)
Última Hora (La Paz)

Ecuadorian Newspapers Consulted through Servidatos, Diario Hoy's newspaper database

El Comercio   (Quito)
Diario Hoy   (Quito)
El Telégrafo (Guayaquil)
El Universo   (Guayaquil)

Interviews

BOLIVIA

Individual Interviews (all in La Paz unless otherwise stated)
Aimaretti, Marco Antonio (CEJIS, Santa Cruz), July 1, 1997.
Albó, Xavier (CIPCA), October 18, 1995; May 22, 1997; and August 2, 1997.
Aranibar, Sonia (USAID), May 21, 1997.
Arias, Iván (Director, Apoyo a los Pueblos Indígenas), May 27, 1997.
Barrientos, Bonifacio, July 2, 1997; July 24, 1997; and July 25, 1997 (CABI, Santa Cruz).
Bravo, Nestor (CSUTCB), October 24, 1995; July 4, 1997; and July 9, 1997.
Calla, Ricardo (TAIPI), May 27, 1997; July 4, 1997; and August 4, 1997.
Calvo, Luz María (Subsecretary of Asuntos Etnicos in Secretaría Nacional de Asuntos Etnicos, de Género, y Generacionales) October 31, 1995 and August 9, 1997.
Canqui, Sonia (ICAB/Aywi-Aroma, Machacamarca Sur), July 19, 1997.
Cárdenas, Víctor Hugo (Vice President of Bolivia), June 19, 1997.
Castillo, Oscar (CPIB, Santa Cruz), July 25, 1997.
Choque Quispe, María Eugenia (THOA), May 21, 1997.
Conde Mamani, Ramón (THOA), June 25, 1997.
Contreras, Manuel E. (Universidad Católica Boliviana), October 23, 1995 and May 30, 1997.
Crespo, Mónica (CIPCA, Cochabamba), June 23, 1997.
De la Cruz, Juan (CSUTCB), October 24, 1995.

Bibliography

Delgado, Sergio (Fondo Indígena), October 20, 1995.

Fabricano, Marcial (former President of CIDOB and CPIB; vice presidential candidate for MBL in 1997 elections), October 31, 1995; November 2, 1995 (Santa Cruz); June 13, 1997; and June 20, 1997.

Flores, Jenaro (former Secretary General of CSUTCB), October 24, 1995; October 30, 1995; November 3, 1995; May 26, 1997; and June 10, 1997.

Gray Molina, George (UDAPSO), May 23, 1997.

Guasebi, José (CPIB, Trinidad), October 26, 1995.

Iturralde, Diego (Fondo Indígena), October 19, 1995; October 20, 1995; May 23, 1997; June 16, 1997; and August 13, 1997.

Lavadenz, Isabel (INRA), August 4, 1997; August 5, 1997; and August 15, 1997.

Layme Escalante, Diomedes (ICAB), June 12, 1997; June 17, 1997; and July 9, 1997.

Lehm, Zulehma (CIDDEBENI, Trinidad), October 26, 1995 and August 1, 1997.

Lima, Constantino (former leader of Indianista movement), June 16, 1997 (El Alto); June 17, 1997 (El Alto); and July 15, 1997 (El Alto).

Loayza, Román (CSUTCB), June 11, 1997 and June 19, 1997.

Machado, Freddy (CIDDEBENI, Trinidad), October 27, 1995.

Mamani, Belizario (Secretary General of Aywi-Aroma, Machacamarca Sur), July 19, 1997.

Mamani, Carlos (THOA), June 2, 1997 and June 16, 1997.

Mamani, Liño (ICAB and Aywi-Aroma), July 9, 1997.

Molina, Carlos Hugo (Secretaría de Participación Popular), July 17, 1997.

Molina Ramiro (as Secretary of the Secretaría Nacional de Asuntos Etnicos, Genero, y Generacionales), October 23, 1995 and October 25, 1995; and (as Scholar at Ministerio de Justicia), May 28, 1997 and May 30, 1997.

Molina, Wilder (CIDDEBENI, Trinidad), July 29, 1997.

Morales, Evo (leader of cocalero movement and national deputy in Congress), July 15, 1997 and August 6, 1997.

Morales Ramos, Gerarda (ICAB), June 17, 1997.

Múñoz, Jorge (UDAPSO), May 31, 1997.

Murillo, David, Roberto Rozo, and Luis Antonio Rodríguez (joint interview at UNDP), June 9, 1997.

Noe, Ernesto (CPIB), July 25, 1997.

Pérez, Federica (President of la Federación Departamental de Mujeres, Bartolina Sisa/CSUTCB), July 17, 1997.

Pinelo, José (Semilla), June 4, 1997; June 10, 1997; and July 8, 1997.

Rojas, Gonzalo (Secretaría de Participación Popular), October 19, 1995 and May 27, 1997.

Romero Bonifaz, Carlos (CEJIS), July 1, 1997 (Santa Cruz) and July 29, 1997 (Trinidad).

Rufina Quispe Yumpace, Lucy (ICAB), July 9, 1997.

Torranza, Carlos (ILDIS), October 23, 1995 and May 30, 1997.

Urañabi, José (CIDOB), July 2, 1997.

Vadillo, Alcides (Oficina de Asuntos Etnicos), October 31, 1995 and (Legal Director, Secretaría de Participación Popular), June 11, 1997 and June 13, 1997.

347

Vare Chávez, Lorenzo (CIDDEBENI, Trinidad), August 1, 1997.
Vargas, Humberto (CERES, Cochabamba), June 23, 1997.
Velasco, Arminda (SIPADEM), June 24, 1997 and August 7, 1997.
Veliz, Alejo (Presidential Candidate for ASP in 1997 elections), June 10, 1997; June 11, 1997; and July 18, 1997.
Yandura, Oscar (CABI, Santa Cruz), July 28, 1997.
Zolezzi, Graciela (APCOB, Santa Cruz), July 2, 1997.

Community Interviews
Community discussions in several communities in Department of Santa Cruz; conducted by Marcial Fabricano, José Urañabi, and Felicia Barrientos (representatives from CIDOB) (June 27–30). Discussions held in Camiri among Guarani (June 28, 1997); in Villamonte among Weenhayek (June 29, 1997); and in Monteagudo among Consejo de Capitanes de Chuquisaca (June 30).
Community discussion with Aywi Aroma (youth group) in Lahuachaca, Department of La Paz, July 10, 1997.
Discussion with community leaders from Llojlla Chico, Llojlla Grande, and Llojlla Pampa (July 10, 1997).

ECUADOR

Individual Interviews
Bottasso, Juan (Salesian priest who has worked in various capacities with Ecuador's indigenous movements), Quito, November 17, 1995 and November 22, 1995.
Buñay, Francisco (President of Unión de Inca Atahualpa, Tixan, Chimborazo), April 22, 1997.
Cabascango, José María (former president of FICI, former elected leader of CONAIE for human rights and lands, and temporary president of CONAIE, Quito), November 27, 1995; March 19, 1997; March 26, 1997; and April 23, 1997.
Cerda, César (President of OPIP, Quito), May 6, 1997.
Conejo, Roberto (Member of Centro de Estudios Pluriculturales [CEPCU], Otavalo), March 12, 1997.
De la Cruz, Pedro (President of FENOC-I, Quito), December 8, 1995.
Díaz, Carlos (researcher at Centros de Estudios y Difusion Social [CEDIS] working with Unión de Inca Atahualpa, Tixan, Chimborazo), March 31, 1997.
Grefa, Ignacio (former president of FOIN, Tena, Napo), December 6, 1995.
Grefa, Valerio (former president of CONAIE and Secretary General of COICA; involved in various capacities in the Movimiento Pachakutik, Quito), November 29, 1995 and March 18, 1997.
Hurtado, Osvaldo (former President of Ecuador, Quito), December 1, 1995.
Ibarra, Hernán (researcher on indigenous affairs, Quito), February 22, 1997.
Karakras, Ampam (indigenous activist and researcher who has worked in various capacities with the Amazonian organizations and CONAIE, Quito), November 26, 1995; February 20, 1997; and April 7, 1997.
Larrea, Carlos (researcher on poverty and inequality, Quito), March 5, 1997.

Bibliography

Leon, Jorge (researcher on indigenous affairs, Quito), February 17, 1997.

Lluco, Miguel (National Deputy in National Congress and former president of ECUARUNARI, Quito), March 13, 1997; March 26, 1997; and April 30, 1997.

Lluilema, Anselmo (member of Unión de Inca Atahualpa, Tixan, Chimborazo), March 21, 1997.

Macas, Luis (former president of CONAIE and national deputy in the National Congress, Quito), May 6, 1997.

Maldonado, Luis (CONAIE and President of CEPCU), March 12, 1997.

Merino Gayes, Tito (General Coordinator of 1992 OPIP march; interview at OPIP conference, Alishungu, Pastaza), April 3, 1997.

Ortiz Crespo, Gonzalo (Secretary to the president during the Rodrigo Borja administration, Quito), February 27, 1997 and March 11, 1997.

Pacari, Nina (formerly part of directorate of CONAIE; at time of interview, she was providing legal advice to the recently elected indigenous members of the National Congress, Quito), March 5, 1997.

Ramón, Galo (researcher on indigenous affairs, Quito), March 20, 1997 and April 28, 1997.

Rosero, Fernando (researcher on indigenous affairs, Quito), March 11, 1997 and March 18, 1997.

Shutka, Juan (Catholic priest who helped to found the Shuar Federation, Quito), November 24, 1995.

Tapuy, Cristóbal (former president of FOIN, CONFENAIE, and CONAIE), November 24, 1995 and February 18, 1997.

Torres, Ramón (Coordinador Programa Derechos Pueblos Indígenas at CEPLAES [Centro de Planificación y Estudios Sociales], Quito), November 21, 1995 and March 5, 1997.

Tovar, Benjamín (Director Nacional de Desarrollo Campesino, Ministerio de Agricultura y Ganadería), December 1, 1995.

Vargas, Antonio (President of CONAIE, Quito), February 28, 1997 and March 4, 1997.

Viteri, Cecilia (researcher at Centro de Estudios y Difusión Social [CEDIS], Quito), February 27, 1997.

Viteri, Leonardo (OPIP and Director of Amazangas, Quito), March 6, 1997.

Yamberla, Carmen (President of FICI, Otavalo, Ecuador), March 12, 1997.

Wray, Natalia (researcher. Interview in offices of COICA, Quito), November 23, 1995.

Group Interviews

Anonymous group discussion outside of Puyo, Pastaza on May 2, 1997 and May 3, 1997.

Federación de Organizaciones Indígenas de Napo (FOIN) in Tena, Napo on December 6, 1995 with Ignacio Grefa, Blas Chimbo Chong, and Víctor Coyafeo.

Unión de Inca Atahualpa, Tixan, Chimborazo on March 14, 1997 with President Francisco Buñay, Secretary Augustín Vargas, José Guacho, and Vice President Albino Chicaisa.

Unión de Inca Atahualpa, Tixan, Chimborazo on April 21, 1997 with fourteen anonymous individuals.
Unión de Inca Atahualpa, Tixan, Chimborazo on April 22, 1997 with four anonymous individuals.

Participant Observation at Meetings
OPIP conference, Primera asamblea ordinaria de los pueblos quichua y shiwiar de Pastaza, Alishungu, Pastaza, April 3, 1997.
Taller de Jóvenes organized by the Centro de Estudios Pluriculturales (CEPCU), Otavalo, April 22, 1997.

PERU

Interviews in La Paz, Bolivia about UNCA
Cruz Alanguía, Bonifacio (UNCA), June 22, 1997; June 24, 1997; July 9, 1997; July 17, 1997; August 6, 1997; August 7, 1997; and August 14, 1997.
Jose Pinelo (Semilla), July 8, 1997.

Interviews in Lima, Peru
Aroca Medina, Américo Javier. Jefe del Programa Especial de Comunidades Nativas, Defensoría del Pueblo. Interview conducted for this book by Maritza Rodríguez-Seguí, September 16, 1999.
Cantalicio, Julio (President of CNA), August 20, 1997.
Inoach, Gil (President of AIDESEP), August 19, 1997.
Nukjuag, Evaristo (former-president of AIDESEP), August 18, 1997; August 19, 1997; August 20, 1997; and August 21, 1997.
Sarasara, César (President of CONAP), August 20, 1997.

Group Interviews in Peru
ADECAP, anonymous group interview, August 19, 1997, Lima.
UNCA, collective discussion with an estimated twenty-five community leaders and Executive Council, Puno, Peru on August 21, 1997.
UNCA, collective discussion with twenty community members in Desaguadero (Puno), Peru on August 22, 1997.
UNCA, group discussion with President (Héctor Velasquez) and Executive Council in Puno, Peru on August 21, 1997 and August 22, 1997.

Index

Index

Index

Index

Index

Made in the USA
Middletown, DE
25 August 2023

37376617R00231